BROKERING PEACE
IN NUCLEAR ENVIRONMENTS

BROKERING PEACE IN NUCLEAR ENVIRONMENTS

U.S. Crisis Management in South Asia

Moeed Yusuf

Stanford University Press
Stanford, California

Stanford University Press
Stanford, California

© 2018 by the Board of Trustees of the Leland Stanford Junior University.
All rights reserved.

Printed in the United States of America on acid-free, archival-quality paper

Library of Congress Cataloging-in-Publication Data

Names: Yusuf, Moeed, author.
Title: Brokering peace in nuclear environments : U.S. crisis management in South Asia / Moeed Yusuf.
Description: Stanford, California : Stanford University Press, 2018. | Includes index.
Identifiers: LCCN 2017050825 (print) | LCCN 2017055156 (ebook) | ISBN 9781503606555 (ebook) | ISBN 9781503604858 (cloth) | ISBN 9781503611580 (pbk.)
Subjects: LCSH: Nuclear crisis control—South Asia. | Crisis management—United States. | Nuclear warfare—India—Prevention. | Nuclear warfare—Pakistan—Prevention. | United States—Foreign relations—India. | India—Foreign relations— United States. | United States—Foreign relations—Pakistan. | Pakistan—Foreign relations—United States. | India—Foreign relations—Pakistan. | Pakistan—Foreign relations—India.
Classification: LCC JZ6009.S64 (ebook) | LCC JZ6009.S64 .Y87 2018 (print) | DDC 327.1/7470954—dc23
LC record available at https://lccn.loc.gov/2017050825

Cover design: Tandem Creative

To my family
with utmost love, affection, and gratitude

Contents

Acknowledgments

THIS BOOK HAS HAD A LONG JOURNEY. ITS GENESIS lies in a paper I wrote back in 2003 on the 2001–2002 India–Pakistan military standoff. The paper left me unsatisfied—with myself for not being able to fully rationalize crisis behavior in light of the Cold War–era literature that continued to inform scholarship on the subject, but even more so with this body of literature itself. Something was missing; I didn't quite know what. This "something" kept me intrigued, but it was not till 2007 that I was able to crystallize the intellectual puzzle in my mind: the missing piece, I realized, was a deep dive into the role of external actors in influencing nuclear crisis behavior. Cold War literature was largely silent on these third-party roles. The puzzle became a passion and, today, the journey has culminated in this book—an attempt to articulate an original theory of crisis behavior that is centered on third-party mediation in regional nuclear settings.

This work would not have been possible without the constant encouragement and support of my mentors, peers, assistants, and family and friends. Four individuals deserve special mention. Each of them has had a larger-than-life role in my professional development. Adil Najam at Boston University is the reason for my professional existence. Without him, this book, and much else, would have been impossible. Words cannot express my gratitude for his constant mentoring and trust in me. No one has looked out for me and promoted me more than Ejaz Haider, Pakistan's strategic expert par excellence and my first newspaper editor. Ejaz picked me up as a twenty-something nobody and taught me to think, write, and speak like a strategist. He has been my sounding board for all things related to international relations—and I could not have had a better one. Stephen Cohen, the legendary American expert on Pakistan, was my first boss in the field. Steve has trained hundreds of scholars over the years, but my bond with him has been special. Through thick and thin, Steve has been the anchor that has kept me moored despite the rough seas of Washington's policy circuit. But for Steve, I may not have persevered with my interest in the policy world I belong to today. Finally, Ali Sultan, my childhood friend, sparring partner, and uncompromising critic. He has been there for me in the best and worst of times—and this book saw both.

I started researching for this book in earnest in 2009. I wish to thank Timothy Crawford and Sophia Perez for their guidance and advice. Tim has been especially crucial to this project. His seminal work, *Pivotal Deterrence: Third-Party Statecraft and the Pursuit of Peace*, and my many conversations with him provided the building blocks for this endeavor. This project traveled with me to the U.S. Institute of Peace (USIP) in 2010. USIP has been a fantastic professional home for me ever since. Even though this book was not part of my USIP portfolio per se, I was extremely fortunate to have unconditional support and encouragement from the institute's leadership. I owe special gratitude to my colleague, friend, and inspiration, Andrew Wilder, who allowed me the flexibility to complete this book while working full-time at the institute. There is absolutely no way it would have been completed without his understanding, and for this—and much more—I shall remain indebted to him.

Parts of the book rely on primary information gleaned from interviews of senior American, Indian, and Pakistani interlocutors. I am grateful to the interviewees for their willingness to speak to me, and to colleagues and friends who helped arrange these conversations. The Delhi Policy Group in New Delhi, India, convened a special roundtable with senior Indian ex-officials and experts to discuss my project. I am also grateful to Peter Jones and Nicole Waintraub, organizers of the Ottawa Dialogue Track II process between India and Pakistan, and to Feroz Hasan Khan, a frequent convener of table-top exercises involving Indians and Pakistanis under the auspices of the U.S. Naval Postgraduate School, for inviting me to their deliberations as these settings created avenues for several of my interviews. I also wish to thank Happymon Jacob, Ajay Darshan Behera, General Aditya Singh, and Brigadier Arun Sahgal for the hospitality and networks they offered during my research trip to India.

Many scholars and practitioners were kind enough to read and reread parts of the manuscript for this book at various stages. I am grateful to all of them. Without their feedback, the book would not have attained its true depth and perspective. In addition to Stephen Cohen, Ejaz Haider, and Tim Crawford, I must mention Dinshaw Mistry at the University of Cincinnati and Jason Kirk at Elon University, who became my go-to people for impressions of the work along the way. Jack Gill at the U.S. National Defense University, my USIP colleague Colin Cookman, Rabia Akhtar at the University of Lahore, Arsla Jawaid, and Happymon Jacob at the Jawaharlal Nehru University also provided valuable feedback toward the end of the project. The input of all these individuals is responsible for drastic improvements to earlier drafts of the book. So is the feedback I received from the anonymous reviewers who evaluated the manuscript.

Throughout this project, I have been fortunate to receive substantive and administrative assistance from very diligent and able research associates. Eric Auner, Huma Rahman, Muhammad Faisal, Abhay Kumar, and Shalini Prasad all helped advance the project at different points. Shahzad Atta deserves special praise for supporting me over the past four years through meticulous research, fact checking, data collation, and editing. Together, we regularly burned the midnight oil. He complained and groaned but never let me down. Equally crucial for my sanity was my friend Arshad Khurshid, who has gone through this manuscript more than anyone but me. As someone who is technologically challenged to the core, I cannot overstate the importance of his support in preparing the illustrations in this book, formatting the work, and ensuring data consistency and security. I am also grateful to Ahmet Selim Tekelioglu, Pamela Aall, and Lauren McNally for making important reference material available to me in the last stages of the project.

This book is fortunate to have found a home at Stanford University Press (SUP). I must thank Scott Sagan, Peter Jones, and Riffat Hussein for generating interest in my project at SUP. Led by Alan Harvey and his associate Leah Pennywark (and before her Micah Siegel), the team at Stanford made the publications process remarkably seamless.

Finally, I owe immense gratitude to the most important people in my life—my family. They saw me literally eat, sleep, and breathe this project for years, often at the cost of my responsibilities toward them. My parents are truly special people. They have always been a source of constant and unflagging support. From my mother's perennial concern that I was neglecting my health as I sat for hours in front of my computer typing, to my father's meticulous attention to ensuring a comfortable work environment during the many months I hid at home to write, this book is as much theirs as it is mine. My elder sister, Rushdia, has taught me to pursue my dreams and my younger sister, Aminah, did much to help and kept me in good spirits throughout this process. My children, Sereen, Ahmed, and Hamza, are too young to realize their real contribution to this book. The project was a means for me to demonstrate to them the value of dedication, hard work, and perseverance. They allowed me to do so by giving up their play time with me. And I cannot but mention my mother's and mother-in-law's constant prayers, which were a source of much-needed spiritual inspiration for me along the way.

Most of all, I am indebted to my wife for making this book possible. Words will not do justice to what Shanza has meant to this journey. For convincing me that the finish line was near when it wasn't, and for making me believe in myself when it seemed pointless, I owe the world to her. She is the reason I persevered not only with the book but also with a career in this field. For that, she put her own professional life on hold and disproportionately shouldered the burden of raising our children. All this without batting an eye and with a smile that makes her the absolute gem that she is. I know she is glad this is finally done.

BROKERING PEACE
IN NUCLEAR ENVIRONMENTS

Introduction

Regional Nuclear Crises in a Unipolar World

EW POLICY ISSUES DESERVE GREATER ATTENTION
than the need to prevent nuclear war. No other pair of nuclear
rivals has worried the world more consistently in this regard since the end of
the Cold War than India and Pakistan. These adversaries tested nuclear weapons in May 1998 and within a year they were fighting a war in the disputed
territory of Kashmir. This marked the first ever crisis between two regional
nuclear powers and earned Kashmir the tag of being "the most dangerous
place in the world."[1] As the conflict began, alarm bells rang instantly; no one
could predict how these nascent nuclear powers would handle crisis situations. The world had long feared that nuclear proliferation would lead to such
scenarios, but its entire understanding of nuclear crises had been informed
by the Cold War. Would the Cold War playbook apply to regional powers? Or
would their behavior depart in important, and perhaps dangerous, ways from
what we had come to expect based on the bipolar world's experience?

All Cold War nuclear crises involved one or both superpowers and were
shaped by their competition. Even though the superpowers had to constantly
factor the security of their allies into their deterrence equations, scholars
largely examined these alliance considerations as extensions of the superpower rivalry. Virtually all modeling and empirical examinations of nuclear
crisis behavior during the Cold War therefore assumed a bilateral context and
were based on two-actor models. The post–Cold War regional nuclear context
is fundamentally different in this regard: unlike the superpowers, regional

nuclear states involved in a crisis operate in a unipolar world and contend with the preferences of the unipole and other strong states.

The Indian and Pakistani crisis experiences confirm this. These South Asian rivals faced a real prospect of major war at least three times in their first decade as overt nuclear powers. Third parties, principally the United States, played an undeniable role in mediating these episodes. Yet, there has been surprisingly little effort to theorize third-party involvement in nuclear-ized regional crisis environments and to understand its effects on traditional thinking about nuclear crisis behavior. Much has been said about *what* a third party may have done in a particular India-Pakistan crisis but far less has been done to understand *why* and *how* the third-party dynamic plays out. Specifically, how does the presence of stronger third parties alter the crisis behavior of regional nuclear powers? And what implications does this have for crisis management, stability, and outcomes? The literature provides few answers.

This book theorizes third-party roles in regional nuclear crisis settings and tests the theory by examining U.S.-led crisis management in South Asia. Its relevance flows from two of the most significant international developments since the end of the Cold War. The first is the emergence of regional nuclear rivalries. While India and Pakistan are the only pair of regional rivals to have been embroiled in an active nuclear rivalry to date, the chilling prospect of future proliferation, and fresh nuclear contests, remains ever present. The second is the shift from the Cold War's bipolar context to today's unipolar international setting. Projections about the waning power of the United States and the rise of China and a resurgent Russia notwithstanding, the United States remains the only state that has "global interests which it can care for unaided."[2] Its military preponderance remains all but absolute, and even "economic, technological, and other wellsprings of national power . . . are concentrated in the United States to a degree never before experienced in the history of the modern system of states."[3] While competitors like China and Russia are exhibiting increased issue-based cooperation and talk about a growing threat from them to American preponderance has been energized in recent times, there are no signs yet of any broad balancing coalition emerging with the objective of eclipsing the U.S. position as the leader of the world.[4] Even if such an effort were to evolve, the power differential between the United States and its competitors makes it materially impossible for them to achieve a decisive break from unipolarity in the foreseeable future.[5]

The implications of the combination of regional nuclearization and unipolarity for nuclear crises are not fully understood. This void has serious consequences in a world where the United States may frequently have to get involved in regional crises in nuclear environments to manage tensions. Indeed, the central argument of this book is that crises between regional nuclear powers will be heavily influenced by the overbearing interest of the unipole (and other strong powers) in preventing a nuclear catastrophe. These crises can be conceptualized as "brokered bargaining": a three-way bargaining framework where the regional rivals and the "third party" seek to influence each other to behave in line with their crisis objectives and in so doing, affect each other's crisis choices. The theory of brokered bargaining posited in this book unpacks the processes and mechanisms that underpin this trilateral interaction and explains the patterns of state behavior during crises. While it speaks to crisis outcomes inasmuch as these processes and mechanisms shape them, at its core, brokered bargaining is a theory of *process*.

Brokered bargaining marks a fundamental departure from bilateral deterrence models that have dominated thinking on nuclear crises since the onset of the Cold War. These models discount many of the effects of third parties on non–superpower crisis behavior. Derived from the classical (rational) theory of nuclear deterrence, they explain behavior as being driven by the need of the antagonists to balance between signaling resolve to the adversary and exercising caution to avoid nuclear war. The three-way interaction underpinning brokered bargaining introduces a parallel dynamic focused on the third party and driven by a "combination of sensitivities," the third party's to escalation risks and the regional rivals' to third-party preferences given its power to tilt the crisis decisively against them. Crisis behavior of the antagonists is marked by a constant tension between their incentives to pursue their maximalist objectives and their compulsion not to defy the third party completely. The third party, on the other hand, seeks to heighten the antagonists' sensitivity to its preference for de-escalation ahead of their ideal crisis outcomes. Successful escalation management requires the third party to get the regional rivals to defer to its preferences over any autonomous decisions that could escalate hostilities. This three-way dynamic introduces risks of misperceptions and inadvertence due to the challenges inherent in signaling to multiple audiences simultaneously. Traditional deterrence models do not account for these.

A Focus on South Asia

This book applies brokered bargaining theory to the three major crises between India and Pakistan since their overt nuclearization in 1998: the Kargil conflict in Kashmir, 1999; the 2001–2002 India-Pakistan military standoff; and the Mumbai crisis, 2008. These represent the universe of crises between regional nuclear powers since the dawn of the unipolar era that set in at the end of the Cold War. Each of these episodes risked escalation that could have spun out of control and forced these South Asian rivals into major war.

The India-Pakistan rivalry is multifaceted. A territorial dispute over the state of Jammu and Kashmir has epitomized their broken relationship. Each controls part of Kashmir but both claim its entirety.[6] The two sides have been involved in multiple wars and crises over this disputed land.[7] Pakistan also went through the trauma of its dismemberment as a state in 1971. Years of discriminatory domestic policies led to a civil war in the eastern wing of the country. India aided and abetted the insurgents and a short India-Pakistan war ultimately forced East Pakistan's surrender.[8] Pakistan's India-centric security establishment internalized the episode as confirmation of its deeply held view that India would waste no opportunity to undo Pakistan.[9] This episode also significantly influenced Pakistan's decision to pursue nuclear weapons.[10] Bilateral tensions continued thereafter, deteriorating into significant crises at least four times between 1971 and 1998.[11] The Indian and Pakistani nuclear tests in May 1998 provided a fresh jolt to the relationship. Another three major crises and multiple bouts of moderate tensions have occurred since.

India and Pakistan have an interesting history of engagement with stronger third-party actors. Throughout the Cold War, India championed non-alignment but favored the Soviet Union, receiving significant military and economic assistance in return.[12] Yet, the Indian strategic elite remained strongly wedded to the concept of strategic autonomy. In this discourse, third-party engagement for dispute resolution is an anathema. Specifically with regard to Pakistan, India tended to stick to its preference for bilateralism with a "religious fervor."[13] India's international stature has risen exponentially since the turn of the century, bolstered by a strategic partnership with the United States.[14]

Pakistan was allied with the U.S.-led Western bloc during the Cold War and keenly sought U.S assistance to offset India's greater military might. Even though this assistance was instrumental in allowing Pakistan to maintain a semblance of parity with India throughout the Cold War, the partnership was marked by tremendous angst and disappointment on both sides.[15] It broke down at the end of the Cold War, but was revived after a decade, courtesy of Pakistan's frontline role in the post-9/11 War on Terror. The United States again provided significant assistance to Pakistan, this time as a quid pro quo for its support of the U.S. military campaign in Afghanistan, but the mutual mistrust nonetheless deepened. The United States blames Pakistan for actively abetting the Taliban insurgency fighting the United States and its allies in Afghanistan.[16] On its part, Pakistan harbors a perennial concern that the United States has not fully reconciled with its nuclear capability and that it has an eye on forcibly dismantling it.[17] Its apprehension has grown as the world has frequently raised concerns about the safety and security of Pakistan's nuclear weapons in the post-9/11 period.[18] China has been Pakistan's more enduring ally. Its own tensions with India have made the Sino-Pakistan engagement a natural one.[19] Unlike its disappointment with the United States, Pakistan considers China an "all weather friend."[20] Critically, China assisted some aspects of Pakistan's nuclear weapons development.[21]

Their distinct views on third-party engagement notwithstanding, India and Pakistan can most accurately be described as states that have maintained active working relationships with the world's great powers throughout their history. Even though both countries were internationally sanctioned due to their nuclear tests when the Kargil conflict erupted, they continued to engage diplomatically with the United States and other major powers during this period. They were involved in far more intense partnerships with the unipole by the time of the 2001–2002 and Mumbai crises. They have traditionally seen their relations with the United States as a zero-sum game vis-à-vis the other, but the United States has tried hard in the post-1998 period not to allow its partnership with one to upset its relations with the other.[22]

Brokered Bargaining in South Asia: Evidence from the Crisis Case Studies

An analysis of the Kargil, 2001–2002, and Mumbai crises finds strong evidence of behavior predicted by the brokered bargaining framework. In each episode, the concern about escalation forced the United States to engage, largely unsolicited, and use a mix of rewards (or promises of) and punishments (or threats of) with the regional rivals to achieve de-escalation—ahead of any of its broader regional or global policy interests. U.S. crisis mediation was complemented by efforts from other strong powers. Both India and Pakistan eagerly engaged the United States and oscillated between manipulating the risk of war and deferring to American preferences in a bid to gain its support for their crisis objectives. The *process* encompassing this dynamic interaction explains both the specific choices and overall crisis behavior of the three actors.

In the Kargil crisis, this entailed the United States and other major powers ignoring Pakistan's efforts at manipulating the risk of war and its pleas for support to help terminate the crisis while it was in possession of forcibly occupied territory in Indian Kashmir. Instead, they deemed Pakistan's unilateral withdrawal to be the most realistic and efficient way of ensuring crisis termination and threatened it with international isolation and economic consequences if it refused. India reacted militarily to Pakistan's provocation but kept its actions limited to retain international goodwill and get the third party to make efforts to ensure Pakistan's withdrawal.

In the 2001–2002 standoff, the third party played down the middle. India threatened to unleash its military might on Pakistan but pulled back at critical junctures as the United States acted as a guarantor of Pakistan's promises of eliminating anti-India terrorism from its soil. The United States also raised India's costs, for instance by issuing travel advisories that caused significant losses to the Indian economy. Pakistan promised retaliation against any Indian military action and demonstrated its ability to harm the then recently initiated U.S. military campaign in Afghanistan by withdrawing some of its forces that had been deployed on the Pakistan-Afghanistan border in support of the U.S. mission. However, this autonomous behavior was trumped by its propensity to oblige the United States by accepting some responsibility for anti-India militancy and taking tangible action against terrorist outfits. These moves, in turn, allowed the United States to convince India of the merits of exercising military restraint.

In the Mumbai crisis, otherwise predicted to boil over given the spectacular nature of the terrorist attacks that had triggered the episode, India, Pakistan, and the United States exhibited an even greater sense of familiarity with the opportunities and limitations associated with the trilateral crisis bargaining framework. Despite threatening military action at times, India relied almost exclusively on the United States to do its crisis bidding. Without boxing it in completely, the United States breathed down Pakistan's neck and once again forced it to take actions against terrorists believed to be linked to the attacks, and used this to pacify India. Notably, concerns over emboldening the Indian decision makers to use force against Pakistan kept the United States from backing India unequivocally even though U.S. citizens had died in the Mumbai carnage and despite U.S. suspicions that rogue elements within Pakistan's spy agency, the Inter-Services Intelligence (ISI), or its former personnel may have had some involvement in the attacks.

Each of these three crises ended without large-scale hostilities. However, a number of risks peculiar to the three-party interaction were apparent and made peaceful outcomes probabilistic at best. For one, the likelihood of third-party involvement in regional nuclear crises creates a moral hazard problem that makes crisis recurrence more likely.[23] The false expectation of supportive third-party involvement was partly responsible for Pakistan's decision to instigate a crisis in Kargil. India's equally flawed assumption of receiving third-party support in the 2001–2002 standoff contributed to its brinkmanship, marked by a full-scale military mobilization. The South Asian crises also exposed the risks of the regional rivals misperceiving the extent of the third party's leverage over their adversary and its willingness to use it. Indian thinking during the 2001–2002 crisis reflected the dangerous belief that the United States would not allow an expanded war and would be able to prevent Pakistan from using nuclear weapons. On the other hand, India could have discounted third-party leverage over Pakistan (or believed that the United States was unwilling to use it) in the Kargil crisis, where it came perilously close to expanding the conflict as Pakistan initially stood firm in the face of U.S. pressure.

In each crisis, the third party played a crucial role as an information conduit between the rivals. This role puts a high premium on timely intelligence and information gathering, and on clear communication and messaging to the rivals. In the 2001–2002 standoff, India was reportedly on the verge of acting militarily against Pakistan and was restrained only by a diplomatic frenzy made possible by U.S. satellite imagery confirming that Indian forces had moved into war-fighting positions. Later in the crisis, however, the United States was unaware of a mismatch between Indian and Pakistani perceptions about the most likely scale of any Indian attack and the fact that the Indian military had planned an all-out offensive that could easily have crossed Pakistan's threshold for using nuclear weapons. The case studies also highlighted how inherently prone the third party's information provision can be to misperceptions and miscommunication. The Mumbai episode provided a vivid illustration of the difficulty in communicating clearly in fast paced crisis environments when a hoax call attributed to the Indian foreign minister risked igniting war. Finally, the Kargil conflict also provided an example of the three-way interaction's potentially negative implications for bilateral crisis management. Pakistani interlocutors believe that the United States' conciliatory signaling toward India during the crisis hardened India's stance and enabled its decision to pull out of a serious bilateral diplomatic effort to end the conflict.

Significance of the Book

The importance of preventing escalation of crises in nuclearized environments can hardly be debated. Episodes of crisis in South Asia are especially relevant because the region represents the intersection of nuclear weapons with state fragility and terrorism. That heightened crises present the riskiest scenario in terms of "loose nukes" makes successful crisis management in South Asia even more imperative for Western policy makers.[24]

This book breaks new ground in several ways. It is the first attempt to: 1) present a theory of nuclear crisis behavior centered on third-party mediation; 2) conduct a systematic comparison of the three major India-Pakistan crises since overt nuclearization in 1998, including the virtually unstudied Mumbai crisis; and 3) shed light on "learning" in nuclear crisis management in South Asia across a decade-long time span. The book's findings also offer lessons for crises between potential nuclear rivals in the Middle East, on the Korean peninsula, and between China and India.

This work speaks to policy makers in India and Pakistan, and in countries that could be future regional nuclear rivals. The policy conclusions are especially relevant to the United States and other third-party states. The analysis stresses the need for U.S. policy makers to appreciate their centrality to regional nuclear crisis management. This book's analysis will help them more accurately interpret crisis dynamics and identify crisis management options. The findings also highlight a counterintuitive aspect of great power politics by suggesting that strong states will prefer to complement U.S. efforts to prevent escalation of a regional nuclear crisis rather than using regional rivals as proxies to undercut each other's influence. The United States should invest in third-party coordination mechanisms in anticipation of such crisis management roles. The overriding interest in avoiding any nuclear catastrophe in regional nuclear contexts also has direct implications for alliance credibility given the constraints this compulsion promises to impose on third parties that might otherwise be expected to wholly back their regional partners in crisis situations. Perhaps the most consequential policy implication of this work, however, is to point to the need for third parties to invest in deeper dispute resolution between regional nuclear rivals as the most assured way of preventing crises from occurring. This is crucial since crisis management in contexts with multiple audiences will always involve inherent risks that make trajectories of these episodes unpredictable and prone to escalation.

The book also makes several scholarly contributions. It explores the otherwise undertheorized role of third parties in preventing war and introduces brokered bargaining as one of the few truly three-actor bargaining frameworks. The analysis also adds significant value by moving beyond the dichotomous debate between nuclear deterrence optimists and pessimists that is consumed by rank ordering the importance of nuclear versus nonnuclear factors in explaining crisis outcomes. In contending that the dynamic *process* of trilateral interaction encompassed by brokered bargaining explains crisis behavior, and in turn, trajectories and outcomes, the findings are distinct from the views of both optimists, who link crisis results causally to bilateral nuclear deterrence, and pessimists, who point singularly to third-party presence to explain these outcomes. This research has also opened up the possibility of the emergence of a new strand of literature that focuses on the stabilizing and destabilizing effects of three-way bargaining on crisis dynamics and their impact on crisis stability. Finally, this work engages scholarship on subjects often considered to be beyond the nuclear realm, primarily mediation, unipolarity theory, and sociological literature on "evaluation" by external audiences.

Structure of the Book

The book is divided into three sections. Section I comprises two chapters. Chapter 1 introduces the theoretical foundations of nuclear crises and surveys the literature on nuclear crisis behavior. Chapter 2 introduces brokered bargaining, propositions that underpin the framework and theory, and the methodology applied to the case studies. Section II forms the core of the analysis. Each of the three chapters in this section contains a detailed case study:

Chapter 3 studies the Kargil crisis; Chapter 4 is dedicated to the 2001–2002 standoff; and Chapter 5 examines the Mumbai crisis. Section III draws lessons from the case studies and explores their implications. Chapter 6 summarizes the findings and examines their implications for nuclear crisis behavior and crisis stability in South Asia, and generalizes the findings to future South Asian crises. Chapter 7 examines the relevance of brokered bargaining beyond South Asia. Chapter 8 highlights contributions of this work to theory and practice and provides specific recommendations for regional and third-party policy makers.

SECTION I
CONCEPTUAL AND THEORETICAL ISSUES

1 Understanding Nuclear Crisis Behavior

A Survey of the Literature

SEMINAL SCHOLARSHIP ON NUCLEAR WEAPONS DEVEL-oped in the Cold War era and was centered on the superpower competition. The major Cold War crises provided empirical tests for the theoretical work done during this period. Even though the end of the Cold War made the superpower rivalry obsolete and nuclear proliferation introduced regional nuclear powers dissimilar to these global hegemons, the world's understanding of nuclear competition continued to be influenced by frameworks developed to explain the superpower calculus.[1] Some specialist literature has extended these original formulations and tested their applicability to regional contexts. Yet, no existing theories of nuclear deterrence center on third-party mediation.[2] This chapter surveys the theoretical and empirical literature on nuclear crises from the Cold War and post–Cold War periods, with a focus on third-party roles.

Cold War Expectations of Nuclear Crisis Behavior

Crises are exercises in coercion through which adversaries seek to enhance their relative bargaining strength vis-à-vis their opponents.[3] Crisis management is the art of preventing "systematic or significant violence from occurring or escalating."[4] The quantum and speed of destruction associated with nuclear weapons give special meaning to this desire to avoid major conflict by making deliberate all-out war rationally unthinkable.[5] This is why *nuclear deterrence*, aimed at preventing the opponent from contemplating major conflict by threatening use of nuclear weapons, became the cornerstone of all rational nuclear theory developed during the Cold War.[6] Throughout, the superpowers operated under an overarching bilateral deterrence context; even as their intense positional competition directly or indirectly forced them into crises regularly, they had to remain mindful of the prohibitive costs of uncontrolled escalation. Deterrence optimists who embody an unflinching belief in the efficacy of *deterrence stability*—the idea that rational actors would be dissuaded from major conflict because the anticipated costs of nuclear war will always tend to outweigh any benefits—credit nuclear weapons with preventing wars between the superpowers during the Cold War.[7]

The deterrence prism lends primacy to a player's intent, resolve, and nerve over relative capabilities that are central to conventional military contexts.[8] A nuclear crisis is often seen as competition in heightening the fear of the consequences of war for the opponent rather than actually inflicting maximum damage through war-fighting. Crisis behavior is more about issuing threats to use force than about its actual employment.[9] Crisis strategizing aims to convince the adversary that the challenger is serious about its threats and has the resolve to carry them out. Specifically, to get the opponent to alter its behavior, a player may threaten to use nuclear weapons in retaliation for the adversary's aggression in pursuit of deterrence or it may threaten to initiate hostilities as part of a strategy of compellence—deterrence's offensive variant that seeks to get the opponent to act in a desired manner or undo a course of action it may be pursuing.[10] For these strategies to work, the threats associated with them must be credible.[11]

Since "credibility-of-commitment" is essentially about creating desirable images of one's resolve in the opponent's mind, it puts a premium on communication. Crisis communication could entail actions and force demonstrations involving conventional or nuclear forces and verbal declarations and statements.[12] These "signals" could be aggressive and aimed at communicating intent to punish the rival ("resolve signals") or relatively measured and meant to convey calm ("prudence signals"). The clearer and more specific a commitment conveyed through a signal, the more credible it is likely to be but the lesser the space it leaves to retract the commitment without causing reputational damage to an actor's credibility-of-commitment.[13]

The credibility conundrum received much attention in deterrence literature produced during the Cold War.[14] Scholars grappled with the obvious difficulty in establishing credibility given that nuclear threats are inherently risky to the party making them: the costs of provoking a nuclear capable opponent into retaliation can be prohibitive. This problem was central to the Cold War where both superpowers espoused the doctrine of mutually assured destruction (MAD) that all but guaranteed their annihilation in a tit-for-tat nuclear exchange.[15]

The most prominent solution to the credibility problem offered by nuclear thinkers entailed playing on the "autonomous risk" of a nuclear launch despite an actor's desire to avoid it.[16] The challenger essentially leaves the risk of escalation to nature rather than to deliberate strategy. The credibility of this implicit threat flows from the belief that actors involved in a crisis are never in full control of the developments—"force of events" tends to create a dynamic of its own.[17] The concept is embodied in Thomas Schelling's notion of "threats that leave something to chance" whereby states raise the prospect of an unintended nuclear launch—sometimes this may even require seeming irrational to create enough fear in the adversary's mind—and in the process, hope to convince the opponent of the high costs of continuing the crisis.[18]

The Centrality of Brinkmanship

"Brinkmanship" was the most studied behavior pattern that centered on autonomous risk in nuclear crises.[19] A brinkmanship game involves playing chicken in an environment when both opponents are uncertain of the other's credibility of resolve and each believes that it is more resolute than the adversary.[20] Although the formulation does not envision outright recklessness, an element of provocative and tit-for-tat moves, possibly including limited use of violence, is built into the dynamic. The conflicting parties intentionally manipulate the risk of war by upping the ante to suggest that things *may* escalate to the nuclear level inadvertently or through a desperate action. The goal is to get the adversary to blink and accept accommodation on terms unfavorable to it. Brinkmanship ultimately banks on the efficacy of the notion of deterrence stability. Even as it puts a premium on actively exploiting the space below the nuclear threshold by employing credible threats or limited force, it assumes that adversaries will be mindful of the need to avoid moves that could force the opponent to act preemptively. At least theoretically then, nuclear crises should exhibit serious attempts at coercion by the rivals and possibly escalate, but the actors involved should stop short of major war.[21]

In addressing the credibility problem during the Cold War, the superpowers deemed it necessary to possess credible nuclear options against each other for virtually every realistic limited and all-out war scenario.[22] For the United States, this resulted in an enormous arsenal featuring elaborate first and second strike capabilities and limited war-fighting options including use of battlefield nuclear weapons in defense of its European allies.[23] U.S. extended deterrence guarantees to NATO partners posed a special credibility challenge because the United States had committed to using nuclear weapons against a debilitating Soviet conventional attack in Europe knowing that the conflict could escalate to a mutually destructive strategic nuclear exchange between the superpowers.[24] The United States' solution, aimed at both reassuring its allies and credibly threatening Moscow, was to deploy thousands of tactical nuclear weapons on the frontlines in Europe and posture them in ways that made their use on the battlefield, and in turn escalation to a direct U.S.-Soviet nuclear exchange, almost inevitable in a conflict even if neither side wished for such an outcome.[25] Even though damage-limiting war involving nuclear weapons was built into the U.S. strategy, the real aim of the U.S. nuclear buildup always was to deter the Soviet Union by signaling a tacit acknowledgment that too much was being left to chance to believe that any war would remain limited.

The superpowers empirically tested risk-taking escalation management theories in the first decade of their rivalry; brinkmanship remained the defining feature of the most high-profile superpower crises during this period. The United States and the Soviet Union retained provocative nuclear postures, they undertook tit-for-tat escalatory steps, and they regularly communicated the risk of escalation during these episodes.[26] The world came closest to nuclear war during the Cuban missile crisis. The United States and Soviet Union put their conventional and nuclear forces on alert and threatened all-out conflict. Several risks of escalation induced by miscalculations, incomplete information, and misinterpretation of signals were not recognized at the time but they brought the two sides perilously close to a major global disaster.[27] Previous episodes like the Berlin Deadline crisis of 1958–1959 and the Berlin Wall blockade of 1961 did not reach such epic proportions but they too saw both sides playing up the autonomous risk and making repeated tit-for-tat threats of all-out nuclear attacks.[28] The only Cold War crisis between nuclear powers that escalated to significant direct armed clashes was the 1969 Sino-Soviet Ussuri River conflict over the disputed island of Damansky/

Chenpao. The pattern of tit-for-tat resolve signaling and war preparations was on display, and in this case, a shooting war ensued as part of the brinkmanship exercise. The Soviet Union repeatedly hinted, and actually contemplated, a preemptive strike against the Chinese arsenal, sending the Chinese into a frenzy and forcing them to prepare underground tunnels and shelters to deal with any eventuality. Ultimately, the uncertainty of this mission deterred the Soviets.[29]

Brinkmanship was theoretically and intuitively appealing, but the inherent uncertainties associated with crisis dynamics made it impossible to guarantee that the conflicting parties would not end up overcooking provocativeness and forcing the autonomous risk to actually take effect and lead to uncontrolled escalation.[30] Psychological, perceptual, organizational, political, and technical deficiencies can drastically lower crisis stability—a measure of countries' incentives not to launch a nuclear first strike—in the fog of war and make deliberate, inadvertent, unauthorized, or accidental use of nuclear weapons a realistic possibility.[31] Unexpected behavior can also be a function of reputational concerns of the crisis actors.[32] Since statesmen are believed to be overly concerned about establishing and enhancing their reputation as resolute bargainers to extract future benefits,[33] their own behavior and their expectations about the opponent can lead to decisions that may not seem entirely rational—and thus make them more susceptible to misjudgment—in a particular context.

These concerns influenced Cold War nuclear thinking immensely. The early crisis experiences forced the superpowers to recognize the difficulty in clearly defining escalation thresholds and controlling the process even as metaphorical escalation ladders had been created to show an orderly buildup of a conflict and the various ways nuclear war could be won.[34] A recognition quickly set in that no one could guarantee the discipline, meticulous control, and self-restraint presumed in escalation control models to keep wars limited.

The Cuban missile crisis initiated a period marked by U.S. and Soviet efforts to create rules and norms to reduce the risk of nuclear conflict. Over time, both sides began shying away from brinkmanship in their neighborhoods; they avoided attempts at forcibly altering the territorial status quo in the central theaters of competition, principally Europe, instead competing through proxy wars in peripheral areas elsewhere in the world; and concluded a number of arms control and risk reduction protocols that contributed to stabilizing their deterrence relationship.[35] The history of the Cold War ended up being a schizophrenic one: massively overblown U.S. and Soviet arsenals and constant planning of scenarios involving nuclear war ran in parallel to the deeply held "common knowledge" among political leaders on both sides that any use of nuclear weapons was profoundly undesirable.[36]

The predominant verdict on the Cold War maintains that the caution-inducing attributes of nuclear weapons ultimately led to prudence at critical crisis moments.[37] Yet, many less sanguine voices rightly point out that the force of events still nearly resulted in deterrence failure on a number of occasions across these crises.[38] These "pessimists" have remained influential in shaping Western nuclear policy debates. Therefore, even as the rational view of deterrence and frameworks like brinkmanship have continued to inform the prevailing understanding and expectations of threat-making and escalation management in nuclear crises, the extreme concern for risks associated with the nuclear weapons enterprise has retained a special place in U.S. nuclear thinking.

The Two-Actor Bias in Cold War Models

Third-party roles remained important for the superpowers throughout the Cold War. The typical examination of third parties was in the context of formal alliance politics and the extended deterrence guarantees superpowers provided their respective nonnuclear allies. These committed them to defending the ally (protégé) against conventional or nuclear aggression by its adversary (challenger), using all means at their disposal. Literature on alliance politics concerned itself with questions of alliance credibility as well as the possibility of ambitious protégés behaving in undesirable and unexpected ways that could make crises more dangerous and force the superpowers into direct confrontation.[39]

Yet, this third-party aspect did not take away from the overbearing reality of the superpower rivalry defining the bipolar global order. The superpowers' hegemonic competition ensured that virtually all modeling of nuclear crises during the Cold War approximated two-actor models. Even where third-party roles were inherent, these models tended to assume that the superpowers could take control of their client's actions, essentially transforming the situation into a superpower crisis. For instance, the literature examining extended deterrence equations almost reflexively modeled only two players, the third party (defender) and the challenger, leaving out the protégé as a strategic actor.[40] None of this literature explicitly factored in the nuclearization of regional powers.

The neatness of these models exaggerated the superpowers' control over their allies. But they were made possible in part by the fact that NATO allies in Europe largely remained passive-defensive and never raised too many concerns about acting belligerently independent of the United States.[41] Even Britain and France posed their nuclear weapons capabilities as contributions to the central strategic balance between the superpowers.[42]

The nature of regional conflicts in peripheral theaters further reinforced two-actor oriented thinking. Crisis episodes with the most intense superpower involvement bore stark resemblance to direct superpower crises. For instance, during the 1956 Suez crisis, both superpowers resorted to brinkmanship, with the Soviet Union threatening use of nuclear weapons if France and Britain did not withdraw from Egypt and the United States responding with full alerting of its nuclear forces and a commitment to respond in kind.[43] The U.S. nuclear forces also went on alert during the 1973 Middle East crisis as Washington threatened Moscow to deter its intervention on Egypt's behalf.[44] In the Vietnam conflict, the United States hinted at potential nuclear weapon use—later determined to be a bluff—in 1969 if the Soviet Union failed to force North Vietnam to accept a U.S.-dictated outcome.[45] At much lower levels of intensity and commitment, the superpowers also acted as third parties in conflicts in South Asia. Both openly used threats of direct military intervention and undertook force demonstrations to coerce their rival great power into reining in its regional partner.[46]

The primacy of furthering their global hegemonic interests led the superpowers at times to shy away from swift crisis termination. However, irrespective of the stakes involved for their global competition, at no point did they ignore the reality that their involvement in regional crises carried the risk of direct superpower confrontation. They therefore balanced moves aimed at forcing the rival superpower to back down with arduous efforts to control escalation in these episodes. This even led them to coerce their own allies into accommodation at times. This was the case in the crisis in Laos in 1961–1962 where the United States avoided use of military force partly to forestall a confrontation with the Soviet Union, and in Vietnam, where it sought to exploit Sino-Soviet tensions but constrained itself due to the fear of Chinese intervention in the conflict.[47] Though the Sino-Soviet Ussuri River conflict is not strictly comparable to these crises given that one of the superpowers was a direct party, the concern about superpower confrontation also colored the U.S. approach to this episode. The United States held back from playing any major role even as the crisis presented an opportunity to forge closer ties with China against the Soviet Union.[48]

Glenn Snyder's seminal work on alliances modeled such superpower behavior in war-avoidance roles. Snyder's "straddle strategy" within his "composite security dilemma" considers the use of a third party's coercive leverage to signal possible abandonment to the ally and direct opposition to its adversary in a bid to strike a balance between unnecessarily emboldening the ally to contemplate aggression and making its opponent feel so insecure that it chooses to act out of desperation.[49] Here too, however, Timothy Crawford points out that Snyder's operationalization of this scenario unnecessarily creates two separate, seemingly independent games—between the third party and the ally and the third party and the ally's adversary—rather than a truly three-actor one.[50]

Even in the minority of cases where state-level alliances were considered to be totally absent, the thrust of attempts at theorizing third-party roles was largely the same. Virtually all literature on "triads" is based on game theoretic formulations that either explicitly assume or approximate a two-against-one scenario. Analysts either assume two parties to be collaborating against the third or view each of the three in a zero-sum confrontation but where two of them ultimately form a coalition to isolate the third.[51]

Third Parties as De-Escalators: Post–Cold War Treatment

A rich body of literature seeking to move away from the Cold War's two-actor bias and to account for regional nuclearization under the unipolar global setting has emerged since the end of the Cold War. Four strands of literature that focus on third-party war-avoidance roles are most relevant to the discussion here. Combined, these provide the building blocks for a theory of brokered bargaining. Individually however, none of them capture unipolarity and regional nuclear dyads while focusing on third-party roles.

One strand of literature entertains unipolarity and nuclear proliferation. At the broadest level, Nuno Monteiro's seminal work on unipolarity theory fills a great void by positing possible U.S. options to prolong the unipolar moment and the implications of each of the options for conflict around the world.[52] While he studies the effects of nuclear proliferation on unipolarity, his focus is restricted to the nuclear capability of great powers and to the increased incentive for recalcitrant minor powers (Iran and North Korea) to acquire nuclear weapons to deter the unipole. Neither fits the India-Pakistan dyad: they are neither great powers looking to act as counterweights to the unipole, nor its direct adversaries. On regional nuclear states, Monteiro predicts U.S. efforts at using force to prevent states for acquiring nuclear weapons but has little to say about the unipole's options when regional rivals possess operational nuclear capabilities. Prior to Monteiro, some authors, such as Sumit Ganguly and Devin Hagerty, scrutinized unipolarity theory's application to a regional nuclear setting by examining the U.S. role in South Asian crisis management.[53] However, they did not theorize third-party involvement further.

A second strand of literature looks at third parties and may at times entertain the nuclear aspect but it does not tackle unipolarity directly. It includes a set of hypotheses that are not systematically developed, theorized, or tested. In terms of preventing nuclear war, Peter Lavoy presents the "nonproliferation hypothesis" of the theory of nuclear revolution: that "foreign powers will become actively involved to manage crises involving nuclear-armed states, to reduce pressures for military escalation, and to discourage any state from leveraging the fear of nuclear war to change the territorial and political status quo."[54] Others have coined terms such as "dual deterrence" to describe the situation where the United States is seen to be deterring two conflicting parties by threatening each with outright opposition if they resort to force and have summarily highlighted the problems in achieving this.[55] Also relevant is Patrick Morgan's idea of "collective actor deterrence," which applies most neatly to multilateral efforts at crisis management usually authorized by the UN or a powerful coalition of states.[56] Morgan entertains various types of collective security arrangements, also examining, but discounting as largely theoretical, the possibility of a global hegemon allowing a concert of states to play a consequential role in crisis management.[57]

The most comprehensive framework focused on third parties is Crawford's "pivotal deterrence." The framework significantly overlaps in its assumptions with those underpinning this book's focus on brokered bargaining. Crawford's theory includes the pivot's (third party's) "manipulation of threats and promises in order to prevent war . . . by making potential belligerents fear the costs, by confronting them with risks they do not want to run."[58] The third party's ability to maintain peace is predicated on two factors, the "uncertainty effect" and the "ingratiation effect" (or the desire to avoid isolation). Uncertainty forces the antagonists to confront the possibility that the pivot may behave in ways that lead to their defeat. Ingratiation amounts to the rivals offering concessions and avoiding provocations in a bid to "woo the pivot's allegiance."[59] Focusing on outcomes, Crawford teases out different scenarios to examine the probability of success of the pivot's crisis management. Central to his framework are alignment options available to the antagonists: pivotal deterrence is less likely to succeed when the rivals have recourse to other third-party patrons that can offset the influence of the pivot.[60] For instance, he explains America's inability to prevent a war between India and Pakistan in 1965 by pointing out that both rivals had other partner states (the Soviet Union for India and China for Pakistan) they could rely on.[61] Frank Zagare and D. Marc Kilgour challenge Crawford's finding on alignment options by contending that third-party success is most likely when a protégé's threat to realign is "most credible."[62] Although the authors model all three actors in a tripartite crisis game and usefully highlight the interdependence between the third party and the antagonists, their analysis is limited to extended deterrence contexts.

Crawford's focus on examining third parties with requisite leverage to influence conflict dynamics and outcomes and operating in war-avoidance roles without being strictly beholden to alliance politics overlaps neatly with the context of today's regional nuclear settings. However, his most systematic application of the theory is limited to conventional military crises, and he only examines the relevance of pivotal deterrence in a unipolar global setting obliquely. Even as he talks about the India-Pakistan "compound crisis" of 1990, which some have termed South Asia's first nuclear crisis owing to speculation that both sides possessed some operationalizable capabilities,[63] his analysis does not fully entertain the consequences of the presence of nuclear weapons.[64] As Yusuf and Kirk highlight in their study examining pivotal deterrence's relevance to South Asia, the nuclear factor demands a reconsideration of Crawford's expectations in fundamental ways.[65]

The third strand of relevant scholarship is owed to Vipin Narang's posture optimization theory.[66] Like the present book, Narang's work focuses on regional nuclear powers and attempts to go beyond the Cold War–centric understanding of nuclear states. But neither unipolarity nor third parties are central to his analysis. Narang's main contribution is to link deterrence to various nuclear postures adopted by regional powers. One of his posited postures, *catalytic*, is explicitly centered on a regional power's desire to exploit the threat of nuclear use to force favorable third-party intervention in crises.[67] However, in explaining the posture, Narang wavers close to the world of alliance politics, predicting that a catalytic stance would be driven by the presence of a powerful patron. He also seems to ascribe agency almost wholly to the regional actors, leaving third-party patrons to merely react to the regional actor's posture-induced solicitation. Moreover, Narang all but discounts third-party roles in the two postures he ascribes, respectively, to Pakistan and India in their overt nuclear phase, *asymmetric escalation* and *assured retaliation.* While he predicts that the country with the asymmetric escalation posture would tend to initiate crises more often, he sees this as being driven by the deterrent effect of nuclear weapons rather than by any consideration of a third-party role in the crisis.[68]

Finally, and perhaps most relevant, is post–Cold War literature that is focused specifically on the India-Pakistan dyad and recognizes third-party involvement in South Asian crisis episodes. This body of work is exceptionally strong in terms of empirics on India-Pakistan crises. However, attempts at developing new theories have been rare.

These works tend to recognize that "India and Pakistan are no longer free agents to pursue their quarrels as they please."[69] There is acknowledgment that third parties—primarily the United States—will likely find reason to enter crises given their concern about escalation.[70] Others, however, warn that third-party roles are context dependent: U.S. considerations in past crises may have been driven by its immediate security interests in the region but this cannot be counted on in the future. Those who foresee U.S. involvement debate its precise posture—whether it would remain neutral or seek to back one of the two parties to "win" the crisis—with some arguing that the third party will be forced to oppose the provoker in every crisis situation.[71] Hints of the United States' keenness to manage tensions in a nuclearized South Asia were provided by its role in the 1990 compound crisis. While the status of Indian and Pakistani nuclear weapons was unknown at the time, and neither of the two rivals believed that the opponent had an operational capability, the United States took the supposedly nuclearized environment into account in shaping its crisis strategy.[72] U.S. deputy national security advisor Robert Gates made a special trip to the region toward the tail end of the crisis, signaling the futility of war and urging de-escalation.[73] Although India and Pakistan were already contemplating crisis termination when Gates arrived, his mission is believed to have had a positive impact in terms of lowering tensions.[74]

The recognition of the South Asian nuclear calculus being a "three-dimensional deterrence system" notwithstanding,[75] the approximation to the two-actor models characteristic of the Cold War literature has also made its way into analyses of the India-Pakistan rivalry. There is still a tendency to treat third parties as exogenous to the calculus of the antagonists and focus on Indian and Pakistani strategies rather than the third party's. The one exception is Yusuf and Kirk's earlier-mentioned effort to extend pivotal deterrence theory to South Asia and examine the U.S. role as a "pivot" in the post-overt-nuclearization period.[76] For the most part, analysts tend to debate the applicability of Cold War notions of stability to South Asia within the deterrence optimism-pessimism frame and remain disproportionately focused on crisis outcomes rather than unpacking processes shaping crisis behavior.

Optimists have seen Indian and Pakistani ability to survive nuclear crises without significant escalation as evidence of strategic stability.[77] Ganguly and Hagerty argue that bilateral nuclear deterrence continues to explain South Asian crisis outcomes far better than factors such as third parties and conventional deterrence.[78] Pessimists tend to focus on nonnuclear aspects including third-party presence to explain successful escalation management. Some like Bhumitra Chakma, S. Paul Kapur, and Dinshaw Mistry, among others, specifically single out the United States as the principal explanatory factor for de-escalation and argue counterfactually that escalation would have likely occurred without its presence.[79] Still, pessimists converge with optimists in equating long-term stability with the presence of robust bilateral escalation control mechanisms among regional rivals. Third-party-induced de-escalation is considered suboptimal.[80]

The ability and incentive of the regional rivals to alter their behavior specifically to attract third-party attention are also recognized by existing studies. Conflicting parties could create "demonstration crises" deliberately by using provocativeness to entice third-party actors to intervene. Studying the India-Pakistan case, Sumit Ganguly and R. Harrison Wagner argue that these rivals may see an interest in creating conflicts to force the third party to reveal its intentions.[81] Kapur establishes that the risk of nuclear escalation has allowed the weaker, revisionist Pakistan to be belligerent and thereby trigger third-party presence in crises.[82] Even though some like T. Negeen Pegahi disagree, arguing that the conditions under which weaker states are emboldened by nuclear weapons to pursue revisionist aims are far more restrictive than Kapur's rather deterministic "rational pessimism" would suggest,[83] Kapur's is the more accepted view. Chakma and Ganguly and Wagner also appreciate the interplay between Pakistani behavior and third-party concerns about inadvertent escalation.[84] Others do not single out Pakistan but point to a similar crisis dynamic. Mistry predicts that the anticipation of third-party involvement would make it likelier for regional nuclear powers to resort to violence and less likely for them to back down in a crisis.[85] Feroz H. Khan's "independence-dependence paradox" posits that while India and Pakistan believed that nuclear weapons would accord them greater strategic independence, the acquisition of these capabilities has made them more dependent on the United States. As he puts it, "both countries hurl themselves into crises that deepen, escalate, and reach a point of spiraling out of control, only to unwind with outside intervention—notably by the United States."[86]

To be sure, the Pakistani and Indian tendency to solicit third-party support by engineering crises predates their nuclearization. For instance, the 1965 India-Pakistan War was an effort by Pakistan to ignite a rebellion in Indian Kashmir and elicit third-party support to wrest the area from India.[87] However, the outreach to third parties during this period was carefully calculated to exploit great power wedges and tensions. India and Pakistan often tailored their crisis signals to convey their propensity to invoke alternative alignment options, should the superpowers disappoint them. Pakistan used the Chinese alternative effectively to get the United States to focus on the 1965 war.[88] India shed its cloak of nonalignment and reached out with pleas of help to the West as the Soviet Union leaned toward China during the Sino-Indian War of 1962.[89] Kapur clarifies that the presence of nuclear weapons removes the requirement of prior alliances and relationships for third-party intervention, possibly further incentivizing demonstration crises.[90] The presence of nuclear weapons may also shift the demands on solicited third parties from supporting regional partners to fight and win wars to helping them achieve their crisis objectives without an all-out conflict. As Satu Limaye notes, "in using brinkmanship both India and Pakistan want ultimately [to be] held back while having the United States push their interests forward."[91] Yusuf and Kirk's analysis of South Asian nuclear crises also confirms this attitude.[92]

This post–Cold War literature considerably expands the horizon of the superpower-fixated bilateral deterrence models by recognizing third-party roles beyond alliance politics, including in nuclear South Asia. The third party's interest in crisis management irrespective of alliances, the incentives for regional actors to exhibit belligerence to solicit the third party's presence, a recognition of the third party's leverage over the antagonists given their interest in avoiding isolation, and the limits a nuclear capability may impose on their strategic independence are all individual components that can be pieced together to theorize third-party roles. However, important gaps still exist. A theory of third-party involvement in regional nuclear crises in a unipolar world must directly engage the effects of unipolarity on the frequency of U.S. involvement in crises, the specific conditions under which it may intervene, the link between its interest in intervening and its global policy agendas, the likely reaction of other strong powers to these crises, the tools available to the United States to leverage desirable behavior from the regional antagonists, and the implications of all this for the success of the United States' crisis management efforts. Such a theory must also more fully expound on the various motivations of the regional rivals for seeking third-party support and the type of crisis choices that may help them achieve this. It should also shed light on the tension between the strategic independence associated with nuclear weapons on the one hand and the limits third-party leverage places on the options available to the regional nuclear rivals on the other, and the effect of this dynamic on overall crisis behavior and outcomes. Further, it ought to posit the link between this dynamic and the inherent deterrent effect of nuclear weapons in influencing crisis-related decisions of the regional rivals. The next chapter develops this theory.

2   Setting Up the Inquiry

An Introduction to Brokered Bargaining

THE CURRENT LITERATURE LEAVES US WITH INSUFFI-
cient knowledge of the various factors at play in regional nuclear
crises. This is a void with potentially serious practical consequences, including an inability of U.S. policy makers to fully appreciate the various crisis
management options available. To rectify this, a theory centered on third-
party involvement and specifically tailored to today's global context is needed.

This chapter introduces brokered bargaining as a three-actor model that
explains patterns of state behavior in regional crises in a unipolar global setting. It unpacks and illustrates the *processes* that make these patterns fundamentally different from those anticipated during the Cold War. In doing
so, it opens the black box of crisis behavior beyond the traditional deterrence optimism-pessimism frame and exposes its limitations in understanding regional nuclear crisis dynamics. The chapter begins by presenting ten
propositions that collectively shape crisis behavior of third-party actors and
regional adversaries. Building on these, the brokered bargaining model is subsequently introduced and a comparison drawn between it and bilateral deterrence models. The last part of the chapter presents the methodology employed
to conduct the case studies that follow in Section II of the book.

Propositions for Crisis Behavior

The first task is to identify how regional nuclearization and unipolarity may affect the third party's outlook on nuclear crises and the crisis choices made by it and the regional rivals involved. The key factors shaping these decisions are presented as a set of propositions below. Each proposition constitutes a specific, observable behavior pattern. The last two propositions deal, respectively, with the iterative quality of the posited crisis dynamic and its implications for crisis stability and outcomes.

Factors Shaping the Third Party's Crisis Behavior

The first proposition is that crises between regional nuclear states will tend to induce the unipole's involvement in pursuit of de-escalation and crisis termination. This goes against the post-Cold War literature that predicted that the unipolar world, free from the overriding concern about superpower competition, would accord the United States more freedom to choose its interventions.[1] More recent work on unipolarity like Monteiro's ties the likelihood of U.S. involvement in regional crises to specific unipolar strategies, but he too leaves open the possibility of a disengaged superpower.[2] As mentioned in Chapter 1, even though literature centered on South Asia recognizes the third party's impulse to engage, it also continues to warn of scenarios where the United States may not intervene, leaving India and Pakistan to do their own crisis bidding.[3]

Yet, the nuclear factor in crises between regional nuclear dyads ought to eliminate a unipole's freedom for sporadic intervention, irrespective of global and regional alliance dynamics and the unipole's overall strategy to preserve its preponderance. This is especially true for the United States, whose institutional memory of the Cold War lends itself to an overbearing impulse to prevent escalation of crises in nuclear environments. "Anything that smells remotely nuclear" tends to set off alarms within the U.S. government bureaucracy.[4] The "working assumption [is] that something can go wrong . . . and that the U.S. must do everything conceivable to prevent a nuclear exchange."[5]

Several post–Cold War realities ought to reinforce this orientation. Foremost among them is the sheer threat of direct harm to U.S. global interests from nuclear use anywhere on the planet. No other event would cause a bigger shock to the international system and shatter its stability as instantly. The physical destruction of cities and accompanying infrastructure and the breakdown of technical communication networks so central to trade and finance would lead to massive global economic shocks. Millions more would fall into poverty over time as global production and trade suffer irreparably.[6] These economic losses would be dwarfed by the environmental consequences of nuclear war. Recent studies have shown that the fallout from even a limited regional nuclear war would be far worse and longer lasting than was believed during the Cold War.[7] James Doyle confirms that "a quite limited exchange of nuclear weapons against urban areas could trigger or accelerate global climatic catastrophe (cooling rather than warming), leading to the deaths of millions who had been uninvolved in the conflict itself."[8] Specifically with regard to South Asia, Alan Robock and Owen Toon argue that "regional nuclear war between India and Pakistan could blot out the sun, starving much of the human race."[9] These facts make the traditional definition of direct harm focused on a state's physical territory largely irrelevant. Even the most reserved unipole would not be able to ignore the reality that any nuclear exchange, even thousands of miles from the homeland, promises to cause unbearable pain for the entire planet. Altruistic and humanitarian concerns that have traditionally had significant impact on U.S. decision making should further punctuate the compulsion to intervene to prevent nuclear escalation.[10]

The United States also has an intrinsic stake in preserving the taboo on nuclear weapons use, one of the strongest but still fragile global norms in the world. Thinking around this taboo has always cautioned that "extraordinary measures would need to be taken to restore and reconstruct the world" once the taboo is broken given that it may set a precedent and make others feel less burdened by the need to avoid nuclear use.[11] This belief was a major reason the world took pains to delegitimize the use of nuclear weapons during the Cold War. As the sole superpower, whose overwhelming global conventional military superiority allows it to benefit disproportionally from the taboo,[12] the United States has a strong incentive to ensure its permanence.

Proposition 1: As the unipole, the United States will tend to see a direct interest in preventing escalation of regional crises to the nuclear level.

The dire implications of any nuclear use should not only create an incentive for the unipole to intervene but one can also expect it to maintain a low risk threshold in making intervention decisions. Inasmuch as the risk of escalation may grow as a crisis lingers, the United States can be expected to seek intervention early on. This expectation is reinforced by the deep-seated concerns among Western policy makers across the political spectrum about the dangers of deliberate, and even more so, inadvertent use of nuclear weapons by nascent nuclear powers.

During the Cold War, these risks were mitigated through conscious unilateral and bilateral efforts by the superpowers. They ensured special direct communication protocols, built redundant command and control, allowed increasing transparency in their doctrines and postures over time, concluded and faithfully implemented a number of arms control treaties, and avoided direct conflict.[13] These agreements on the rules of the game were important in reducing major crises after the Cuban missile crisis.[14] The bipolar international structure meant simplicity for the global order and made it easier for the two strongest powers to negotiate and implement these measures. The superpowers also had the luxury of being separated by thousands of miles, had no direct territorial disputes, and had unquestioned control over their respective territories. Still, these rivals came close to having several serious mishaps and on occasion were only saved by good fortune.[15]

The assumption of instrumental rationality in superpower behavior is deemed to be somewhat exceptional by Western policy minds. New regional nuclear powers are seen as confronting fundamentally different challenges, which casts doubts over their ability to manage their weapons responsibly.[16] Typical concerns flow from their lack of experience in nuclear management, the fact that their smaller arsenals could be vulnerable to preemption, and their limited economic resources, which may force them to prioritize a nuclear buildup at the cost of robust operational safety and security requirements crucial to ensuring crisis stability. Regional nuclear rivals like India and Pakistan are also geographically contiguous, which reduces decision and reaction times in crises. Regional nuclear antagonists may also suffer from unsettled borders, be part of long-standing rivalries with religious or ideological overtones, and may lack robust direct communication and political dialogue needed to build the necessary trust to agree to risk reduction measures and rules of engagement during crises. Moreover, domestic political instability is rife in a number of regions with potential nuclear aspirants. This offers the prospects of military-dominated nuclear programs getting trapped in path dependent mindsets and leading to poor crisis choices, emergence of unpredictable rogue leaders, and potentially weak state control over their territories that raises the specter of "loose nukes."[17]

These factors could lead to learning patterns among new nuclear states that diverge from those of the Cold War superpowers.[18] Since learning tends

Setting Up the Inquiry   31

to be influenced by the operating context and informed by the interpretation of one's experiences,[19] weak political and military cultures in these countries could lead to interpretations that are less reassuring than those derived during the Cold War. Consequently, new nuclear rivals may either forego the opportunity or remain unable to engage in the kind of rules and norms-setting pursued by the superpowers.

The U.S. approach to regional nuclear powers is deeply influenced by these concerns. In fact, the mindset is entrenched and reflexive—to the point that any change in it will require no less than an overhaul of the very psychological processes that underpin the present culture of nuclear policy thinking and decision making in the United States (and other important Western countries).[20] This outlook implies susceptibility to an exaggerated estimation of the risks involved in regional nuclear crises. The upshot should be a greater urge to intervene early.

Further, contrary to the general leaning of the current literature on the issue of third-party involvement, intervention by the United States need not necessarily be linked to a direct demand for its presence by the conflicting parties. Given its pronounced sensitivity to nuclear risks, the United States can be expected to enter the fray unsolicited by the antagonists if it perceives that a crisis may escalate. It ought to do so irrespective of the root cause or the immediate trigger of the crisis or even the force postures of the regional rivals involved. These factors would likely influence its specific crisis choices and may impact the probability of achieving peaceful outcomes, but they should not deter it from intervening per se.

Proposition 2: The United States is likely to maintain a low risk threshold in choosing to intervene in regional nuclear crises. It can be expected to enter the fray, even unsolicited, as soon as it recognizes the presence of a crisis with escalatory potential.

The United States' crisis demeanor will inevitably be affected by global developments at the time, its broader foreign policy interests, and its relations with the regional rivals, among other such concerns. Inasmuch as these interests could be complemented with efforts to ensure swift crisis de-escalation, the unipole can be expected to pursue them. However, wherever they contradict the de-escalation agenda, the overbearing concerns about the risks involved in a potential nuclear exchange ought to be strong enough to fix attention on the immediate need for crisis termination. All the United States' prior preferences, including its equities in its bilateral relations with the antagonists, would thus be accorded secondary importance during the crisis moment. This may leave one or both regional rivals dissatisfied with the United States' crisis behavior, and with the crisis outcome. The unipole can be expected to return to its broader strategic interests once the crisis is over.

Proposition 3: The larger foreign policy interests and equities of the United States vis-à-vis the regional rivals that do not complement the goal of swift crisis de-escalation will likely be overridden by this immediate need during the crisis period.

The combination of U.S. preponderance and nuclear risk is likely to introduce a largely ignored, yet refreshing and possibly persistent feature of great power politics in regional nuclear crisis settings: all strong powers besides the unipole would likely be driven by their genuinely shared interest in preventing a nuclear catastrophe. Rather than seeking positional gains vis-à-vis the unipole or their peers, all strong states can therefore be expected to reinforce the unipole's crisis termination efforts. While the prospects for direct coordination between the United States and other important third parties would be influenced by the nature of Washington's relations with these states, the United States should welcome this, and where possible, seek to cultivate such support and actively use it during crises. In its most coordinated form, the situation could amount to a "collective actor" intervention whereby a plurality of third parties coalesce and overcome their competitiveness to help achieve crisis de-escalation.[21] The convergence of interest in swift crisis termination among third-party states should reduce the ability of regional rivals to seek alternative alignment options that could otherwise complicate U.S. crisis management efforts.

Proposition 4: Strong powers can be expected to align with U.S. efforts to ensure crisis de-escalation. The United States should see an interest in utilizing this support.

Intuitively, the urgency of de-escalation should prompt the third-party actors to bring all their resources to bear on the crisis in pursuit of this objective. The United States' wide and overbearing array of military, economic, and diplomatic leverage could reasonably be expected to feature in an effort to force the conflicting parties into submission. The situation would then conform to Crawford's pivotal deterrence where direct coercion by the third party is central to war avoidance and noncoercive techniques like mediation are explicitly dismissed as irrelevant.[22] It would also be reminiscent of superpower roles in regional conflicts during the Cold War where threats of direct military intervention formed an important part of the crisis management toolkit.

Regional nuclearization, however, markedly constrains the options available to the third party. Notwithstanding American preponderance and the complementary presence of other strong powers, this collective third party's tools are blunted by the stakes involved in a nuclearized environment and the regional rivals' knowledge of the third party's acute concern about the risks. For instance, even if the third party's capacity to threaten and employ direct force against one or the other antagonist is never in doubt, its credibility to carry out such an action would be questionable. Any aggressive coercion of this sort could easily induce destabilizing reactions from either of the conflicting parties. The target could perceive it as a gang up against it; it could conceivably buckle and give in, but equally, it could presume an imminent danger of attack and get into the "use 'em or lose 'em" mindset. In fact, any third-party provocation that forces the target to contemplate precipitous action may also unnerve the conflicting party the third party is seeking to benefit. It may prompt this actor to request the third party to back off to prevent panic in the adversary's camp, or seeing the adversary in panic mode, it may act preemptively itself.[23]

The very possibility of a desperate response from either rival makes such behavior on the part of the third party inherently contradictory to its aims. As long as a third party is concerned about the escalatory potential in a nuclear context, it is likely to see moves that could push a conflicting party into self-help mode, and consequently cause it to lose leverage over this actor, as cost prohibitive. More generally, the interest of the third party in avoiding crisis developments that may exacerbate the risks of nuclear use should make complete alienation of either antagonist an unattractive proposition for it.

The theoretical formulation that best fits this somewhat constrained third-party role is "power mediator" or "mediation with muscle."[24] Usually considered to be a noncoercive technique and therefore a poor fit for nuclear crisis situations, mediation is relevant since it explicitly focuses on the third party's role as an intermediary interested in acting as a broker of de-escalation rather than as a patron of one of the conflicting parties seeking to win the crisis.[25] Flowing out of the realist framework, the power mediator—or "manipulator" as this role is also commonly called—can engage in a spectrum of activities from "pure mediation" that may involve facilitation of communication and negotiation between the adversaries or use of reasoning to nudge them toward alternatives to conflict, to actions that bank on the third party's leverage, which denotes resources linked to power and influence over the conflicting parties.[26] Leverage allows the manipulator to offer positive inducements or deprive and sanction the antagonists materially in ways that leave them worse off than they would be if they obliged the mediator.[27]

As the third party uses this "reward-punishment leverage" to manipulate the incentive structures of the nuclear rivals to pull them away from conflict and broker peace between them, it should be expected to focus on positive inducements and nonmilitary sanctions. Facilitation of communication and negotiations, validation or active manipulation of private information, persuasion, promises of concessions and benefits and face savers for the antagonists are most likely to be combined with diplomatic costs and economic deprivation.[28] Direct military threats, much less actual employment of force, which would take the third party's role beyond the remit of mediation, would likely remain absent.[29] In fact, even nonmilitary threats may play out existentially to some extent. The preponderant power's strength and capability of imposing these costs can often be enough to make the conflicting parties sensitive to them.[30]

As a manipulator, the third party may avoid revealing its intentions fully to either antagonist, use its role as information conduit strategically by calibrating the extent, nature, and timing of the information it chooses to share with the antagonists, adopt varying stances in its public versus private signaling, or exaggerate or misrepresent risks in a crisis environment. Ultimately, the third party's posturing and specific choices at any given point in a crisis ought to be dictated by what it deems most useful to further the de-escalation agenda. The mediator also need not necessarily be (or perceived to be) an impartial and/or a trusted broker by the regional rivals.[31] As long as it retains leverage over the crisis actors and context and can continue convincing both antagonists that they would end up closer to their preferred outcomes by banking on the third party, its mediation effort could potentially be effective.[32]

Proposition 5: Third-party actors would have to rely on "power mediation" to ensure de-escalation instead of more coercive strategies. Their use of the "reward-punishment leverage" would likely be dominated by positive inducements and nonmilitary sanctions, calibrated to maximize the chances of de-escalation.

Factors Shaping the Regional Rivals' Crisis Behavior

The first proposition with regard to the behavior of regional rivals stems from rational nuclear deterrence theory and therefore applies to any nuclear dyad. Antagonists will have to balance between achieving their ideal crisis objectives and exercising caution induced by the mutual possession of nuclear weapons. Both the crisis initiator and responder can be expected to manipulate the risk of war to communicate preparedness and resolve to establish the credibility of their deterrent or compellent postures. Depending on the particular context and objectives, they may also employ limited force. At the same time, the need to avoid nuclear war ought to inject prudence and force them to consciously try to remain below the nuclear threshold.

Proposition 6: Regional rivals can be expected to manipulate the risk of war to convey resolve as well as exercise caution given the danger of nuclear war.

In addition, the reality of global politics will force regional powers to confront a set of paradoxes that create contradictory pressures on their behavior. On the one hand, the power effects associated with the possession of nuclear weapons should increase regional actors' space to make independent strategic choices.[33] During a crisis, a nuclear possessor could theoretically choose to stay the course in outdoing the opponent in conveying resolve in pursuit of its crisis objectives. While the principle applies to all nuclear weapon states, it ought to be especially true for regional powers that are otherwise susceptible to pressure by stronger states.

On the other hand, however, there are tangible limits to the freedom nuclear weapons confer on possessors. Cold War literature examining attributes of state power recognized the additional pressure nuclear weapons possession would impose on weak states.[34] The destructive potential and systemic effects of any nuclear weapon use and the earlier-discussed Western concerns about the lack of maturity of new nuclear possessors imply that a regional power will be under far greater scrutiny, especially in times of crises. Outright defiance of the third party's demand to exhibit maturity would be certain to galvanize international opinion against the regional state in question; it would be going against the international community that is often presumed to be speaking of "objective justice" as a collective.[35] The concern about global isolation and the attendant material losses that come with this would be clear and present for the regional rivals. Insofar as states are expected to avoid isolation, especially when they are "confronted with a prospect of war," regional nuclear powers should shy away from intransigence.[36]

The consequences of defiance of strong powers for regional states in today's world can be even greater due to the structure of the global economy. Market-oriented economics has left weaker economies desperate for export markets and foreign direct investment (FDI) while the financial revolution has made states vulnerable to shocks induced by speculation driven by, among other factors, security and stability considerations.[37] FDI can fall merely in anticipation of conflict.[38] Moreover, since international regimes and large investments are heavily influenced by powerful states, any collective effort on their part to target a regional power could devastate the target's economy, and in turn, stability. It follows then that the more interdependent a country's economy, the higher its sensitivity to third-party crisis signals is likely to be. Nonetheless, the most isolated economies tend to be weak and often excessively dependent on access to a very small number of markets or on direct support from a key external patron. A tight squeeze on either of these channels during a crisis could easily present an existential threat to these economies.

Proposition 7: While possession of nuclear weapons should accord regional rivals greater freedom to pursue a resolute course to achieve their crisis objectives, third-party pressure to exhibit maturity ought to act as a serious limiting factor on their ability to utilize this strategic autonomy.

Another set of paradoxical incentives in terms of the antagonists' crisis choices flows from their interest in seeking third-party support. As discussed in Chapter 1, the literature warns that states could employ provocativeness to solicit an external actor's backing against an adversary, and to have it act as a buffer against unwanted escalation.[39] While the antagonist that feels more confident of receiving third-party support due to the specific crisis context or perceives that it has the tools to make the third party more sensitive to its concerns may pursue this course more eagerly, neither rival would want to ignore the third party's presence. Doing so would only allow the opponent uncontested space to curry favor with the mediator; the opponent would now be able to plead its case with greater ease, thereby increasing the chances that the external actor will tilt toward it.[40] This implies that both rivals have an incentive to compete in manipulating the risk of war to attract third-party attention and support. Any belief on the part of an antagonist that the third party ultimately retains sufficient leverage to pull the opponent back from the brink in case of escalation should prompt it to display even greater resolve. Not only that, but a decision to back down from aggressive attention-seeking behavior may be predicated on extraction of concessions from the third party.

These incentives to employ provocativeness to lure third-party support must compete with the opposite pressure to tone down this urge. The third party's instinctive desire for de-escalation implies that risk manipulation will not necessarily be the only means of soliciting its backing. Often ignored in the literature in favor of an emphasis on resolve as a vehicle to seek attention, restrained and prudent behavior can also get the third party to appreciate one's crisis stance and allow an actor to present its opponent as the belligerent party risking escalation. Inasmuch as this could lead third parties to bring more pressure to bear on the aggressive rival, the rival should find it unattractive to allow such a situation to arise in the first place. The dynamic could easily develop into competition between the conflicting parties in projecting prudence and exhibiting restraint.

These opposing tendencies would operate in parallel in any crisis and would feed into the rivals' efforts to calibrate their behavior to maximize the chances of attaining third-party support for their crisis objectives. The precise balance between these impulses will be a function of the specific context and the situational and reputational factors at play and the adversaries' past crisis experience with the third-party actors in question.

Proposition 8: Regional antagonists will compete in attracting third-party support. This may entail attempts to outmaneuver the other in manipulating the risk of war or to use restraint and prudence as a means of obtaining its backing.

The crisis interaction being posited here can be expected to have an iterative quality. The twin conditions of regional nuclearization and unipolarity create a "combination of sensitivities"—the third party's to the escalatory potential in any nuclearized regional context and the regional rivals' to the third party's crisis preferences for de-escalation—that lies at the heart of the trilateral engagement between the antagonists and the third party. As long as these twin conditions exist, the combination of sensitivities should trigger the trilateral crisis dynamic each time. This iterative quality constrains options for a regional rival who may otherwise prefer to bargain bilaterally with its adversary during a crisis episode. Its preference could be driven by a number of situational factors, for instance the rivals' perceptions of relative strength and odds of victory in bilateral settings, their distrust of third-party actors, their past experiences with brokered bargaining, and the domestic dynamics in these countries. Yet, the U.S. impulse to get involved in any crisis, the antagonists' knowledge of the same, their propensity to extract gains from the situation, and the inability of any of the three parties to ignore the others without incurring excessive costs would present serious disincentives for either rival to resist engaging in trilateral bargaining. One can therefore expect a three-way crisis dynamic to play out each time a regional nuclear crisis occurs in a unipolar world.

Proposition 9: Brokered bargaining will tend to be a permanent fixture in regional nuclear crises in a unipolar global setting.

Implications for Crisis Stability and Outcomes

Since three-party interaction provides an alternative route of diplomatic bargaining ahead of the traditionally expected behavior prizing resolve to extract concessions from the adversary, it ought to carry less risk of untoward escalation. As discussed above, the trilateral dynamic also imposes limits on the antagonists in how far they can allow the crisis to escalate without jeopardizing their crisis objectives. In fact, the option of using prudence as a means of soliciting third-party support suggests an incentive for disciplined behavior even at the lower rungs of the escalation ladder. The absence of direct military coercion in the third party's crisis management toolkit ought to further strengthen crisis stability.

While these factors point to an increased probability of relatively peaceful outcomes, successful crisis de-escalation can by no means be considered an over-determined result. The third party's presence introduces dynamics that raise the risks of misperceptions and inadvertence—quite apart from and in addition to the multitude of destabilizing factors known to be present in traditional bilateral contexts and highlighted in literature of the pessimist vein.

The anticipation of the third party's crisis involvement creates a moral hazard problem and incentivizes the creation of demonstration crises simply to get its attention, potentially making crisis recurrence more likely. During a crisis, instability-inducing factors peculiar to the trilateral interaction flow from the "multiple-audience problem" that tends to confuse signaling as actors are forced to convey different messages to different audiences simultaneously.[41] The multiple-audience problem can override the otherwise recognized advantage of a mediator acting as an information conduit to eliminate the two known contributors to the outbreak of war: asymmetric information and misperceptions between antagonists.[42] The three-way crisis engagement is inherently prone to these given that the interaction is premised on regional rivals simultaneously signaling to the opponent and a plurality of third parties, and these external actors signaling to both antagonists at the same time. Not only that, but the intentionally manipulative role of the third party also implies greater risks of confusion as the mediator games its signaling to achieve de-escalation rather than simply facilitating communication by transmitting facts between the two rivals.

Crisis stability can be compromised in several ways. The third party could misunderstand signals from either antagonist and end up making an ill-informed choice that increases the likelihood of escalation. Faulty intelligence on the part of the third party could also produce the same result. On the other hand, the third party, despite accurately comprehending the situation and while trying to avoid such an impression may nonetheless be perceived by one of the conflicting parties as ganging up with the opponent against it. The alienated actor could feel compelled to take matters into its own hands and respond through desperate precipitous action. One could even envision a scenario where the third party perceives a regional actor to be under too much pressure, say due to domestic political compulsions, to hold back from aggressing and therefore encourages it to let off steam by undertaking limited action. The third party would then hope to convince the other regional rival to exercise restraint in return. However, even a commensurate response by this opponent could quickly escalate the crisis.

Furthermore, since the crisis plays out in a framework where the third party may not fully reveal its intentions, the antagonists may see an interest in testing the limits of their autonomy vis-à-vis the third party. Hostilities could break out if either antagonist miscalculates the third party's intentions. An antagonist could wrongly believe that the third party is supportive of its aggression, or could feel forced to momentarily discount the marginal loss in terms of third-party support by making one additional provocative move. This could happen, for instance, if a country's leadership perceives the political or reputational costs of inaction at any point to be unbearable. Hostilities could also result from a regional rival's miscalculation of the third party's leverage over the opponent. A perception that the third party has insufficient leverage to rein in the opponent could incentivize unilateral action. On the other hand, a belief that the third party will eventually force the opponent to back down during a crisis could have an emboldening effect. If the context is one where the conflicting parties have no understanding or prior agreements on limiting wars—an entirely reasonable assumption for new nuclear dyads—the situation could easily spiral out of control.[43]

Finally, the adversaries could also misunderstand each other's signals. Provocative behavior aimed at manipulating the risk of war to attract third-party support could be interpreted by the adversary as an impending attack, potentially leading it to preempt. Even prudence exhibited with an eye on the third party could end up communicating weakness of resolve to the adversary and prompt it to take advantage by launching an attack.

The probability of any of these risks taking over crisis dynamics is highly contingent on particular crisis contexts. Variables such as specific crisis triggers, force sizes and postures of the rivals, domestic political and economic realities and reputational pressures on leaders of these countries, the nature of the relationships of the actors with each other, the rivals' past experiences with third-party crisis management, among other such factors will not undermine the three-way bargaining exercise but they could be important determinants of how some of these risks may actually play out in a crisis. Since these factors will differ from crisis to crisis, the risks involved in a particular context will remain extremely difficult to predict and mitigate.

Proposition 10: The trilateral dynamic imposes constraints on crisis behavior that favor successful de-escalation of crises. Yet, third-party presence, and specifically the multiple-audience problem inherent in these crises, implies that peaceful outcomes cannot be considered over-determined.

The Brokered Bargaining Model

The aggregation of the foregoing propositions constitutes a three-cornered bargaining model that forms the core of the theory of brokered bargaining. It comprises two parallel but intrinsically wedded set of interactions. The first is common to brokered bargaining and bilateral deterrence: the antagonists aim actions and signals at each other, either to deter the opponent from taking an action or to compel it to respond in line with one's crisis objectives. The second is unique to brokered bargaining. It envisages the regional rivals trying to lure the third party to act in certain ways toward them and their adversary while this intermediary attempts to find space to mediate between the rivals to ensure swift crisis de-escalation. Combined, these interactions lead to a *process* marked by a recursive interplay of the perceptions, expectations, incentives, and strategies among the three parties that affects overall behavior and stability, and in turn, the outcome of a crisis.

The regional rivals have to deal with two competing sets of demands on their behavior. They could be prompted to pursue aggressive behavior to establish the credibility of their resolve and to play on the third party's fear of war. The competing need to show prudence is driven both by the dangers in excessive risk-taking in a nuclear environment and by their sensitivity to third-party preferences. The conflicting parties are thus faced with a "resolve-prudence trade-off" with a dual characteristic: vis-à-vis the principal opponent and vis-à-vis the third party.

During any crisis, the regional rivals have an interest in portraying their ability and desire to retain a high degree of autonomy. They would want to make their intent more credible, both for the adversary and the third party, by signaling their willingness to engage in conflict instead of compromising on their objectives to achieve de-escalation. The third party would seek to utilize its "reward-punishment leverage" to chip away at their autonomy while working to minimize the reverse influence the antagonists are able to exert on it. Successful escalation management would require the third party to get the regional rivals to defer to its preferences over any autonomous decisions that could push the crisis over the brink. The third party would have to reorient the antagonists' cost-benefit analysis, making swift crisis termination the most attractive option—ahead of their ideal crisis outcomes and despite the possible political and reputational costs they may incur for settling short of their original objectives. Brokered bargaining should remain relevant even if a major conflict breaks out given the natural interest of the involved actors in keeping the scale of the conflict below the nuclear threshold.

The conflicting parties' sensitivity to third-party preferences could be best described as a desire for "positive evaluation" on their part. The formulation is borrowed from sociological literature and specifically from Jeffrey Rubin and Bert Brown's concept of "evaluation" in bargaining frameworks.[44] It is predicated on the belief that bargaining situations can have "audiences" that act as evaluators who provide performance feedback to the principal bargainers.[45] "The mere presence of an audience (including psychological presence) motivates bargainers to seek positive, and avoid negative, evaluation—especially when the audience is salient to the bargainers."[46] This is driven by the audiences' "apparent readiness to make demands or impose sanctions upon . . . [the bargainers] if their preferences are not pursued to their satisfaction."[47] The need for positive evaluation "puts the bargainer on notice that his behavior is being, or will be, scrutinized, and that the esteem in which he is held is contingent upon the appropriateness of his performance, as this is defined by the particular audience."[48] It develops a sort of accountability toward the audience; accountability in turn provides audiences the requisite leverage to alter behavior.[49] A "dependent" audience that relies on a bargaining exercise's outcome for achievement of its crisis objectives is most likely to hold the bargainers accountable.[50] In the case of brokered bargaining, the third party's dependence on the antagonists to achieve de-escalation puts it squarely in this camp.

To be sure, positive evaluation implies more than just a concern for one's image. It encapsulates the third party's ability to provide tangible concessions and offer gains and inflict material losses. It follows that the more sensitive an actor is to the third party's demands and preferences, the more positive its evaluation—and therefore the greater the likelihood of maximizing gains and minimizing losses—would be. Both rivals can be expected not to lose sight of their need for positive evaluation even as they strive to pursue their crisis objectives. The third party's task, on the other hand, is to play on the regional rivals' desire for this positive evaluation to extract compromises in pursuit of de-escalation.

The positive evaluation lens allows a crisis to be seen as competition between the antagonists to obtain third-party support rather than a context in which they simply react to the fear of direct third-party action against them. The latter was central to the preponderant outsider's behavior in Cold War models. The third party's constraints in terms of its primary reliance on positive inducements and nonmilitary punishment in a regional nuclear setting make a purely coercive prism less relevant.

Brokered Bargaining versus Bilateral Deterrence
The brokered bargaining model presents a much different conceptualization of nuclear crises than bilateral models that flow from the canonical deterrence logic of the Cold War. Table 2.1 summarizes the drivers of the crisis behavior of the antagonists in each case. As it shows, despite considerable overlap, a number of factors at play under brokered bargaining are irrelevant to the traditional models.

The two approaches also lead to different visions of how a prototypical crisis is likely to unfold. Figures 2.1 and 2.2 depict the envisioned crisis paths under each approach.

The explanatory power of traditional deterrence models is limited in regional nuclear contexts given their inability to account for the centrality of

Table 2.1. Drivers of crisis behavior in brokered bargaining versus bilateral deterrence settings

Drivers of resolute behavior	Drivers of prudent behavior
APPLICABLE TO BROKERED BARGAINING AND BILATERAL DETERRENCE	
Need to establish credibility of resolve to act upon threats made as part of coercive crisis strategies	Need to avoid undermining crisis stability and forcing the adversary to take precipitous action
Strategic autonomy attributed to possession of nuclear weapons	Cost-prohibitive outcome in case of nuclear war
Absence of robust bilateral escalation control mechanisms	Importance of exhibiting responsible behavior as nuclear weapon states
Reputational concerns	
APPLICABLE TO BROKERED BARGAINING ONLY	
Risk manipulation to play on the third party's fear of war	Antagonists' sensitivity to the third party's preferences as a means of securing its support
Belief that the third party is supportive of one's aggression and/or that it has enough leverage to prevent the opponent from causing a breakdown of crisis stability	Third party's ability to reward the antagonists' deference to its preferences and to impose costs on them for their defiance
Situational factors linked to third party (e.g., pre-crisis international image of the regional rivals; likelihood of international support based on specific crisis context; perception of the third party's reliance on an antagonist for its broader foreign policy objectives, etc.)	Situational factors linked to third party (e.g., pre-crisis international image of the regional rivals; likelihood of international support based on specific crisis context; perception of the third party's reliance on an antagonist for its broader foreign policy objectives; economic interdependence vis-à-vis third party actors, etc.)

third-party mediation. These models may still seem to rationalize the absence of major escalation in crises by pointing to the caution-inducing effect of nuclear weapons, but this is derived from an inaccurate understanding of the processes and mechanisms underpinning crisis dynamics. Consequently, bilateral models are also unable to correctly identify the risks involved in any given crisis and the means to mitigate them. Brokered bargaining overcomes these gaps and presents a more accurate accounting of crises between regional nuclear powers.

Brokered bargaining does not reject the importance of nuclear deterrence. However, the deterrent effect of nuclear weapons is endogenous to the crisis dynamic encompassed by the three-cornered bargaining framework and therefore operates at a deeper structural level. Pressures to avoid escalation flow from a combination of both strands of the resolve-prudence trade-off described earlier. Since the presence of the third party is also endogenous

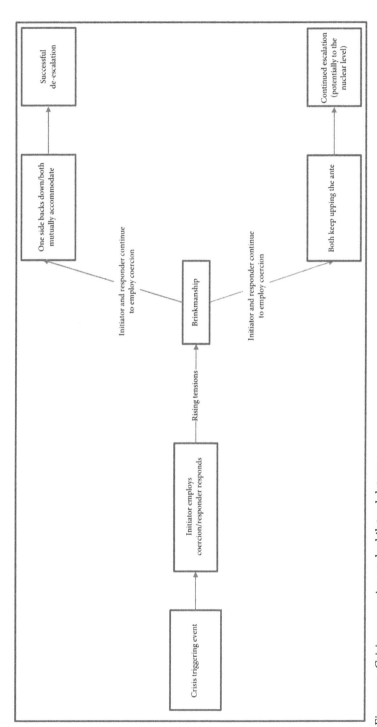

Figure 2.1. Crisis progression under bilateral deterrence

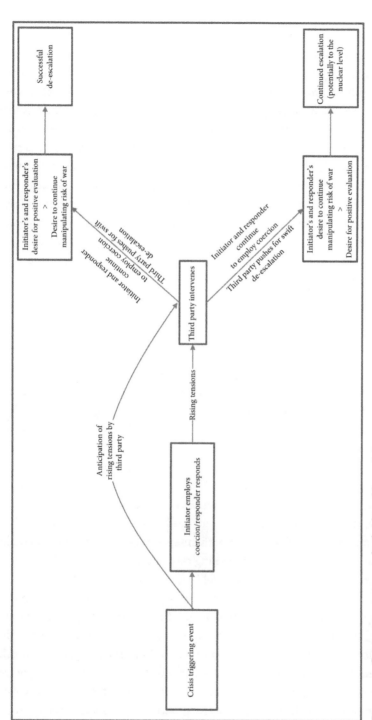

Figure 2.2. Crisis progression under brokered bargaining

to the crisis outlook of the regional rivals, the situation neither lends itself to establishing that nuclear weapons are *the* principal factor at play, nor to a straightforward counterfactual analysis that sees the absence of uncontrolled escalation solely as a function of third-party presence.[51] Studies that have sought to make this case based on straight counterfactuals suffer from an endogeneity problem.[52] The subtle but significant distinction between such analyses and what is argued here must be noted: it is the *process* of trilateral interaction encompassed by the brokered bargaining model, not the exogenous third party's presence alone, that explains crisis behavior, and in turn, crisis trajectories and outcomes. This process cannot be parsed to resemble more familiar two-actor models. Therefore, whenever brokered bargaining is operational, the answer to whether nuclear deterrence would have held in its absence must remain indeterminate.

Methodology

Cases

This book tests the applicability of brokered bargaining by examining three South Asian crises: the 1999 Kargil conflict; the 2001–2002 military stand-off; and the 2008 Mumbai crisis. All other crises involving a regional nuclear power have either featured a superpower as one of the conflicting parties (the 1969 Sino-Soviet Ussuri River conflict), taken place under extended deterrence umbrellas with a nonnuclear protégé (multiple bouts of heightened tensions on the Korean peninsula since North Korea's first nuclear test in 2006), or have occurred under opaque deterrence umbrellas where the antagonists and/or the third party were not convinced of the presence of an employable nuclear capability of one or both antagonists and thus did not take the nuclear aspect into account in making crisis decisions (1987 India-Pakistan "Brasstacks" crisis and 1990 India-Pakistan compound crisis).[53]

Since the cases examined in this book are all part of a single rivalry and span a decade, they can be compared across time to produce cumulative knowledge and aggregate learning in terms of crisis behavior in the first decade of overt nuclearization in South Asia. The analysis is also able to identify how the experience of a particular crisis may have impacted post-crisis decisions and crisis choices in successive iterations. Moreover, the variance over time on some of the situational factors allows for testing whether any of these were significantly correlated to crisis behavior such that they could bring the explanatory power of brokered bargaining into question.

The South Asian nuclear dyad constitutes a "least-likely" case in methodological terms: a case "that seems on a priori grounds unlikely to accord with theoretical predictions."[54] This flows both from India's obsession with retaining its strategic autonomy and wariness of third-party intervention in India-Pakistan disputes, and from Pakistan's long-held concern about the United States' agenda of forcibly stripping it of its nuclear capability, a conviction that ought to make it hypersensitive to any scenario that allows Washington a say or intrusion in its nuclear matters. Therefore, if the case studies provide evidence for crisis behavior predicted by the brokered bargaining framework, this would offer stronger-than-usual substantiation of the theory.

Measurements and Methods

If the primacy of brokered bargaining is to be established, the trilateral dynamic underpinning it must be found to be responsible for shaping crisis behavior. The United States should get involved (proposition 1 [P1]) before significant escalation and without necessarily waiting to be solicited into the mix (P2). It should focus primarily on ensuring swift crisis de-escalation and termination, ahead of its broader foreign policy agenda and bilateral equities vis-à-vis the antagonists (P3). Other strong powers should complement U.S. efforts and, where possible, the United States should be seen actively coordinating and utilizing the presence of these third parties (P4). There should be evidence of third-party mediation—primarily comprising positive inducements and nonmilitary sanctions—remaining central to altering the preferences of the regional rivals during the crisis (P5). Further, crisis choices of the antagonists should simultaneously be aimed at the adversary and the third party. Their propensity to exhibit autonomous decision making must be combined with deference to third-party preferences. The third-party prong of the resolve-prudence trade-off should lead them to actively seek third-party support against the rival (P7, P8). Ultimately, there should be sufficient evidence of the antagonists' desire for positive evaluation, manifested by specific choices linked directly to the third party's use of its reward-punishment leverage. This should hold even if it leaves one or both antagonists with suboptimal results from the crisis. Finally, brokered bargaining should play out in each examined crisis (P9). On the other hand, the theory of brokered bargaining would be falsified if crisis behavior is found to be dominated by bilateral deterrence. Both resolve and prudence signals should be aimed solely at the adversary in this case (P6) and third-party roles should be largely irrelevant to crisis choices of the antagonists (absence of P7, P8).

The central methodological challenge in this inquiry is to separate the crisis choices of the conflicting parties that may be driven by bilateral deterrence concerns from those linked to the *process* underpinning the three-party interaction. Given that behavior patterns for both could lead the rivals to balance resolve and prudence with little explicit indication of the intended audience for their choices, the analysis will not only have to examine crisis developments and actions and statements of the involved actors, but it must also capture the motivations behind these, their intended targets, and the cause and effect between the choices and decisions of each of the three players.

The "structured focused comparison" method is most suited to this task.[55] It involves applying a set of standardized instrumental questions in line with the research objectives and theoretical framework to each case. By doing so, the method allows for systematic comparisons across the cases, but without losing the ability to conduct an in-depth investigation of each case. Each of the earlier-posited propositions directly lends itself to individual instrumental questions. The narrative in each case study will attempt to identify and link relevant crisis behavior patterns to these. The within-case investigation will be conducted using the process tracing technique.[56] Process tracing pays great attention to context and detail and therefore enables the kind of "soaking and poking" required to decipher how the key actors were thinking and acting during each crisis, and why they were doing so.[57]

Data

The case studies rely on a combination of primary and secondary information. The latter is drawn from the rich empirical data and analyses of India-Pakistan nuclear crises since 1998, some of which were recounted in Chapter 1. This literature expounds on the developments during the crises, the planning and strategies behind them, the thinking among policy makers, the military and diplomatic actions taken by India, Pakistan, and the United States and other third-party actors, and the public and private signals transmitted during the crises. This secondary information is complemented by an extensive primary research component. Over eighty interviews and discussions were conducted with Indian, Pakistani, and U.S. officials—these included heads of states, military and intelligence chiefs, and other senior government representatives with key decision-making roles during the crises—and experts with intimate knowledge of the studied cases. The analysis of the case studies also benefits from archival newspaper research used to compile an original database of signals transmitted by officials and other relevant crisis managers during each of the three crises. Relevant news items in Indian, Pakistani, and international press outlets pertaining to each crisis were examined for this purpose.[58] The case studies draw on the content analysis of the compiled signals.[59]

Structure of the Case Studies

The next three chapters are dedicated to the crisis case studies. Chapter 3 examines the Kargil crisis; Chapter 4, the 2001–2002 military standoff; and Chapter 5, the Mumbai crisis. Each chapter begins by providing basic background information on the crisis and laying out the strategic and diplomatic context leading up to it. The crisis behavior of the two antagonists is thereafter examined in turn, first through a bilateral lens without accounting for third-party mediation and then by studying their interaction with the third party. The third party's approach toward the conflicting parties is studied subsequently. This structure sets up each case study as a comparison between traditional deterrence-based explanations and brokered bargaining. While the case narratives test each of the propositions (P1–P10), in the interest of readability, these chapters have not been structured to explicitly pose the propositions as standard questions. The sequence of the narratives also does not always conform to the order in which the propositions were introduced earlier in this chapter; the complexities of the crises do not naturally lend themselves to such a sequence across the three cases. The last section in each of these chapters summarizes crisis behavior, pointing to characteristics associated with particular propositions, and establishes whether their aggregation constitutes behavior in line with brokered bargaining.

SECTION II
INDIA-PAKISTAN CRISES IN THE OVERT NUCLEAR ERA

3   The Kargil Crisis

OCCURRING MERELY A YEAR AFTER INDIA'S AND PAKI-stan's nuclear tests, the Kargil conflict was the first active confrontation between two nuclear-armed rivals since the Sino-Soviet Ussuri River clashes of 1969. The crisis was triggered by a limited land grab operation by Pakistani paramilitary forces in the Kargil district in a remote part of northern Kashmir on the Indian side of the Line of Control (LoC). Between 700 and 1,000 Pakistani troops crossed over undetected in the winter months of 1999 and occupied strategic heights overlooking the all-important National Highway 1A, India's only land access to its forces deployed on the disputed Siachen glacier.[1] For years, Indian troops had created a routine of vacating this area's snow-capped heights during the winter and going back to occupy them after the mountain passes reopened for the summer.[2] Pakistan had hoped to apply the finders keepers rule to these unattended heights and subsequently use this as a bargaining chip to negotiate the Kashmir dispute.[3] India responded by escalating the conflict vertically, eventually throwing as many as 20,000 troops into the contested area and employing ground and air power on its side of the LoC to evict the intruders.[4] After initially offering firm resistance, Pakistani forces were left to face relentless, successful Indian attacks. Fast running out of tactical and diplomatic options, Islamabad eventually agreed to a U.S.-brokered withdrawal. However, this was not before the seventy-five day crisis had etched itself in history as perhaps the bloodiest confrontation between two nuclear powers.[5]

The Road to Kargil: The Strategic
and Diplomatic Context

The timing of the Kargil crisis was crucial. South Asia had been all but ignored by the international community since the end of the Cold War. No foreign policy interests of note had attracted the attention of Western governments to the region. The South Asian nuclear tests of 1998 forced global attention back on India and Pakistan. Fearful of the consequences of nuclearization, the international community responded by imposing sanctions and engaging these two South Asian rivals in nonproliferation diplomacy to persuade them to sign up to arms control and disarmament measures.[6] Their concerns about the nuclear risks in South Asia were heightened by the fact that India and Pakistan had remained locked in an acrimonious relationship throughout the 1990s. Indian Kashmir had been in the grip of a raging violent insurgency that Pakistan was backing clandestinely through non-state proxies, the mujahedeen.[7] Pakistan had hoped that a vibrant insurgency would serve Pakistan's long-term quest to "internationalize" the Kashmir issue by convincing the world of the unsustainability of the territorial status quo and a need for a mediated, compromise solution. India, on the other hand, saw third parties as equalizing forces for the weaker Pakistan and remained deeply distrustful of their involvement. During the 1990s, India managed to keep the international community from backing Pakistan's position; even though there was periodic criticism of India's persistent human rights violations in Kashmir,[8] whatever attention the dispute received during this period tended to reinforce India's preference for a bilateral solution to the issue.

India's and Pakistan's nuclear tests seemed to provide momentary relief in terms of their bilateral competition. Extreme international pressure and calls for a rollback of the nuclear programs forced New Delhi and Islamabad to initiate a peace dialogue to signal their maturity and recognition of the importance of handling nuclear weapons responsibly. Progress was unprecedented. By February 1999, Indian prime minister Atal Bihari Vajpayee and his Pakistani counterpart Nawaz Sharif had signed a broad and comprehensive memorandum of understanding, the "Lahore Declaration," which was intended to stabilize the nuclear relationship and deal with virtually all outstanding issues.[9] Secret backchannel negotiations on the Kashmir dispute were also initiated.[10]

Ironically, this cordial environment made a stealth operation in Kargil that much more unexpected—and thus feasible.[11] Also working to Pakistan's

advantage was Indian strategic thinking that the 1998 nuclear tests had provided India escalation dominance and therefore made an India-Pakistan war
and Pakistan's option of using proxy warfare in Kashmir obsolete.[12] The small
group of senior officers within Pakistan's all-powerful army who planned and
launched the Kargil operation in great secrecy—even without the full knowledge of the other military services and the country's civilian authorities—
sensed the opportunity.[13] Led by the army chief, General Pervez Musharraf,
these individuals had never served in positions that would have afforded them
any real understanding of nuclear strategy.[14] This was the norm at the time;
the clandestine nature of the country's nuclear weapons development had
prevented the military from socializing its officers in nuclear thinking.[15] The
planners of the Kargil operation drew the wrong lessons from South Asian
nuclearization. The operation was initially conceived in the late 1980s in a
conventional environment,[16] and these officers believed that the same tactical, limited land-grab objectives would be more achievable under the nuclear
overhang. There was successful precedent for such tactical actions in Kashmir.
Both Pakistan and India had regularly maneuvered to make minor alterations
to the LoC over the years and Pakistan felt that India had managed to "creep
forward" along this dividing line.[17] More significantly, India had occupied
the Siachen glacier in the north of the disputed state in 1984 through a military operation and Pakistan was forced to accept the outcome.[18] Now, as the
engineers of the Kargil adventure saw it, such an operation would have the
added advantage of alarming the world about Kashmir becoming a "nuclear
flashpoint" and forcing it to call for immediate crisis termination, leaving the
freshly occupied territory in Pakistan's control. More broadly, they hoped that
the demonstration of continued risk of conflict over Kashmir would translate into global pressure on India to negotiate a settlement of the dispute with
Pakistan.[19] The secretive nature of the Kargil operation prevented these officers from receiving broader counsel that may have led them to recognize the
obvious flaw in their assumptions: Pakistan was hoping for international support while challenging the "unwritten law" that nuclear weapon states do not
violate "recognized zones of control."[20]

Nonetheless, India was caught completely unaware by Pakistan's stealth
operation.[21] Its task now was to reverse Pakistan's intrusion without allowing the world to assume a dispute resolution role in Kashmir. Its challenge
was compounded by the fact that global attention was fixated on the risks of
nuclear escalation in South Asia.

As the Conflict Unfolded: Pakistani, Indian, and Third-Party Crisis Strategies

Pakistan

The Land Incursion

Tactically, Pakistan's Kargil operation was a "typical case of salami slicing" whereby Pakistan tried to achieve small territorial gains not significant enough to push India into a general war.[22] Its troops were to occupy various points along ridge lines to control dominating heights overlooking Highway 1A.[23] By early May 1999, these intruders had managed to set up 100–130 posts on various strategic heights five miles deep into Indian Kashmir.[24] Even though this penetration was far deeper than the routine infringements on the LoC that had been ongoing for years, it was still inconsequential as far as any threat to India's heartland was concerned. Pakistani crisis initiators therefore never considered the possibility of a major escalation of the conflict. They also tried to buffer against a disproportionate Indian response by denying direct involvement in the crisis, instead portraying the intrusion as the work of freelance Kashmiri mujahedeen.[25]

Pakistan's plan got off to a perfect start. The Indian military took almost three weeks to determine the true extent and nature of the Pakistani intrusion and lost over fifty soldiers in the process.[26] Fortunes began to change when India introduced its air force into the mix on May 25. Pakistani intruders managed to stand their ground for another fortnight. On June 13, India reclaimed a strategically crucial set of heights in the Tololing Complex, including Point 4590, the closest peak overlooking National Highway 1A that allowed interdiction of the route with direct fire.[27] Control of these heights gave India a foothold inside Pakistan's linear defenses.[28] Bitter fighting continued through early July but during this time, India managed to take back virtually all the critical peaks. The Pakistani military made no attempt to escalate the conflict as the ground situation shifted in India's favor. In fact, it effectively abandoned its men once the Indian air force (IAF) was introduced, only providing them sparing artillery cover. The Pakistan air force (PAF), while on alert and mounting patrols, did not engage IAF in combat.[29] Outside the Kargil region, Pakistan's military moves amounted to little more than force demonstrations. Pakistan activated its second and third lines of defense, including moving armor units, on the international border days after the IAF was inducted and Indian troops and equipment were seen moving toward the international border as part of India's wider mobilization.[30] However, no full-scale mobilization was ordered at any point.[31]

The Pakistani leadership combined the use of force and force demonstrations with frequent verbal messaging, including nuclear rhetoric. These signals had three defining characteristics: a constant attempt to maintain the mujahedeen cover by denying direct involvement in the incursion; offensive and deterrent threats; and an effort to present India as the party resorting to excessive use of force.

The initial period of the crisis witnessed the most intense signaling. At first, when Pakistan enjoyed superiority in the battlefield, it continued to threaten a "befitting response to India, if New Delhi launched any misadventure at the Line of Control."[32] In late May, when India had escalated the conflict vertically and Pakistan was seriously concerned about possible hot pursuit by Indian troops into Pakistani Kashmir,[33] Pakistani foreign secretary Shamshad Ahmad Khan issued the first major deterrent threat by stating that Pakistan "will not hesitate to use any weapon in our arsenal to defend our territorial integrity."[34] Deterrent threats returned in the second half of June. Pakistani prime minister Nawaz Sharif threatened use of the "ultimate weapon" and warned of "irreparable losses" if India crossed the LoC.[35] This was a time when Sharif was convinced that "India was getting ready to launch a full-scale military operation against Pakistan."[36]

Pakistan broached one other nonmilitary avenue during the crisis: it activated the bilateral diplomatic channel with India, seeking mutual accommodation in the form of cessation of hostilities followed by talks. Pakistan twice proposed a meeting of the foreign ministers in late May and again on June 8. The Pakistani foreign minister Sartaj Aziz ultimately visited New Delhi on June 11. It turned out to be a huge embarrassment as a day before Aziz's arrival India released secretly recorded tapes of two conversations between army chief Pervez Musharraf and Chief of General Staff General Aziz Khan, from May 26 and 29, which left little doubt that the Pakistani military had directly planned and executed the Kargil operation.[37] Sartaj Aziz's plea in India for a ceasefire followed by negotiations on the status of the LoC seemed comical and "so totally irrelevant" in the face of this clear evidence of Pakistani instigation of the operation.[38]

The failure of these formal parlays led Sharif to look to quiet diplomacy to produce an acceptable outcome. The backchannel on Kashmir initiated by the two prime ministers immediately after the Lahore Declaration was activated when, in mid-June, the threat of escalation seemed real.[39] After showing some promise, this effort also fell through within two weeks. Pakistani sources alleged that a deal had been struck that would have effectively provided Pakistan with a face saver in return for agreeing to withdraw its forces and reinitiating dialogue as envisioned in the Lahore Declaration.[40] However, the plan was leaked prematurely. India denied that any such crisis termination deal existed.[41]

With battlefield losses mounting, Pakistan agreed to withdraw its troops soon thereafter. The Pakistani and Indian director generals of military operations met on July 11 and reached an understanding on a phased troop withdrawal from Kargil to be completed by July 16.[42]

Centrality of the Third Party in Pakistan's Calculus
The third-party aspect was central to Pakistan's Kargil operation. In fact, the venture can most aptly be defined as a demonstration crisis where Pakistan's military operations focused "at least as much on precipitating international intervention in support of its claims over Kashmir as they did on securing marginal pieces of Indian territory."[43] However, given the failure of Kargil's architects to recognize the inherent contradiction between attempting territorial revisionism and receiving a sympathetic response from a world acutely concerned about the potential for escalation, Pakistan was at an obvious disadvantage. None of Pakistan's moves to obtain the world's support worked at any point during the crisis.

Pakistani planners seem to have considered quick international intervention as an insurance policy against an all-out Indian offensive. This was one major reason they never contemplated preparing for India's vertical and horizontal escalation. Pakistan's mujahedeen cover story also served a dual purpose. Tactically, it sowed confusion among Indian military ranks and thereby delayed their countermoves. But equally, the cover was necessary for Pakistan to escape the charge of obvious duplicity in conducting diplomatic parlays at Lahore while simultaneously planning a massive incursion across the LoC. The importance of keeping the mujahedeen story going was in no small part responsible for Pakistan abandoning its forces rather than engaging the Indian offensive with its own vertical escalation within the Kargil region.

Pakistan's stance was not taken seriously by any third-party actor.[44] According to one account, the United States knew "almost at the beginning" that Pakistani regulars were involved in Kargil.[45] As Pakistan continued to deny its involvement, terming its direct role in the intrusion an "unfounded charge,"[46] it dented its own credibility and further convinced the world of its culpability and duplicity. If there was still any doubt left about Pakistani involvement by the second week of June, India's release of the transcripts of the Musharraf-Aziz conversation removed it. Rather absurdly though, the Pakistani foreign minister stuck to the official line, contending even after this humiliation that Pakistan had "no troops in Held Kashmir" and that the militants were "not under our [Pakistani] control."[47] The foreign minister and the Pakistani public diplomacy machinery recognized the absurdity of their position. Pakistani diplomats had become convinced early on in the crisis that their position was untenable.[48] Having banked on the mujahedeen cover to avoid the world's opposition, however, a formal public admission of guilt at this late stage was deemed to be even more damaging to Pakistan's crisis objectives. Nonetheless, Pakistan was condemned by all Western capitals in unison after this point; their demand was a unilateral Pakistani pullout from Kargil.

If disguising its involvement was one of Pakistan's strategies to elicit a favorable international response, its attempts to portray India in a negative light was another. In a classic display of risk manipulation, Pakistan presented India's response to its incursion as "aggression" that increased the likelihood of escalation of the crisis. Pakistani statements denounced the introduction of the IAF as "very, very serious"; they blamed India for dropping bombs on the Pakistani side of the LoC; and they threatened to retaliate against any air space violations.[49] Pakistan's deterrent threats like the one by Foreign Secretary Khan in late May also served a dual purpose: to signal resolve to India, and to manipulate the risk of war in order to have the world take notice of India's vertical escalation in the Kargil region.

Coupled with these signals was a concerted Pakistani effort to reach out to the international community to seek intervention in the crisis and mediation on the Kashmir issue more generally. While pleas for direct foreign involvement continued from the very outset, including formal requests for "the U.N. Military Observer Group in India and Pakistan (UNMOGIP) to send its observers" and for UN secretary general Kofi Annan to send a special representative,[50] these calls took on a new life after mid-June when Prime Minister Sharif began to sense trouble. Sharif actively sought out countries such as the United States, the UK, China, Russia, friendly Muslim states, and forums such as the Organization of Islamic Countries, in addition to activating the bilateral backchannel with India. His immediate concern around this time was not driven by the battlefield situation but by the growing international pressure and condemnation Pakistan had been facing for days. On June 13, Sharif told Foreign Minister Sartaj Aziz that General Musharraf had "landed us in a terrible mess, but we have to find a way to get out of this impossible situation."[51] At the time, the Pakistani military and media were still very upbeat about the ground situation and Sharif had no information about the impending fall of strategic heights in the Tololing Complex.[52]

Among these outreach efforts, it was the engagement with the United States and China that proved decisive in shaping Pakistan's ultimate crisis choices. Pakistani and U.S. leaders remained in constant touch, both through private and public channels. Till mid-June, while Pakistan remained congenial in its messaging, Sharif stood firm and continued to defy Washington's calls for a withdrawal. At times, Pakistan even sought to build pressure on the United States to rethink its stance by publicly suggesting that its partisan approach (as Pakistan portrayed it) was making Indian leaders inflexible and confident about expanding the war.

Pakistan's tone began to shift gradually after mid-June. In the first sign of a softened position, Prime Minister Sharif wrote a letter to U.S. president Bill Clinton about "meeting with the conditions that India had laid down."[53] Within a week, Clinton dispatched Central Command (CENTCOM) chief General Anthony Zinni and State Department official Gibson Lanpher to Pakistan to convince Sharif and Musharraf to withdraw their troops. Even though their trip coincided with the second burst of Pakistan's aggressive nuclear signaling and emphasis on its resolve to fight back against any expanded Indian offensive, General Zinni's hard talk is believed to have moderated his Pakistani interlocutors. When General Zinni met Musharraf on June 24, the two reportedly discussed the mechanics of a negotiated withdrawal in some detail.[54] General Zinni reports that Musharraf also encouraged Prime Minister Sharif to "hear me [Zinni] out."[55] Even though Pakistan continued to hope for a favorable crisis termination plan, the Zinni mission had caused a rethink in the Pakistani camp. It was no coincidence that Musharraf used the word "withdrawal" publicly for the first time—even though he rejected the idea of a unilateral withdrawal—immediately after Zinni's visit.[56]

As Pakistan worked on the bilateral and U.S. options from mid-June onward, it also reached out to its trusted ally, China. The Chinese message to all visiting Pakistani officials seeking to garner its support was categorical: end the crisis peacefully and bilaterally.[57] This is what General Musharraf was told when he visited China in the last week of May.[58] And this is precisely what the Chinese foreign minister conveyed to Sartaj Aziz, who made an unscheduled one-day trip to China before his fateful June 11 visit to New Delhi.[59] Prime Minister Sharif made a last ditch effort to woo Beijing during a visit shortly after General Zinni departed Pakistan. The Chinese leadership did not budge. Shocked, disappointed, and desperate—also because the bilateral backchannel had just then collapsed—Sharif cut short his trip and returned home on July 1.[60]

The Pakistani prime minister traveled to Washington immediately thereafter and met President Clinton on July 4. As expected, he raised concerns about India's inflexibility and violations in Kashmir and the need for the United States to play a mediatory role.[61] Nothing worked; each of Sharif's attempts to get Clinton to back Pakistan's stance was rejected. In fact, Clinton threatened Sharif with international isolation. Ultimately, the Pakistani prime minister stood down and agreed to a withdrawal. He did, however, extract a face saver in the form of Clinton's promise to take a "personal interest" in the resumption of the India-Pakistan dialogue.[62] The crux of the joint statement issued after the meeting, however, focused on an unconditional Pakistani withdrawal.

Sharif's decision to withdraw merits closer examination for it entailed high political costs for him. Pakistan's right-wing parties and the mainstream press denounced Sharif's decision and accused him of betraying the Kashmiri freedom struggle.[63] Also, as Owen Bennett-Jones notes "many in the military establishment resented the order to pull back."[64] Mistry explains that despite major Pakistani battlefield losses, fighting could have lingered on—Indian strategists felt this could be as long as six months and would have caused additional casualties on their side—before India would have managed to affect a total eviction of the Pakistani intruders.[65] Yet, Sharif recognized Pakistan's growing isolation in Kargil. Clinton's stern approach during their meeting must have reinforced his fears. Also, Pakistan's poor economic health could have heightened his sensitivity to international opinion. In late June, the United States had threatened to force the International Monetary Fund (IMF) to withhold a much-needed $100 million loan to Pakistan pending at the time.[66] Separately, the Pakistani prime minister had been informed by his advisors that "even if the multilateral agencies managed to withstand U.S. pressure to maintain their support for Pakistan, the Kargil hostilities have the potential to run the country's foreign exchange reserves completely dry in the next three months."[67]

Regardless, Sharif's decision to withdraw sealed an all-round military and diplomatic defeat. Pakistan ended the crisis condemned, with only a weak face saver offered by the July 4 Clinton-Sharif meeting to hide behind.

India

Military Response to Pakistan's Incursion

India's response to Pakistan's incursion was an exercise in compellence, aimed specifically at evicting the Pakistani intruders. It can be broken down into three phases. The first phase ran from May 3 to May 25, when the Indian army was unable to fully ascertain the extent of the Pakistani incursion and mistook it for typical mujahedeen infiltration such as had occurred throughout the 1990s. It therefore only took piecemeal actions to dislodge the intruders.[68] The second phase ran from this point to mid-June. The Indian military, despite using significant force in the conflict area, failed to make any significant headway during this period. The third phase proceeded from mid-June till the end of the crisis and proved definitive in determining the outcome of the Kargil crisis in India's favor.

India's military operations only began in earnest after the IAF was deployed along with heavy ground reinforcements on May 25. The armed forces were ordered to "take any action necessary to evict the invaders," but the IAF was also strictly told not to cross the LoC.[69] Still, given that Pakistan had never contemplated an escalatory step involving massive use of Indian air power in its crisis planning,[70] IAF's induction checkmated it. By the time this air campaign was over, Operation Safed Sagar had conducted nearly 5,000 sorties, including 1,200 air strikes, reconnaissance, search and destroy missions, escort missions, and close air support tasks.[71]

In the second and third phases, India also undertook broader mobilization along the international border. As early as late May, "elements of the Indian army's main offensive 'strike force' were loading tanks, artillery, and other heavy equipment onto flatbed rail cars."[72] "Armored units intended for offensive use were leaving their garrisons in Rajasthan . . . and preparing to move."[73] By late June, Indian "mechanized and artillery divisions advanced to forward positions" along the international border and the LoC.[74] India also activated its navy, undertaking the largest amassing of naval ships ever in the region.[75] Even though India did not move its strike corps and mechanized units into final attack positions, it seriously contemplated attacking across the international border. On June 13, the IAF was reportedly "minutes away from launching a full-fledged air attack deep inside Pakistan."[76] This plan to attrit the PAF was part of a significant escalation that would have involved ground operations. Indian political authorities ultimately did not authorize the action and the IAF was asked to stand down at the very last minute.[77] However, the option of using force was not discarded altogether. On June 18, army chief V. P. Malik told his commanders to "be prepared for escalation—sudden or gradual—along the LoC or the international border and be prepared to go to (declared) war at short notice."[78]

Despite the vertical escalation in the Kargil region and force demonstrations along the international and maritime borders, Pakistan remained defiant in the second phase. It was only some days after the Indian military managed to capture Point 4590 in Tololing on June 13 that victories began to flow.[79] Yet, it was not until India captured Tiger Hill, another peak that allowed easy interdiction of Highway 1A, on July 4 that it could claim to have broken the back of the Pakistani intrusion.[80] Victories continued in the following week as India remained firm in its demand for complete Pakistani withdrawal.

Indian military actions during Kargil were supplemented by verbal signaling that sought to balance resolve and prudence. Much like its use of military force, India's rhetoric also hardened as the crisis progressed. Overall, however, Indian signaling, especially statements involving mention of nuclear weapons, were far more measured than Pakistan's. Tellis, Fair, and Medby argue that India did not hype Pakistan's nuclear threats or respond to them in order to avoid increasing the value of Islamabad's ploy of nuclear coercion.[81]

In the early stages, even as the Indian establishment began to realize that the scale of the intrusion was unusual, it sought to avoid creating panic and giving the international community an excuse to intervene in the crisis. The tone began to harden only after more information about the nature of the incursion and the involvement of official Pakistani personnel filtered in. An Indian official hinted at the possibility of a stern military response to the intrusion on May 21, the day India received air surveillance information on the extent of Pakistan's ingress for the first time.[82] He said: "If the Pakistanis are aiding and abetting the alteration of the LoC, there is no reason for us to let it be a localized issue. We too can make gains on the LoC and we may well exercise that option."[83] This was to become a constant feature of Indian messaging throughout the crisis. Indian officials projected maturity and exercised restraint but simultaneously warned that the option to use force across the LoC and the international border remained open. As Indian national security advisor (NSA) Brajesh Mishra put it, "not crossing the border and the LoC holds good today. But we do not know what may happen tomorrow."[84] The frequency of these signals increased in June as the level of fighting escalated and Indian mobilization along the international border began to take shape. A fair amount of chest thumping, aimed at conveying India's firmness and resolve in seeking nothing short of complete and unilateral Pakistani withdrawal, was on display once India had acquired the upper hand in the crisis.

In terms of direct bilateral contacts, India's response to Pakistan's efforts to initiate talks was unflinching: talks would only center on Pakistan's withdrawal and not on the broader Kashmir question. When Prime Minister Vajpayee agreed to Pakistani Foreign Minister Sartaj Aziz's June 11 visit to New Delhi for instance, he made this stance public in a formal address to the nation: "I do want to make it plain: if the stratagem now is that the intrusion should be used to alter the Line of Control through talks, the proposed talks will end before they have begun."[85] During Aziz's visit, India made pointed demands that included immediate withdrawal, reaffirmation of validity of the LoC, abandonment of cross-border "terrorism," and dismantling of militant infrastructure in Pakistani Kashmir where the anti-India mujahedeen were trained.[86] It stuck to this position for the rest of the crisis.

Then came the backchannel. Indian lead R. K. Mishra traveled to Pakistan on June 25 and delivered Prime Minister Vajpayee's blunt message to Prime Minister Nawaz Sharif: India and Pakistan were "one inch away from war."[87] Whether they were at the time, this was a clear signal of India's willingness to up the ante. The threat worked. The Pakistani prime minister immediately outlined a crisis termination plan that entailed an end to the fighting in Kargil—effectively a Pakistani withdrawal—and a return to the understanding reached at Lahore that prized diplomatic solutions to all problems, including Kashmir.[88] The plan was leaked to the press before it could materialize.

Proactive Outreach to the World
The real surprise in India's behavior during the Kargil episode was its eagerness to harness international efforts to influence the outcome of the crisis. Not only had India traditionally remained wary of third-party involvement in India-Pakistan disputes, but it also had lukewarm and bitter relations, respectively, with the United States and China when the Kargil crisis broke out.[89] This should have dampened any keenness on its part to engage outside actors. In reality, India adopted a dual approach, dealing directly with

Pakistan through use of military force and dialogue and simultaneously pursuing an "international strategy" aimed at eliciting favorable third-party support.[90] The *Guardian* aptly described India's approach as a "double act of war and diplomacy."[91]

India's outreach strategy was a mirror image of Pakistan's. Unlike Pakistan, however, India was able to portray Pakistan's incursion as "treachery" and convince the world of its role as the aggressor.[92] It worked hard to expose Pakistan's mujahedeen cover. Its decision to go public with the Musharraf–General Aziz tapes was aimed at exposing Pakistan's duplicity to third-party actors. Indian external affairs minister Jaswant Singh acknowledged this candidly by stating that "the making public of this evidence at this juncture, is to expose the Pakistani game plan to the entire world, to preempt any designs that Pakistan may be nurturing about obscuring the central issue of their involvement, complicity and continued support to an armed intrusion and aggression in which Pakistani regular troops are participating."[93] Simultaneously, India continued to highlight its restraint and couched its own vertical escalation in the Kargil region as a defensive response to Pakistan's aggression. Further, to play to the sensitivities of the United States, the Indian press and other media drew parallels between Washington's concern about terrorism and India's fight against "Islamist terrorists" in Kashmir. Links were also insinuated between the Pakistani state and Al Qaeda leader Osama Bin Laden.[94]

Paradoxically, India even used some of its third-party connections to prevent internationalization of the Kashmir dispute. It invested enormous effort, and was successful, in blocking the UN's attempts to get involved in the crisis in the wake of Pakistani requests to Secretary General Kofi Annan in late May. It also rejected Annan's desire to send an envoy during this phase of the crisis.[95] Instead, India proactively sought assurances from the P-5 in the UN Security Council (UNSC) that the Kargil crisis would not be allowed to become an agenda item at the forum.[96]

Indian external affairs minister Jaswant Singh also visited China at the height of the conflict in mid-June. Though the visit was preplanned and focused on broader bilateral issues, Singh did get a confirmation from the Chinese that they had asked Pakistan to "resolve the problem through peaceful means and dialogue."[97]

It was the United States, however, that proved to be India's unexpected trump card. India's approach toward Washington entailed a mix of direct lobbying for support, manipulation of the risk of war, and a combination of defiance of and deference to U.S. preferences. India lobbied hard through multiple public and private channels—hard enough that the then Pakistani ambassador to the United States, Riaz Khokhar, described its efforts as a "diplomatic earthquake" in Washington.[98]

Most critical to India's outreach were private government-to-government channels. India's first major request to the United States came during a meeting between its external affairs minister Jaswant Singh and U.S. deputy secretary of state Strobe Talbott on May 25. The two officials had developed a warm relationship via the bilateral nonproliferation dialogues the United States had initiated with India (and Pakistan) after the nuclear tests.[99] Singh convinced Talbott to firmly back the Indian position. The two agreed that the United States would push Pakistan to withdraw its forces while India in return would exercise restraint and bar its troops from crossing the LoC.[100]

Given India's traditional distrust of U.S. diplomacy and its engrained psyche that U.S. involvement always tended to benefit Pakistan, it did not take this understanding at face value. Instead, it pressed further by trying to coerce the United States into pressuring Pakistan. As Waheguru Sidhu argues, Indian threats to cross the LoC during the Kargil crisis may have had more to do with pressuring the United States than with signaling resolve to Pakistan.[101] The most obvious example of Indian manipulation of the risk of war vis-à-vis the third party came in mid-June. With bitter fighting still ongoing, NSA Brajesh Mishra was sent to Paris to meet his U.S. counterpart Sandy Berger. Mishra was carrying a letter from Prime Minister Vajpayee for President Clinton. In it was a pointed message warning that India's policy of restraint was reaching its limits and that it was becoming difficult for the government to force the military to keep taking casualties without escalating the conflict to ease the pressure in the Kargil region. Mishra informed Berger that the Indian military might be allowed to cross into Pakistani territory "any day."[102] According to Robert Wirsing, "the letter was a transparent attempt to induce Clinton 'to turn up the pressure on Pakistan.'"[103] Mishra also used the opportunity to press Berger to get the leaders of the Group of Eight (G-8) countries, meeting in Cologne, Germany, at the time, to issue a statement in favor of the Indian position. As the Telegraph reported on June 19, "India has turned to Washington for help to convince the world's richest and most powerful nations—the Group of Eight—of the need to send a strong signal to Pakistan to vacate the armed intrusion in Kargil."[104]

In parallel, India's approach also reflected an acute concern for the third party's signals. As the third party exhibited its intent to cow Pakistan into withdrawing its forces and acted accordingly, India consciously held back from expanding the conflict beyond Kargil. Its decision not to cross the LoC defied military logic since entering Pakistani Kashmir would have allowed Indian troops to interdict the Pakistani supply lines and expeditiously subdue their opponents.[105] It was even more surprising given that Pakistan had neither prepared for nor threatened escalation of the conflict to deter such Indian action.

The predominant explanation for India's decision is that Indian military victories from mid-June onward took away the requirement to escalate the conflict.[106] But this still does not explain why India chose to take avoidable casualties and incur material losses that could have been prevented by crossing the LoC. The question is especially pertinent because this was India's first televised war, which got the entire nation clued in and seething with discontent, and Vajpayee's government was politically challenged and facing national elections.[107] Further, Indian military officers were advocating crossing the LoC; India's National Security Advisory Board had also recommended the same.[108] While multiple factors undoubtedly impinged on the Indian leadership's thinking, a number of Indian officials explained the mindset at the time. Indian high commissioner to Pakistan G. Parthasarathy summarizes the Indian outlook: "We had to get the world to accept that this was Pakistan's fault."[109] India would "keep the moral high ground" by staying on its side of the LoC, thereby making "political gains with the world community."[110] According to Indian army chief General V. P. Malik, Indian "political leaders felt that India needed to make its case and get international support" and that this could best be achieved by showing restraint.[111] Brajesh Mishra opined that restraint meant that "we retained international support and allowed for condemnation of Pakistan's actions by the international community. And ultimately that was important."[112] Hardly any other measure can establish India's concern for third-party support as clearly as its decision to absorb additional casualties.

India's ingrained distrust of third-party involvement and its traditional opposition to internationalization of the dispute over Kashmir would have further incentivized restraint on its part. If Indian leaders felt that external support for its stance in Kargil was merely a result of the third party's belief that backing India was the best means of terminating the crisis rather than of the international community's appreciation for India's overall position on Kashmir, they would have seen third-party sympathy as a function of their measured behavior. Indeed, Indian leaders felt that expanding the conflict would have led to a more forceful international role, including direct UNSC involvement calling for an immediate ceasefire.[113] Hinting at this concern, Jaswant Singh argued that abandoning restraint would have been "a strategic error of incalculable dimensions, principally because of the nuclear status of both India and Pakistan, which for the world was the foremost worry."[114]

This mindset may also explain the virtual absence of aggressive nuclear signaling by India. Its restraint on this count was not limited to verbal statements. India made no mention of intelligence it claims to have picked up at the height of the crisis that pointed to Pakistan's preparation of some missile launching sites, instead quietly taking "some protective measures" such as relocating some of its missiles.[115] It even chose to forego plans to conduct missile flight tests, a common tactic to demonstrate capability and convey resolve to the adversary in crisis situations. India had plans to test its Agni II ballistic missile in early July, just when the Pakistani prime minister and U.S. president were meeting in Washington but army chief General Malik recommended postponement arguing that a test at that juncture would have gone against India's policy of strategic restraint, which had helped garner international support.[116]

India's crisis strategy worked. It emerged from the crisis victorious. As the *Telegraph* noted at the time, "few Indian officials deny that the Kashmir dispute has been internationalized. But they argue that by doing so New Delhi has benefited as most world powers have sided with it."[117] This experience proved to be a watershed for India's view of third-party roles in times of crisis.

The Third Party: Umpiring the Crisis in Pursuit of De-escalation

Western capitals saw the clash in Kargil as a test case of a crisis between two developing countries locked in a long-standing bitter rivalry now managing demonstrated nuclear capabilities with uncertain levels of safety and security. President Bill Clinton took the nuclear dimension of the crisis "very very seriously."[118] Bruce Riedel, Clinton's special assistant in the White House, summarized the sentiment: "We could all too easily imagine the two parties beginning to mobilize for war, seeking third party support . . . and a deadly descent into full-scale conflict all along the border with a danger of nuclear cataclysm."[119] This concern, in the words of Assistant Secretary of State for South Asian Affairs Karl Inderfurth, defined the United States' top crisis management goals: "de-escalation, de-escalation, de-escalation."[120]

The United States remained the principal third-party interlocutor during the crisis. Its foremost worry was that India might cross the LoC and that an expanded conflict could lead to swift escalation.[121] This led the international community to unanimously call for the sanctity of the LoC to be restored and for both sides to show restraint. Pakistan was seen as the culprit: it had acted recklessly and "wrecked the talks" that had been ongoing as part of the parlays between India and Pakistan before the Kargil crisis.[122] Pressuring Pakistan to withdraw its troops unilaterally while persuading India not to expand the conflict horizontally was therefore seen as the legitimate course of action and the quickest and surest way of achieving de-escalation.

U.S. crisis diplomacy began in earnest in late May. The Clinton administration issued its first set of demarches on May 24 as soon as the veil of confusion about the nature and scale of the intrusion and Pakistan's role in it began to lift and it became clear that the situation was not business as usual on the LoC.[123] Thereafter, the crisis received daily attention through dedicated meetings in Washington that involved all relevant U.S. government agencies.[124] In addition, U.S. and Indian and Pakistani leaders remained in constant contact through phone, letter, and shuttle diplomacy.

Washington's signaling conveyed three key messages in the first three weeks or so of its involvement: Kashmir is a bilateral issue; Pakistan is to blame for the crisis and so Pakistani forces must withdraw; and as a logical extension, the United States is willing to back India's position in the crisis. Pakistan was blamed, first in private and then in public. Privately, U.S. officials were categorical in multiple interactions with the Pakistani ambassador to the U.S. Riaz Khokhar in late May that the United States would be forced to put all the blame on Pakistan publicly if it did not withdraw from Kargil.[125] U.S. assistant secretary Inderfurth acted on this threat days later by issuing Washington's first public call for Pakistan's withdrawal: "Clearly, the Indians are not going to cede this territory that militants have taken. . . . They have to depart and they will depart, either voluntarily or because the Indians take them out."[126] The U.S. Congress also joined in to complement the Clinton administration's messaging. In late May, Democratic congressman Frank Pallone, founder of the India caucus on the Hill, compared India's predicament to Israel's, asserting that "India has every right to defend against them [terrorist forays into India from Pakistan] and do what is necessary to prevent them."[127] In a letter to the Pakistani prime minister on June 3, President Clinton indicated that withdrawal of Pakistani forces had to be a precondition for any hope of U.S. diplomatic involvement in Kashmir.[128] Days later, Congressman Gary Ackerman urged Congress to put Pakistan on its annual list of state sponsors of terrorism unless it ceased its support for "Islamic terrorists in the Kargil/Dras area of Jammu and Kashmir and withdraws its forces from the region."[129] Others also piled on the blame and censured Pakistan. UN secretary general Kofi Annan, despite having proposed an envoy in line with Pakistan's request, candidly stated on May 29 that Pakistan was "violating the Line of Control."[130]

India was universally acknowledged as the victim; it received understanding and support from across the world. Even though it was constantly pushed to exercise restraint and avoid expanding the conflict, its use of force within the immediate area of the conflict was considered justified. Specifically for the United States, the biggest challenge was to win India's trust as a broker whose role could prove beneficial for New Delhi's crisis objectives. The U.S. leadership recognized that it bore the burden of proof. India would otherwise remain suspicious of its intentions and expect it to lean toward Pakistan if the situation became critical.[131] The United States addressed this by banking on full transparency in its crisis management approach. It regularly shared information of its crisis dealings with Pakistan with Indian leaders, thus allowing them to judge the U.S. role for themselves and recognize Washington's genuine inclination to act as a supportive force.

U.S. backing for India's position remained consistent. It started from Strobe Talbott's assurance of a firm U.S. stance in India's favor during his May 25 meeting with External Affairs Minister Jaswant Singh. Talbott's pledge surprised the Indians but they welcomed and appreciated it nonetheless. By May 29, all permanent members of the UNSC except China had assured India that they would not allow the Kargil issue to be raised in the Security Council.[132] President Clinton personally worked to block any move by the UN secretary general to appoint a formal envoy or to mediate the crisis.[133] On May 30, U.S. secretary of state Madeline Albright assured Jaswant Singh that the United States was aware of Pakistani complicity in the Kargil operation.[134]

U.S. diplomacy truly heated up from mid-June onward when India and Pakistan had mobilized well beyond Kargil, and both Indian and Pakistani leaders remained steadfast in their stance. The United States stood behind India even more firmly. At the same time, however, worried that a larger Indian offensive might cross Pakistan's redlines and make it impossible for the United States to prevent it from retaliating,[135] the U.S. leadership continued to call on India to show restraint. President Clinton talked to Prime Minister Vajpayee on June 14 to convey his appreciation for India's restraint, to urge its continuation at all costs, and to confirm that the United States would persist in its position that Pakistan must withdraw from Kargil and return the situation to the status quo ante. He also prodded Vajpayee to talk to the Pakistani leadership directly.[136]

Simultaneously, Washington continued to harden its position vis-à-vis Pakistan. It regularly put out public calls for a Pakistani withdrawal and reinforced its ask through private messaging. President Clinton demanded this in a call to Prime Minister Sharif on June 15.[137] Meanwhile, in what is evidence of the United States' increasingly firm public stance with Pakistan at the time, Assistant Secretary Inderfurth stated categorically that the "Line of Control has to be respected, (and) the intruders would have to first leave what they had occupied."[138] Jaswant Singh recalls this as the first unambiguous U.S. articulation of its position on the LoC.[139] The State Department also issued other statements squarely blaming the Pakistani incursion for the crisis.

U.S. diplomacy was forced to go into even higher gear after the Mishra-Berger meeting on June 16. As Mishra claimed, the United States took the Indian prime minister's message "quite seriously";[140] it initiated immediate measures to reduce the possibility of an expanded war. Berger assured Mishra that U.S. action would come "in days, not weeks."[141] Moreover, in line with India's demands, the United States pressed the G-8 countries to issue a strong statement favoring New Delhi.[142] Even though the statement left enough room for Pakistan to find some respite by calling for a ceasefire and resumption of dialogue between India and Pakistan, in reality it was an indictment of Pakistan's actions. Most notably, the statement termed "any military action to change the status quo as irresponsible."[143] Vajpayee's claim shortly thereafter that "India had the world community's understanding"[144] suggested that the United States had managed to satisfy the Indian leadership and buy time to put more pressure on Pakistan to withdraw.

It was also Prime Minister Vajpayee's letter to President Clinton that was responsible for prompting the U.S. president to dispatch General Zinni on his mission to Pakistan.[145] Zinni's task was to get Pakistan to agree to withdraw. He clearly signaled that the Pakistanis could not count on the United States to protect them. In his meeting with Musharraf, he warned: "If you don't pull back, you're going to bring war and nuclear annihilation down on your country. That's going to be very bad news for everybody."[146] Zinni's prodding must have convinced Musharraf that continuing the conflict risked isolation. Then U.S. ambassador to Pakistan William Milam who was present in the meeting felt that Musharraf's "body language clearly indicated a desire to withdraw."[147] As a potential face saver, Zinni offered to arrange a Clinton-Sharif meeting, but only after Pakistan agreed to a withdrawal.

As the United States kept up public and private pressure on Pakistan following Zinni's mission, it let it be known that Pakistan might have problems in receiving a $100 million IMF loan it desperately needed at the time.[148] The international community also threatened further economic isolation and imposition of a ban on aid from international organizations.[149]

Gibson Lanpher, who had accompanied Zinni on his trip, was sent to New Delhi from Pakistan in keeping with the United States' decision to maintain transparency in its crisis dealing with India.[150] Lanpher conveyed an honest recounting of his understanding of what had transpired between Zinni and the Pakistani leadership: that Pakistan had all but agreed to India's desired outcome of an unconditional withdrawal.[151] In tandem, he reiterated Washington's emphasis on the need for continued Indian restraint.[152] Incidentally, this visit coincided with the breakdown of the India-Pakistan backchannel negotiations, prompting some Pakistanis to insinuate that the United States' reassuring message to India caused it to pull out of direct negotiations. Some have even gone far enough to allege that the United States actively dissuaded India from pursuing the backchannel further as a means of punishing Pakistan.[153] American officials had been aware of the backchannel and thus could not have been totally oblivious to the implications of its messaging to India, but the fact is that it never considered the status of the backchannel to be promising enough to deliver a breakthrough.[154] Lanpher may therefore have discounted the possibility of any negative fallout from his messaging in New Delhi.[155]

Arguably the single most important element of the United States' crisis engagement was its role in crisis termination. The White House's management of the July 4 Sharif-Clinton meeting was the most pronounced manifestation of the use of the third party's punishment leverage attempted during the crisis. In advance of the meeting, the White House made it known that "any proposal for a supervised withdrawal by the U.S. or even the U.N. Military Observer Group for India and Pakistan (UNMOGIP) is a non-starter."[156] This was a preemptive strike against the Pakistani prime minister's predictable attempt to convince the U.S. president to agree to further internationalizing the crisis. Also, in a strategy blessed by the Saudi Arabian government, a close traditional ally of Pakistan, the Clinton White House asked the Saudi ambassador to Washington to act as an intermediary and soften Sharif up immediately before his meeting with Clinton.[157] Others like British prime minister Tony Blair also weighed in to stress the need for Pakistan's withdrawal.[158]

During the meeting, Clinton refused Sharif's request for U.S. mediation in the Kashmir dispute. Clinton knew that this would be unacceptable to New Delhi. In fact, he told Sharif, "If I tell you what you think you want me to say, I'll be stripped of all influence with the Indians. I'm not—and the Indians are not—going to let you get away with blackmail, and I'll not permit any characterization of this meeting that suggests I'm giving in to blackmail."[159] The president also raised the stakes by letting Sharif know that his team had already prepared two draft statements, one of which had to be released after the meeting. One bluntly put all blame for the crisis and for supporting terrorism on Pakistan while the other was more conciliatory and provided face-saving language.[160] A unilateral withdrawal, Clinton promised, would be followed by his efforts to nudge India to restart dialogue on Kashmir (but not mediation).[161] Plainly put, Clinton had given Pakistan the choice of withdrawing and leaving some hope of post-crisis U.S. assistance, or of continuing to fight, possibly with outright U.S. backing of the Indian position.

Clinton's master stroke was still to come. Just before the meeting, the CIA presented Clinton with what Bruce Riedel later described as "disturbing evidence that the Pakistanis were preparing their nuclear arsenals for possible deployment."[162] With the potential for further escalation already on their minds, this information would only have reinforced the United States' worst fears. Clinton informed his team that he would use the information "to scare the hell out of Sharif" during the meeting.[163] Accordingly, he confronted Sharif by asking him if he was aware that his military was readying the nuclear arsenal.[164]

There is great deal of controversy about the authenticity of Riedel's claim. While Riedel suggests that the intelligence was as authentic as it could be,[165] Pakistanis, and even Indians, dismiss the information as deliberately manipulated to pressure the Pakistani prime minister to give in and agree to a withdrawal.[166] Regardless, Clinton's diplomacy worked. The Pakistani prime minister, already beleaguered and unsure of his military's intentions given that his army chief's Kargil plan had failed miserably, agreed to the withdrawal and accepted that the sanctity of the LoC must be maintained. Sharif only asked for one specific line to be included in the joint statement in return. It read: "The President would take a personal interest to encourage an expeditious resumption and intensification of those bilateral efforts [agreed as part of the Lahore Declaration] once the sanctity of the Line of Control has been fully restored."[167] The U.S. team agreed.

Persisting with the spirit of transparency with India, Clinton and his team kept the Indian leadership fully updated on the progress of the July 4 meeting in real time.[168] President Clinton also previewed the joint statement with Vajpayee before sealing the deal with Sharif.[169] The coordination was so close and surprising for the Pakistani team that some of them believed that the United States received direct and significant input from New Delhi on the text of the statement.[170] Interestingly however, the United States did make one important exception to its "full transparency with India" strategy during the crisis by concealing intelligence about Pakistan's alleged nuclear movements from it. This was deliberate, driven by concerns that the information could force India into preemptive action.[171]

While Pakistan remained under the scanner throughout, the United States was not oblivious to the danger of alienating it totally. Between mid-June and the end of the crisis, the United States balanced its stern messaging to Pakistan by providing some concessions. For instance, during the Berger-Mishra meeting, Berger was cautious in responding to Mishra's demand to isolate Pakistan.[172] He stressed the need to provide Pakistan a face saver to back down. The United States also felt that such an outlet was necessary for Pakistan to be able to return to the Lahore process after the crisis, something that Washington had constantly eyed.[173] The call for a ceasefire in the G-8 statement emerging from the Cologne meeting also provided Pakistan space to stress that it had the ear of the international community. Unsurprisingly, Pakistan latched on and put a positive spin on the statement. Declaring it "a serious diplomatic setback" for India's efforts to garner the G-8's support, the Pakistani Foreign Office claimed that the statement amounted to a "virtual endorsement of Pakistan's stand" since the group "had expressed its deep concern on the continuing military confrontation in Kashmir and has called for an end to military action."[174] It presented the statement's call for the warring parties to talk to each other as an endorsement of "the need for intensifying efforts for a final settlement of the Jammu and Kashmir dispute."[175] The spin went unchallenged by the G-8. The third party's threats of economic sanctions and withholding of multilateral loans were also relaxed once the objective was accomplished. Pakistan's debt servicing was rescheduled within days of the Sharif-Clinton meeting.[176] Also contributing to the decisions to loosen the economic squeeze on Pakistan would have been the country's feeble economic situation—ironically, one of the reasons that made Sharif more sensitive to U.S. threats during the July 4 meeting—which kept the United States worried about a collapse of the Pakistani government, or worse yet, the country.[177]

The most obvious example of the U.S. concern about Pakistan's complete isolation was that it went into the July 4 meeting seeking Pakistan's troop withdrawal but also fully prepared to offer Sharif a tangible face saver. The U.S. team believed that political cover was necessary for Sharif to order a withdrawal and see it through, given his tensions with the military over the Kargil blunder.[178] This is why President Clinton readily agreed to the one-line addition to the joint statement requested by the Pakistani side. The full joint statement also contained a mention of Clinton's desire to visit South Asia in the near future.[179] Since it did not single out India, Pakistan could present this as an indication that it was being treated evenhandedly. Equally, the United States prevented India from misconstruing the results of the meeting to paint Pakistan as internationally isolated. Furthermore, when India subsequently attempted to suggest that the United States had agreed that an end to all cross-border infiltration from Pakistan should be a prerequisite for dialogue with Pakistan, the State Department immediately rebutted India's claim.[180]

The U.S. crisis management at Kargil proved crucial. The United States' own assessment was that it had "played a critical role in ensuring that the situation didn't spin out of control."[181] Its hand was strengthened through-out by other strong powers who complemented the de-escalation agenda. This convergence among third-party actors could not have been predicted ex ante. In fact, as the United States took note of the Kargil crisis, it was concerned that, akin to the Cold War, Pakistan and India would get their respective backers—China and the Arab countries for Pakistan and Russia and Israel for India—to support them against each other.[182] In reality, the United States and its allies like the UK actively coordinated their crisis management efforts. Others including China, Russia, France, and even much of the Muslim world reinforced these efforts by advocating restraint and backing U.S. calls for Pakistani withdrawal with varying degrees of candor. China's role was most crucial. Chinese interests only partially overlapped with those of the United States given that the two were competing for regional influence in South Asia. Yet, the de-escalation agenda seems to have taken precedence in Beijing's calculus. Its refusal to back Pakistan's stance came as a shock to Islamabad given China's tradition of support. It would have even surprised India, whose strategic elite almost reflexively internalize a pro-Pakistan Chinese role in such scenarios, including foreseeing the possibility of Chinese military intervention on Pakistan's behalf in an expanded conflict.[183] Nonetheless, while China's public messaging remained neutral, in private it asked Pakistan to defuse tensions on the LoC. This signal became firmer once the Indian military began clocking victories on the ground and the rest of the world pressed Pakistan to pull back. Swaran Singh argues that the Chinese role may have been the single most important factor in prompting the Pakistani leadership to seek to terminate the crisis quickly.[184]

Brokered Bargaining in South Asia: Implications of the Kargil Conflict

The Advent of Brokered Bargaining

The Kargil conflict was the first ever confrontation between two regional nuclear powers. There was great uncertainty about how India and Pakistan would behave during the episode. Brokered bargaining was neither natural to the crisis nor could this trilateral dynamic have been considered a preferred choice for the parties involved. India and Pakistan had freshly acquired their nuclear status. An urge to exhibit a more emboldened and independent stance should therefore have been intuitive. Moreover, the Indian strategic elite's deep-rooted suspicion of third-party intervention and staunch opposition to internationalizing Kashmir militated against any serious deference to a third-party role. This was also an unprecedented situation for the United States. There had been virtually no debate till this time on how specifically the unipole might react to a Kargil-type scenario. Real interest in third-party roles in regional nuclear crisis management developed only as a consequence of the crisis.

As the Kargil episode unfolded, the third-party angle was inherent in its very conception. Pakistan created a demonstration crisis specifically to lure third-party support. The United States entered the fray due to its "immediate and continuing" concern that the "conflict would escalate into a nuclear exchange."[185] It was aware that Pakistan was hoping for international attention and that intervening in the crisis could play into its hands. However, there is no evidence of any U.S. thought not to get involved simply to avoid creating a moral hazard problem. Rather, the United States engaged as soon as the opaque phase of Pakistan's incursion began to give way to the recognition that the Kargil operation had the makings of an India-Pakistan crisis. This was despite the fact that the United States and much of the Western world had no broader regional interests in South Asia at the time. The United States was also preoccupied with a war in the Balkans, and by efforts to enforce UN resolutions on Iraq and to manage fresh developments in the Arab-Israeli peace process.[186]

As the circumstances around the Kargil incursion became clear, the United States concluded that the most assured way of achieving de-escalation was to pressure Pakistan to withdraw. Its initial apprehensions of a divided, competitive mediation effort by third-party states proved unwarranted. All important states complemented U.S. messaging. This collective weight of the international community blocked Pakistan's alternative alignment options. It was important as the Pakistani leadership desperately tried to garner support from multiple sources, and only after all its potential partners, most importantly China, had refused to back its position did Prime Minister Sharif agree to terminate the crisis through U.S. intercession.

The third party's decision to pin the blame for the conflict squarely on Pakistan could have made it seem biased in India's favor. In reality, the third party was still acting as an "umpire, calling the plays as it saw them."[187] The United States coerced Pakistan while simultaneously seeking India's assurance that it would not expand the conflict outside the Kargil theater as long as the third party maintained outright support for its stance. The transparency built into the United States' crisis management proved critical in convincing India of its sincerity in operating as an honest intermediary. The United States not only backed the Indian position seeking Pakistani troop withdrawal, but it also promised not to allow Pakistan to link the Kargil crisis to the broader Kashmir dispute. Importantly, however, Washington never signaled unconditional support to New Delhi. Its promises of support operated in parallel with its demands for Indian restraint. While these messages were persuasive, not coercive, at no point did the United States guarantee consistency in its stance if India shed its restraint and triggered fresh escalation by expanding the conflict. A more explicit use of the third party's punishment leverage was never required given the Indian leadership's propensity to provide time and space for U.S. efforts to force Pakistan's withdrawal.

The United States was far more direct in its signaling to Pakistan. It used its diplomatic and economic clout to raise Pakistan's costs of defiance. Underlying the U.S. messaging throughout was an implicit threat that Pakistan could not count on Washington's support in case of an expanded conflict. At the same time, however, U.S. crisis managers remained cognizant of the dangers of sending Pakistan into oblivion. Otherwise easily overshadowed by the general direction and tone of U.S. crisis engagement at Kargil, a number of inducements, cited earlier, were on offer for Pakistan as quid pro quos for obliging the United States on its demands during the crisis. President Clinton also made efforts to prod the Indian prime minister to consider reengaging in dialogue with Pakistan after the crisis in line with his promise to Prime Minister Sharif.[188]

The United States accorded only secondary importance to larger foreign policy interests and agendas. Issues such as the Kashmir dispute or the desire to improve the Indo-U.S. relationship hardly ever made it into conversations among U.S. crisis managers. The United States did not back Pakistan's revisionist position on Kashmir as doing so would have undermined its crisis leverage with India. At the same time, it accepted India's position that the LoC was inviolable, but did not support its interpretation that Washington had made an end to all cross-LoC infiltration a prerequisite for talks on Kashmir. It worried that acquiescing to this would have negated the very face saver that was to allow Prime Minister Sharif sufficient cushion to oversee the implementation of his troop withdrawal order. By the same token, the fact that the Indo-U.S. relationship gained tremendously from the Kargil experience was, at best, a positive spinoff from Washington's crisis engagement.[189] Equally, Pakistan's ties with the United States suffered but the face savers it received had little to do with any effort to mend the relationship; any soothing effect they may have had on bilateral ties were collateral dividends from an action driven foremost by the crisis de-escalation agenda.

India's and Pakistan's behavior in the Kargil crisis exhibited the dual attributes of the resolve-prudence trade-off. Both sides sought to extract concessions from each other by employing military force, force demonstrations, and aggressive rhetoric while exhibiting restraint in terms of expanding the conflict. This aspect of their demeanor resembled a classic limited war under a nuclear umbrella and could easily be construed as substantiation of bilateral deterrence: Pakistan indulged in salami-slicing tactics and signaled its intent to inflict greater punishment on India if it continued to refuse a negotiated settlement to the Kashmir dispute; India stood firm and responded with military force in the war theater; at the same time, both sides kept the scope of the conflict limited by restricting the quantum and type of force used and initiated bilateral negotiations to seek a way out of the crisis and prevent further escalation.[190]

The third-party strand of the resolve-prudence trade-off played out vividly as well. Both rivals exhibited a mix of decision-making autonomy and sensitivity to third-party preferences. Pakistan, while pleading for support, continued to bank on plausible deniability to paint India as the aggressor and to ward off international pressure, and defied calls for withdrawal until the later part of the crisis, even seeking to suggest that U.S. support of India was adding to the risk of an expanded war. It was only when the international community reinforced its calls for withdrawal after mid-June and the battlefield situation turned against Pakistan that it began to seek a way out rather desperately. Ultimately, Pakistan was hamstrung by the fact that its crisis objectives could not have been met without outright third-party support. Having failed to achieve this, and instead being portrayed as a "reckless, adventuristic, risk-acceptant, untrustworthy state,"[191] Pakistani leaders had to be alive to the possibility that continued defiance could have forced the third party's hand into carrying out its threat of further tightening the squeeze on Pakistan. This concern drove the Pakistani prime minister to terminate the crisis despite the significant political costs his decision entailed.

Notably, India also actively exploited the third-party angle even though its approach internationalized the crisis. The United States' vocal sympathy and support for its stance meant that it did not have to budge from its demand for Pakistani troop withdrawal as a precondition for crisis termination, and instead greatly strengthened its position by aggressively and successfully using the media to expose Pakistan's involvement in the Kargil operation. That said, India also indulged in risk manipulation. Most obviously, India's decision to continue mobilizing its military to prepare for a larger offensive and its conscious efforts to signal its intent to expand the conflict ran in the face of third-party preferences. These autonomous decisions were balanced by India's deliberate choice to defer to U.S. efforts to coerce Pakistan into reversing its intrusion. As mentioned, hardly anything could provide clearer evidence of the importance India accorded to third-party preferences than its decision to hold back from crossing the LoC even though this defied military logic and considerations of political expediency.

Brokered Bargaining and the Escalation–De-escalation Dynamic

The Kargil crisis ended without escalating into a major war. On the one hand, global sympathy eliminated pressure on India to soften its position and ensured that it incurred no "evaluation costs" tied to its vertical escalation within the Kargil sector. On the other hand, however, the need to maintain this very international empathy and support in pursuit of its crisis objectives acted as a restraint on any Indian urge to expand the conflict horizontally. India's task was made simpler by the fact that its objectives were limited to restoring the territorial status quo ante. As long as Indian decision makers were convinced that the third party was working sincerely to deliver a Pakistani withdrawal and believed that it had the leverage to pull it off, they had little to gain by defying the third party outright. India's aversion to internationalizing the Kashmir crisis also predisposed it to avoiding excessive belligerence. While India gained tremendously by portraying Pakistan as reckless during the crisis, in so doing it also ran the risk of implying high escalatory pressures in South Asia, and reinforcing the world's fears about instability in such crisis contexts. India's efforts to downplay the nuclear factor despite Pakistan's deterrent threats ought to be seen in this vein.

As for Pakistan, its misplaced assumption of third-party support created an inbuilt buffer against prolonging the crisis or exhibiting belligerence in defiance of international opinion. Pakistan's crisis goals had predisposed it to seeking third-party support, but its failure to garner the world's backing forced it to rely on diplomatic intervention for crisis termination. The relentless international pressure on Pakistan and the obvious American tilt toward India made abundantly clear that there was little space for Pakistani leaders to salvage the situation through further aggression. The de-escalation objective benefited from this Pakistani predicament.

These stability-inducing dynamics notwithstanding, the Kargil episode was also rife with significant risks associated with the presence of the third-party mediation. Foremost, the incident demonstrated the role of flawed assumptions and poor decision making in creating crises under the nuclear overhang. Pakistan's intrusion was a shocking miscalculation of the world's likely reaction to its action. Flowing from a sheer lack of understanding of the true diplomatic implications of fighting a war in a nuclear environment on the part of the Kargil operation's planners, this display of bounded rationality was especially risky given the general aura of unpredictability that went with the first real-life experience of a regional nuclear crisis. India, caught completely unaware by Pakistan's intrusion and suspicious of third-party mediation in general, could have easily panicked and adopted a far more forceful response, risking swift escalation in the process.

The trilateral interaction during the crisis also offered much to be concerned about. Even as India patiently tested the United States' sincerity in its crisis management, its general suspicion of the United States and sensitivity to its historical leaning toward Pakistan meant that U.S. crisis managers had no room for error. As the conflict progressed into mid-June and Pakistan remained steadfast, India could have concluded that the United States was unwilling or unable to force Pakistan to back down. Worse yet, Indian leaders could have felt that the international community might give in to Pakistan's intransigence and ask for a ceasefire with the ground situation frozen in Pakistan's favor. Or equally, they could have misperceived third-party backing of their stance throughout the crisis and convinced themselves that the world would show understanding for an Indian decision to expand the conflict. Indeed, Indian leaders seem to have come dangerously close to drawing one of these conclusions in mid-June. Lavoy contends that India would have expanded the conflict through ground forces had it not captured vital heights in mid-June.[192] Perhaps the air force would also have received the go ahead to execute its plans to strike inside Pakistan on June 13, had India not managed its first set of successes in the Tololing Complex that day. Had India acted upon either of these plans, there would have been serious risks of instant vertical escalation.

On the flip side, Pakistan's view that the U.S. tilt was emboldening India's crisis stance could have led its leadership to perceive the situation as a gang up against it. The Pakistani military's perennial fear of Indian designs to dismember the country could have quickly molded perceptions of the unfolding scenario and led Pakistan to react to defend itself through all means at its disposal.[193]

The third party's failure to finely balance its signaling to India and Pakistan could also have induced instability. For instance, a less transparent U.S. posture would likely not have succeeded in convincing India of the world's sincerity about ensuring a Pakistani withdrawal. On the other hand, transparency created a certain expectation in New Delhi and put a premium on consistency of the strategy. The United States' supposed manipulation of intelligence about Pakistani nuclear movement during the Sharif-Clinton meeting could have had unintended consequences in this regard. Had India found out that the United States had withheld this important information from it, its leadership may have begun to have second thoughts about trusting America's overall mediatory role. On the other hand, a decision by Washington to convey the information to India could have led it to take precipitous action. This information was also delicate as it could conceivably have led the Pakistani prime minister to confront his military, which Clinton had suggested was behind the nuclear movements, and, in turn, triggered a total meltdown of their already-tense relationship. This may have made it impossible for Sharif to get the army to carry out his withdrawal order. At the very least, the breakdown would have prolonged the crisis and kept the prospects of its further escalation alive.

Finally, the Kargil episode also hints at the potential negative implications the third party's role can have for efforts at bilateral crisis management. While there is not conclusive evidence to support the Pakistani allegation that the United States deliberately tried to scuttle the backchannel, the Indian decision makers and press did take note of the U.S. pressure on Pakistan and its reassuring messaging to India with some enthusiasm. Key Indian crisis managers like External Affairs Minister Jaswant Singh also believed that there was no way Pakistan would have sent General Zinni back with a "no response" to his demand for withdrawal.[194] Inasmuch as this mindset may have influenced India's outlook toward the backchannel, Washington's lack of appreciation for this dynamic may well have dented the prospects for a deal through these secret parlays.

In retrospect, as Pakistani ambassador to the United States Riaz Khokhar put it, "Kargil was a most irresponsible adventure by a newly turned nuclear power."[195] Pakistan's revisionist aim to cement an altered territorial scenario lost out to India's preference for the status quo. The lesson was that attempts to use the nuclear umbrella to affect a change in territorial distributions were likely to lead to an instant loss of positive evaluation from key third-party actors. India, on the other hand, stood out as the maturer nuclear power in the eyes of the world. This fact contributed to its swift global rise after the crisis.

4 The 2001–2002 Military Standoff

THE 2001–2002 STANDOFF CAN BEST BE EXAMINED IN two phases, the first running from December 13, 2001, to the spring of 2002 and the second from May 14, 2002, to October 2002. The crisis was triggered by a terrorist attack on the Indian parliament in New Delhi on the morning of December 13, 2001. Five armed militants managed to breach security and kill seven people and injure eighteen before being shot dead.[1] The motive of the attack, as later established, was to kill Indian political leaders.[2] The Indian government swiftly blamed Pakistani-based militant outfits Lashkar-e-Taiba (LeT) and Jaish-e-Muhammad (JeM) for the carnage and alleged that the attackers were operating at the Pakistani state's behest.[3] Both these groups were known for their close ties to Pakistan's intelligence agency, the Inter-Services Intelligence (ISI), but this did not necessarily translate into state control over their individual acts.[4] Pakistan denied responsibility for the attack but India launched Operation Parakram (Valor), an exercise in full-scale military mobilization. Pakistan responded with a counterdeployment, and when complete, the two sides had nearly a million soldiers eye ball to eye ball on the international border.

Tensions ebbed and flowed, rising in the days following the attack on the parliament and again in the wake of a May 14, 2002, attack on a bus and an Indian army camp nearby in the town of Kaluchak in Jammu, which killed 31 people, mostly family members of army personnel.[5] The Kaluchak attack marked the second peak of the crisis—thus the frequent use of the term "twin peaks" to refer to the standoff.[6] India alleged that the Kaluchak attackers were Pakistanis belonging to LeT.[7] Eventually, the crisis subsided without an active war when the Indian military undertook "strategic relocation"—read demobilization—on October 16, 2002.[8] Indian prime minister Atal Bihari Vajpayee, having won reelection after the Kargil crisis, offered a "hand of friendship" to Pakistan on April 18, 2003.[9]

From Kargil to Twin Peaks: The Strategic and Diplomatic Context

The Kargil crisis ended in a clear military and diplomatic victory for India. Yet, it left New Delhi deeply reflective of the implications of overt nuclearization for the India-Pakistan relationship. If India was going to be forced to restrain itself in response to Pakistani sub-conventional military aggression, it risked conveying that its conventional superiority had been neutralized. This called the credibility of India's nuclear deterrent into question and amounted to a "strategic paralysis."[10] India's response was a rather vague conception of "limited war under the nuclear umbrella" against Pakistan. The doctrine, as expounded by Defense Minister George Fernandes, posited that India could "fight and win a limited war, at a time and place chosen by the aggressor," and while acknowledging limitations due to risks of escalation, suggested that conventional war had "not been made obsolete by nuclear weapons."[11] The premise was that Pakistan had been using nuclear blackmail as "bluff and bluster" to exaggerate the risks in any crisis—its bluff had to be called.[12]

The state of India-Pakistan relations after Kargil kept India focused on this thought. Bilateral ties had deteriorated further as levels of infiltration and militancy in Indian Kashmir rose sharply.[13] Pakistan-based militant outfits upped their anti-India rhetoric, promising attacks not only in Kashmir but also in mainland India. Such attacks did take place, including a major one on the iconic Red Fort in Delhi in December 2000, less than a year after LeT chief Hafiz Saeed had singled it out as a target in a public statement.[14] Even conciliatory bilateral overtures like a de facto ceasefire on the Line of Control (LoC) in late 2000 and a major effort at diplomacy marked by the July 2001 Agra summit, which brought Indian and Pakistani leaders together for a dialogue on bilateral issues for the first time since the Kargil conflict, failed to make any headway.[15]

Adding to India's confidence vis-à-vis Pakistan was the fact that India's behavior during the Kargil crisis had ushered in a new era in terms of the country's international standing. The India-U.S. relationship now promised a multifaceted strategic engagement. India's strategic elite and public still maintained the deep-seated suspicion they had harbored toward the United States throughout the Cold War.[16] However, the post-9/11 context also worked to convince Indian decision makers that the change in global outlook toward countries facing terrorism had now bound India and the United States together because of a common grievance that would bring them global support—even for waging war.[17] India could now portray Pakistani support for the insurgency in Indian Kashmir as an obvious case of "terrorism" and hoped to convince the world that this justified a proactive response to compel Pakistan to reverse its policy.[18] The combination of India's strategic outlook and a favorable post-9/11 environment meant that it was able to enter the 2001–2002 crisis openly committing itself to punishing Pakistan directly if terrorist attacks like the one on the Indian parliament continued to occur.

Pakistan, on the other hand, had walked away from the Kargil crisis convinced that it could not trust the United States as an honest mediator.[19] Its fortunes were to dwindle further in the wake of a military coup in October 1999 that brought General Pervez Musharraf, the architect of the Kargil war, to power. The Pakistani state was also under the scanner for a massive nuclear proliferation scandal—not made public by the United States at the time—involving Pakistan's nuclear kingpin, A. Q. Khan, who had transferred nuclear technology and hardware to various countries.[20] There were also suspicions of Pakistani nuclear scientists assisting Al Qaeda and the Pakistan-backed Taliban regime in Afghanistan.[21] Coupled with the presence of a milieu of militant outfits on Pakistani and Afghan soil, these developments had also begun to create fears of the possibility of "loose nukes" in Pakistan.[22] The Pakistani leadership had to make repeated public assertions to assure the world of the safety and security of its arsenal in the weeks following 9/11.[23]

Pakistan's only respite was that the 9/11 attacks had catapulted the country to the status of a frontline U.S. ally. Pakistan offered the United States an invaluable transit route into landlocked Afghanistan, and it deployed troops on its western border, and provided critical intelligence to complement America's post-9/11 military campaign next door.[24] In fact, Pakistan was only just finishing deployment of over 100,000 troops to the Pakistan-Afghanistan border when the December 13 parliament attack occurred.[25] During the twin peaks crisis, the U.S. military would also establish a physical presence in Pakistan, including bases in western Pakistan, to support its operations across the border.[26] Interestingly though, Pakistan saw its partnership with the United States as one of compulsion rather than choice. President Musharraf feared that his refusal to assist America in Afghanistan would allow India to manipulate the situation to its advantage and might also offer Washington an opportunity to forcibly neutralize Pakistan's nuclear arsenal.[27] He later revealed that the United States had warned of bombing Pakistan "back to the Stone Age" if he refused to cooperate.[28]

When the terrorists struck the Indian parliament on December 13, 2001, Pakistan found itself in an awkward position. On the one hand, it realized that the world had not forgotten its behavior in Kargil and that its policies worried most world capitals, even more so in the wake of the 9/11 attacks and international concerns about its nuclear weapons. On the other hand, however, Pakistan remained intrinsically wedded to Kashmir and the Pakistani security establishment still believed strongly in the merits of its proxy strategy vis-à-vis India.[29]

The United States was in a delicate situation. The U.S. government, now under Republican president George W. Bush who had taken over from Bill Clinton earlier that year, had been actively promoting its post-9/11 doctrine of preemption against terrorism that justified the use of military force against regimes and countries perceived to be posing a threat to U.S. national security, even if the threat was not imminent.[30] This should have logically implied U.S. receptivity to India's characterization of the Kashmiri insurgency as "terrorism" and sympathy for India's view that it was justified in taking the fight to the source of militant infiltration in Pakistan. But the United States now also needed Pakistan for the success of its campaign in Afghanistan. This made its concern about an escalated India-Pakistan nuclear crisis, and of a subsequently distracted Pakistan, even more salient. Worryingly, during the crisis, the CIA's assessment confirmed a high risk of inadvertent escalation in South Asia given India's and Pakistan's lack of clear understanding on how and when a conventional war could escalate to the nuclear level.[31] In essence, India's fixation on calling Pakistan's nuclear bluff to avoid further reputational losses to its deterrent credibility ran up against a Pakistan that had become vital for U.S. global security interests.

As the Standoff Unfolded: Indian, Pakistani, and Third-Party Crisis Strategies

Phase I: The First Peak

India

QUEST FOR COMPELLENCE

The initial days after the parliament attack were extremely tense. The Indian government produced a list of specific demands for Pakistan. It wanted a stop to LeT's and JeM's activities; a closure of their offices and freezing of their assets in Pakistan; and detention of the groups' leaders.[32] About two weeks into the crisis, New Delhi asked for the extradition of twenty other alleged criminals wanted for heinous crimes in India.[33] On December 15, the Indian Cabinet Committee on Security (CCS), the highest decision-making body on national security issues, authorized military mobilization.[34] Indian decision makers discussed various military options during this period. While a consensus was elusive, the political leadership seemed to be favoring limited operations involving "hot pursuit" or "punitive use of force."[35] The military, however, presented plans for a "short and intense war" that envisioned primarily targeting Pakistani Kashmir through multiple thrusts across the LoC to inhibit infiltration in tandem with full-scale mobilization along the international border to take on any Pakistani offensive, should it expand the war theater in response.[36] This was perhaps the closest the Indian military had come to specifying the hitherto vaguely defined doctrine of "limited war under the nuclear umbrella."

On December 18, Prime Minister Vajpayee asked his military service chiefs to prepare for war, albeit without giving them specific direction on what he expected to achieve from it.[37] The result was Operation Parakram, India's largest military mobilization since the 1971 India-Pakistan War. It brought half a million Indian troops to the international border and activated India's air and naval forces.[38] Within a week, the Pakistani military's assessment was that Indian preparations had reached a stage where they could launch an attack within 24 hours.[39]

Early January 2002 was the defining period in terms of India's efforts to raise the stakes. Reportedly, Indian troops had taken "advanced attack" positions in the first week of January and "were on the point of launching a full scale war" at the time.[40] An operation "to hit and seal off major terrorist launching pads in Pakistan occupied Kashmir" was also believed to be ready to launch, but was called off at the last minute.[41] In fact, after U.S. satellites picked up Indian II Corps' movement into strike positions and confronted India with evidence supposedly suggesting an imminent attack, New Delhi abruptly removed Lt. General Kapil Vij, the corps commander, for having gone beyond orders.[42] V. K. Sood and Pravin Sawhney argue that the move signified the Indian political leadership's backtracking on their approval of military action rather than a case where General Vij may have exceeded his authority.[43] Next came Pakistani president Musharraf's January 12 televised speech in which he promised to act against militant outfits and announced a ban on LeT and JeM. Abruptly, the worst of phase I was over. Even as the Indian military remained mobilized and in position to execute its military plans and continued signaling resolve—most prominently through a test of its Pakistan-specific Agni I nuclear capable ballistic missile on January 25[44]—Indian posturing suggesting an imminent danger of war subsided after this point.

India matched its military mobilization with aggressive rhetoric throughout the first month of the crisis. Immediately after the parliament attack, the Indian cabinet threatened in a unanimous resolution that India would "liquidate the terrorists and their sponsors wherever they are, whoever they are."[45] The government continued to up the ante, with Prime Minister Vajpayee declaring that the attack was a challenge to the Indian nation's very "existence and honor" and thus "other [military] options are also open."[46] Meanwhile, in a major diplomatic move, India recalled its high commissioner to Islamabad on December 21 and a week later cut the strength of its mission in Islamabad and Pakistan's in New Delhi by half.[47] Direct bilateral communication remained virtually nonexistent throughout the crisis. A backchannel involving R. K. Mishra and retired Pakistani army general Mahmud Durrani was initiated. Durrani and Mishra met several times and were seriously considering a plan for the demobilization of Indian troops. However, Durrani pulled out of the process after the Pakistani security establishment expressed reservations about Mishra's authority to strike a deal on the Indian prime minister's behalf.[48]

Nuclear signals were also provocative even though India continued to reinforce its no-first-use policy on nuclear weapons.[49] While discussing the nuclear calculus on the floor of the Indian parliament on December 18, India's junior minister for external affairs Omar Abdullah stated that "geographical features should not leave anyone in doubt so as to who would recover from such an [nuclear] attack."[50] Relentless deterrent threats continued over the next fortnight. Significantly, on January 2, 2002, a time when the Indian military was allegedly preparing to launch an offensive against Pakistan, the Indian prime minister stated ominously: "No weapon would be spared in self-defense. Whatever weapon was available, it would be used no matter how it wounded the enemy."[51]

It was not until the week of January 7, when India was confronted with information about its II Corps being on an active war footing, that Defense Minister George Fernandes sought to ease the tension by stating that "no surgical strike has been planned against anyone."[52] On January 10, Indian deputy prime minister L. K. Advani reassured his audience during a visit to Washington that India "will not abandon restraint and the country would stand by its assertion of no-first-use of nuclear weapons."[53] The next day, Fernandes sent his second prudence signal in four days but this time it was aimed at clarifying the Indian army chief General Padmanabhan's provocation earlier in the day. In an authorized statement, Padmanabhan threatened a devastating nuclear strike if Pakistan was "mad enough" to launch a nuclear strike.[54] Fernandes immediately rebutted the statement, arguing that "the use of nuclear weapons is far too serious a matter that it should be bandied about in a cavalier manner."[55] On January 13, India responded with cautious optimism to Musharraf's pledge to clamp down on militant outfits made during his speech but declared that it would keep its military mobilized until it saw tangible signs of a reversal of militant infiltration from Pakistan.

Eyeing Third-Party Support

Accompanying this brinkmanship exercise was India's deliberate and proactive outreach to the world. The Indian leadership made instant efforts to goad the third party and signal its right to punish Pakistan. By promising to "liquidate the terrorists and their sponsors wherever they are, whoever they are," the Indian leadership was taking a leaf out of America's post-9/11 doctrine of preemption. India's behavior over the next month simultaneously conveyed resolve to Pakistan and signaled to the United States that it would have no option but to take direct action unless the world was willing to pressure Pakistan to fulfill Indian demands.[56] The Indian leadership sought to build pressure on the United States publicly in the early days of the crisis. In a finely balanced statement that demanded U.S. support while signaling the possibility of unilateral action, Vajpayee stated: "We are being counseled to exercise restraint. Our neighbor should be asked how long this ugly game of cross-border terrorism will go on. They [U.S.] need our neighbor right now but the same advice should be given to it also." He added, "We expect there will be action. . . . We are not relying only on diplomacy. We are confident that international opinion is on our side. We will fight on our own."[57]

Privately, India worked the diplomatic channels both in New Delhi and Washington. U.S. ambassador to India Robert Blackwill was constantly prodded by Indian leaders and he continued to impress upon Washington that India, as one official put it, had "moral parity" with the United States on the issue of terrorism.[58] A number of senior officials, including Deputy Prime Minister L. K. Advani, External Affairs Minister Jaswant Singh, and Defense Minister George Fernandes, also visited Washington at the peak of the crisis during December 2001 and January 2002. The Indian message was that "this is serious—[the] Government of India would take steps without hesitation. . . . We don't care if Pakistan has nuclear weapons—there is a price to be paid."[59] In a view reflective of the Indian belief at the time, former Indian army officer General Ashok Mehta predicted in an interview published on December 31, 2001, that U.S. interests in the region guaranteed that India's "coercive diplomacy . . . will, sooner than later, force the US to put the brakes on Pakistan."[60]

Influential Indian strategists and the Indian military had even factored in the third-party angle in contemplating the possibility of military action against Pakistan. The evidence lends itself to a very different understanding of the Indian military's earlier-discussed confidence that a "short but intense" war could be fought with Pakistan without risking escalation to the nuclear level. Writing at the time, K. Subrahmanyam, considered to be the godfather of Indian strategic thinking, argued that a limited war was thinkable since the U.S. presence in Pakistan ensured that it would promptly intervene to de-escalate and if need be, physically prevent Pakistan from launching nuclear strikes.[61] Sood and Sawhney also point to the view within the Indian military that a conflict "could well be short depending on when India or Pakistan succumbed to world pressure to end war."[62] Rajesh Basrur argues that the very Indian threat to attack Pakistan was based on confidence in the United States' interest and ability to restrain Pakistan.[63]

India's engagement with the third party simultaneously imposed several constraints on its behavior. Even as it upped the ante through its expansive military mobilization and aggressive rhetoric, there were strong voices cautioning Indian leaders not to squander the favorable international opinion it had carefully cultivated in recent years.[64] Two critical junctures in early

January 2002 that eventually proved to be game changers in phase I crystallize India's sensitivity to this dynamic. The first was the United States' concern about General Vij's corps, which resembled a formation ready to attack
across the border. The United States, on Pakistan's prodding, captured satellite images of the troops and confronted India with the information, forcing the Indian political leadership's alleged U-turn.[65] The Indian government
found itself in an embarrassing situation when the press picked up on the
story on January 20, and questioned the link between India's decision and
U.S. pressure.[66]

The second was India's deference to U.S. calls to exercise restraint before
Musharraf's January 12 speech. In a display of quiet diplomacy, U.S. deputy
secretary of state Richard Armitage met the Indian ambassador to Washington, Lalit Mansingh, just days before the speech and asked him to convey to
his capital that "Musharraf will make an important statement, and you will
be very pleased, just wait."[67] Mansingh later recalled that he saw the United
States acting as a "guarantor for Musharraf's promises."[68] Brajesh Mishra,
India's national security advisor (NSA), also acknowledged later that the
United States had asked New Delhi "to be patient and to listen to what Musharraf said."[69] British prime minister Tony Blair arrived in India a week before
Musharraf's speech to reinforce the third party's desire that India put on hold
any military plans.[70] To New Delhi's embarrassment, a *New York Times* story
a day before Musharraf's speech confirmed that India had hinted to Washington that "it would take no unprovoked military action against Pakistan as long
as American-led diplomatic efforts to defuse the crisis were continuing."[71]

The pattern of Indian nuclear signaling during these days also ought to be
recast in light of the third party's efforts. George Fernandes's statement that
"no surgical strike has been planned against anyone" in the immediate aftermath of General Vij's removal, otherwise out of sync with India's aggressive
signaling pattern to this point, can now be more accurately seen as reassurance to the United States that India would not attack Pakistan. The contradictory messages from Indian army chief Padmanabhan and Fernandes on
January 11 were also likely targeted at both Pakistan and the United States.[72]
Coming a day ahead of Musharraf's speech, the combination of signals reiterated India's commitment to the third party to restrain itself while putting
both Islamabad and Washington on notice and reminding them that India's
future actions would depend on what Musharraf said in his address. The
Indian CCS reportedly read Musharraf's speech as courageous. As Indian

intelligence chief Vikram Sood recalled, "we felt . . . let's give him another chance and see if there is a decline in terrorist activity."[73] India knew that the speech had shut the window on its use of force.[74] But it had shifted the onus of extracting tangible results from Pakistan on to Washington.

Pakistan

A DEFIANT BALANCING ACT

Pakistan began the crisis by denying any links to the parliament attack, blaming India for stage-managing the episode, and offering an impartial inquiry.[75] Simultaneously, it displayed its conventional military preparedness in the face of Indian mobilization. Orders were passed down to respond to any Indian military aggression and initiate at least one counteroffensive.[76] Pakistan's countermobilization included, much to Washington's dismay, an eastward redeployment of parts of the two corps it had stationed on its western border to assist America's campaign in Afghanistan.[77] Simultaneously, Pakistan signaled that it was only reacting to the mobilization of India's superior military might and that its buildup was defensive in nature. In an official statement representative of an effort to project this, the Pakistani president's spokesperson stated on December 27: "They (India) have moved all their formations to the border. We know it. We are monitoring that and as minimum defensive measures, we will just move minimum troops if we have to."[78] This public posturing continued even as Pakistan mobilized fully to match the Indian deployment.

Pakistan also generated movement around its nuclear sites. Reports suggested that Pakistan may have moved its Chinese-supplied M-11 nuclear-capable missiles in early January 2002.[79] In mid-January, the press quoted U.S. intelligence-based information alleging that Pakistan was preparing five launch sites for these missiles.[80] Pakistani officials have continued to deny any such movement to this day.[81] Nonetheless, on-the-ground military preparations during the first month of the crisis confirmed that both Pakistan and India were on a war footing and prepared for an outbreak of conflict.

The most counterintuitive aspect of Pakistani behavior was the way it went about signaling its intent. Pakistan wasted no opportunity to convey its commitment to retaliate in kind to any Indian military action. In terms of deterrent threats, however, it signaled maturity when tensions were at their peak in the first month after December 13. The first noticeable mention of nuclear weapons came on December 21 when Musharraf responded to a question on the security of Pakistan's weapons during a press interview: "I can say they [the nuclear and missile assets] are absolutely secure. We have no doubt."[82] He again conveyed calm amid aggressive Indian rhetoric by stating on December 27 that Pakistan would "step very cautiously . . . as we are a responsible state of 140 million people with nuclear capabilities."[83] Keeping up with the pattern of prudence signaling, Foreign Minister Abdul Sattar stated on December 29: "Nuclear weapons are awful weapons and any use of these weapons should be inconceivable for any state."[84] He further added the next day that Pakistan's nuclear weapons were meant for defense and deterrence, and that it "did not want a local, general or nuclear war."[85]

Pakistan also made an attempt to signal its nuclear threshold for using nuclear weapons in January. This was the first time it had done so since the May 1998 nuclear tests. General Khalid Kidwai, the de facto head of Pakistan's nuclear establishment, enunciated Pakistan's red lines while talking to a group of Italian scientists who were allowed to make these public: Pakistan would employ the nuclear option if India attacks Pakistan and takes over a large part of its territory (space threshold); if it destroys a large part of Pakistan's land or air forces (military threshold); if it proceeds to strangle Pakistan economically (economic threshold); or if it pushes Pakistan into political destabilization or creates a large-scale internal subversion in Pakistan (domestic threshold).[86] While many have seen this as a provocative signal emphasizing Pakistan's commitment to using nuclear weapons first, it was a clever message that conveyed resolve but was equally meant to allay concerns that Pakistan would choose to employ its nuclear capability early on in a conflict.[87]

The key to de-escalation in phase I was Pakistan's seeming accommodation of India's demand that Pakistan take action against cross-border terrorism. After its initial recalcitrance, Pakistani authorities proceeded to round up at least fifty militants belonging to LeT and JeM by the end of December 2001.[88] President Musharraf's January 12 speech proved to be the defining moment. Musharraf affirmed that Pakistan was threatened by militant groups and that he would no longer tolerate them in any form. He announced the banning of five militant organizations including LeT and JeM and vowed not to allow Pakistani soil to be used for militancy in Indian Kashmir. While he pledged to continue "moral, political, and diplomatic" support for the Kashmir cause and refused to hand over the twenty alleged criminals demanded by India, his speech signaled an unprecedented recognition of ongoing infiltration into Indian Kashmir from Pakistani soil.[89] The Pakistani state followed up this pledge immediately after the speech by detaining 1,430 alleged militants and closing down as many as 390 offices suspected of links to militant organizations.[90] Even though a number of these individuals were released soon thereafter, and infiltration rose again during the spring of 2002, Musharraf's speech and these detentions bought crucial time and helped ratchet down tensions.

DIPLOMATIC MANEUVERING

Pakistan's post-December 13, 2001 countermobilization was driven by a genuine belief on the part of its military that India would attack if Pakistan's conventional deterrent was not on display in full.[91] But its leadership wasted no opportunity to leverage third-party actors in tandem. President Musharraf and his team conducted a flurry of diplomatic activity with leaders of both Western and Muslim countries to gain support. Pakistan's outreach to the world centered on four messages: it had nothing to do with the December 13 attack; Indian mobilization had unnecessarily raised tensions and needed to be reined in; Pakistan would have no option but to respond with force if India acted militarily; and the international community should help mediate a resolution to the Kashmir dispute.

Pakistan quite deliberately raised the stakes for the third party in an effort to get it to force India to back down. This aspect of its strategy was most evident in its messaging to the U.S. diplomatic mission in Islamabad. After initially blaming India for stage-managing the December 13 attack, the Pakistani military began using its trump card—its role in Afghanistan—within the first week of the crisis. On December 20, the chairman of Pakistan's Joint Chiefs of Staff Committee, the country's senior-most military official, hinted to his American counterpart that an Indian provocation may affect Pakistan's ability to assist U.S. operations in Afghanistan.[92] A more forceful case was made in special meetings summoned by the Pakistani army leadership the next day when the military provided an intelligence picture of Indian mobilization and shared its belief that India could launch a general attack within 24 hours.[93] On December 22, Pakistan informed the U.S. embassy that it had intelligence suggesting that India would attack before dawn on December 23.[94] The next day, the army let it be known that Pakistan would respond with "full force" to any Indian provocation.[95] Pakistan's vice chief of army staff asserted that the military would pull troops from the western border as it could not "manage two threats at the same time" and had to "deal with the most serious one first."[96] Despite constant U.S. pleas and reassurances, Pakistan moved its forces eastward at the turn of the year.[97] Pakistani messaging also hinted that an expanded war with India might force them to ask the United States to vacate the Pakistani airfields it was allowed to use after 9/11.[98]

Simultaneously, Islamabad sought to convey calm and exhibit deference to third-party demands. Pakistan's relatively restrained nuclear signaling during this phase of the crisis was influenced by its military's damaged image since the Kargil crisis. By emphasizing that Pakistan would only consider using nuclear weapons after exhausting its conventional deterrent and if a general breakdown in the situation was impending—this is what General Kidwai's red lines amounted to—the Pakistani military sought to dispel the common perception that it was a risk taker and might prove to be trigger happy when it came to employing the nuclear option against India.[99] In terms of actions, Musharraf's decision to begin rounding up LeT and JeM militants in December 2001 and to include in his January 12 address an admission of guilt as far as militant infiltration was concerned, can both be attributed to third-party pressure. Musharraf, on his part, believed, correctly as it turned out, that obliging the United States would prevent it from backing the Indian position and prompt it to oppose India's military option. As Musharraf worked closely with American officials on the January 12 speech, receiving detailed input into the content of his remarks, the United States again assured him that it would continue opposing any Indian military designs.[100]

After the January 12 address, although the United States leaned heavily on India to de-escalate, it also kept pushing Musharraf to follow up on his pledge regarding cross-border infiltration. Its efforts were only partially successful though as positive movement on this front was reversed in the months that followed. However, Musharraf never defied U.S. demands. Instead, he pledged lack of capacity to produce instant results in terms of quashing the cross-border flow of militants.

The Third Party: Playing Down the Middle
If part of the goal of the Indian military mobilization was to manipulate the risk of war to force the third party to take notice, it was perhaps unneeded. Even though the United States' energies were focused on Afghanistan at the time, there was hardly any dissent among Washington's decision makers on the desirability and need of instant U.S. involvement in the crisis.[101] The salience of one "abiding concern in the U.S.—that an Indian military response to cross-border terrorism from Pakistan could escalate the confrontation between the two nations to the nuclear level" was unmistakable.[102] Intrinsically linked was the concern that continued tensions would compromise

Pakistan's efforts to support the U.S. campaign in Afghanistan. Yet, the primacy of the de-escalation objective above and beyond Afghanistan was uncontested in the minds of the U.S. crisis managers.[103] As U.S. Deputy Secretary of State Richard Armitage, arguably the most influential third-party crisis manager during the standoff along with his boss, Secretary of State Colin Powell, recalled, there was "absolutely no question about it. This [crisis diplomacy] was about nuclear."[104] Asked how centrally Afghanistan featured in the crisis conversations with India and Pakistan and among Washington's principals, his response was categorical: "Not at all. Not in any conversation with them [Pakistan and India] or in [Washington] DC."[105] In reality, the relative importance accorded to these two concerns was bifurcated between top decision makers and their working-level staff in Washington and at the U.S. embassies in India and Pakistan. Working-level officials entrusted with Pakistan portfolios had been consumed by the Afghanistan War since 9/11 and continued analyzing how best to protect U.S. equities there.[106] This was overridden by the top leadership's fixation on the risk of escalation of the India-Pakistan crisis. These principals ultimately scripted U.S. crisis signaling and communications. This proved crucial in avoiding mixed messages from Washington that could have complicated its crisis management efforts.

As in the Kargil crisis, the United States took the lead in managing the 2001–2002 standoff but it worked closely with its partners with influence over India and/or Pakistan to carefully coordinate messages.[107] The UK was the most active and maintained a round-the-clock control room to monitor crisis developments.[108] At the very onset of the crisis, the United States and the UK choreographed a strategy whereby they ensured that a high ranking U.S. or British official was ready to go to the region at short notice. Secretary of State Colin Powell later recalled: "We had sort of a duty roster out there for who is going tomorrow to keep these clowns from killing each other."[109] Other European capitals were regularly engaged to complement the roster.[110] China was also kept fully informed throughout the crisis.[111] It once again ended up complementing these efforts, and using its good offices to reinforce the requests and demands being made by Washington and other Western capitals.[112] Beijing remained in close contact with the Pakistani leadership throughout and welcomed several visits by its officials, including three by Musharraf, but it did nothing to tangibly back their position.[113]

The third party's strategy was to "play for time," to delay any Indian plans for an offensive, thereby letting the law of diminishing returns set in for New

Delhi.[114] It urged restraint on India's part while recognizing its right of self-defense and promising continued support against terrorism. According to U.S. NSA Condoleezza Rice, the U.S. aim was to "acknowledge the right of others to do what we had done in responding to the attack on the Twin Towers [use military force] but also convince them not to actually do it."[115] At the same time, the United States pushed Pakistan to curb the export of militants to India but not so forcefully that it would draw an adverse reaction from Pakistani leaders.[116] Its private message to Pakistan was that it wanted swift and visible movement against terrorists. American officials were also being quoted by the U.S. press in the first week of the crisis confirming that they were planning to tighten the screws on Islamabad. In public however, the U.S. tone and demands remained to Pakistan's liking for the most part. The U.S. State Department hinted early on that it could not blame the Pakistani state for the attack in the absence of hard evidence of its complicity.[117] On December 16, Secretary of State Powell publicly asked India to desist from military action.[118] The United States continued to convey this message over the next week, suggesting that India must avoid any action that makes "more difficult the fight against terrorism in the region."[119] On December 21, President Bush warned that any military action "could really create severe problems for all of us that are engaged in the fight against terror."[120] The same day, the White House suggested that the parliament attack was aimed at harming Pakistan and its growing relations with the United States.[121]

As Musharraf began to oblige the United States and rounded up militants, Washington took the opportunity to praise him. President Bush noted Musharraf's moves and stated on December 31 that "he's cracking down hard [on extremists]" and that this was "a good sign."[122] Colin Powell followed up days later by stating: "Pakistan has done a great deal since this crisis started on the 13th of December—first by arresting the leaders of the two terrorist organizations most closely linked to being the perpetrators of this act."[123] Washington also reinforced its public appreciation for Musharraf's efforts in its private messaging to New Delhi. For instance, while on a visit to Washington in late December, L. K. Advani was told that Musharraf had taken "some steps" and that the United States was waiting to see what "additional action he has taken."[124]

The third party simultaneously sought to balance some of this conciliatory messaging toward Pakistan. The United States' closest third-party partner, the UK, reprimanded Pakistan to compensate for Washington's seemingly soft public attitude. On December 16, the day Powell publicly called on India to exercise restraint, the British high commissioner to India insinuated Pakistan's role in anti-India terrorism and urged it to stop aiding militancy.[125] On December 28, Foreign Secretary Jack Straw all but discounted Pakistani efforts against LeT and JeM by berating Pakistan and demanding that it take "more effective" steps against terrorist groups and suggesting that there had been "complacency, if not ambiguity" in Pakistan's attitude toward cross-border terrorism, which had resulted in an attack on the very "heart of Indian democracy."[126]

The United States also displayed positive outreach to India and took tangible steps in its favor. After December 13, the uptake of the Indian saber-rattling in Washington was that New Delhi wanted it to weigh in and pressure Pakistan to act against terrorism. In the days following the attack, U.S. officials remained in constant touch with their Indian counterparts, conveying sympathy and offering assistance in the investigations.[127] At the forefront, and often ahead of Washington in appreciating India's position, was U.S. ambassador Robert Blackwill. He drew parallels between December 13 and 9/11 by stating that the parliament attack was "no different in its objective from the terror attacks in the U.S. on September 11th."[128]

On December 20, Washington announced that it was putting LeT on its terrorist list and freezing its assets.[129] A week later, it formally declared LeT and JeM terrorist outfits.[130] Then came the two critical junctures of phase I. The incident involving General Vij occurred on the heels of the United States' message to India that Musharraf was acting against militants. Interestingly, U.S. intelligence was divided on whether Indian force movements were deliberate and intended as preparations for an attack.[131] The United States never sought clarity and assuming the worst, simply asked the Indian leadership to back off, leaving it to choose between obliging or essentially accepting that they had deliberately authorized war footing despite U.S. assurances that it was doing India's bidding with Pakistan. Washington also saw Musharraf's January 12 speech as a major opportunity to buy more time from the Indians, if not to affect de-escalation of the crisis.[132] The speech was a direct function of America's, specifically Colin Powell's, pressure on Musharraf to make a public pronouncement to comfort India. But for Powell, "there would never have been a January 12 speech."[133]

Immediately after the speech, Colin Powell came out publicly in support of Musharraf, expressing appreciation for his "bold and principled stand to set Pakistan squarely against terrorism and extremism both in and outside of Pakistan" while asking both antagonists to show restraint.[134] President Bush also congratulated Musharraf on his "firm decision to stand against terrorism and extremism" and got other third-party partners to do the same.[135] When India responded positively, President Bush thanked Prime Minister Vajpayee for his measured take on the speech.[136] The United States simultaneously kept up the pressure through Powell's shuttle diplomacy. In Pakistan, he pressed Musharraf to fulfill his pledge and in India, he was once again providing de facto guarantees of Musharraf's sincerity. He confirmed to the Indian leadership that the Pakistani leader was working to follow up on his promise to curb cross-border terrorism.[137] He suggested that infiltration levels would continue to decline, hinting that the United States could be counted on to keep pressing Pakistan.[138] Implicit here was also the continuing disapproval of Indian use of force. This led India away from contemplating war.[139] On January 18, 2002, Indian journalist Jawed Naqvi reported on the success of Powell's mission in the Pakistani English daily *Dawn*: "A much milder India and an equally reassured United States seemed to be the main outcome on Friday of three days of sustained high pressure diplomacy between the triad of US Secretary of State Colin Powell and Indian and Pakistani leaders, all engaged earnestly for once to end the looming menace of war between the two nuclear armed states of South Asia."[140]

After this point, as tensions eased, so did the frequency of third-party probing. The United States sought to refocus Pakistani attention on the Afghan border even as concerns grew in Washington's intelligence community over the spring that Pakistan was not doing enough to end infiltration into Kashmir. Pakistani receptivity to U.S. prodding on its support of the Kashmiri militancy also seems to have declined somewhat after the imminent threat of war subsided. The focus of the diplomacy and public signaling broadened from immediate crisis management to larger strategic objectives during this period of decreased tensions. Pakistan publicly talked about a resolution of the Kashmir dispute and the need for a mediator.[141] India expectedly rebuffed such suggestions.[142] The United States continued to stress the need for a political settlement to the issue, but without clearly backing either side.

The other aspect of note during this period was the United States' emphasis that it remained committed to strengthening its strategic partnership with India. In parallel to crisis diplomacy, the United States and India continued to talk about avenues for expanding defense ties. In early May, in what was described as evidence of growing strategic cooperation between the two sides, they also undertook their largest joint army and navy exercises, respectively, Balance Iroquois and Exercise Malabar.[143]

Phase II: The Second Peak

India

COMPLEX BEHAVIOR

As the spring season made conditions conducive for renewed infiltration, the cross-LoC movement of militants into Kashmir began to soar. Pakistan had reportedly released as many as 1,800 of the 2,000 individuals it had eventually rounded up in January.[144] By April, about 60 militant camps were estimated to be operating in Pakistani Kashmir; as many as 2,000 militants allegedly crossed over into Indian Kashmir by May.[145] On what turned out to be the eve of the May 14 Kaluchak attack, Indian external affairs minister Jaswant Singh publicly claimed that Musharraf had broken his promise and that militants had been freed to operate again.[146]

The implications of the Kaluchak attack could potentially have been more far-reaching than the December 13, 2001, assault because it targeted the families of Indian army personnel. Also, between January and May 2002, the Indian military had rethought its offensive plans, arguing that a "short but intense" war was most feasible when India enjoyed the element of surprise. It now backed a full-scale conventional attack designed to deliver a sledgehammer blow and enter deep inside Pakistan to fight a war of attrition. To make this possible, the army had moved an additional strike corps to the border to complement the two corps already stationed there as part of the initial mobilization in December 2001.[147]

In the days following the Kaluchak attack, India sent several additional fighter jets to forward bases, five of its most sophisticated ships were deployed with its western fleet, and its sole aircraft carrier was placed on alert.[148] On May 17, the Indian army commenced heavy shelling across the LoC and Prime Minister Vajpayee cancelled a planned vacation to attend military briefings.[149] There was also a growing sentiment within Indian military circles in favor of using force.[150] Toward the end of May, the Indian press was reporting that an attack on Pakistan was planned for mid-June.[151]

Despite the seeming imminence of war, the outcome in phase II was identical to phase I. President Musharraf made a speech on May 27 in which he reaffirmed his pledge not to allow cross-border infiltration into Kashmir.

India did not use force and by mid-June, Indian officials were acknowledging that war had been averted. Shelling on the LoC fell by 90 percent soon thereafter. While infiltration levels were to rise again by the autumn, the peak in phase II had long passed. India eventually demobilized its troops in October 2002.

Part of India's verbal signaling was unsurprisingly hawkish. Indian leaders made a number of threats and repeatedly hinted at the imminence of war in the days following the Kaluchak attack. Perhaps the most provocative were Prime Minister Vajpayee's statements on May 22. Speaking to Indian soldiers, he conveyed a message akin to a troop commander's motivational speech before combat: "the time has come for a decisive battle and we will have a sure victory in this battle"; "the enemy has thrown us a challenge by waging a proxy war. We accept it and pledge to give it a crushing defeat."[152] Just two days after his rallying message, in a move that surprised most observers and one that must have left Indian troops confused about the government's intent, Vajpayee left for the five-day vacation he had postponed a week earlier.[153] No obvious development related to the crisis had occurred to affect this seeming change of heart. In fact, on the day Vajpayee went on vacation, the U.S. press warned of Indian plans to attack Pakistani Kashmir.[154] Nonetheless, there was a visible shift in India's signaling posture after this point. While hard-hitting rhetoric continued and the threat of war remained very high for another fortnight, New Delhi now spent considerable energy explicitly addressing the international community.[155]

In tandem with this internationally oriented messaging, India issued nuclear signals that conveyed a mix of resolve and prudence and were blatantly contradictory at times. A glaring example came in early June. On June 3, the Indian Defense Ministry stated: "The government makes it clear that India does not believe in the use of nuclear weapons. Neither does it visualize that it will be used by any other country."[156] The same day, however, Yogendra Narain, India's defense secretary, responded to aggressive Pakistani rhetoric during this period by threatening that India would retaliate with nuclear weapons if Pakistan used its atomic arsenal: "Everything is finalized. It is in the hands of the civilian government and we don't expect any delay in issuing orders."[157] A quick clarification was, however, issued by the same ministry: "India does not believe in the use of nuclear weapons." "India is a responsible country and it feels it will be imprudent to use such weapons."[158]

RELIANCE ON THE THIRD PARTY

In phase I, India's belief that world opinion was certain to back its position and remain sympathetic to its threat of military action proved incorrect.[159] After the May 14 attack, Indian leaders invested even more energy in trying to convince the international community to pressure Pakistan and to portray it as irresponsible—even as India flexed its own muscles by contemplating full-scale conventional war and backed it by a we-mean-business rhetoric in the fortnight following the Kaluchak attack. As India's belligerent rhetoric took off, Prime Minister Vajpayee made his displeasure with the situation known to President Bush in a direct conversation the day after the Kaluchak attack. From Vajpayee's perspective, New Delhi had trusted Washington as the guarantor on Pakistan's behalf in phase I, but the third party had failed to rein Pakistan in and force a reversal of its Kashmir policy.

Vajpayee's political party's spokesperson made New Delhi's expectations from the United States amply clear in a statement on May 15: "War cannot be ruled out." "We do not think that the U.S. can restrain Pakistan, and if Pakistan is not restrained the Americans may as well forget about their dream of ridding the world of terrorism."[160] Junior External Affairs Minister Omar Abdullah threw United States' own mantra back at it: "America is either with us or with the terrorists."[161] On May 22, Brajesh Mishra demanded from U.S. NSA Condoleezza Rice that Washington pressure Pakistan to give in to Indian demands or be ready for direct Indian action. His specific ask, however, was interesting and pointed to his recognition of the limits of the concessions he felt India could extract. When Rice asked Mishra what it would take for India to be satisfied with Pakistani sincerity on terrorism, he only demanded "a guarantee" that Pakistan would be made to end cross-border terrorism.[162] Coming at a time when India was threatening to launch a military attack without delay, the demand for immediate and tangible action by Pakistan or indeed, U.S. backing for Indian use of force, would have been more fitting. India also decided to give more time to third-party diplomacy by waiting for the results of the upcoming visit of Secretary of State Colin Powell and his deputy Richard Armitage. This context helps explain Vajpayee's decision to proceed on his vacation on May 24.[163] Musharraf's May 27 speech seems to have further reinforced this outlook. A *New York Times* article captured the context aptly: "Indian officials are clearly pleased that Secretary of State Colin L. Powell, Foreign Minister Jack Straw of Britain and 'no less a person than President Bush' . . . have publicly lectured General Musharraf about the need to deliver on his promises to halt the infiltration."[164] Alex Stolar reports that Brajesh Mishra believed that the May 27 speech was the turning point.[165] Mishra recalled that India felt it needed to give Musharraf another chance and that it would have only gone to war after this point if it had been forced to.[166]

If the period from General Vij's removal to Musharraf's January 12 speech crystallized India's deference to the third party in phase I, it was India's concern about the impact of travel advisories issued by third-party countries and its response to Richard Armitage's June 7–8 mission to India that did so in phase II. On May 31, the United States and the UK—followed by a number of other countries, including Japan, France, Germany, and Israel—issued travel advisories for India and Pakistan based on their assessment that the possibility of nuclear war could not be completely ruled out.[167] The impact of the advisories on India was significant given its relatively high dependence on inflow of capital for its foreign-investment-led service sectors that were crucial to its claim of being a rising power. Foreign direct investment in the following six months declined by over 30 percent compared to the preceding six months and quarterly GDP growth slowed to roughly 0.5 percent.[168] Indian leaders saw the advisories as a deliberate move and blamed Washington and London for unnecessarily exaggerating the risks of escalation to shock the Indian public and rattle the Indian stock market.[169] On June 5, Defense Minister Fernandes claimed that the advisories had a "special agenda of their own" of creating panic and affecting investment flows into India.[170] Ironically, this Indian perception would have only further confirmed to Indian leaders the world's reluctance to allow them to drag the crisis. Kanti Bajpai suggests that New Delhi saw its continued defiance after this point as risking its larger strategic partnership with the United States; it would have alienated not only the U.S. administration but also Western investors and tourists.[171]

Then came Armitage's visit to India and Pakistan that was responsible for starting the de-escalation process. Armitage's objective was to get India the "guarantee" Brajesh Mishra had asked of Condoleezza Rice a fortnight earlier. He arrived in India on June 7 from Pakistan with the news that Musharraf had agreed to put a permanent stop to militant infiltration.[172] He maintained that Musharraf was sincere but added that his government did not have full control over cross-border militant movement.[173] India asked Armitage to go public with Musharraf's pledge, and in return accepted this as enough of a guarantee even though it was no better than what it had received in phase I.[174] There was an almost instant drop in tension. India even agreed to begin pulling back some of its ships from forward deployment in the Arabian Sea.[175] Indian officials also acknowledged that Musharraf had ordered the ISI to curb infiltration and that positive actions were already being noticed.[176] Mistry maintains that India ended up preferring to use U.S. diplomacy over direct military action even though the strategy only delivered a temporary reduction in infiltration.[177]

India, after dragging its feet, ultimately tied its decision to demobilize to the Jammu and Kashmir state elections in September 2002, arguing that these elections were indicative of positive developments in Kashmir and had pre-sumably removed the need to maintain the troop deployment.[178] In reality, the summer months saw growing international pressure on India to pull back its troops.[179] New Delhi could not have ignored this nor the danger that the longer it kept its forces mobilized, the more space Pakistan would have found to present itself as the peace aspiring party, and India as keeping South Asia one mishap or accident away from a catastrophe.

It was sometime after the crisis that Vajpayee provided his most candid acknowledgment of India's sensitivity to third-party preferences during the twin peaks crisis. Speaking to a U.S.-based academic, Vajpayee stated that "all preparations were made for attacking Pakistan to punish it for the attack on Parliament. But America gave us the assurance that something will be done by Pakistan about cross-border terrorism, both in January and in May 2002. America gave us a clear assurance. That was an important factor."[180] Jaswant Singh also acknowledges in his memoirs that "to some degree, success was a function of India's ability to work with the United States."[181] India's deference to the third party was so obvious that it even led some to posit that India was never serious about the military option, and was only truly focused on attract-ing third-party attention and support.[182] While this may be an unreasonable assumption given that India spent a whopping US$1.3 billion on its military mobilization,[183] it nonetheless highlights just how proactively and unambigu-ously India engaged the third-party actors.

Pakistan

PERSISTENT DEFIANCE

Pakistan had grounds to see itself as having emerged ahead of India from phase I. Even though Musharraf had to acknowledge infiltration, India could not launch an offensive. Pakistan repeatedly blamed India for initiat-ing the military mobilization, but it exhibited restraint in nuclear signaling during the first peak of the crisis. And most importantly, the international community, while expressing support and sympathy for India, never backed its plans to use force. Yet, Pakistan was on the defensive again as India blamed the Kaluchak attack on LeT.

As tensions soared after the attack, Pakistani troops were fully alerted and remained ready to launch.[184] Reports surfaced that Pakistan had also relocated its nuclear capable Shaheen missiles closer to the border.[185] Chatter around Pakistan's nuclear movements within the first week after the Kaluchak attack led India's junior external affairs minister to state that "Pakistan will be stupid to consider [the] nuclear option."[186] Nonetheless, in what was a deliberate signal to India, Pakistan conducted three missile tests in quick succession between May 25 and 28 to demonstrate its first-strike capability.[187] These tests were prompted by Pakistani intelligence reports about offensive Indian military deployments that indicated that an attack may have been imminent.[188] Even though Pakistani assessments suggested that India would realistically only be able to launch limited strikes at this stage, a message to counterattack if the Indians crossed the LoC or the international border was transmitted on an open line by Pakistani officials in the hope that India would intercept it and be deterred.[189] Musharraf had also ordered the Pakistani air force to hit back immediately—but conventionally only—should India attack.[190]

Pakistan's signaling behavior in phase II was more aggressive, especially in the last week of May when Pakistan was convinced an Indian attack was impending. In addition to transmitting offensive threats confirming resolve to use conventional force against any Indian military action—this carried over seamlessly from phase I—the nuclear signals were also bolder. Just prior to the May 25–28 missile tests, Pakistan reminded India of its nuclear red lines. On May 23, the India's water resources minister had issued a veiled threat hinting at scrapping the bilateral Indus Water Treaty, which would create a "drought in Pakistan and the people of that country would have to beg for every drop of water."[191] Pakistan termed any such moves "economic strangulation,"[192] one of the nuclear red lines enunciated by General Kidwai in phase I. Immediately after the first missile test on May 25, Pakistan officially boasted that "all sensitive Indian places including its nuclear centers of Nagpur, Jullundur and Jesselmir are now within reach of Pakistani missiles."[193] This was followed by another provocative statement by Pakistan's UN ambassador Munir Akram in New York: "Pakistan had to rely on the means it possessed to deter Indian aggression. . . . If India reserved the right to use conventional weapons, how could Pakistan—a weaker power—be expected to rule out all means of deterrence?"[194]

Interestingly, however, as officials around him transmitted resolve signals, Musharraf took on the task of conveying prudence. Analogous to his January 12 speech, Musharraf delivered a speech on May 27 at the height of tensions in which he reiterated his pledge to change Pakistan's pro-militancy tactics: "I . . . give the assurance that no infiltration is taking place across the Line of Control. . . . Pakistan is doing nothing across the Line of Control and Pakistan will never allow the export of terrorism anywhere in the world from within Pakistan."[195] Even though New Delhi dismissed Musharraf's address as "disappointing and dangerous," there were some signs of the infiltration abating in early June.[196]

Musharraf also sought to balance the aggressive deterrent threats emanating from Islamabad at the time. On May 26, in an interview with a Western press outlet, he reiterated his military's conventional strength and preparations to rebuff an Indian attack but on nuclear weapons, he affirmed: "[I] really don't think we will ever reach that stage and I only hope that we—I hope and pray that we will never reach that stage. It's too unthinkable."[197] A week later he sought to embarrass India when speaking of reports in the press that Pakistan may have mobilized its missiles at the time. Refuting this claim, he stated that "If India has moved their missiles this is extremely dangerous and a very serious escalation . . . the international community must take note of this because you can't distinguish what is conventional and what is unconventional."[198] Other prudence signals followed till the importance and frequency of nuclear rhetoric decreased (from both sides) after mid-June.

OUTREACH TO THE THIRD PARTY

Like India's leaders, the Pakistani leadership continued to liaise with the international community in phase II, openly calling for third-party intervention to stall what it consciously painted as India's aggressive intent. Within the first week of phase II, Pakistani leaders hinted at their desire to seek UN Security Council intervention to force India to pull back.[199] On May 23, with the threat of war at its peak, Musharraf warned that India's aggressive rhetoric could not be ignored and the Pakistani Foreign Office reported that it had formally reached out to the UN.[200] Privately, Islamabad kept its channels with the third party open to reiterate that the international community should get India to demobilize. President Musharraf also dispatched five special envoys to Western and Muslim country capitals at the end of May 2002 to elicit support for Pakistan's position.[201]

To the United States, Pakistan continued to emphasize that it would have no option but to retaliate if India attacked.[202] In a clever twist, its messaging tied the United States' support to India with heightened possibility of escalation and war. The argument was that India was looking for international backing to launch a military offensive; if war was absent, it was only because New Delhi could not find unequivocal U.S. support. Islamabad's loudest message to Washington, however, was meant to play on the possibility of immediate harm to U.S. security interests. Even more vociferously than in phase I, Pakistani interlocutors conveyed that they would have to pull out more troops from their western border if India did not back down. Musharraf announced: "We are very seriously contemplating moving some elements . . . on to the east, if at all tensions remain as high as they are now."[203] On May 29, the Pakistani military refused a U.S. request for reinforcements on the Afghanistan border and maintained that it could not spare more than two brigades in light of India's war preparations in the east.[204]

Simultaneously, Pakistan showed sensitivity to U.S. preferences. This was most evident in the run up to Musharraf's May 27 speech. That Musharraf had been influenced by the third party's blunt messaging to him became obvious when he confided in his cabinet shortly before his speech that Pakistan was losing its standing with key third-party interlocutors. He argued that the world was firmly on India's side and was no longer willing to distinguish between terrorists and freedom fighters.[205] He conceded that Pakistani diplomatic efforts to make this distinction had failed and concluded that the only way forward for Pakistan was to shut down militant camps operating on its soil.[206] Therefore, Musharraf ordered the ISI to pull back from militants engaged in cross-border activity. This was a difficult decision with potentially serious consequences and elicited an angry reaction from the militant enclave. They blamed Musharraf for having betrayed Kashmiris after having done the same to the Afghan Taliban in the face of U.S. pressure after 9/11.[207] As Mistry notes, Pakistan's concessions would likely not have come in the absence of U.S. pressure.[208]

Pakistan's relatively sterner posture in terms of issuing deterrent threats in phase II could have been driven by a number of factors. Foremost, Pakistani planners genuinely thought an Indian attack could take place and therefore would have sought to signal resolve to put India on notice. At the same time, however, they could not have been oblivious to the fact that the May 14 Kaluchak attack had allowed India to remind the world of the persistence of anti-India terrorism emanating from Pakistan and to put Pakistan under the international scanner again. Pakistan was also acutely aware of global concerns about the security of its nuclear weapons and about the possibility of their deliberate or inadvertent use. This rationalizes Musharraf's effort to continue conveying calm to offset the aggressive nuclear rhetoric of his colleagues. After all, Musharraf was the army chief and chairman of the National Command Authority, the apex body in charge of operational command and control of nuclear weapons—essentially the only man who had the right to press the nuclear button—and most frequently in touch with the third-party interlocutors. His receptivity to the U.S. message was evident when Colin Powell called him out on Pakistan's aggressive nuclear rhetoric in late May by pointedly telling him: "All this chatter about nuclear weapons is very interesting, but let's talk general-to-general."[209] "General, you are scaring the crap out of everybody, so you've got to cool it."[210] Musharraf responded by saying, "I understand."[211] Pakistan's deterrent threats fizzled out quickly thereafter.

As tensions subsided, Pakistan's focus once again shifted to stressing the need for a political dialogue on Kashmir and for third-party involvement in the effort. It also kept up messaging aimed at painting India as being reluctant to improve bilateral relations. The other feature of Pakistani behavior in this period was identical to phase I. As the U.S. receptivity to Indian messaging decreased and the United States urged Pakistan to focus on the Afghan border, Islamabad let its pledges on infiltration take a backseat. Musharraf also openly challenged the U.S. claim, discussed shortly, that distanced Washington from a commitment to help get India to negotiate sincerely on Kashmir. The Pakistani leadership believed that the United States had agreed to press India on the Kashmir issue as a quid pro quo for their concessions, but that the United States had not kept its end of the bargain.[212]

The Third Party: Persisting with the Middle

The third party was extremely concerned about the potential for escalation at the onset of phase II. It perceived Indian threats immediately after the Kaluchak attack to be credible and believed that barring visible action against militants from Pakistan, New Delhi would escalate the crisis.[213] U.S. sources also picked up signs that India had made full preparations to initiate military hostilities.[214] Interestingly, however, Nayak and Krepon reveal that U.S. secretary of state Colin Powell believed that the crisis was fundamentally political and that both India and Pakistan ultimately wanted the United States to act as a "separator."[215] In this spirit, the United States and the UK, along with other amenable international actors—China, France and Russia being the most notable parties in phase II—undertook a flurry of diplomacy. The arrangement of having foreign dignitaries visit the region at regular intervals that was instituted between the United States and its partners in phase I remained intact.

The principal message carried over from phase I. India was urged to show restraint and Pakistan was pushed to deliver on the pledges Musharraf had made in his January 12 speech. However, Pakistan received much more public sanction in phase II. U.S. diplomacy intensified after Brajesh Mishra's demand for a guarantee from Condoleezza Rice. A series of conversations were initiated with Musharraf to push him to ensure a permanent resolution of the issue of cross-border infiltration. These diplomatic efforts culminated in Musharraf's May 27 speech and a reaffirmation of his pledge to show visible movement against terrorism directed at India.[216]

Concerned that a mere speech might not have been enough, especially since the CIA station chief in Islamabad had conveyed his assessment to Washington that he expected war within a day or two around this time,[217] the third party continued harsh public signaling, demanding more tangible gains for India than had been managed in phase I. The British foreign secretary Jack Straw visited Islamabad a day after Musharraf's speech and got the Pakistani president to reaffirm his pledge against cross-border infiltration.[218] President Bush himself used "very firm language" with Musharraf on a number of occasions.[219] On May 31 for instance, Bush said: "He [Musharraf] must stop the incursions across the Line of Control. He must do so. He said he would do so. We and others are making it clear to him that he must live up to his word."[220] A day earlier, Colin Powell, perhaps the softest voice on Pakistan in phase I, had berated Musharraf publicly in delivering much the same message as President Bush: "We were receiving assurances from President Musharraf that infiltration across the LoC would be ended. . . . But unfortunately we can still see evidence that it is continuing."[221]

Like phase I, both game changing developments in phase II also had visible third-party roles. The travel advisories emanated from the shared belief between the American ambassador and British high commissioner in New Delhi that there was a higher-than-zero possibility of a conflict breaking out and escalating to the nuclear level.[222] Recognizing the direct consequences of such a development, the UK had been convening its experts to determine if the plumes from a nuclear exchange would reach London.[223] The concern was shared in Washington where the Pentagon was also busy calculating radiation plumes and medical treatment requirements in case of a nuclear war.[224] Nonetheless, coming amid extreme third-party private and public pressure on Pakistan, the advisories surprised India. While their issuance suggested just how sensitive Western decision makers remained to the specter of an escalated conflict, and how real they thought this possibility was, Indian leaders saw this as too convenient a time to issue such warnings. They had a point. Even though the intent of the advisories was not as Machiavellian as the Indians believed, U.S. interlocutors did not shy away from using them to further the de-escalation agenda.[225] Before issuing them publicly, U.S. officials informed Pakistan's ambassador to the United States, Maleeha Lodhi, that the advisories would go into effect and should have a numbing effect on India.[226] Deputy Secretary Armitage also declined an Indian request to remove them immediately after they were issued.[227] The move even surprised Pakistan, whose calculations suggested that the threat of full-scale war at the time was lower than at the peak of phase I.[228] Regardless, by one stroke, the United States and the UK had signaled to India that it could not hope to continue threatening war without serious consequences for its economy. India's tourism industry and business confidence, both so critical to the country's new-found economic success and positive global image, were shaken and the Indian government was brought under pressure from its business community, including through a joint petition by national and state-level chambers of commerce and industry, to consider the economic fallout of a lingering crisis.[229] The logic of India's provocative behavior had fallen flat once it was clear that the advisories were causing significant domestic commotion. Nayak and Krepon report that U.S. officials believed India was essentially seeking a face saver to exit the crisis after this point.[230]

The second defining moment was Richard Armitage's visit. On the sidelines of an Asian security summit in Kazakhstan, and just two days before Armitage arrived in Pakistan on June 6, Russian president Vladimir Putin had made a strong, albeit unsuccessful, attempt to help the Indian and Pakistani premiers find a breakthrough.[231] In its wake, on June 5, President Bush spoke to the Indian and Pakistani leaders and the White House issued a statement carrying the United States' well-rehearsed position as a prelude to Armitage's mission: "The [U.S.] president reiterated [to] President Musharraf that the United States expects Pakistan to live up to the commitment Pakistan has made to end all support for terrorism. The president emphasized to

Prime Minister Vajpayee the need for India to respond with de-escalatory steps."[232] President Bush also hinted at American willingness to resolve the "many underlying issues" between India and Pakistan.[233] Perfectly worded, the phrase suited the U.S. interest to keep both sides expectant of positive results from the deputy secretary's visit; it could have been interpreted as a promise of support against terrorism by India and a signal of U.S. willingness to involve itself in Kashmir politically by Pakistan.[234]

Armitage's astute diplomacy over the next three days surpassed expectations. He selectively and carefully utilized information from his interactions in Islamabad and New Delhi to get the two sides to lower tensions.[235] During his meeting with Musharraf, he walked away confident that he had received an assurance that Pakistan would curb militancy once and for all.[236] At least in Musharraf's view, Armitage had also promised that the United States would help get India to negotiate on the Kashmir dispute.[237] In India, Armitage told his counterparts that he had received an unequivocal promise from Musharraf that infiltration would stop permanently.[238] But by also emphasizing that the Musharraf government was not capable of stopping all infiltration of militants from Pakistan,[239] Armitage had signaled Washington's tacit acceptance of this Pakistani position and dodged the need for a firm, measurable commitment as a guarantor of Pakistan's promises. This was identical to what Colin Powell had done in phase I.

The Indians, already under intense pressure from international actors and business interests, accepted this explanation.[240] However, they still needed to show that their compellence strategy vis-à-vis Pakistan had worked. They therefore demanded that Armitage make this information public. He did, though in a formulation that would have irked Musharraf. In what is perhaps the most widely quoted statement credited for finally beginning the de-escalation process in the twin peaks crisis, Armitage stated that there is a "commitment to the US by Musharraf to end permanently, cross-border, cross-LoC infiltration."[241] "The President of Pakistan has made it very clear that nothing is happening across the Line of Control. . . . We're looking for that to hold in the longer term."[242] Armitage had deliberately focused on what the Indians wanted to hear, leaving out what Pakistan thought was the real deal: his pledge of a U.S. role in getting India to talk about Kashmir.[243] Equally though, Armitage required a visible gesture from India to compensate Musharraf and convince him that his ploy had worked. This came in the form of India's agreement to call some of its ships away from Pakistan. The move allowed Armitage and Colin Powell, traveling with Armitage at the time, to inform Musharraf that India was responding positively.[244]

Interestingly, given the experience of phase I, U.S. interlocutors knew that India would not take Pakistan's pledge at face value.[245] However, they also realized that by acting as Musharraf's guarantors and by promising to and visibly applying more serious pressure on Pakistan than in phase I, they would make it difficult for India to reject their plea. This was despite the fact that most in Washington, including Armitage, saw Musharraf's promise as mere expediency.[246] In fact, Armitage was careful not to suggest to the Indians that he believed Musharraf's pledge. Instead, when Indian officials pushed him on the veracity of Musharraf's claims, he simply asked them to use their own sources to check if infiltration levels were dropping.[247] Armitage's diplomatic maneuvering points to the tactical nature with which Washington was approaching its role; it needed de-escalation first and foremost, and was willing to subordinate the actual implementability of its assurances to this objective.

The crisis had all but subsided by the end of June 2002 even as Indian mobilization remained intact. The United States lifted its travel advisories on July 22.[248] Thereafter, Washington continued its balancing act but with a broader strategic horizon in mind. It called on India to demobilize troops and formally end the crisis; stated its preference for India and Pakistan to initiate dialogue to resolve their differences without firmly pressuring India to do so; simultaneously reiterated India's importance for the U.S. and continued discussions with India on sales of advanced-technology equipment for special forces to bolster its counterterrorism capacity—these conversations were held during the peak of phase II as well[249]—along with other efforts to expand bilateral ties; and pushed Pakistan to refocus energies on the Afghanistan border and periodically praised Musharraf for his pledges against terrorism to signal a move away from its blunt attitude toward him at the peak of phase II. When Indian officials prodded the United States to push Pakistan harder to fulfill its promises, they got little receptivity in this period.[250] As in the Kargil crisis, the United States ended the crisis believing that its efforts had prevented India and Pakistan from going to war.[251]

South Asia's Second Attempt at Brokered Bargaining: Implications of the Twin Peaks Crisis

Brokered Bargaining at Play

Like the Kargil crisis, the 2001–2002 standoff exhibited a dynamic three-way interaction between India, Pakistan, and the U.S.-led third-party actors. If India's proactive efforts to engage the third party offered substantiation for brokered bargaining in the Kargil crisis, Pakistan was an equally unlikely case to operate within the trilateral framework during the twin peaks crisis. Disappointed by America's stance on the Kargil crisis and virtually isolated internationally after the episode, deeply suspicious of overall U.S. designs in South Asia, and forced into a partnership with it through a do-or-die ulti-matum just months before the crisis, it would not have been unreasonable to expect the Pakistani military regime to chart a more autonomous path dur-ing the crisis. While Pakistan's crucial role in the United States' campaign in Afghanistan accorded it obvious leverage, this could not have completely overshadowed its deep mistrust of the United States and its growing belief that Washington had developed a strategic bias in India's favor. Yet, Pakistani leaders could ill-afford to ignore the fact that a circumspect approach toward the U.S. crisis management role would only have strengthened India's hand and further assisted its efforts to portray itself as a victim of terrorism. There-fore, even though New Delhi led the way in attracting third-party attention by initiating full-scale mobilization and aggressive rhetoric, Islamabad actively sought to outmaneuver its rival throughout the crisis by painting it as the aggressor.

The United States' involvement was far less surprising this time round. The Kargil experience had reinforced the Western world's conviction of the dan-gers associated with crises between these nascent nuclear powers. Therefore, as Armitage put it, "the international community was frightened to death that we were on the verge of nuclear war" during the 2001–2002 standoff.[252] Addi-tionally, Washington now had vital and immediate interests in the region courtesy of its military campaign in Afghanistan. The two acted as mutually reinforcing drivers of its intervention in the crisis. That said, U.S. principals quite consciously distinguished between their concern about escalation from the importance of Afghanistan as a foreign policy priority. Their involvement in the crisis was centered on the former, with the latter only operating in the background to complement it inasmuch as swift crisis termination was also the preferred outcome for the Afghanistan context. Given how preoccupied the United States was with 9/11 and its newly launched War on Terror in Afghanistan at the time, this speaks to just how secondary everything but the risk of escalation tends to become in nuclearized environments.

The United States entered the fray without delay and without any explicit solicitation by either of the regional rivals. While the de-escalation agenda benefited by plainly calling out Pakistan for the Kargil incursion, during the twin peaks crisis, the goal was better served by accepting and confirming Islamabad's position that it did not have any direct association with the parliament and Kaluchak terrorist attacks. Therefore, U.S. crisis management was marked by a persistent effort to play down the middle without revealing its intentions fully to either side. This had both antagonists working the third-party channel throughout in the hope of obtaining its backing ahead of the rival.

Devoid of brokered bargaining, the third party's signaling would risk appearing schizophrenic. It constantly switched between appreciating and pressuring India and Pakistan, and between the need to get both sides to climb down from their aggressive posturing while allowing them enough decision-making autonomy to retain requisite leverage over them. In a classic balancing act, the United States was sympathetic with India but opposed any military action. It used the "nuclear factor as the pressure point" to get India to "cool down."[253] It forced Pakistan to tackle anti-India terrorists and continued to hint at the possibility of greater alignment between the U.S. and Indian stances through private and public signaling but did not box it in completely by setting strict deadlines to ensure cessation of militant infiltration into India. All along, it kept conveying to both sides that it was making headway in pleading their respective cases to the other and carefully and selectively shared information to reinforce this claim. Washington utilized its punishment leverage effectively to get Musharraf to acknowledge the need to put his own house in order and to take some tangible steps to lower cross-border infiltration. With India, this leverage was used to oppose its claim that it had the right to tackle Pakistan-based militants directly and to pressure it, for instance through the travel advisories, to demobilize its troops.

The United States also managed to produce inducements in the form of potent face savers. Both Musharraf's speeches provided India the justification for deferring the military option. In phase II, Armitage's public statement confirming Musharraf's pledge to end infiltration was key to getting India to back off. The international community also played along as India tied its demobilization to the September 2002 elections in Jammu and Kashmir and ultimately endorsed the elections, thereby providing the Indian leadership a domestically palatable way of withdrawing from the crisis.[254] As for Pakistan, India's inability to act militarily was Musharraf's opening. Even though he had to admit that infiltration was taking place from Pakistani soil, he had an obvious wedge with which to extract himself from the crisis. Also, the United States never cast any judgments on who came out ahead in the crisis. It simply allowed India to shift the onus of forcing Pakistan to deliver on ending cross-border militancy on to the third party and let Pakistan point to its deterrent capability to take the credit for India's demobilization. The ability of both sides to have enough on offer to claim victory meant that they could terminate the crisis without losing face.

The United States closely and proactively coordinated its crisis management with other third-party actors, such as the UK, often to the level of specific actions. For the second crisis in succession, China's decision to complement U.S. efforts ahead of its regional alignment with Pakistan was driven by the specter of nuclear escalation in South Asia.[255] Its role was counterintuitive this time given its discomfort with America's muscular ingress in the region post-9/11. All other third parties also relegated their regional equities to the background during the crisis.

Broader foreign policy questions even apart from Afghanistan were entertained only if they could reinforce the principal crisis management objective. The United States was deeply interested in its strategic partnership with India, but it disappointed New Delhi by its reluctance to paint anti-India terrorism with the same brush as terrorism directed at itself. It was careful not to entertain India's strategic revisionism that eyed forcibly and permanently eliminating Pakistan-linked terrorism directed at India even though this aligned neatly with the United States' post-9/11 anti-terrorism agenda. The United States recognized that backing India's desire to use the U.S. preemption mantra to act directly against Pakistan ran smack in the face of the objective of de-escalating the crisis. Meanwhile, the United States stressed its commitment to its relationship with India by offering military sales and defense cooperation but ensured that this did not complicate the crisis dynamic in any way. With Pakistan, the United States used its long-standing wish for a negotiated settlement of the Kashmir dispute cleverly, leaving enough ambiguity in its approach to let Musharraf believe that the United States' deeper engagement on Kashmir was on the table as a quid pro quo for his deference to third-party preferences, but without having any real intention to sincerely pressure India on the issue.

India and Pakistan worked the bilateral and third-party aspects of the resolve-prudence trade-off simultaneously in pursuit of their respective crisis objectives. Sans the third party's presence, Indian and Pakistani behavior could easily be construed as a case of classic coercion and bilateral brinkmanship: full military preparations were backed by aggressive rhetoric aimed at conveying resolve. Nuclear saber-rattling was overt and far more pronounced than during the Kargil crisis.[256] Seen through this lens, Pakistan's actions against anti-India militants would signify success of India's compellence strategy. India's threats of military aggression could be construed as having forced Pakistan to accommodate its most important demand.

In reality, the third party was as much a target of Indian and Pakistani signaling. They used it as a "court of appeal"[257] to get a verdict in their favor. India's compellence strategy led it repeatedly to exhibit resolve during the crisis. Some of its autonomous choices even directly clashed with the United States' regional security priorities. Most notably, its decision to mobilize troops and retain the deployed posture for ten months was a major drag on American interests in Afghanistan. At critical junctures, however, India's sensitivity to third-party preferences prevailed, pulling it back from the brink of war in phase I and forcing it to start the de-escalation process in return for a meager U.S. promise on Pakistan's behalf in phase II. Its failure to secure third-party support for its ultimate crisis objective, an end to anti-India terrorism emanating from Pakistani soil, also forced it to rely on the United States as the face-saving intermediary to terminate the crisis.

India's decision to prioritize third-party preferences implied significant costs for the credibility of its commitment to act against Pakistan. India had entered the crisis determined to reverse its reputational deficit in terms of suffering from a strategic paralysis against Pakistan. Its crisis behavior also had all the markings of a country set to follow through on its threats. Yet, it ended the crisis having reconfirmed its problematic image by preferring to use U.S. mediation over direct military action even though the strategy had little hope of delivering any permanent gains.[258]

Pakistan too ignored the United States' number one concern by redeploying troops from its western border and clearly signaled that the move was directly linked to Washington's inability to get India to demobilize. At the same time, the Pakistani leadership recognized that it had to be seen as acting against terrorism to keep the third party from adopting a harsher stance against it. It therefore obliged the third party, most significantly by publicly acknowledging cross-border infiltration and promising action against militants after years of denial. Pakistan's primary interest in merely returning to the status quo ante in the crisis—which amounted to preventing Indian military action without being forced to chase the goal of permanently eliminating all anti-Indian terrorists in the short run—also allowed it greater space to exhibit prudence to the third party's liking. Even as it undertook tit-for-tat countermoves on the military front then, it simultaneously sought to convey calm, especially in the nuclear realm in phase I. Also, while Musharraf pushed the United States to get India to negotiate on Kashmir as part of Pakistan's crisis diplomacy, he ultimately played along with the United States' tactical use of the Kashmir question as a crisis-management tool as long as it was moving the crisis toward de-escalation.

Brokered Bargaining and the Escalation–De-escalation Dynamic

Indian, Pakistani, and U.S. crisis choices loaded the dice in favor of de-escalation during the 2001–2002 standoff. India's growing relationship with the United States posed an interesting dilemma for it. On the one hand, India's warm relations with the United States and its improving global image contributed to its confidence that it could elicit support for its compellence strategy. On the other hand, however, the importance of India's bilateral partnership with the United States accentuated its need to retain its positive image. India's efforts to manipulate the risk of war to solicit third-party support and its desire to maintain its image of a responsible nuclear power were inherently contradictory. As soon as it employed a combination of aggressive military posturing and resolve-inducing rhetoric, its reputation as a mature actor in competition with a more reckless Pakistan was open to challenge. In fact, by transmitting prudence signals in phase I, Pakistan came across as relatively more restrained. Pakistan's active efforts to portray itself as the defender against potential Indian aggression further strengthened this depiction. The de-escalation agenda benefited from this Indian paradox.

In Pakistan's case, the opposite reality helped ease escalatory pressures. The Pakistani military's image of an outfit prone to risk-taking, reinforced by its recklessness during the Kargil crisis, implied that it needed to do less to convince the adversary and the world of its resolve. To the contrary, its reputation demanded that it reassure the international community that it had learned the right lessons from Kargil and recognized its responsibilities as a nuclear power; this would have incentivized some of its prudent signaling during the crisis. Pakistan's preference for the status quo during the crisis would have further complemented this. Incidentally, Pakistan's behavior during the standoff also challenges the conventional wisdom that military decision makers are more likely to support committal tactics to establish resolve at all costs and thus are liable to force themselves into a commitment trap.[259] While this may have been the case for the Pakistani military in the Kargil crisis, during the 2001–2002 standoff, it was the Indian political leadership more than Pakistan's military regime that seemed to have over-committed itself by mobilizing troops and backing it up with display of political resolve as soon as the crisis got underway.

Even though these factors helped end the twin peaks crisis without an active confrontation, the crisis was not without significant risks linked to the trilateral interaction between India, Pakistan, and the third party. To the extent that India's initial mobilization and saber-rattling were conducted with an eye on the third-party prong of crisis bargaining, the United States' anticipated involvement had a destabilizing effect. More importantly, it represented a flawed assumption on India's part that the post-9/11 environment would force the United States to acknowledge it as a fellow victim of terrorism and underwrite its compellence strategy to punish Pakistan. Further, if Sood and Sawhney are correct in asserting that the Indian political leadership had authorized military action in the first week of January 2002 and only reversed the decision due to U.S. pressure,[260] this too would imply an initial Indian belief that the United States would accept, if not support, its use of force or that the marginal loss of positive evaluation caused by U.S. opposition to this action would be bearable. Nayak points out that one of the assumptions underlying India's military mobilization was that if the United States was unable to force Pakistan to stop cross-border terror, it would be sympathetic to an Indian attack across the LoC.[261] Equally problematic was the seeming confidence in India that the United States, first, would not allow a war to drag on, and, second, would even prevent Pakistan from using nuclear weapons. All these represented misperceptions on India's part. The United States remained strictly opposed to Indian use of force throughout.

If India was reading too much into U.S. sensitivity to its plight with terrorism, Pakistani military leaders may have put too little faith in a third party they both distrusted and doubted in terms of its leverage over India. Their genuine belief that India planned to launch a conventional military operation after the parliament attack prompted their immediate countermobilization. This deployment, its leadership's orders to the military to respond with force to any Indian attack, increased activity near missile and nuclear sites, and its reported missile movements all added to the already-heightened risk of escalation caused by India's military moves.[262]

Phase II also exhibited possibilities of misunderstandings, most obviously in terms of a mismatch of perceptions whereby the Indian military had planned for an all-out offensive aimed at destroying Pakistan's war-making capability while the Pakistani military reportedly believed that a full-blown successful Indian military attack was less feasible in this period.[263] Any massive Indian ingress may therefore have surprised the Pakistanis. More importantly, such an Indian thrust would have risked flirting with the military and space thresholds identified in General Kidwai's enunciation of Pakistan's nuclear red lines earlier in the crisis. The United States revealed its own impression about its limitations as a crisis manager by reportedly providing India with specific information about its presence on the Jacobabad air base in Pakistan's western Baluchistan Province—the United States was using the base at the time to support its military operations in Afghanistan—to ensure that India did not strike its personnel in case of war.[264] It was a dangerous signal that suggested that the United States was not ruling out the possibility of war and Indian strikes deep inside Pakistan. This could have easily emboldened New Delhi and reinforced its misperception of the third party's tacit acceptance of its use of force as long as it avoided targeting the U.S. presence in Pakistan.

The full mobilization of military forces during the crisis put a far greater premium on the third party's crisis management role than in Kargil given the ease with which India and Pakistan could have stumbled into major war from the very beginning. The U.S. role as the conduit for information sharing between the two rivals was also more crucial since Indian and Pakistani leaders made virtually no effort to communicate directly during this crisis. More than simply facilitating information exchange between the rivals, the United States remained deliberately manipulative in its messaging and sought to use information selectively to convince both antagonists that it was doing their bidding. While it managed to choreograph this successfully, a number of risks were inherent in its approach. For instance, Pakistan was aware of the readiness of Indian troops in early January and also knew that the United

States was working to force the Indians to stand down. However, this was also a time when the Pakistani military was convinced of India's resolve to act and uncertain of Washington's ability to dissuade it. Even the slightest inkling in Islamabad that India had defied U.S. requests at the time could have forced Pakistan to act to seize the initiative. This could have happened even if India's defiance was only aimed at extracting further concessions from the United States and it had no actual plans to use force. Pakistani decision makers had no way to decipher true Indian intentions but their deep-seated mistrust of India could easily have led them to assume the worst.

The crisis also demonstrated the unpredictability of the consequences of crisis-management decisions. The travel advisories proved to be a catalyst for de-escalation. However, neither the United States nor the UK had originally thought of them as a crisis management tool, nor did they expect their action to have the kind of impact it did on Indian thinking.[265] The positive results surprised them.[266] While it worked desirably in this case, in reality, the greater-than-expected impact on India could also have had a negative effect. Sensing India's predicament, Pakistan could have felt emboldened to take a firmer stand on its demand for dialogue on Kashmir during Armitage's visit to India that closely followed the issuance of the advisories. Musharraf could also have decided to challenge Armitage's selective reporting of his demands and promises in New Delhi. Armitage's diplomacy would have been rendered less effective and the crisis would likely have prolonged further.

The 2001–2002 standoff constantly threatened to spiral out of control but ultimately none of these risks managed to overtake the crisis dynamic. India got Pakistan to accept its link with militant infiltration but failed to compel Pakistan to force a permanent end to this activity. The crisis ended with the status quo ante intact. Brokered bargaining remained central to the crisis. While India and Pakistan competed in coercing and cajoling the third party to back their respective crisis objectives, the third party successfully played down the middle to ensure crisis termination.

5   The Mumbai Crisis

INDIA AND PAKISTAN FOUND THEMSELVES EMBROILED
in their third major crisis in a decade courtesy of a series of terrorist
attacks in the Indian metropolis of Mumbai in November 2008. Ten terrorists entered Mumbai on November 26, 2008, and by the time the last shot was
fired on November 29, the attack had become the longest terrorist incident in
India's history.[1] It left 174 people dead, 26 foreigners including U.S. citizens
among them, and 311 injured.[2]

The Mumbai attackers were all Pakistani nationals. The Lashkar-e-Taiba
(LeT) had conceived, planned, and executed the operation. Ajmal Kasab, a
young Pakistani from Faridkot in Punjab, was the sole attacker to be captured
alive. Within hours of the attacks, the Indian media were pointing fingers
at Pakistan. The Indian government, now led by Prime Minister Manmohan
Singh from the left-of-center Congress Party, and law enforcement agencies
confirmed a Pakistani link based on information provided by Kasab.[3] Many
in the Indian media drew parallels between 26/11, as the Mumbai attacks
were called, and 9/11 and advocated a muscular response similar to the U.S.
response in Afghanistan.[4] Ultimately, the crisis never escalated to the level of
the clash in Kargil or the 2001–2002 standoff. While there was genuine fear
of escalation at the outset, India ended up exercising restraint. Neither side
mobilized its armed forces extensively, nor were there any skirmishes. Nuclear
rhetoric and posturing were all but nonexistent. Tensions faded gradually as
both sides launched investigations into the attacks and Pakistan took some

actions against the perpetrators. India had held back again, this time in the face of the most spectacular provocation in the history of anti-India terrorism emanating from Pakistani soil, and that too by an outfit it believed to be a direct proxy of Pakistan's intelligence agency, the Inter-Services Intelligence (ISI).

From 2001–2002 to Mumbai: The Strategic and Diplomatic Context

The period between the 2001–2002 standoff and the Mumbai crisis saw unprecedented progress in India-Pakistan relations. Indian prime minister Atal Bihari Vajpayee's "hand of friendship" after the twin peaks episode led to a comprehensive bilateral peace process. This "composite dialogue" continued till the eve of the Mumbai attacks and produced noticeable progress, including a ceasefire on the Line of Control (LoC) in Kashmir.[5] Pakistani president Pervez Musharraf's orders to check anti-India militancy during and after the 2001–2002 standoff also ensured a major dip in cross-border militant movement.[6] Pakistan's own energies after the twin peaks affair were consumed by a raging Islamist insurgency and widespread terrorism, largely a fallout of the lingering war in Afghanistan, which were challenging the state's writ across the country.[7] While the Pakistani state acknowledged that some slippage of militants may have still been occurring across the LoC, it pleaded lack of capacity due to its preoccupation with maintaining internal law and order rather than any lack of will to ensure its complete elimination.[8]

The Pakistani argument did not sit well with India as, from its perspective, it meant continued infiltration of militants, even if at a lower level. The case of LeT troubled India most. Pakistan had banned the outfit after the twin peaks crisis but it still managed to continue operating relatively openly.[9] Therefore, even though the logic of the bilateral peace process led the Congress government in New Delhi to adopt an overall dovish attitude toward relations with Pakistan, it also continued to stress that it would not tolerate recurring attacks from Pakistani soil. This sentiment hardened as terrorist incidents in India picked up again after 2005, and especially in the aftermath of a July 7, 2008, attack at the Indian embassy in Kabul, which killed 41 people, including India's defense attaché.[10] The Indian government defied domestic pressure to end the peace process after this incident, instead choosing to continue engaging with Pakistan's new, but weak, civilian government that had replaced Musharraf's rule. Nonetheless,

U.S. strategist Neil Joeck captured the virtually universal consensus among the Indian strategic elite just months before the Mumbai crisis: "[Another] violent action even two steps removed from ISID [Pakistan's Inter-Services Intelligence Directorate] may be enough to compel India to go after the source rather than the immediate perpetrator of a terror attack."[11] Such a possibility was extremely worrying given the doctrinal developments in the Indian army since the twin peaks crisis. The army had responded to the failure of its full-scale mobilization strategy in the 2001–2002 standoff by floating Cold Start, a Pakistan-specific limited war-fighting doctrine that envisioned reduced mobilization and execution times to enable India to inflict swift and limited punishment before Pakistani forces could mobilize fully and before the international community could pressure India to back off.[12] Even though Cold Start was not fully operational when the Mumbai attacks occurred, there were fears that India might attempt to employ it.[13]

India's and Pakistan's relations with the United States added another interesting dynamic to the Mumbai crisis. India's swift global rise continued after the twin peaks episode. Economic and defense ties between India and key third parties grew exponentially, including a flagship Indo-U.S. civilian nuclear deal that allowed India to access dual-use technology in defiance of global norms.[14] Yet, when it came to an India-Pakistan crisis, the Indians saw the United States as a constraining factor. New Delhi perceived the Bush administration's success in preventing the Indian leadership from acting against Pakistan in the 2001–2002 standoff and its unwillingness to press Pakistan sufficiently on the anti-India terrorism issue thereafter to have emboldened the Pakistani security establishment to persist with its proxy warfare strategy.[15]

Pakistan had continued to serve as the frontline U.S. ally in the campaign in Afghanistan but this partnership was overshadowed by their lingering trust deficit. Islamabad was widely reviled for playing a "double game" by simultaneously supporting the United States and encouraging anti-U.S. Afghan insurgent operations from its soil.[16] Pakistan, on its part, had grown even more suspicious of Washington's growing ties with India. Pakistani leaders were especially rankled by the Indo-U.S. nuclear deal. They saw this exceptional treatment as confirmation of U.S. determination to bolster India as a strategic partner, even at the cost of negatively affecting regional stability in South Asia.[17] In addition, continuing U.S. concerns about the safety and security of Pakistan's nuclear arsenal, reinforced due to Pakistan's rising domestic instability, kept alive Pakistani worries about U.S. designs to forcibly neutral-ize its capability.[18]

The United States faced a dilemma. As in 2001–2002, it maintained imme-diate foreign policy interests in Afghanistan and did not want Pakistan's attention diverted from this theater. It had been trying hard to get Pakistan to do more to support U.S. efforts against Afghan insurgent groups.[19] At the same time, it had made India the lynchpin of its broader South Asia policy and wanted to avoid damaging its larger relationship with New Delhi. Yet, it knew that both India and Pakistan felt that it was partial toward the other, and that they might not trust its mediation during a crisis. The United States was also all too aware of predictions that India might shed its restraint in the face of another major provocation from Pakistani soil. The context presented an acute challenge for Washington's crisis managers.

As the Crisis Unfolded: Indian, Pakistani, and Third-Party Crisis Strategies

India

A Strategy of Military Restraint
India's reaction to the Mumbai carnage was marked by a mix of relatively subdued military behavior, aggressive signaling, and introspection about the failure of its internal counterterrorism measures. Tensions rose immediately after the attacks. Large sections of the Indian media demanded a hard-hitting response; an "enough is enough" attitude was palpable.[20] The political costs of inaction for the Congress government were deemed to be great. They were up for reelection soon and Prime Minister Singh's administration had already been called out for having soft-peddled on Pakistan-linked terrorism. India's claim of "clear and incontrovertible proof" of ISI support of LeT's leadership further increased the pressure on the government to act forcefully.[21] As George Friedman observed immediately after the Mumbai attacks, it was "very diffi-cult to imagine circumstances under which the Indians could respond to this attack in the same manner they have to recent Islamist attacks."[22] Inaction, Friedman argued, would potentially lead to a fall of the Singh government. He therefore predicted that India might ignore any calls to hold back.[23]

Some senior Indian officials did advocate an overt military response.[24] However, the Indian leadership defied the odds and exercised military restraint. Prime Minister Singh met his military services chiefs only once in the initial period after the attacks.[25] He ruled out an Operation Parakram–style mobilization at the outset.[26] Even as discussions about the pros and cons of various military choices continued, and limited options like surgical strikes against terrorist camps in Pakistani Kashmir were seriously considered, no specific military plans were drawn up.[27] The only military moves of note entailed alerting the Indian air force (IAF) after the attacks and extending the stay of two army brigades involved in peacetime exercises on the Pakistani border at the time.[28] While some within the Indian decision-making enclave believe that India still came "fleetingly close" to war with Pakistan, they credit the uncertainty of Pakistan's response and the risk of an expanded conflict for the Indian leadership's choice to defer any firm decision on taking the military course.[29]

The Indian prime minister started off by promising his nation that "we will go after these individuals and organizations and make sure that every perpetrator, organizer and supporter of terror, whatever his affiliation or religion may be, pays a heavy price."[30] Yet, puzzlingly, India made its intent not to wrest the initiative through swift action against Pakistan known early on. By the first week of December, Indian officials were acknowledging that they had "decided that we will collate all the information, piece together the picture and then act."[31] Although diluted somewhat by clarifications by unnamed officials suggesting that the military option was open,[32] India's external affairs minister Pranab Mukherjee confirmed publicly on December 2: "Nobody is talking about military action." "We will await the response of Pakistan."[33] He reiterated ten days later, "I am making it quite clear that it [war] is not a solution."[34]

The tensest period of the crisis was to follow, however. It started with Pakistan's allegation that Indian jets had intruded into its airspace in Pakistani Kashmir and over the border city of Lahore on December 12 and 13, 2008.[35] India promptly denied this and Defense Minister A. K. Antony emphasized on December 16 that India did "not plan to take any military action."[36] Two days later however, India angrily dismissed Pakistan's claims about the IAF intrusion as a "disinformation campaign" and Pranab Mukherjee stated that India would be obliged to consider "the entire range of options" to protect itself from terrorism.[37] On December 22, he affirmed that India was prepared to "take all measures necessary, as we deem fit, to deal with the situation."[38] In the same week, Stratfor, a U.S.-based private intelligence firm, revealed that India had set a one-month deadline at the onset of the crisis for Pakistan to take significant action against militants. It claimed that "Indian military operations against targets in Pakistan have in fact been prepared and await the signal to go forward."[39] India denied having conveyed any such ultimatum but the Pakistani media reported Indian troop movement along the international border and beefed-up security around Indian airstrips. India also subsequently put its Border Security Force on alert, it warned villagers in the border areas to be prepared for war, and it declared travel of Indian citizens to Pakistan unsafe.[40] During this period, the Indian prime minister also held meetings with his military services chiefs and of the Nuclear Command Authority to "discuss all the options available" to India.[41] Ultimately, tensions cooled down. On December 28, the Indian and Pakistani director generals of military operations spoke to clear the air.[42] Two days later, India released 66 Pakistani prisoners in its custody for reasons unrelated to the Mumbai crisis as a goodwill gesture.[43]

The Indian leadership's real focus during the crisis remained on nonkinetic options. India employed aggressive and threatening rhetoric to gain concessions from Pakistan. Its demands were strikingly similar to those in the 2001–2002 standoff: 1) hand over for interrogation and prosecution the Pakistani ring leaders involved in the Mumbai attack; 2) as in 2001–2002, India produced a list of twenty fugitives—the list was later expanded to forty[44]—wanted by India in connection with pending terrorism-related or other criminal cases. It also wanted them extradited; and 3) permanently dismantle the LeT terrorist infrastructure in Pakistan.[45] On December 1, India served two demarches to the Pakistani high commissioner in New Delhi, formally laying out some of these demands.[46] The Indian government stressed, both through direct channels and public messaging, that this time it would not be satisfied with token promises and had to see tangible and lasting action for it to persist with its posture of restraint.

India also sought to build pressure on Pakistan through a concerted public messaging campaign. Within a week of the Mumbai attacks, Mukherjee was calling Pakistan out for not having responded to India's diplomatic protests nor to its demand for extradition of the named individuals.[47] Even as Pakistan moved to crackdown on LeT (and its charity front cum alias Jama'at-ud-Dawa [JuD]) just days later, India kept up the pressure, with at least one government official calling the Pakistani actions "eyewash" that did not address the core concerns.[48] A major part of the Indian effort during the crisis was to prepare findings of its investigation into the Mumbai attacks and share these with Pakistan. This information was also used to pressure Pakistan further through the public domain. On January 5, 2009, India handed over to Pakistan a 69-page dossier containing detailed information on the attacks and demanded that Pakistan take decisive action against the perpetrators based on this evidence.[49] All along, the Indian government kept stressing its belief that the Pakistani state was involved in the attacks.[50]

As the crisis subsided over the next month, India continued to accuse Pakistan of not doing enough to address its demands and intermittently peppered its criticism with various threats. Even the most far reaching of these threats, however, amounted to no more than mild diplomatic censures. This highlights just how minor this crisis turned out to be in light of the nature and scale of the provocation that had triggered it. India had quite openly given Pakistan time to act against the perpetrators of the Mumbai carnage, predicating its ultimate response on Islamabad's actions. By January 19, officials from the two governments were involved in a "friendly handshake."[51] While India continued to demand that Pakistan respond to its concerns, the debate now revolved entirely around the technicalities of Indian and Pakistani investigations into the attacks, Pakistan's measures in response to India's dossier, and the legal mechanisms to bring the perpetrators of the attacks to justice. On February 19, after Pakistan had shared the findings of its own preliminary investigation with India and the press and in doing so had finally acknowledged that the plan was hatched in Pakistan by Pakistanis, Mukherjee declared victory by suggesting that diplomacy had "prevailed" and that India would continue pressing Pakistan to dismantle the terrorist infrastructure in a "verifiable and credible" manner.[52]

Focus on the Third Party
The Indian leadership's military restraint, their propensity to publicly acknowledge their intention not to take retributive action involving use of force, and their decision to merely repeat diplomatic demands that India had been making for years without much success were highly surprising given the pre-crisis mindset in Delhi, the nature of the provocation in Mumbai, and the Indian claim of Pakistani state involvement in the attacks.[53] The Indian government's eye on the third party as the principal vehicle to compel Pakistan to deliver on its demands rationalizes its crisis demeanor.

India neither made any pretense of resisting third-party involvement, nor did it hide the fact that it was willing to opt out of bilateral brinkmanship in favor of using international support to achieve its objectives in the Mumbai crisis. In the words of a U.S. diplomat, "India's Plan A, B, and C was to rely on the US."[54] India's message to the third party was threefold: 1) get Pakistan to permanently end anti-India terrorism emanating from its soil; 2) keep the pressure on Pakistan's leaders since Pakistan was a deliberate sponsor of terrorism and untrustworthy when it came to its promises to tackle militants; and 3) recognize that, given intense domestic pressure, India would not be able to restrain itself in the event of another attack. Indian officials were categorical in direct conversations with third-party interlocutors about their desire to avoid use of force and their willingness to give Pakistan time to act against militants before deciding their future course. Indian Foreign Secretary Shiv Shankar Menon and National Security Advisor (NSA) M. K. Narayanan both confided in David Mulford, the U.S. ambassador to New Delhi, in separate meetings in the days following the attacks that India did not intend to take military action against Pakistan. Narayanan even suggested that doing so would "let Pakistanis off the hook."[55] Menon expressed a similar sentiment to visiting U.S. deputy secretary of state John Negroponte by suggesting that India "wouldn't do them [Pakistan] that favor."[56] These messages hint at India's concern that using force could have played into Pakistan's hands.[57] As Menon explained later, an Indian attack would have obscured the focus on Pakistan's link to the terrorist attacks and pushed the world to see the incident as part of the larger India-Pakistan dispute and to split the blame between the two rivals.[58] India's moral standing would have been diminished.[59] Instead, India focused on retaining international goodwill and support and asked the third party to do its bidding. Nayak and Krepon's reflection on the Indian message to U.S. secretary of state Condoleezza Rice during her December 3 visit to India aptly sums up the crux of this strand of New Delhi's messaging: "Look at the pressures we are facing. We don't want to take military action; we don't want escalation. Do something that will help us satisfy the considerable blood lust that's out there. You need to pressure Pakistan to take actions."[60]

India simultaneously kept up public pressure on third-party actors. Prime Minister Singh encapsulated India's messaging in this vein on December 12. Dismissing the world's assurances of support, he argued that "the political will of the international community must be translated into concrete and sustained action on the ground."[61] Indian leaders also suggested in public that their patience was not unlimited. For instance, amid heightened tensions, on December 22, External Affairs Minister Mukherjee acknowledged India's dependence on the third party for crisis diplomacy but also hinted at New

Delhi's frustration: "We have so far acted with utmost restraint and are hopeful that the international community will use its influence to urge [the] Pakistani government to take effective action. While we continue to persuade the international community and Pakistan, we are also clear that ultimately it is we who have to deal with this problem. We will take all measures necessary, as we deem fit, to deal with the situation."[62] Coming at a time when the perceived risk of a military confrontation was at its peak, this was perhaps the most obvious public effort at risk manipulation vis-à-vis the third party on New Delhi's part.

India's efforts to paint Pakistan's anti-militant actions as insufficient reinforced pressure on the third party to lean harder on Pakistan. After the initiation of Pakistan's crackdown on militants on December 7, Indian leaders publicly called for the UN to designate JuD as a terrorist organization.[63] They also stressed to U.S. interlocutors that Pakistan had a history of detaining accused militants merely to buy time and pointed to the absence of any legal prosecutions in the days immediately following Pakistan's crackdown and lack of positive Pakistani response to India's December 1 demarches.[64] Indian lobbying in world capitals like Washington was also paying off. The U.S. House of Representatives passed a resolution shortly after Pakistan initiated its crackdown that expressed support for the people of India and called on Pakistan to cooperate fully with New Delhi and to prevent its territory from "serving as a safe-haven and training ground for terrorists."[65]

In the run up to the January 5 handover of the Indian dossier to Pakistan, Indian leaders again emphasized to Washington that tangible results from its intercession with Islamabad were still awaited.[66] After presenting the dossier to Pakistan, Foreign Secretary Shiv Shankar Menon specially briefed fifty Delhi-based foreign envoys through detailed presentations, starting with representatives of nations that had lost citizens in the Mumbai attacks and subsequently speaking to an expanded group of representatives of important countries.[67] According to Menon, this effort made a "huge difference" by making it difficult for the world to entertain Pakistan's denials of its links to the Mumbai attacks.[68] Home Minister Chidambaram also traveled to the United States during this period "armed with evidence about involvement of Pakistan-based terrorists in the Mumbai attacks" as part of efforts "to drum up international pressure for nailing Islamabad's lies."[69]

Overall though, India never sought to defy the third party openly during the Mumbai crisis. Rather, Indian leaders were comfortable in explicitly acknowledging to American officials that they could "count on our [India's] pressure on you [the U.S.] to help you do it [pressure Pakistan]."[70] At times, the candor was even accompanied by uncharacteristic acknowledgment of helplessness. External Affairs Minister Mukherjee told U.S. Deputy Secretary Negroponte on December 12: "We deeply appreciate the efforts you are taking" noting that "what little steps [Pakistan] is taking is because of you."[71] Three days later, Indian NSA Narayanan told U.S. Senator John Kerry that India's pressure on Pakistan was unlikely to work and that "the U.S. and UK can help since they provided much of it [evidence]. You might be able to persuade Pakistan unlike how we can."[72] Narayanan was referring to the extensive support U.S. Federal Bureau of Investigation (FBI) and British intelligence agencies had provided to assist the investigations of the Mumbai attacks. Incidentally, acceptance of such widespread assistance in itself was an indication of India's deference to third-party crisis involvement as it had consistently refused such support in the past.[73]

When third-party actors pushed India to tone down its rhetoric during the tensest period of the crisis in mid-December, Indian interlocutors were quick to point to New Delhi's overall restraint and inaction as far as the military option was concerned. Even on developments like the IAF incursions into Pakistani airspace, India chose to deny them rather than confront the third party when Indian leaders were approached with concerns about the incident. India's U-turn on its public demand for extradition of the Mumbai accused was also influenced by third-party demands. Washington's warning to India not to set itself up for failure by making its extradition demand nonnegotiable led Indian officials to confirm to U.S. interlocutors as early as mid-December that they would be willing to settle for less.[74] After some flip flopping, the Indian government also accepted publicly that it would be satisfied with trials of the Mumbai accused in Pakistan.[75] Finally, India softened its no-dialogue-with-Pakistan stance after the Mumbai attacks in response to U.S. persuasion to move away from this position.[76] This was despite the fact that insinuations that the Indian government had buckled under U.S. pressure had earned Prime Minister Singh's government significant domestic criticism.[77] Bilateral dialogue resumed in July 2009 even though Pakistan had released some of the key accused in the Mumbai affair.

Pakistan

A Familiar Crisis Response

Pakistan responded to the Mumbai carnage with a combination of expressions of sympathy and promises of support to India, denial of any involvement in the attacks, action against militants, and aggressive rhetoric and force demonstrations. All along, Islamabad sought a way to wriggle out of the crisis without engaging in conflict or facing diplomatic isolation.

Pakistani decision makers perceived the possibility of Indian use of force to be high after the Mumbai attacks. Pakistan's NSA General Mahmud Durrani recalled that the Pakistani leadership felt there was a "50–60 percent chance Indians would do something militarily."[78] ISI chief General Ahmed Shuja Pasha also acknowledged: "At first we thought there would be a military reaction . . . as the Indians, after the attacks, were deeply offended and furious."[79] For the Pakistani president Asif Ali Zardari, this belief almost turned into reality when he received what has been described as a hoax call attributed to Indian external affairs minister Pranab Mukherjee on November 28.[80] Zardari took the caller's ultimatum of an impending Indian military attack extremely seriously and immediately requested his military leadership to assess the threat.[81] Around this time, Chinese intelligence sources were also reportedly conveying to Pakistan a concern about the real possibility of a flare up of the crisis.[82]

Pakistan alerted its air force, which began patrolling the skies over Islamabad with live ammunition even though the Pakistan army and ISI leadership had concluded that India was unprepared to attack immediately.[83] Even as the Pakistani civilian and military principals met repeatedly during the early days to assess the environment, they simultaneously attempted to convey calm, even vouching for India's prudent behavior in the process. The Pakistani military's spokesperson confirmed on November 30 that "no unusual [Indian military] activity has been witnessed so far [on the international border]."[84] The army also maintained that the LoC "ceasefire is holding."[85]

Pakistan's rhetoric hardened only in the wake of the alleged IAF incursions into Pakistani air space in mid-December. While the Pakistani government was deliberate in trying to publicly downplay the incursions, with Information Minister Sherry Rehman confirming that her government had accepted India's version that the violations were "inadvertent," it was also categorical in noting that incursions 2–4 kilometers deep into Pakistani territory had indeed taken place.[86] The Pakistan Air Force (PAF) scrambled its jets and its spokesperson cautioned that his service was "fully alive to the situation and capable of giving a befitting reply in case of a misadventure."[87] A war of words ensued over the next fortnight. The Indian external affairs minister's suggestion during this period that India was keeping all options on the table elicited a flurry of responses from Pakistan suggesting that it did not want war but "will be compelled to respond" if India aggressed in any manner.[88] Such signals continued as talk of possible Indian surgical strikes grew in the press and media. The Pakistani army chief, General Ashfaq Parvez Kayani, warned that Pakistan would respond "within minutes" to any such Indian provocation.[89] Leader of the House in the Senate Raza Rabbani emphasized that the Pakistani government would consider an Indian surgical strike an act of war and "give a befitting response if war is thrust on it."[90]

Pakistan's resolute rhetoric during this period was backed by sparing military moves. Mukherjee's provocation on December 22 hinting at the military option being open for consideration led the PAF to once again mount patrols over several major cities.[91] Within the week, Pakistan put its navy, air force, and army on "red alert," cancelled leaves of its military personnel, and deployed more troops on its border with India.[92] As India warned its citizens not to travel to Pakistan and the Indian prime minister consulted his services chiefs on options, reports surfaced that Pakistan had also begun redeploying some of its forces from the Afghanistan border.[93] However, tensions cooled down abruptly shortly thereafter.

These military moves notwithstanding, like India, Pakistan followed a non-kinetic strategy during the Mumbai crisis. Through multiple public statements, President Asif Ali Zardari took the lead in condemning the Mumbai attacks and in conveying Pakistan's intent to support India in investigating them. Pakistani NSA, Mahmud Durrani, specifically broached the idea of a joint investigation with his Indian counterpart M. K. Narayanan as the attacks were unfolding.[94] Pakistan would continue to hold out this offer as a way forward throughout the crisis. Perhaps most significant, however, was the symbolically crucial promise (ultimately rescinded) by Pakistani prime minister Yousaf Raza Gilani to send the ISI chief, General Pasha, to India immediately after the attacks.[95]

Pakistani officials also spent considerable time and energy attempting to distance themselves from the Mumbai plot. In a statement representative of Pakistan's stance, Foreign Minister Shah Mahmood Qureshi reiterated on November 29 that Pakistan's "hands are clean, we have nothing to hide, we have nothing to be ashamed of."[96] Even after India had confirmed a Pakistani connection to the attacks and served formal demarches on December 1, Islamabad simply continued to deny that any Pakistanis were involved or that the plan was hatched on its soil.[97] Pakistan would deliberately maintain this stance well beyond the peak of the crisis even though the Pakistani and international media had revealed Kasab's identity by the second week of December.[98] The Pakistani state's crackdown against LeT/JuD in the face of Indian demands for action against militant outfits was also in obvious contradiction to its public denial of involvement of Pakistanis in the attacks. Starting from December 7, Pakistan made multiple arrests including that of Zaki-ur-Rehman Lakhvi, the Mumbai episode's alleged mastermind, and sealed a number of LeT/JuD offices.[99] Hafiz Saeed, the outfit's leader was put under house arrest on December 11 and JuD was formally banned on December 13.[100] Pakistan continued to investigate the Mumbai attacks internally and in fact bought considerable time and space by showing some results once the crisis was past its peak. On January 15, Pakistani interior minister Rehman Malik announced that a special investigation team was being set up to conduct a formal investigation of the attacks and claimed that Pakistan had shut down five JuD camps and detained as many as 124 accused terrorists.[101] Pakistan found more respite when it shared the salient findings of its investigation in mid-February and finally acknowledged that the Mumbai plan was hatched in Pakistan.[102] It followed this up by formally initiating legal proceedings against those it had apprehended in connection with the attacks.[103]

The fact that Pakistan was forced to admit that the Mumbai attacks were masterminded by LeT on its soil was not trivial from the Indian and third-party perspectives. In reality, however, Pakistan was only doing enough to avoid a break in Indian restraint. In parallel with investigating the attacks, Pakistan took pains to highlight the complexity of the facts surrounding the Mumbai episode to keep neutral observers from fully accepting India's version of the event. As the crisis progressed, Pakistan's position became increasingly tied to the legal hurdles that were preventing it from moving swiftly against the Mumbai suspects. This included a persistent complaint that India had not provided sufficient information and evidence for Pakistan to successfully prosecute the accused.[104] By the spring of 2009, the familiar pattern of terrorists being rounded up and later released by the Pakistani state was being repeated.[105]

Efforts to Utilize the Third Party's Leverage

Pakistan complemented its strategy vis-à-vis New Delhi by utilizing third-party presence with candor and vigor similar to India's in its engagement with the outside world. Pakistan's principal preoccupation was to get the third party to prevent India from using force against it.[106] Immediately after the attacks, the Pakistani leadership reached out to the United States, China, Turkey, European countries, Gulf states, and other partners with a set of scripted talking points.[107] The gist of these is aptly summed up by NSA Mahmud Durrani's message to Washington while the attacks were still ongoing: Pakistan is sorry about the attacks; both India and Pakistan have terrorist threats and need to fight them together; they should avoid playing into the hands of the militants by escalating tensions; Pakistani leaders had spoken to their Indian counterparts and extended their support; and the Pakistani leadership had agreed to send their investigators to India to help move the investigation along.[108] Pranab Mukherjee's supposed ultimatum of war during the hoax call also prompted Pakistani president Zardari to reach out frantically to a number of key world capitals, starting with Washington.[109] Meanwhile, the Pakistani Foreign Office gathered envoys of a number of important third parties in Islamabad on December 2 and emphasized the need for India to exercise restraint, or risk an expanded conflict.[110]

Pakistan's effort to distance the state from non-state actors and argue that the attack took place without any official knowledge was a central element of its messaging strategy. While it could not challenge India's universal characterization as the victim, it worked to keep the world from declaring the Pakistani state as the aggressor. There is some evidence that third parties agreed with the argument that it would have been irrational for the Pakistani state to authorize a terrorist operation that would target and kill foreigners. The U.S. embassy in Islamabad conveyed to Washington that this Pakistani defense was entirely logical and believable.[111] Working in Pakistan's favor was the fact that Western intelligence sources had found no evidence of ISI authorization of the attacks even though they were not willing to rule out the possibility of involvement of rogue or former ISI personnel.[112]

Pakistan sought to capitalize on this to counter the Indian diplomatic onslaught aimed at pinning the blame on the ISI. Immediately after the attacks, Pakistani interlocutors requested the United States to make public the fact that no direct ISI role had been identified in the Mumbai plot.[113] U.S. crisis managers seem to have obliged. On December 1 and 2, leading U.S.

newspapers carried stories with strikingly similar language attributed to unnamed intelligence sources that stressed this point.[114] The view was also emphasized in an official White House statement.[115] Unsurprisingly, President Zardari triumphantly declared in a much-publicized interview on CNN that "the state of Pakistan is, of course, not involved." "Even the White House and the American CIA have said that today. . . . we are part of the victims."[116] In due course, the Pakistani intelligence leadership shared more facts about the attacks with key third parties. The aim was to confirm the absence of any ISI direction or role in the attacks. In a meeting with CIA director Michael Hayden, ISI chief General Pasha acknowledged that former ISI personnel operating in their individual capacity may have "engaged in some broad training of the attackers."[117] However, he rejected any institutionalized ISI role, instead suggesting that the ISI had failed to identify the timing of the plot and prevent the attackers from traveling to India.[118]

The two most important aspects of Pakistan's strategy vis-à-vis the third party were manipulation of the risk of war and accommodation of its demands. The latter was more pronounced. In terms of raising the stakes for the third party, Pakistan's trump card was an obvious one: the continuing U.S. need for Pakistani troop presence and support on the Afghanistan border. Even as Pakistan showed understanding for India's predicament and promised cooperation, Pakistani media reported a day after the Mumbai attacks ended that the United States had been informed that continuing tensions with India would force Pakistan to divert its troops from the western border.[119] During his early December trip to Pakistan, Chairman of the U.S. Joint Chiefs of Staff Admiral Mike Mullen also received explicit ultimatums from the civilian and military leadership that the Indian threat would take precedence over America's Afghanistan campaign.[120] Pakistan would raise the specter of relocation of its troops again when tensions seemed to be reaching the tipping point in late December. The press quoted unnamed Pakistani officials who confirmed that the military had actually begun to pull its troops from the western border, supposedly because of "new intelligence suggesting that India might launch an attack inside Pakistan."[121] Nayak and Krepon observe that this move was "guaranteed to focus US as well as Indian attention."[122]

Islamabad's signals that it would respond with force to any Indian provocation were also issued with an eye on the third party. The IAF incursions into Pakistani air space in mid-December were dealt with sternly through private third-party channels even as they were downplayed in public. Pakistani NSA

Mahmud Durrani reached out to his U.S. counterpart Stephen Hadley immediately with a pointed message: India had violated Pakistani air space; Pakistan had interpreted this as a threat; if India attacks, no Pakistani government would be able to survive inaction, and it would therefore respond with force; and Pakistan would do so even at the cost of expanding the conflict.[123] Durrani was deliberately making a "veiled threat" to the third party and through it, to the adversary.[124]

A week later, when Admiral Mike Mullen returned to Pakistan to help lower the temperature and echo India's demand for greater action against those accused of involvement in Mumbai, he was greeted by PAF sorties over major cities.[125] Pakistan also responded to rumors that Mullen had arrived with a proposal that would allow India to let off steam and ratchet down tensions by carrying out a symbolic surgical strike inside Pakistan.[126] While Pakistani leaders were not certain if the rumors had any basis, their concerns would have been heightened by the fact that influential U.S. senator and presidential candidate in the 2008 U.S. elections John McCain had broached the idea of surgical strikes against LeT's headquarters in the densely populated town of Muridke close to the international border with Pakistani interlocutors when he visited the region in early December.[127] In an obvious bid to raise the stakes and signal the impermissibility of any such Indian action, army chief Kayani told Mullen categorically that even the slightest act of military aggression by India would receive an immediate response.[128] He was not bluffing: Pakistan had pre-marked targets to strike in India and had decided to do so immediately in the event that the rumored Indian strike occurred.[129] General Kayani's and House Leader Raza Rabbani's statements during this time that Islamabad would treat an Indian surgical strike as an act of war ought to be seen in this light. The Pakistani parliament also came out backing a strong response if India struck.[130] By making this a public debate, the Pakistani leadership was able to portray itself as being hostage to public opinion and to the political pressure it would face in choosing its course in response to Indian adventurism.

What ultimately allowed Pakistan wiggle room to escape the crisis relatively unharmed was its sensitivity to third-party demands. All Pakistani leaders were in sync throughout in confirming their commitment to attend to the international community's principal demands: sincerely investigate the Mumbai attacks and decisively act against non-state actors, specifically LeT. The Pakistani leadership recognized that it had to do something—in the words of President Zardari, "arrest them; get them locked up"—against those involved in Mumbai.[131] Therefore, they took tangible actions at key moments to ease the otherwise relentless pressure they faced from the United States. By the first week of December, Pakistan was beginning to apprise third-party interlocutors of its plans and actions to oblige them. Senator McCain's congressional delegation heard from the Pakistani prime minister during their trip that Pakistan had begun the process of trying to arrest individuals specified by U.S. secretary of state Condoleezza Rice in her meetings in Islamabad earlier in the week. He was also candid about the fact that Pakistan had not objected to the UN's designation of LeT/JuD members and affiliated charity organizations as terrorists as proof of its sincerity.[132] For some time the UN had been prevented from labeling LeT/JuD as terrorist organizations courtesy of a Chinese "hold" on the process, a move believed to have been requested by Pakistan.[133] Soon, Pakistan would also have progress to report on arresting some of those accused by India. That the Pakistani crackdown occurred almost simultaneously with the UN's listing of LeT/JuD members and affiliates was no coincidence.

The United States had also been instrumental in creating an arrangement for information sharing on the Mumbai case, keeping itself at the center and sanitizing material it received from Pakistan and India before passing it on to the other.[134] Pakistan was sharing substantive, interrogation-based information about the Mumbai attacks through this mechanism by early January 2009. It was doing so deliberately to signal its commitment to work constructively with India.[135] Washington saw this as a sign of goodwill on the part of Pakistan and as an indication of its seriousness to cooperate. Pakistani officials also continued telling U.S. interlocutors that they were willing to act on information provided by India in its dossier and by U.S. intelligence sources.

Pakistan's decision to go public with the announcement that it was setting up an investigation task force in January and with the findings of its investigations the following month also bought it time by alleviating some of the pressure coming from India and the third party. There were signs that Islamabad's efforts to convince the third party of the seriousness of its efforts and its political constraints were working. A U.S. embassy cable from Islamabad to Washington after Pakistani interior minister Rehman Malik's announcement of the task force noted: "Malik . . . is trying to produce concrete results every day for the international community. At the same time, he is trying to build domestic support by framing the process in a way that makes the GOP

[Government of Pakistan] (not India or the U.S.) appear to be the demandeur."[136] The U.S. embassy was again reporting its appreciation of Pakistan's efforts to investigate Mumbai before key findings of the investigation were released in February. It also reinforced the Pakistani contention that lack of evidence from India was holding up further progress.[137]

The Pakistani leadership believed that the United States was "a big support in calming the situation."[138] Yet, they never fully acquiesced to U.S. demands on potentially game-changing issues. For instance, their propensity to drag their feet on accepting that the Mumbai plan was hatched in Pakistan by Pakistanis complicated the crisis dynamics in the initial weeks. Similarly, despite intense U.S. pressure, Pakistan only allowed piecemeal access to suspects accused of involvement in the Mumbai affair. Interior Minister Malik agreed to allow the FBI access to the investigation immediately after India handed over the dossier to Pakistan on January 5 under the promise that the arrangement would be kept discreet, but he later cited domestic political sensitivities to refuse access to suspects identified during the Pakistani investigation. Instead, he promised to send a team to Washington to share all relevant information with U.S. officials.[139] This was despite the fact that Washington had continued to call Pakistan out on the issue, at one point even insinuating that Pakistan might be holding back on access to the likes of Zaki-ur-Rehman Lakhvi because it had something to hide.[140] As the legal prosecution stalled and some militants were released in summer of 2009, Pakistani authorities kept blaming India for lack of evidence and pointed to legal lacunas, without doing much to fix them.[141] Pakistani leaders seem to have calculated, rightly it turned out, that they could take this liberty once the threat of Indian military action, or of Pakistan's international isolation, had waned.

Pakistan exited the crisis reviled. The Mumbai episode reinforced the world's view of Pakistan's troubling links with terrorism. But importantly from its perspective, Pakistan had done just enough to achieve its immediate crisis objective of keeping the status quo ante intact.

The Third Party: Perfecting the Brokered Bargaining Game
The relatively subdued nature of the Mumbai crisis has led many to argue that the episode never realistically threatened to escalate to a major war. At the time, however, the Mumbai attacks had worried the international community immensely. U.S. leaders could not help drawing parallels between the Mumbai attacks and 9/11 and recall how deeply compelled they had felt to go to

war because of the attacks on the U.S. homeland.[142] The U.S. embassy in New Delhi was also reporting "war fever" in India as the crisis got underway.[143] Even though there was a view in the U.S. mission in Islamabad that Pakistan might respond to any Indian attack in a graduated manner and may even wait a day or two to see the international response,[144] for others, the possibility of Pakistan's preemption of any Indian effort to employ force could not be ignored.[145] The extent of Washington's concern was reflected by the swiftness with which President Bush's administration got involved. The U.S. intervention was marked by an effort to "get out in front of events."[146] Notably, this was despite the fact that the Mumbai attacks took place at a time when virtually all U.S. principals were distracted by the major Thanksgiving national holiday, and were not present in Washington.[147]

The magnitude of the attacks and the circumstances surrounding them complicated Washington's position by bringing the third party's role as an honest broker into sharp focus. India was once again seen as the undisputed victim of gruesome terrorism. The United States also believed that the ISI had been supporting and protecting LeT.[148] Moreover, the United States and a number of other Western countries had lost their citizens in the carnage. This imposed a legal responsibility on them to investigate and prosecute those responsible for their deaths. The context was therefore logically set up for a partisan U.S. approach in India's favor.

In reality, the third party took pains to avoid doing just that. For the United States, Mumbai posed a "crisis management situation [it was] trying to de-escalate" by identifying "what short term steps [could] be taken at the time to defuse the crisis."[149] President Bush explicitly asked his team to "do what you have to do to prevent a war between Pakistan and India."[150] Crisis management was about providing India a good enough "excuse to back down."[151] For the second crisis in succession, the goal of de-escalation neatly overlapped with crucial U.S. interests in Afghanistan. However, even as the U.S. leadership was "unarguably trying to manipulate the situation," the focus of Washington's crisis diplomacy "wasn't to save Afghanistan."[152] "It was solely for de-escalation."[153] In fact, the U.S. National Security Council working under NSA Stephen Hadley was bifurcated between the directorates that handled India-Pakistan versus Afghanistan affairs. Notably, the latter was not involved in crisis management during the Mumbai episode.[154] Like the 2001–2002 standoff, the Afghanistan issue continued to operate in the background. Even the importance of the death of U.S. citizens was overshadowed by the urgency to achieve de-escalation. The issue did not feature in Washington's conversations about managing the crisis despite longstanding public commitments by U.S. governments that the death of American citizens in terrorist incidents would be a key determinant of their response. As one U.S. official recounted, "We wouldn't have done anything different even if U.S. citizens weren't killed."[155] "That [death of U.S. citizens] is the sort of thing that never comes up [in such crisis management discussions]."[156]

U.S. officials have talked of having operated from a notional "playbook" during the Mumbai episode that was derived from America's past crisis management experiences.[157] They decided on a very clear game plan and choreographed messages, phone calls, and visits, all of which took place regularly throughout the crisis. U.S. interlocutors were assigned their principal counterparts in India, Pakistan, and other third country capitals and they were responsible for engaging them as needed.[158] U.S. officials who visited South Asia worked off a "completely and totally coordinated" messaging script.[159] Washington also received support from other third-party actors. Senior officials from the UK, China, and Saudi Arabia, and the UN secretary general made trips to the region during the crisis.

The United States led with messages of outright sympathy for India and pushed Pakistan to issue statements and take steps that would help lower the temperature of the crisis.[160] Various U.S. officials condemned the attacks instantly. Even when the United States was forced to make choices that were likely to worry India, it took New Delhi into confidence and sought its consent in advance. For instance, in stark contrast to the twin peaks crisis, Washington forewarned the Indian leadership that it had an obligation to its citizens to issue a travel advisory in the prevailing environment, but it promised that it would do so as "sensitively as possible."[161] The advisory, issued on November 27 without any real hype, asked U.S. citizens to "defer travel to Mumbai for at least the next 48–72 hours."[162] The FBI also worked with Indian intelligence agencies to prepare a situation report to assuage the concerns of the business sector within 24 hours of the Mumbai attacks.[163]

Equally important, messages were simultaneously being sent to India "to not take precipitous action" and instead to first determine all the facts surrounding the event.[164] Washington's decision to oblige Pakistan on its request to publicly acknowledge that the Pakistani state was not complicit in the Mumbai carnage immediately after the attacks was the first clear public signal to India that the United States was unlikely to challenge Pakistan on this count without evidence to the contrary. President Bush had also informed Prime Minister Manmohan Singh directly of this position.[165] However, CIA officer and key crisis manager during the Kargil episode Bruce Riedel interprets the earlier-cited U.S. press stories that suggested the absence of Pakistani state involvement as an "orchestrated campaign to downplay any ISI link to remove India's justification for retaliation."[166] While the CIA denies having sourced these stories,[167] Riedel observes that such use of intelligence information would likely be "fully coordinated between CIA and WH [White House]."[168] Nevertheless, third-party interlocutors continued to remind India throughout the crisis that there was no evidence to back its view on Pakistani state complicity and even asked Indian leaders to tone down its public rhetoric aimed at amplifying this claim. To India's dismay, they even pressured it publicly on the issue. While visiting India in mid-January, British foreign secretary David Miliband was categorical: "I have said publicly that I do not believe that the attacks were directed by the Pakistani state. And I think it is important to restate that."[169]

The first occasion where the crisis seemed to be slipping out of control was in the wake of the hoax call attributed to Pranab Mukherjee. According to a U.S. official, this "changed everything—[it] risked having all spin out of control."[170] U.S. secretary of state Condoleezza Rice got involved instantly and headed off the immediate threat of war through phone diplomacy. She talked to Mukherjee, who plainly denied having made the call.[171] This was quickly conveyed to the Pakistani leadership to assuage their concerns. Immediately afterward, President Bush dispatched Secretary Rice to the region to help calm tensions.[172] Rice's early December visit was closely coordinated with British interlocutors.[173] Her messaging during the trip succinctly captures the crux of third-party signaling to India and Pakistan throughout the crisis. She assured India that Pakistan was being pressured to act against those involved in Mumbai. Publicly too, she came down hard on Pakistan and affirmed that Pakistan had a "special responsibility" and needed to take "direct and tough" action since "non-state actors remain a matter of responsibility if it's in your [Pakistan's] territory."[174] At the same time, she insisted on the need for Indian restraint. Her recounting of her first encounter with a visibly perturbed Indian NSA M. K. Narayanan is telling: she offered sympathy by drawing parallels between 9/11 and the Mumbai attacks but then quickly advised that India needed to "concentrate on preventing the next attack" rather than contemplating aggression at the time.[175] She also warned of "unintended consequences" of any Indian military action in her public statements.[176] The Indians saw Rice's visit to the region as "helpful [and] timely."[177] On her part, she had managed to convince the Indian leadership of the merits of holding back and relying on U.S. crisis management efforts.

U.S. and other third-party interlocutors who followed on the heels of Rice's visit reinforced her message. Senator John McCain, whose trip was coordinated with the U.S. administration,[178] was perhaps most explicit in reassuring his Indian hosts by suggesting that the United States was "one-thousand percent behind India" and that he would carry direct and tough messages to Pakistan.[179] Interestingly, however, and even though McCain would go on to Pakistan and convey that an Indian military attack was highly likely, he was categorical in opposing any Indian action modeled on the U.S. intervention in Afghanistan.[180] Nor did the United States bite when India attempted to nuance its position on Pakistani state complicity by emphasizing that it was not blaming the Pakistani civilian government for the attacks, but only its security establishment.

One of the key levers of U.S. diplomacy during the crisis was its ability to mediate the information exchange related to the legal investigation of the attacks. Washington saw the legal intervention and its offer of FBI assistance to India as serving a crisis-management function: it provided space for lowering the temperature and "slowing down the decision making process in Delhi."[181] While the law enforcement/legal aspect of the crisis remained important throughout, the third parties managed to ensure a law enforcement/legal-only focus by early-to-mid-January 2009. The United States praised Indian efforts to compile the information dossier and share it with Islamabad. U.S. ambassador Mulford declared the information contained in the dossier as "credible" enough and promised that the United States "will pursue this matter to its conclusion."[182] Simultaneously, however, India was also asked to give Pakistan time to act on the evidence. Once the active crisis subsided, the discussions focused almost exclusively on Pakistan's prosecution efforts. Even as Pakistan's delivery faded, the United States chose to emphasize the progress it had made in law enforcement cooperation with India and in forcing Pakistan to accept its links to the attacks. Indian complaints of dwindling prospects for prosecution in Pakistan were met with understanding and promises that LeT would not be allowed to get away with terrorist attacks on India.[183]

U.S. crisis mediation with Pakistan was built around getting it to say and do the right things that could then be carried back to India as proof of progress and reason enough for it to keep trusting the third party. The United States collated India's asks, eliminated what could cause misunderstandings or was deemed to be unrealistic, and then confronted Pakistan with a list of seven demands: prevention of repeat attacks; sincere investigation of the Mumbai affair; arrests and prosecution of those involved, including LeT chief Hafiz Saeed; access to verifiable information for the FBI; information sharing with India; assurance that Pakistan would not escalate tensions; and crackdown on LeT, and on terrorism overall.[184] Throughout, "phenomenal pressure" was kept up on Pakistan to deliver.[185] Intermittently, however, efforts to warn Pakistan of the potential consequences of ignoring American demands and of the high level of anger in India were peppered with platitudes to avoid any impression that the United States was wholly aligned with New Delhi against Islamabad.

Washington started by asking Pakistan to crackdown urgently on any individuals who could potentially execute another attack. Some U.S. crisis managers believed that a second attack could dissolve Indian restraint and "undo the whole [US diplomatic] ball game."[186] Simultaneously, Washington built pressure on Pakistan to demonstrate its willingness to cooperate with India within 24 hours of the attacks by urging it to send ISI chief General Pasha to India.[187] As Pakistan first obliged and then backtracked after Pakistani army chief General Kayani refused to allow Pasha to travel for fear that it would set the wrong precedent of India summoning Pakistani intelligence chiefs,[188] pressure was kept up—unsuccessfully—to follow through on the commitment. U.S. interlocutors cautioned Pakistani officials that not doing so would signal lack of sincerity to make good on promises of cooperation.[189]

Hard-hitting messages hinting that the United States would not tolerate Pakistani inaction continued to pour in privately to Pakistani leaders even as Washington publicly absolved the Pakistani state of involvement in the attacks. On the same day that the U.S. press carried reports suggesting the absence of any formal ISI role in Mumbai, U.S. officials were busy issuing a demarche to Pakistan that contained sanitized intelligence information with names of LeT operatives believed to be involved in the attacks.[190] Washington pressed Pakistan hard to recognize that it increasingly saw LeT as a direct threat to it and wanted to see action aimed at dismantling the group—not just rounding up a handful of individuals. In addition to arresting its leadership, it specifically asked that Pakistan shut down LeT camps, dismantle its infrastructure, and curtail its finances.[191] Pakistani ambassador to Washington Husain Haqqani's assessment of this environment was that Pakistan's expectations of immediate monetary assistance from international financial institutions to shore up its economy could suffer unless demonstrable action was taken in line with U.S. demands.[192]

Third-party pressure was kept up by the slew of visitors who arrived in Pakistan from the first week of December onward. Admiral Mike Mullen brought a clear message to prevent any repeat attacks and rein in LeT.[193] Secretary of State Rice followed with pointed demands to act against those connected to Mumbai and suggested that America stood with India and needed Pakistan to provide New Delhi enough reason to maintain restraint.[194] The Pakistani leadership was also asked not to try blocking the UN effort to blacklist individuals connected to Mumbai.[195] Washington's success in pushing through the UN listing helped increase India's confidence in U.S. crisis engagement.[196]

A classic example of the third party's manipulative mediation was provided by Senator John McCain's signaling after he arrived in Pakistan from India in the first week of December. McCain reached Pakistan to tell Anne Patterson, the U.S. ambassador in Islamabad, that "this is the biggest international crisis since the Cuban missile crisis."[197] In a bid to jolt the Pakistani leaders into anti-terrorist action, he went to the point of affirming that the Indian prime minister was "visibly angry" and had conveyed to him that he could authorize use of force against Pakistan "within a matter of days" if Pakistan did not act swiftly against the terrorists. He also explicitly warned that the United States would not be able to stop India from doing so.[198] His choice of making these comments in front of a group of specially invited Pakistani journalists confirms that this was a deliberate attempt to signal publicly.[199] As a U.S. diplomat recounted, McCain "over-dramatized the degree of Indian upset, which was useful. He got their [Pakistan's] attention."[200] McCain also rather controversially broached the specific possibility of a surgical Indian strike against LeT's headquarters and asked senior Pakistani interlocutors how Pakistan might react. It was never clear whether the scenario had come up in his discussions in India or if he was raising this on behalf of the Bush administration. Tellingly though, his trip had the blessings of the U.S. leadership and, at least on one occasion, he raised this issue in the presence of the U.S. State Department's Special Representative for Afghanistan and Pakistan, Richard Holbrooke, who made no attempt to clear the air.[201]

The initial days of the Mumbai crisis also saw a significant Chinese role. While China promised general support to Pakistan, it called upon both India and Pakistan to talk and cooperate to ensure regional peace.[202] More importantly, China, on U.S. prompting, communicated to Pakistan its unwillingness to hold back the UN listing and sanctioning of militants and pressed Pakistan hard to arrest the Mumbai accused.[203] In a public statement, the Chinese Foreign Ministry even offered to join hands with India to help it hunt down terrorist groups involved in the Mumbai attacks.[204]

The Pakistani crackdown against LeT/JuD operatives that was initiated during this time was critical to addressing New Delhi's concerns. The third party pressured Pakistan into acting against militants and then expectedly greeted the crackdown with much private and public praise. The United States officially commended Pakistan by stating "there is no doubt that Pakistan has taken some positive steps. It's critically important now . . . that we continue to work together, the Indians, the Pakistanis, the United States and our allies to prevent follow-on attacks after the attacks in Mumbai."[205] The European Union and others joined in with their own praise.[206] The first spike of the Mumbai crisis had been managed effectively.

During the second spike, the United States worried that increased tensions marked by the IAF incursions could quickly slip out of control.[207] Even though facts were not immediately obvious, Washington privately questioned India's denial of the incursions. NSA Stephen Hadley promptly acted upon his Pakistani counterpart's "veiled threat" by confirming from Indian and U.S. sources that no Indian military attack was imminent and conveyed it back to Islamabad with a message urging calm and restraint.[208] As tensions continued to rise nonetheless, U.S. interlocutors pointed fingers at Pakistan publicly and asked for greater acceptance of Pakistani links to the attacks, and for action against the Mumbai accused. In the third week of December, Secretary Rice implored Pakistan in a statement representative of this effort: "You need to deal with the terrorism problem. And it's not enough to say these are non-state actors. If they're operating from Pakistani territory, then they have to be dealt with."[209]

Simultaneously, both sides were urged not to take actions that risked increasing tensions.[210] Pakistan's claim in late December that it had begun to move forces from its western border also seems to have worked, as U.S. calls for restraint intensified immediately after this development. The U.S. president was on the phone urging Indian and Pakistani leaders to avoid escalatory moves and building pressure by making public that "all three leaders . . . agreed that no one wanted to take any steps that unnecessarily raise tensions."[211] India was also subsequently asked to "tone down" its war rhetoric while Washington assured it that it was "not giving them [Pakistanis] any breaks" as far as the demand to eliminate LeT completely was concerned.[212]

Other third-party actors reinforced these messages. Once again, British and Chinese interlocutors were especially visible. They urged restraint but also weighed in heavily to convince Pakistan to provide something tangible to help ratchet down tensions. When the Chinese deputy foreign minister He Yafei was dispatched to Islamabad in late December to conduct crisis diplomacy, some in the Pakistani military leadership believed that Beijing was acting on a U.S. request.[213] Chinese influence seems to have had an effect again as Pakistan issued statements assuring calm, including importantly one by General Kayani immediately after his meeting with He Yafei in Islamabad on December 29.[214] Other Pakistani allies like Saudi Arabia had been sufficiently sensitized by New Delhi and were also active in pushing Pakistan to act against those suspected of involvement in the Mumbai attacks.[215]

By mid-January, third-party actors had succeeded in pushing crisis dealings squarely into the law enforcement/legal domain. Their engagement was now about continuing to press Pakistan to thoroughly investigate the attacks, build a strong case for prosecutions, and share all relevant information with India. As the crisis subsided and Pakistan slowly drifted in its commitment to prosecute and punish the Mumbai accused, the third party did little more than reiterating its demands. The focus immediately began shifting back to priorities on the Afghanistan front.[216] The United States, however, maintained a close eye on ensuring there would be no further attacks in India. With confirmed intelligence pointing to the potential for fresh incidents in the summer of 2009, it renewed calls on Pakistan and rehearsed India's ultimatum that "the people of India will expect us [the Indian government] to respond" in the event of another attack.[217] Meanwhile, the Mumbai crisis proved to be a watershed in the hitherto lackluster Indo-U.S. counterterrorism cooperation. The United States shifted attention to cementing this aspect of the bilateral relationship soon thereafter. For the third crisis running, U.S. crisis managers walked away from the crisis believing that Washington had played a crucial role as a "broker, an interlocutor, a validator" in pursuit of de-escalation.[218]

Brokered Bargaining in South Asia: Implications of the Mumbai Crisis

Defining Crisis Behavior at Mumbai

The Mumbai carnage was easily one of the greatest terrorist provocations India had experienced from a Pakistan-based outfit. The attacks were the starkest reminder yet that the threat of cross-border terrorism emanating from Pakistan remained clear and present. India's desire to indulge in brokered bargaining therefore remained an open question. The fact that Western citizens had been targeted provided grounds for India to believe that it might receive strong third-party support. Yet, India's move toward exploring limited war options able to circumvent third-party pressure after the twin peaks crisis, its disappointment with the U.S. role during that crisis, its view that the American partnership with Pakistan was continuing to enable Pakistan's troubling behavior toward India, and intense pressure on the Manmohan Singh government to act forcefully in the wake of the Mumbai attacks made for a perfect cocktail that could easily have led it to prize direct action over engaging the United States. Certainly, the pre-crisis predictions about India's decisive reaction to a Mumbai-type scenario suggested a great likelihood of India pursuing its crisis objectives independent of the third party. Pakistan's wariness of the U.S. strategic vision for South Asia, specifically its tilt toward India, could also have made Pakistani leaders circumspect in terms of accepting a U.S. mediatory role. In reality, the Mumbai crisis provided a vivid exposé of brokered bargaining. All three sides seemed to settle into the trilateral framework seamlessly, exhibiting a greater sense of familiarity with the opportunities and limitations associated with the three-way interaction than they had in previous crises.

The U.S. response to the crisis manifested the lessons it had drawn from past episodes. Perhaps the most consequential of these was reflected in the swiftness and decisiveness with which it engaged the antagonists. Worried about the dangers associated with the prevailing environment, Washington entered the fray while the attacks were still ongoing, without any calls from either India or Pakistan to get involved. As in the twin peaks crisis, U.S. foreign policy interests in Afghanistan dovetailed nicely with the de-escalation objective at Mumbai. Washington's propensity to prevent India from using force and to avoid boxing Pakistan in completely complemented its interest in focusing Pakistan's attention back on Afghanistan. Yet, the latter was not driving Washington's crisis engagement. From the outset, the conversations among U.S. principals revolved around India's possible military action and the dangers this posed in a nuclear-ized environment. The fact that the attacks took place during a national holi-day period when most senior American officials were celebrating the occasion outside Washington, an obviously suboptimal circumstance in terms of crisis response coordination possibilities, did not seem to affect their desire to inter-vene or the conviction with which they did so.

The United States remained at the forefront, mediating between the antag-onists in conjunction with other third parties. It worked hand in glove with the UK. Other key actors, including China, also played a critical role in back-ing the crisis de-escalation agenda. In fact, perhaps also a reflection of lessons from previous crises, there was virtually no effort from either India or Paki-stan to explore or signal alternative alignment options to offset the U.S. role. Neither was there any evidence of U.S. concerns that other third parties might look to compete with its crisis intervention.

The United States positioned itself down the middle. With India, Wash-ington relied almost exclusively on pleas and persuasion for restraint in return for promises that it would continue to pressure Pakistan to deliver on Indian demands. However, neither the deaths of Western citizens in Mumbai and the world's reflexive outpouring of sympathy for India and finger pointing at Pakistan nor the suspicion of rogue or former ISI personnel being involved in the Mumbai attacks was deemed sufficient to consider ganging up with India to punish Pakistan. Rather, the third party diluted Indian justifications for military action by confirming absence of Pakistani state complicity and prais-ing its investigation and crackdown on LeT/JuD.

The third party's real genius in the Mumbai episode was to push the focus of the crisis toward the law enforcement/legal framework. It used its role as the principal communication conduit to great effect, utilizing the informa-tion it was transmitting to both sides as a means of keeping them apart. This altered the tenor of the debate and kept India's attention on investigating the episode rather than thinking of acting militarily against Pakistan. Interest-ingly, the U.S. stance was in glaring contradiction to its own insistence on the war (rather than law enforcement) approach to countering terrorism glob-ally, which it had used to justify its post-9/11 military interventions, including the one in Afghanistan.[219] Importantly though, hypocritical as it may have seemed, its posture at Mumbai supported the de-escalation agenda.

The third party's punishment leverage was more clearly employed against Pakistan. The United States applied immense pressure on Pakistani leaders to seriously investigate the Mumbai affair and to act visibly against terrorists. It constantly warned them that it would be unable to prevent Indian use of force if they failed to oblige. That said, the United States never went further. A harsher approach risked being counterproductive for the de-escalation goal. Washington's willingness to use its coercive leverage may also have been partly muted by concerns about Pakistan's fragility at the time. Misplaced as these predictions proved to be, Western analysts were projecting a dire future for Pakistan during the 2008–2009 period, with some even warning of an imminent collapse or the possibility of a jihadist takeover of the Pakistani state.[220] Brian Jenkins captures the third party's dilemma vis-à-vis Pakistan: "Pakistan's principal defense against external pressure is . . . its own political fragility—its government's less-than-full cooperation is preferable to the country's collapse and descent into chaos."[221] Nonetheless, even though the United States managed to win no permanent gain for India and left many in India questioning just "how effective is the implied quid pro quo [that] you, India, should not attack, and we, the US, will sort these Paks out" for New Delhi,[222] it achieved its immediate crisis termination objective by getting just enough out of Pakistan to convince India of the merits of continued restraint during the crisis moment.

Larger third-party interests that may have clashed with the goal of early crisis termination were relegated to the background during the crisis. For instance, the United States could conceivably have manipulated the situation in terms of leveraging greater Pakistani support on the Afghanistan front in return for U.S. efforts to prevent Indian military action. There is no evidence of this strategy being considered even though the United States had spent the months before the Mumbai crisis working hard to force a shift in Pakistan's Afghanistan policy to its liking.[223] On the other hand, U.S. crisis managers could have seen the crisis as an opportunity to further prioritize the future of the Indo-U.S. relationship, or at the very least, signal this possibility to Pakistan to extract greater concessions from it during the crisis. Hardly any attention was paid to this aspect either. Expectedly, Afghanistan returned to the fore as the crisis wound down, and was largely responsible for Washington's relative indifference to Pakistan's decreasing commitment to prosecuting the accused militants thereafter. India was compensated by close counterterrorism cooperation, de facto aimed at preventing terrorism from Pakistani soil. This was an unexpected byproduct of the U.S. and India's positive intelligence sharing experience during the Mumbai crisis. Bilateral cooperation on this count has blossomed ever since.

India and Pakistan utilized both strands of the resolve-prudence trade-off. The relatively hawkish rhetoric from India threatening to shed restraint at the outset of the crisis, its consideration of military options, the tit-for-tat signaling by both sides during the second half of December 2008, and limited military movements during the crisis fit within the traditional characterization of bilateral coercion. The real puzzle over the Mumbai crisis, however, was the prudence both sides exhibited in avoiding brinkmanship of the kind witnessed during the 2001–2002 standoff even though the circumstances surrounding the Mumbai attacks could have easily propelled them in that direction. The centrality of the third-party strand of crisis management helps explain this seeming anomaly.

Mumbai represents an example of regional rivals competing for third-party support by putting restraint ahead of behavior aimed at risk manipulation. For one, unlike the Kargil and twin peaks crises, Washington's immediate entry into the fray meant that neither rival had to exhibit resolve to attract third-party attention at the front-end of the crisis. India willingly deferred to the United States to do its crisis bidding and was quite candid in acknowledging this to third-party interlocutors. It relied on direct pleas to get the third-party actors to pressure Pakistan harder but waited patiently for them to deliver. Indian leaders also remained extremely careful not to allow Pakistan to dent the global consensus in their favor during the Mumbai crisis. As discussed, one reason for their decision to forego the military option seems to have been their desire to avoid giving Pakistan the opportunity to claim it was the victim. This prudent behavior overshadowed India's parallel use of implicit threats of shedding restraint in case of the third party's indifference or its inability to get tangible results from Pakistan.

Prudence was also the dominant feature of Pakistan's demeanor even though it ended up presenting a somewhat more even mix of autonomous decision making and deference to third-party preferences. As in the 2001–2002 standoff, Pakistan leveraged its importance in Afghanistan by threatening to redeploy troops from the Afghanistan border, and by actually doing so at the tail end of the crisis. It also stood firm and played on its domestic political costs of inaction when confronted with rumors that the United States might not be opposed to an Indian surgical strike inside Pakistan. Pakistani leaders also dragged their feet on the legal investigation. Far more important in shaping Pakistan's ultimate behavior, however, was its leadership's realization that the circumstances surrounding the Mumbai attacks had left them with little room to defy the third party. Therefore, Pakistan presented virtually all its resolve signals and sparing military movements as well as its inability to do more on the legal front as driven either by the threat of Indian military action or by domestic political pressures. More importantly, it made a number of conciliatory gestures in direct response to third-party demands. The ISI's move to acknowledge involvement of Pakistanis in the attacks and to promise necessary action much before Pakistan's public acceptance of the origins of the attacks, the politically difficult choice of initiating a fairly expansive crackdown and legal inquiry, the decision to share the findings of the inquiry publicly, and Pakistan's lack of active resistance to the UN's listing and sanctioning of LeT/JuD members and affiliated organizations, temporary and tactical as they were, communicated seriousness on Pakistan's part during the most crucial periods of the crisis. This proved instrumental in preventing major escalation.

Brokered Bargaining and the Escalation–
De-Escalation Dynamic
The Mumbai crisis featured a happy convergence between structural and situational factors that generated pressures to de-escalate and kept the crisis largely under control. Unlike the Kargil and twin peaks episodes, neither antagonist needed to exhibit any belligerence at the outset of the crisis simply to seek third-party attention. Indian prime minister Manmohan Singh's rejection of full-scale military mobilization reflected an important lesson from the 2001–2002 standoff that such excessive display of resolve in nuclearized environments is neither likely to force the nuclear-armed opponent to buckle, nor likely to elicit the third party's backing. Instead, it may dilute one's position as the defender even if the global environment is conducive to sympathy for victims of terrorism. In the Mumbai crisis, India benefited from the global consensus in its favor but maintaining this required it to remain sensitive to third-party calls for restraint throughout the crisis. More broadly too, much like the 2001–2002 standoff, India's growing international standing and economic stature that had otherwise increased its leverage on the global stage created a paradox that constrained its resolve options. Potential economic fallout from the crisis was on Indian minds throughout. Having learned from the twin peaks crisis, India not only teamed up with the FBI to produce an initial situation report to prevent panic within the business sector immediately after the attacks, but it also brought in private sector entities for

classified and unclassified briefings in the following days to further reassure them.[224] The concern about the economy would have created a strong incentive for India to keep tensions limited.

Pakistan's precarious position during the Mumbai crisis was equally responsible for holding it back. Thoroughly embarrassed by the context of the Mumbai attacks, it had little room to defy third-party actors without opening up a real possibility of pushing them firmly into India's camp. The best Pakistan could hope for was to get out of the crisis unscathed, and to do so with the status quo ante intact. This required a mix of promises and evidence of tangible actions in line with Indian/third-party demands, not belligerence and brinkmanship that would have heightened escalatory risks.

Western concerns about Pakistan's fragility as a state and the weakness of its civilian government also benefited the de-escalation agenda. It would have made the third party more sensitive to the implications of a prolonged crisis, let alone war, for Pakistan's long-term ability to tackle terrorism and maintain control of its nuclear weapons. Some have argued that even Indian decision makers were wary of pushing Pakistan over the edge.[225] Interestingly, for Pakistan, the third party's concerns about its weakness opened up greater space to point to domestic pressures and costs in justifying its reluctance to do more to satisfy India. While this would have reinforced the third party's inclination to settle for partial Pakistani responses to India's demands, it also paradoxically kept India dissatisfied with Pakistan's actions, in turn, making the third party's ability to achieve early crisis termination more challenging.

Like the Kargil and twin peaks crises, significant risk factors attributable to the multiple-audience problem were at play during the Mumbai episode. At one level, the Mumbai crisis was the perfect scenario for India to redress its seeming impotence in the face of terrorism emanating from Pakistani soil without denting its positive evaluation. The instant sympathy and understanding India received from the world could have emboldened it to act. Limited punishment would also not have run any real risk of irreparably rupturing the Pakistani state and society's internal fabric. Conversations about the United States potentially contemplating a symbolic Indian surgical strike to let off steam may have been perceived as the international license to do just that. Such an Indian action would have unleashed a dangerous escalatory dynamic as Pakistan had planned to respond in kind.

The third party's immediate involvement and conscious offer to do India's bidding, but in return for its restraint, was crucial in shaping Indian minds

to the contrary. A more partisan third-party approach would have been especially risky given that the context surrounding the Mumbai crisis would have
made Pakistan hypersensitive to a gang-up scenario. It could therefore have
been more prone to misperceiving any U.S. moves to lean heavily in India's
favor. For instance, a U.S. effort to actually pressure Pakistan to accept the
idea of a symbolic Indian strike may have been sufficient to panic the Pakistani leadership. The fact that Pakistani leaders felt that India was going to
employ force at the outset of the crisis also created a similar possibility. An
actual Indian military action at the time would have reinforced Pakistan's
perception that the United States was unwilling to restrain India. Or Pakistan's leaders may have concluded that the United States did not have sufficient leverage to do so. Either way, it would have diminished their faith in
third-party mediation for the rest of the crisis.

Once again, the third party's most crucial role was in terms of information
sharing. Its importance was highlighted on multiple occasions, but so was the
extreme challenge this role entails. The Mukherjee hoax call saga provides a
vivid example of the multiple risks poor communications can inject in a tense
situation. Even though U.S. facilitation of information exchange proved effective in allowing the moment to pass peacefully, the episode wasn't uneventful.
U.S. secretary of state Condoleezza Rice had initially failed to reach Mukherjee and had started contemplating whether he was deliberately avoiding her to
buy time for India to act on his ultimatum to attack Pakistan.[226] A prolonged
delay in getting through to him could have created panic in Washington and
increased Pakistan's apprehensions. Fortunately, this did not occur. But even
Rice's confirmation of Mukherjee's denial would not have totally reassured
Pakistan. The Pakistani apparatus remained unclear about the origins of the
call. Pakistan's immediate investigation had traced the number back to India's
External Affairs Ministry.[227] However, the Pakistani military top brass suspected all along that the call was fictitious. The ISI considered possibilities that
someone from India other than Mukherjee may have tried to spark a conflict
or that the United States may have engineered this to test Pakistan's response
to such an ultimatum.[228] Further confusion was created as Mukherjee, while
denying the call, had suggested to Rice that the Pakistani foreign minister
Shah Mahmood Qureshi may have misinterpreted Mukherjee's earlier warning to him that Pakistan was leaving India with no choice but war.[229] Qureshi
had not conveyed any such ultimatum from Mukherjee to his leadership and
was not involved in Pakistani deliberations on the hoax call.[230] Secretary Rice

herself was not totally convinced of Mukherjee's explanation, nor that he had not in fact made the call.[231] It was months after the crisis that Pakistani authorities discovered that the call was made by Omar Saeed Sheikh, a jailed Pakistani terrorist linked to Al Qaeda and other militant outfits, in hopes of escalating the crisis.[232]

Nonetheless, had the Pakistani military not separately concluded that India was not in a position to attack it instantly after the call, these uncertainties may well have created doubts in the minds of Pakistani leaders about Rice's assurance, and indeed, Washington's sincerity as a mediator. Their preexisting distrust of the United States could have easily colored their judgment, and fearing deliberate information manipulation by the United States to obfuscate an impending Indian attack, they could have taken precipitous action.

The question of Pakistan's plausible deniability in terms of state complicity during the Mumbai episode also placed the United States in an extremely delicate position. Washington confirmed the absence of Pakistan's state involvement to encourage Indian restraint. It was able to do so based on the evidence it had in hand. CIA chief Mike Hayden also recognized the fact that his ISI counterpart, General Pasha, had just taken over as ISI chief and thus felt that "a lot of what he was picking up [about Mumbai] was discovery learning on his part."[233] But what if the U.S. had reached a different conclusion in terms of ISI's institutional involvement in the attacks? Revealing such information to India would have been dangerous as it may have felt even more justified to act directly against Pakistan. On the other hand, withholding it would have brought Washington's credibility into question, especially if India were able to decipher this information independently. Given that the United States anchored its entire crisis management strategy in its role as the information conduit, such a scenario could have collapsed the whole arrangement.

Even though constraints on escalation attributable to brokered bargaining ultimately prevailed during the Mumbai crisis, none of these risks were trivial. Neither Indian and Pakistani restraint nor third-party leverage to ensure this was a foregone conclusion at any point during the episode. Views that have projected the Mumbai crisis as never having carried the kind of escalatory potential associated with the Kargil conflict or the 2001–2002 standoff underestimate the crisis's potential to spiral out of control.

SECTION III
LESSONS AND IMPLICATIONS

6 Brokered Bargaining

Observations and Lessons for South Asia

THE PRECEDING THREE CHAPTERS HAVE OPENED THE black box of crisis behavior in nuclearized regional environments. How well does the brokered bargaining framework apply to the South Asian nuclear crises and what implications does this have for crisis stability? What is the validity of brokered bargaining for future crisis scenarios in South Asia? These issues are examined in this chapter.

The South Asian Experience with Brokered Bargaining

The cases examined in the preceding section of the book confirm the propositions introduced in Chapter 2, which discussed the key factors shaping crisis behavior of the third parties and regional rivals in brokered bargaining contexts. They also demonstrate the iterative quality of brokered bargaining across crisis episodes and highlight the stability and instability-inducing dynamics associated with the trilateral bargaining framework. The key lessons and implications from the South Asian crisis experiences are summarized below.

Third-Party Roles in the South Asian Crises
In Chapter 2, five propositions were posited as shapers of the third party's outlook on regional crises and its crisis choices under the twin conditions of

regional nuclearization and global unipolarity. These are: 1) the United States' direct interest in preventing escalation of a regional nuclear crisis; 2) a low threshold for crisis intervention, potentially unsolicited; 3) primacy of the goal of swift de-escalation over America's larger foreign policy interests and equities vis-à-vis the regional rivals; 4) complementary efforts of the unipole and other strong powers to achieve de-escalation; and 5) reliance on "power mediation" (principally positive inducements and nonmilitary sanctions) as the third party employs its reward-punishment leverage in pursuit of de-escalation. Each of these factors dictated the third party's crisis choices across the studied cases.

U.S. Interest in Preventing Escalation

The United States' concern about the risks involved in nuclear environments led it to engage without hesitation in each of the three crisis episodes. Each time, it prioritized de-escalation and swift crisis termination as the primary intervention objective. U.S. involvement left its crisis managers open to the critique that they were unnecessarily hyping nuclear dangers in South Asia. India hinted at this most notably in the wake of the travel advisories in the 2001–2002 standoff. The predictability of U.S. crisis interventions also created a moral hazard problem and an incentive for Pakistan and India to manipulate the risk of war to attract Washington's attention and support. The United States considered this an acceptable cost. U.S. policy makers radiate an inviolable belief that *all* nuclear contexts carry a greater-than-zero risk of deliberate or inadvertent escalation.[1] That is why they did not risk leaving crisis management to the antagonists even during the Kargil crisis when India and Pakistan could only field basic operationalizable nuclear capabilities. Moreover, even though the threat of direct harm to the United States—most obviously from an adverse impact on its military campaign in Afghanistan during the 2001–2002 and Mumbai crises—was not lost on U.S. crisis managers, they had deeper considerations in responding with alarm to the studied crises. Washington was driven by a deep sense of responsibility as the leader of the world; its decision makers believed that no other third party could mediate the crises as effectively.[2] Indeed, its willingness to get involved, its superior intelligence capabilities, and its ability to coordinate an international effort positions it uniquely to intervene as the principal intermediary in such crisis contexts.[3]

Low Intervention Threshold and Unsolicited Involvement
While attention-seeking efforts like Pakistan's creation of a demonstration crisis in Kargil and India's belligerence at the front-end of the twin peaks crisis reinforced Washington's desire to get involved, its engagement across the three crisis iterations was unsolicited for the most part. Furthermore, the United States maintained an extremely low risk threshold in choosing the timing of its intervention. The swiftness with which it involved itself increased with each passing crisis. In the Kargil crisis, the United States entered as soon as it was clear that the Pakistani incursions had created a situation with escalatory potential, but this was over two weeks after India detected Pakistani intruders across the Line of Control in Kashmir. In the twin peaks crisis, it got involved in earnest immediately after the December 13, 2001, attack on the Indian parliament and before India began its military mobilization. In the Mumbai crisis, the United States had initiated active crisis management even before the terrorist attacks were over.

Primacy of De-escalation over Competing Events, Broader
Interests, and Relations with the Regional Rivals
U.S. presidents dealing with the Kargil, 2001–2002, and Mumbai crises were faced with multiple competing global and domestic priorities. These included the Balkans war, UN sanctions on Iraq, and the Arab-Israeli peace process in 1999, the post-9/11 invasion of Afghanistan in 2001, and the ongoing Afghanistan and Iraq wars internationally and the national Thanksgiving break during the Mumbai episode. In none of the crises did this issue competition affect U.S. resolve to get involved in pursuit of de-escalation.[4]

The United States' fixation on de-escalation held despite varying American policy interests and equities in South Asia. Decision making dominated by immediate U.S. security interests in the region or driven by the state of U.S. bilateral relations with India and Pakistan could have easily led Washington to adopt a less favorable stance toward India at Kargil when New Delhi was still consumed by its deep antipathy toward any U.S. role in India-Pakistan disputes. To the contrary, the context at Mumbai begged for a more supportive third-party role toward India. Similarly, Pakistan's inability to extract greater benefits in the 2001–2002 standoff despite its pivotal role in Afghanistan cannot be easily explained through a typical foreign policy lens. Notwithstanding Washington's obvious interest in trying to dovetail its regional interests with the goal of de-escalation during the twin peaks crisis, there was never any doubt about the prioritization between these. As discussed in the case studies, the fact that the Indo-U.S. relationship gained tremendously from the Kargil experience, that their counterterrorism cooperation blossomed courtesy of the Mumbai crisis, or that Pakistan was allowed to escape crises with insignificant or partial retribution were mere collateral spinoffs from Washington's crisis mediation aimed at preventing escalation.

In terms of broader foreign policy demands of the antagonists, the risks entailed in backing one antagonist at the cost of its adversary's alienation forced the United States to leave both of them dissatisfied with its approach toward their larger strategic objectives. The United States sought to appease both, but only insofar as such behavior complemented the de-escalation goal. Ultimately, the United States did not back Pakistan's revisionist position on Kashmir in any crisis nor did it second India's contention that cross-border terrorism justified unilateral action against Pakistan or its total diplomatic isolation. Instead, the United States soothed Pakistan by promising to nudge India to initiate dialogue on Kashmir during the Kargil and twin peaks crises and promised India in each crisis iteration that it would keep pressuring Pakistan to ensure a permanent end to anti-India militancy. While it wished for both to happen, it was unable to invest in either with any sense of urgency once the crisis was over. Instead, the United States prioritized reverting to its broader foreign policy concerns, forging better ties with India after the Kargil crisis, and working with Pakistan to secure victory in Afghanistan while attempting to de-hyphenate its relations with these rivals after the 2001–2002 and Mumbai crises.[5]

Cooperation between the United States and Other Strong Powers
The case studies also have confirmed the "convergence effect" of the twin conditions of regional nuclearization and unipolarity on the crisis stances of the unipole and other strong powers. Prior to the Kargil crisis, expectations of third-party involvement were still driven largely by the Cold War experience of alliance politics. The United States was therefore seriously concerned about competitive third-party intervention during the Kargil crisis.[6] In reality, each of three studied crises demonstrated complementary, even coordinated, efforts by external actors. The United States actively collaborated with other countries, coordinating down to the messaging protocols and schedules for regional visits by third-party officials with key allies like the UK. All external actors complemented Washington's de-escalation agenda, irrespective of the nature of their relationships with it, or with India and Pakistan. Arguably the most counterintuitive was China's propensity to stand "shoulder to shoulder

[with the U.S.] in counseling restraint" despite its otherwise competitive relationship with the United States, including wariness to its ingress into Beijing's South Asian backyard.[7] China's demeanor was especially revealing given its traditionally partisan stance on the India-Pakistan rivalry and its continuing diplomatic support for Pakistan during peacetime. Its concern about nuclear conflict suspended this foreign policy leaning during each crisis.[8] The third party's complementary crisis management was crucial in terms of depriving Pakistan and India of alternative alignment options that are otherwise known to impede successful third-party-led crisis management efforts.[9]

Power Mediation and Use of the Reward-Punishment Leverage
The third party's crisis management tools were limited to positive inducements as incentives and quid pro quos for the antagonists' deference to its preferences and sanctions in the diplomatic and economic realms. Specifically, the third party's behavior comprised two complimentary roles: of a balancer, and a face saver.

As a balancer, the third party used a mix of "pure mediation" and manipulation as it attempted to provide each antagonist an impression that it stood by it as long as it agreed to descend down the escalation ladder. Without revealing its intentions fully to either rival, the United States absorbed and conveyed signals from and to both sides through public and private channels, selectively shared intelligence information at critical junctures, and made commitments as a guarantor on behalf of one or the other adversary. None of the commitments, however, were fixed and time bound in a way that they could bring its leverage into question or suggest to either antagonist that it was leaning decisively in the opponent's favor and contemplating ganging up with it. Washington's propensity to act as a guarantor of Pakistan's promises to end militant infiltration during the 2001–2002 standoff provides the most vivid illustration of this aspect of third-party mediation. The third party's demeanor held even in contexts such as the Mumbai crisis where the instant wave of international sympathy for India and the death of third-party citizens could have intuitively led to stronger backing for New Delhi's position.

Still, the third party's punishment leverage kept the conflicting parties worried about the prospect of serious U.S. opposition that could tilt the crisis in their opponent's favor. The United States used this leverage most prominently in its dealings with Pakistan during the Kargil crisis. During the twin peaks and Mumbai iterations too, Washington signaled its inability to prevent Indian military action if Pakistan failed to respond positively to Indian and third-party demands. India experienced the punishment leverage during the 2001–2002 standoff and even during the Kargil crisis inasmuch as U.S. backing for its stance was implicitly presented as a quid pro quo for its measured behavior. The third party's economic influence over both sides was also on display, most prominently in the threat to hold up a $100 million International Monetary Fund loan to Pakistan during the Kargil crisis and through the travel advisories that directly affected India's crisis calculations in the 2001–2002 standoff.

As a face saver, the third party rewarded both sides by allowing them to shift the onus of their suboptimal crisis outcomes to the United States whenever such a move was conducive to de-escalation. Pakistan received face savers in the form of President Clinton's promise of assistance in supporting an India-Pakistan dialogue on Kashmir during the Kargil crisis, and through praise for its crackdown against militants in the twin peaks and Mumbai crises. India managed to save face in the twin peaks crisis courtesy of Pakistan's acknowledgment of cross-border infiltration under third-party pressure and when the third party played along with its tactic of tying its troop demobilization with the September 2002 state elections in Jammu and Kashmir. In the Mumbai crisis, the United States succeeded in forcing Pakistan to conduct a serious enough investigation into the attacks for India to declare victory.

Behavior of the Conflicting Parties in the South Asian Crises
The propositions posited in Chapter 2 to explain the demeanor of the conflicting parties suggested that regional rivals engaged in brokered bargaining must exhibit behavior aimed simultaneously at the adversary and the third party. They must also combine autonomous decision making and deference to third-party preferences, and these choices ought to be directly linked to the third party's use of its reward-punishment leverage. Indian and Pakistani behavior across the three crises bears this out. They exhibited the dual characteristic of the resolve-prudence trade-off by balancing these aspects of crisis behavior vis-à-vis the other and simultaneously competing in seeking the third party's backing. To varying degrees across the three crisis iterations, both antagonists manipulated the risk of war and reached out with direct pleas to the United States for support in hopes of extracting concessions in line with their respective crisis objectives. Throughout, they retained a fair degree of autonomy and were careful not to signal either to the adversary or the third party that they were willing to stand down completely. In fact, the limitations

of third-party leverage to ensure desirable behavior of the antagonists were constantly exposed, for instance through Pakistani decisions to redeploy its troops from its western border during the 2001–2002 and Mumbai crises and India's prolonged full-scale mobilization during the 2001–2002 episode. Ultimately, however, Indian and Pakistani sensitivity to the third party's "evaluation" potential was important in consistently pulling them back from the brink at critical junctures, if not staying well short of these high-risk moments in the first place. Even when India and Pakistan indulged in risk manipulation, such moves were portrayed as compulsions or options of last resort necessitated by the adversary's behavior, which they inevitably characterized as provocative and aggressive.

The need for positive evaluation also proved to be strong enough for India and Pakistan to settle for partial fulfillment of their immediate crisis objectives. In the process, they even accepted significant political and material costs, and in India's case, also overbearing reputational losses associated with its inability to respond to sub-conventional provocations emanating from Pakistan. The Indian decision not to cross the LoC at Kargil in defiance of military logic, its decision to defer plans of employing military force against Pakistan in the 2001–2002 standoff, and even its choice to "contract out" its crisis diplomacy to the United States for all practical purposes during the Mumbai crisis were all influenced by evaluation concerns.[10] So were Pakistan's choices to accept the terms of crisis termination at Kargil and to make public promises and take action against militant outfits during the 2001–2002 and Mumbai episodes. Indian and Pakistani behavior across the three crises also suggests a reluctance to hold the crisis outcome hostage to their larger foreign policy interests—a permanent end to sub-conventional provocations from Pakistani soil for India and negotiations on Kashmir for Pakistan. Each time, they ended the crisis with little concrete in hand on these counts.

The Permanence of Brokered Bargaining

Evidence from the South Asian case studies also confirms the iterative quality of brokered bargaining. These experiences not only demonstrated Washington's unsolicited interventions, but they also highlighted the regional rivals' seeming compulsion to operate within a trilateral framework even when the immediate crisis context suggested their possible preference for a bilateral approach. A number of situational factors that could have impeded the trilateral crisis dynamic were present across the crises. However, none of them affected the centrality of brokered bargaining. They also varied considerably from crisis to crisis, and therefore cannot be considered alternative explanations for crisis behavior and outcomes. These factors included the state of India's and Pakistan's relations with the United States, their past experiences with brokered bargaining, their pre-crisis preferences in terms of crisis strategies, domestic political dynamics, and economic and security conditions that impinged on crisis decisions.

Third-Party Relations, Past Crisis Experiences, and Pre-Crisis Outlooks
India and Pakistan's inclinations to engage in the trilateral framework seemed unaffected by their relationship with the United States or their experience with brokered bargaining in the previous crisis iterations. The United States was never considered truly impartial or fully trusted as a mediator by either side in any of the three studied crises. For Pakistan to have continued engaging a third party that was seen as a potential aggressor against its nuclear assets, both at a time when bilateral ties were all but nonexistent (Kargil) and when it was a frontline ally (2001–2002 and Mumbai) was counterintuitive. Equally, its propensity to eagerly engage the third party in the twin peaks crisis even though it had left Kargil seething with discontent and to trust the United States during the Mumbai crisis despite obvious grounds for it and other third parties to back India cannot be explained purely by the situational factors at play. India's case is even more intriguing given the deeply ingrained reservations of its strategic elite about third-party mediation in general. India's outreach to the United States during the Kargil crisis when it was still invested in its "fetish of bilateralism"[11] took everyone by surprise. In addition, India shed its pre-crisis resolve to punish Pakistan in the 2001–2002 and Mumbai iterations despite the significant reputational costs this decision entailed. As puzzling as this may be from a traditional nuclear crisis behavior perspective, India continued to prize positive evaluation over establishing the credibility of its resolve to employ force.

Domestic Political Factors
Variations in political factors central to crisis decision making also did not undermine India and Pakistan's propensity to engage in the three-cornered framework. India was led by a nationalist, right-wing government during the Kargil and 2001–2002 crises and a left-of-center government during the Mumbai iteration. Moreover, elections were scheduled in India within a few months of the Kargil and Mumbai crises; during the Kargil crisis, the Vajpayee

government was acting as a de facto caretaker set up.[12] Pakistan experienced both civilian and military-led regimes during the examined period. The contrast in the state of its civil-military relations from crisis to crisis was also stark: an active civil-military tussle colored its actions during the Kargil crisis; General Musharraf's military government made the civilian domain completely irrelevant during the 2001–2002 standoff; and a freshly inducted but weak civilian government was in charge during the Mumbai episode.

One might expect these political factors to affect the leaders' levels of sensitivity to public pressure, and in turn, their inclination to stay the course or back down in crises. For instance, a democratic government is believed to be more beholden to domestic audience pressure than those operating in undemocratic environments.[13] Furthermore, a civilian government seeking reelection or one seen as dovish on foreign policy can be expected to be far more concerned about satisfying domestic audiences than a military or a politically secure civilian government. This makes Indian prime minister Manmohan Singh's restraint during the Mumbai crisis even more counterintuitive. In fact, his demeanor has led many to attribute the absence of war in this crisis primarily to his personality.[14] This line of argument essentially makes leaders' qualities and inclinations the principal explanation for crisis choices and outcomes.[15] In reality, evidence from South Asia suggests that all leaders—civilian or military, right or left-leaning—tended to see domestic audience costs similarly. They pointed to domestic pressures primarily as a risk-manipulation tactic aimed at attracting greater third-party attention and letting off steam. Ultimately, however, they seem to have had little trouble in pursuing choices that maximized the possibility of attaining third-party understanding and support ahead of satisfying these internal pressures. This explains India's equally eager engagement of the third party under Prime Ministers Singh and Vajpayee even though they represented very different political constituencies, as well as Pakistan's unwavering interest in eliciting third-party backing under civilian and military governments.

Economic and Security Factors

India and Pakistan experienced widely divergent economic and domestic security fortunes during the decade spanning the studied crises. India became one of the world's fastest growing economies during this period and was deeply engaged in expanding business and economic ties with global powers.[16] Pakistan, on the other hand, went from being a relatively peaceful state to an excessively violent one that worried the world about its potential collapse. Interestingly, both India's rise and growing integration in the global economy and Pakistan's economic weakness and consequent need for foreign assistance made them more sensitive to third-party preferences. The costs of defying the third party seem to be directly proportional to a country's dependence on global economic relationships, and both good performance and a weak economy tend to increase this.

Pakistan's increasing political and institutional weakness and global concern about the safety and security of its nuclear arsenal seemed to further reinforce three-way bargaining. Broadly, worries about any country's extreme weakness ought to force third parties to take a relatively softer approach toward it. It should instill greater caution in terms of avoiding measures that may push the country over the precipice. This more careful third-party engagement implies an additional disincentive for it to lean heavily in the stronger antagonist's favor irrespective of the specific crisis context. At the same time, an internally weak conflicting party must account for the relatively severer consequences for it if the third party were forced squarely into the opponent's camp. This represents an additional factor that ought to discourage the weak antagonist from contemplating an autonomous crisis posture that ignores the third party. The stronger rival's knowledge of the third party's concern about the weakness of its opponent should also signal to it the greater-than-usual likelihood of the third party's disapproval for any of its actions that risk pushing its opponent over the edge. This aspect would have worked to further constrain India's choices for unilateral action against Pakistan, most of all during the Mumbai crisis when Pakistan was faced with serious internal challenges. In fact, to generalize, any factors that add to the third party's inherent constraints in terms of adopting an outright partisan approach to crisis management and generate added incentives for the regional rivals to resort to third-party mediation ahead of unilateral actions should work to reinforce the centrality of brokered bargaining.

INDIA'S COMPELLENCE DILEMMA

The above observation is also relevant to another popular explanation for India's behavior in past crises that seemingly challenges the explanatory power of the trilateral bargaining framework. The Indian strategic elite argues that India has faced a "compellence dilemma" vis-à-vis Pakistan: Pakistan's weakness implies that Indian military action risks its implosion, and an attendant fallout that would provide even greater space to terrorists to operate in the region.[17] They ascribe India's restraint in the twin peaks and Mumbai crises principally to this factor. While there is recognition that a limited military action would not threaten Pakistan's collapse in any way, the argument is that restricted action would not hurt Pakistan sufficiently to compel it to put a permanent end to cross-border militancy. In other words, there is a mismatch between Indian crisis objectives and the realistic military options available to it.[18] As conceived by its proponents, this compellence dilemma is a key reason for India to entertain the third-party factor: were Pakistan's weakness not a consideration, India could have ignored the United States and proceeded to call Pakistan's nuclear bluff.[19]

Even if taken at face value, this contention does not undermine the centrality of the trilateral crisis interaction. While a stronger Pakistan may well eliminate India's compellence dilemma in the minds of the Indian strategic elite, any hint of an Indian desire to undertake major military action would only work to heighten U.S. concerns about a possible breach of Pakistan's nuclear red lines. This would likely force it to intervene with an even greater sense of urgency, albeit in an extremely challenging crisis management context given India's increased temptation to flex its muscles. More generally, the idea that good military options free of the risk of escalation, and therefore able to avoid exacerbating the concerns of the third party, can exist in any regional nuclear context is mistaken. The combination of the innate risk in a nuclearized environment and the third party's acute sensitivity to regional nuclear crises eliminates this possibility—regardless of the military capabilities or the internal cohesion of the antagonists in question. Indeed, a number of Indian interlocutors privately acknowledged to the author that no provocative crisis moves in South Asia are likely to go unnoticed by the United States.

The Quest for De-Escalation: Brokered Bargaining and Crisis Stability

At the heart of brokered bargaining lies the constant tension between the third party's efforts to heighten the antagonists' sensitivity to its preferences without backing either's stance such that it would alienate the other completely, and the antagonists' incentives to maximize autonomy without denting their evaluation by the third party. This tension tends to constrain destabilizing behavior that can lead to uncontrolled escalation, but it also induces significant risks that threaten to unleash exactly this dynamic. The three South Asian crises provide confirmatory evidence for both aspects.

Stability-Inducing Aspects of Brokered Bargaining

Evidence gleaned from the case studies suggests that the combination of sensitivities—the third party's to the escalatory potential and the antagonists' to third-party preferences—that triggers brokered bargaining is inherently limiting in terms of the escalatory risks in any given crisis context. On the one hand, the third party's quest to retain leverage over both rivals limited its flexibility and created an incentive for the antagonists to exercise a greater degree of autonomy to force the third party to divulge more information about its intentions—read, support their respective stances. At the same time, however, the balancer's compulsion to avoid completely isolating either rival was key to preventing conditions that might have prompted Pakistan or India to act precipitously. This constraint was responsible for the absence of a more coercive, and potentially destabilizing, U.S. posture against Pakistan during the Kargil and Mumbai crises, and perhaps against India during the 2001–2002 standoff, even though the immediate circumstances offered the United States an opportunity to adopt a more forceful approach.

The antagonists' desire for autonomy was also reined in by their quest for positive evaluation, specifically their concern that excessive autonomy could force the third party into stauncher support of the adversary. In every instance across the three studied crises where either India's or Pakistan's actions threatened major escalation, they eventually ended up deferring to third-party preferences, compromising on their ideal crisis objectives in the process. The case studies have identified the link between a number of these Indian and Pakistani decisions to forego autonomy and the third party's use of its reward-punishment leverage. Also at play was the reality that as long as the third party remains the broker of de-escalation, defying it by upping the ante beyond a certain point only raises the reputational costs of using its good offices to climb down later. In avoiding any major military moves during the Mumbai crisis, India seems to have drawn this lesson from its 2001–2002 military mobilization.

Significantly, India's and Pakistan's sensitivity to third parties tended to hold irrespective of their international stature. Both good and bad crisis-specific or broader international images seem to make the conflicting parties more responsive to third-party preferences. For India, if global sympathy opened up space to exhibit autonomy and eliminated the compulsion to soften its position during the Kargil and twin peaks crises, the need for keeping the international community's empathy simultaneously acted as a restraining factor. The Indian case provides a vivid example of how a country's economic rise can make it more concerned about its evaluation by third-party actors. New Delhi's eagerness to shift the onus of achieving its objectives on to the United States in phase II of the 2001–2002 standoff was in no small part affected by the economic losses triggered by the travel advisories. Its efforts to preempt any economic fallout during the Mumbai crisis by reassuring the private sector immediately after the attacks flowed from the same concern.

In Pakistan's case, it was the negative international opinion during the Kargil and Mumbai crises that increased its concern about third-party preferences. Its decision makers could not have ignored the fact that defiance of the third party in such adverse circumstances risked decisively strengthening India's hand. More generally too, Pakistan's reputation as a military-dominated state deemed to be capable of extreme risk-taking during crisis situations seems to have forced it to feel the need to negate this impression, especially after the Kargil episode. Pakistani behavior during the 2001–2002 standoff reflected a recognition of this factor. Perversely, its image also meant that it needed to do less to convince its adversary or the world of its resolve to employ force in any eventuality—another potentially calming influence on its crisis posturing. Furthermore, Pakistan's weak economic base and dependence on external support worked to increase its sensitivity to Washington's economic leverage. This was most evident in the Kargil crisis.

Instability-Inducing Aspects of Brokered Bargaining
These stability-inducing dynamics notwithstanding, the South Asian crises also entailed a number of risks inherent in the trilateral bargaining framework. These were often accentuated by the specific circumstances surrounding the crisis episodes. The moral hazard problem was at play, as was the multiple-audience problem. The latter was exacerbated by the use of suboptimal communication protocols. Peacetime policy choices of the third parties and regional rivals created additional risks.

MORAL HAZARD PROBLEM
The South Asian experiences confirmed the presence of the moral hazard problem, which tends to incentivize demonstration crises, thereby making crisis recurrence more likely.[20] The fact that each South Asian crisis terminated with the status quo ante intact reinforced this likelihood. While status quo preferences played a role in deterring revisionism and diminishing the urge to employ extraordinarily provocative behavior, as was the case for India in the Kargil crisis and Pakistan in the 2001–2002 and Mumbai iterations, cessation of these crises in this manner also implied that the provoker—the

state of Pakistan in the Kargil crisis and non-state actors in the subsequent two crises—managed to escape relatively unharmed. The situation most obviously suits a provoker seeking to create a demonstration crisis without any immediate revisionist goals in mind. Non-state actors behind the 2001–2002 and Mumbai crises may consider themselves winners in this case: even if a war did not ensue, they managed to grab the limelight by causing an international crisis that sucked in the world's powers.

Moreover, each time a demonstration crisis occurred or when an antagonist exhibited provocativeness to lure the third party to intervene, it made the crisis more threatening even as the subsequent third-party intervention played a pacifying role. The Kargil crisis is perhaps the most obvious example where absent Pakistan's desire for the demonstration effect, the crisis—and therefore concerns of escalation—would never have occurred. At the same time, however, the third party's involvement and the sensitivity of the antagonists to its preferences helped keep the crisis limited. India's initial mobilization and saber-rattling was responsible for the same paradox in 2001–2002. The ideal scenario from the de-escalation perspective played out in Mumbai where the rather instantaneous induction of the third party eliminated any real need for attention-seeking behavior by the rivals at the front-end of the crisis.

MULTIPLE-AUDIENCE PROBLEM

The multiple-audience problem kept the risks of misperceptions and misunderstandings high during each crisis. India may have read too much into the post-9/11 global anti-terrorism consensus in undertaking its military mobilization in the 2001–2002 standoff,[21] but Pakistan's belief that India would attack militarily unless Pakistan deployed its conventional forces suggested a perception that the post-9/11 context may in fact allow India to acquire third-party backing or to defy it in using force against Pakistan. This disconnect forced Pakistan's countermobilization and eventually resulted in a million Indian and Pakistani troops keeping South Asia on the verge of war for ten long months. Even later on, India's thinking that the U.S. presence in Pakistan would limit any war and that the United States could physically prevent Pakistan from using nuclear weapons pointed to a potentially disastrous misperception. Had the United States not reacted decisively to signal its disapproval when India was prepared to attack Pakistan in January 2002, the outcome could have been catastrophic. During the Kargil and Mumbai crises as well, the overwhelmingly favorable crisis context for India could have led it to believe that a decision to use force against Pakistan would be tolerated by the third party. On the other hand, India could have made the same choice based on its perception that the third party was either unwilling or unable to persuade Pakistan to act as India desired. These assumptions seem to have brought India perilously close to expanding the war theater in Kargil in mid-June 1999. To the contrary, discussions of possible U.S. support for Indian use of force, for instance through a surgical strike during the Mumbai crisis, was an obvious occasion for an already under-pressure Pakistan to feel vulnerable to a possible gang up scenario.

SUBOPTIMAL COMMUNICATION PROTOCOLS

India's and Pakistan's crisis communication protocols made their experiences even more worrisome. Despite the presence of hotlines between civilian and military officials, these rivals relied heavily on public signaling during crises. This channel is known to be prone to misinterpretations in the presence of multiple audiences. Even greater was their dependence on the United States to communicate with one another, and increasingly so over time. The hoax call episode during the Mumbai crisis exposed how one phone conversation in a context marked by an absence of predictable communication procedures could risk spiraling a crisis out of control. The episode also highlighted the difficulty in ascertaining and validating facts in an environment fraught with mistrust. Strikingly, these experiences do not seem to have left either antagonist discontented with the use of indirect communication. In fact, the author's conversations with Indian and Pakistani crisis managers suggest that their perceived need to keep working the third-party channel seems to have been reinforced.[22]

Playing the go-between also allows the third party greater control over the crisis dynamics. The third party's use of private information played a positive role in successful de-escalation across the three crises. In each episode, Washington's ability to buy time, to force the antagonists' to climb down from maximalist demands, and to convince them that they would be better off allowing the third party to do their bidding than contemplating unilateral action was driven in no small part by its role as the transmitter of messages and its carefully calculated use of information received from either of the antagonists or through its intelligence channels.[23] Yet, the potential for misperceptions emanating from the third party's selective use of information cannot be ignored. For instance, Washington's handling of intelligence about Pakistan's nuclear movement at the tail end of the Kargil crisis; its possible decision not to confront India with evidence of its forces adopting war-fighting positions in January 2002 given that U.S. intelligence was unsure of Indian intentions; its potential inability to delicately balance its promises of forcing Pakistan to end militant infiltration into India, but without fixing timelines; or a scenario in which the United States perceived direct ISI involvement in the Mumbai attacks could all have led to potentially explosive results. The Kargil episode also highlighted the possibility of third-party and bilateral crisis management efforts working at cross-purposes. The U.S. communication channel may, in part, have been responsible for precipitating the breakdown of the direct backchannel negotiations between India and Pakistan during the crisis.

PEACETIME CHOICES AS RISK EXACERBATORS

The peacetime behavior of the antagonists and the United States also posed a challenge to crisis stability in South Asia. Since brokered bargaining plays out solely as a tactical crisis management tool, the third party's propensity to put its own and the antagonists' broader foreign policy priorities on the back-burner is limited to the crisis moment. In South Asia, the United States left business unfinished in terms of the deeper Indian and Pakistani demands in each of three crises. This meant that the most likely trigger for crises (terrorism) as well as the underlying cause for them to recur (the Kashmir dispute) remained intact. Not only that, but the specific U.S. foreign policy choices in the inter-crisis periods ended up adding to its crisis management challenge in the subsequent crisis iterations. As the United States worked to strengthen its relations with India after the Kargil crisis, it entered areas of cooperation, most notably the civilian nuclear deal and broader support for India's defense modernization, which further increased Pakistan's suspicions about U.S. designs in South Asia.[24] Meanwhile, India continued to view Washington's ongoing support of Pakistan as a frontline ally after 9/11 as a key reason for Pakistan's ability to get away with piecemeal efforts against anti-India terrorist outfits. These factors impinged on Pakistani and Indian crisis thinking.

India's inter-crisis efforts to win the next iteration by undoing its military weaknesses exposed in previous crises resulted in its limited war doctrine after the Kargil crisis and Cold Start after the failure of Operation Parakram. The common denominator was the desire to find autonomous options that could punish Pakistan without crossing its nuclear red lines, and in Cold Start's case, to do so while explicitly keeping the third party at bay. Pakistan, on its part, continued to undertake military modernization, especially after the twin peaks crisis, including integrating its nuclear capability more fully into its force planning.[25] These developments added to the challenges of crisis management.

The fact that crises in South Asia ultimately ended without major wars despite these pressures does suggest the potency of the earlier-mentioned combination of sensitivities in limiting the incentives for escalation. Yet, the instability-inducing factors identified here came close to overpowering these pacifying influences on several occasions across the three crises. Also, the relative importance of the various risks involved and the form they took was so dependent on the specific crisis context that they could not have been accurately predicted in advance. This is a generalizable observation. It implies that all regional nuclear crisis environments will likely carry risks directly attributable to the trilateral interaction, but it will remain difficult to mitigate them ex ante.

The Future of Brokered Bargaining in South Asia

The foregoing analysis has established the centrality of brokered bargaining in explaining behavior in South Asia's past crises under the nuclear overhang. This section analyzes the framework's validity in future crisis iterations. Two scenarios are entertained. The first examines whether brokered bargaining would hold if an India-Pakistan crisis were to erupt today. The second, set within a two decade or so time horizon, depicts a more futuristic, but realistic, context that assumes the induction of new technologies and expanded conventional and nuclear arsenals in South Asia.

The Next India-Pakistan Crisis: Will Brokered Bargaining Hold?

On September 29, 2016, the Indian army triumphantly declared that it had conducted "surgical strikes" inside Pakistani Kashmir in retaliation for a terrorist attack by Pakistani militants that had killed eighteen Indian soldiers in an Indian army camp in Uri in Indian Kashmir a fortnight earlier.[26] Many had already predicted that incumbent Indian prime minister Narendra Modi, known for his hard-line nationalist credentials and hawkish stance on Pakistan, would shed his predecessor Manmohan Singh's restraint in the face of terrorism emanating from Pakistan.[27] Some even cautioned of a "distinct possibility now that the Indian response [would] be immediate, harsh, and lethal."[28]

India's surgical strikes have been presented as a paradigm shift in its approach to Pakistan.[29] Yet, a closer look reveals that the playbook has remained fundamentally unaltered, and so too the efficacy of brokered bargaining in explaining the choices of the involved actors. Details of the strikes clarified that India's action was largely indistinguishable from the cross-LoC raids that have been employed for years as tactical means of pricking Pakistan as part of the tit-for-tat efforts by both sides to raise each other's costs along the LoC.[30] The major difference this time was India's public acknowledgment of its action.[31] Unlike the past, Indian leaders had carefully thought through their decision with an eye on gaining political mileage, while avoiding escalation to a full-fledged crisis and preventing negative third-party reactions. That is why India quite deliberately chose to describe its strikes as being specifically targeted at terrorist "launch pads" even though Indian troops had also engaged Pakistani military posts along the LoC.[32] Furthermore, it declared the action as a one-off preemptive strike undertaken in self-defense to prevent further terrorist attacks and emphasized that it had no desire to escalate.[33]

India took great care in covering the third-party flank. It had initiated contact with U.S. officials immediately after the Uri attack to build support and requested that the U.S. condemn the attack and Pakistan's link to it.[34] While India did not take the United States into its confidence on its plans to conduct the strikes, Indian officials briefed their U.S. counterparts—as well as numerous other governments in New Delhi and in their home capitals—immediately afterward.[35] Their focus was to confirm the limited nature of the action—India presented it as a justifiable, proportionate response to the Uri attack—and to assure the United States that India wanted the episode closed.[36] U.S. intelligence sources were convinced that the Uri attack was linked to Pakistan-based militant outfits and therefore came out with a strong statement critical of Pakistan and its inaction against terrorists.[37] This was a major signal that sought to clarify the public record and put Pakistan on notice. Other important third-party actors reinforced the sentiment. Russia went furthest by supporting India's surgical strikes as an act of self-defense.[38]

The United States simultaneously worked on Pakistan through multiple senior-level contacts to urge military restraint and prod Pakistan to take real action against the terrorists operating from its soil.[39] It conveyed its confidence that India was not looking to escalate the situation, but it also signaled its leaning toward India, implying that Washington might take a firmer public position should Pakistan choose to respond with force to the Indian strikes.[40]

Tellingly, Pakistan absorbed the Indian strikes and simply denied their occurrence.[41] Crucially, the United States avoided challenging this Pakistani characterization, concerned that doing so would only build domestic pressure on the Pakistani leadership to respond.[42]

U.S. messaging also struck the familiar tone of simultaneously urging caution and restraint on the Indian side.[43] The United States and China, among others, had also consistently called for both sides to lower tensions after the Uri attack, avoiding any signals that may have emboldened India (or Pakistan) to further escalate tensions.[44] Throughout the episode, the principal bureaucratic impulse of U.S. officials to prevent escalation remained firmly in place.[45]

To be sure, New Delhi's post-Uri action was meant to signal the Modi government's intolerance for terrorist attacks emanating from Pakistan. At the same time however, India's demeanor suggested its recognition of the limits on its ability to flex its muscles. Accurately put, its action was more a carefully crafted exercise in messaging than one in compellence. The messaging was designed to maximize domestic political gains by presenting the strikes as proof of Prime Minister Modi's nationalistic credentials while minimizing the diplomatic fallout by signaling "a sense of responsibility and continued restraint" to the international community.[46] Washington's increasing propensity in recent years to publicly censure Pakistan on the issue of terrorism and its belief that India had to be allowed to let off steam given the charged domestic political environment helped New Delhi elicit a sympathetic global response, but there was never any doubt that the third-party actors opposed escalation.

The Uri episode was successfully managed before it could assume crisis proportions. But the threat of future crises looms large. There is a sense that the next major terrorist attack in India could force Prime Minister Modi's hand to act even more forcefully against Pakistan than he did after Uri.[47] Perhaps emboldened by Washington's conciliatory response to India's post-Uri surgical strikes, there also is now an expectation in India that the United States will lean on Pakistan to absorb such Indian action.[48] However, having already expended immense political capital in absorbing the post-Uri Indian action, Pakistan may find it extremely difficult to hold back in a similar future context, especially if the quantum of the Indian use of force is greater than after Uri. The scenario has all the makings of a crisis with a high potential for escalation.[49]

Will brokered bargaining inform crisis behavior if India chooses to go beyond token retribution and signals a desire to push harder? Several simulation and scenario exercises entertaining such India-Pakistan crises shed light on what may follow. Virtually all of them predict an escalated war and demonstrate the ease with which such a situation could lead to a brink-manship exercise involving full-fledged mobilization, and eventually desper-ate or unintended nuclear use.[50] They project no confidence that India and Pakistan will be able to keep a war limited once a major conflict is underway.[51] A number of these exercises have been sponsored by the U.S. government, precisely to understand the risks involved in South Asian crises. Perhaps their biggest contribution is to further heighten Washington's fears and reinforce its number one lesson from previous experiences of managing crisis episodes in the region: that the environment remains highly unstable and ripe for esca-lation. This should translate into an even more alarmed and proactive U.S. response to future crises.

India's and Pakistan's compulsions to engage the third party are also dif-ficult to ignore. In wanting to punish Pakistan through use of force in a cri-sis, Indian leaders require the world to allow it to strike Pakistan and then intervene to force Pakistan to hold back its response.[52] The credibility of the Indian deterrent would take a major hit if Pakistan were able to respond com-mensurately; its ability to do so would deny India the victory it must secure to prove that its military option has not been foreclosed by Pakistan's nuclear deterrent.[53] The trouble for India is that the third party's ability to success-fully pressure Pakistan decreases as the quantum of Indian military force employed against Pakistan increases. U.S. punishment leverage may continue to work after inconsequential symbolic strikes like the one India conducted in the wake of the Uri attack, but it is less likely to hold if any Indian action threatens Pakistan in a more meaningful way. Moreover, as a crisis escalates, the absence of bilateral crisis management mechanisms ought to make India and Pakistan even more dependent on third-party assistance to de-escalate. Indeed, crisis simulation and scenario exercises that account for a Modi-led India and entertain crisis triggers graver than the Mumbai attacks confirm both rivals' resort to third-party mediation in aggravated situations.[54] Pre-cisely because of this dynamic, third-party actors ought to be reluctant to back serious Indian use of force in the first place; Pakistan would undoubtedly look to pressure the third party to ensure this in the wake of any crisis-triggering event. Indeed, lost in the triumphant Indian posturing after the post-Uri military action was the key takeaway that India's space to use force remains circumscribed despite the world's sympathetic view of its position vis-à-vis

Pakistan and the fact that U.S. policy makers are increasingly invested in protecting their country's equities in the Indo-U.S. partnership.

To be sure, neither Indian restraint nor a Pakistani subdued response can be guaranteed in future crisis moments. Should either fail, the context will be fraught with extreme risk. Regardless, brokered bargaining would operate, in the limited as well as heightened escalation scenarios, albeit in an environment that would present a crisis management challenge for the third party that is far more complex than it experienced in any of the previous South Asian crises.

Beyond the Immediate: Force Modernization and
the Future of Brokered Bargaining in South Asia
The three crises examined in this book spanned India and Pakistan's first decade as overt nuclear powers. Both countries only had nascent nuclear capabilities and little experience of handling them. Could positive learning on their part, over time, reduce the world's concerns about their management of nuclear crises?[55] As they go through their learning curves, could they emulate Cold War patterns and begin to approach the need to strengthen bilateral escalation control mechanisms with greater urgency? Furthermore, even as they expand their nuclear arsenals, would it not be reasonable to expect their management and command and control protocols to improve commensurately? And could more secure bilateral protocols and better managed and more transparent programs not generate sufficient confidence among third parties to allow them to stay out of South Asian crises, thereby making brokered bargaining redundant?

This hope of positive learning flows from the view of realist theorists who argue that rivals in possession of nuclear weapons will tend to exhibit a similar "pattern of aggregate behavior."[56] The future ought to resemble the past in terms of the behavior of new nuclear weapon states.[57] However, as constructivist theorists argue, shared beliefs and cultures and social interactions in international relations matter greatly in determining state behavior.[58] Variations in learning can be introduced due to different experiences or dissimilar historical, cultural, or contextual factors that lead states to derive different lessons even when the experiences producing the learning are similar.[59] Apart from the many historical and geopolitical dissimilarities between the South Asian competition and the superpower rivalry,[60] today's international setting is also fundamentally different and lends itself to a learning trajectory that diverges from that of the Cold War. One aspect stands out in particular in the context of this discussion: the superpowers had to seek bilateral recourse in part because no third parties able to influence their crisis behavior existed under the bipolar global order. In South Asia's case, the presence of the unipole and other strong powers and the unipole's keenness to mediate crises offers an obvious avenue for regional rivals to transfer the risks and costs of crisis management to it. It takes away the compulsion to invest in the extremely challenging and often politically costly process of instituting and working through bilateral mechanisms, and incentivizes contracting out crisis management to the third party. At the very least then, the third party's presence ought to protract the learning curve of regional nuclear rivals around the world.

Indeed, even as India and Pakistan have demonstrated some positive learning in terms of crisis behavior, including exhibiting relatively restrained postures in the last of the three studied crises, overall the third-party outlet has "perpetuated strategic and doctrinal immaturity."[61] Their programs remain highly nontransparent and they remain locked in an active tit-for-tat nuclear buildup, including a missile race, they are investing in a number of potentially destabilizing technologies, and they have adopted risky warfighting doctrines.

In terms of Indian and Pakistani force modernization, there are two unmistakable trends. First, Pakistan will find it impossible to match India in the conventional military realm. For the first time ever, the pace of India's conventional buildup is threatening to leave Pakistan with a decisively lopsided conventional deterrence equation. While the many inefficiencies of India's defense sector mean that this is not imminent by any means, Christopher Clary rightly notes that "as long as India continues to grow faster than Pakistan and continues to spend at rates comparable to historical averages (two to three per cent of Gross Domestic Product), there is no doubt that Pakistan will be unable to maintain even a patina of conventional parity over time."[62]

Second, this implies potentially greater insecurities and an even heavier Pakistani reliance on its nuclear capability.[63] Perhaps in recognition of the inevitable, Pakistan has already signaled its move away from its traditional "credible minimum deterrence" nuclear posture to "full spectrum deterrence" that seeks to demonstrate a credible nuclear response option along every rung of the escalation ladder.[64] Since the Mumbai crisis, Pakistan has developed a tactical nuclear delivery option, Nasr, that can be used as a battle-field weapon.[65] Naeem Salik rightly identifies this as an example of nuclear "unlearning"—where an earlier decision to avoid investment in a destabiliz-ing platform has been reversed.[66] India and Pakistan are also pursuing tri-ads. Significantly, the sea-based deterrent's operationalization will amount to permanent deployment of South Asian arsenals. Moreover, India is investing in a ballistic missile defense (BMD) capability that will leave Pakistan at an even greater disadvantage and likely prompt it to strengthen its own offensive capabilities.[67] Further instability will be introduced as counterforce target-ing enters the mix and cruise missiles with precision capabilities, already an integral part of the delivery options for both countries, become the norm in a context marked by extremely short flight times.[68] Combined with an Indian move toward developing multiple independently targetable re-entry vehicles (MIRV), a conversation no longer alien to South Asia, this will further shift the offense-defense balance in India's favor and make use of force options more attractive to it.[69] Some scholars have also advocated an Indian move toward tactical nuclear weapons to match Pakistan.[70] Worryingly, India has already begun to debate the efficacy of its no-first-use policy, instead consider-ing an offensive "preemptive nuclear counterforce" strategy,[71] while Pakistan has remained steadfast in its first-use posture.

All this would grossly increase the command and control and safety and security challenges in South Asia. Any gains from the likely improvement in the dependability and safety of the next generation of weapon systems, the lesser concerns about preemption associated with larger arsenals, assured sec-ond strike capabilities through sea-based platforms, and even any potential progress in instituting bilateral escalation control mechanisms will likely be more than offset by these negative trends.

What implications does this expected trajectory have for brokered bar-gaining? Two observations are pertinent. First, these developments point to significantly greater risks during crises. Specifically, the combination of Paki-stan's eroded conventional deterrent and a potentially emboldened Indian psyche flowing from this makes a rethink of South Asia's presently recessed nuclear postures far likelier. Pakistan's nuclear use threshold will inevitably be lowered. It may consider active readying and deployment of tactical nuclear weapons. If reaction times get further compressed, even pre-delegation of launch authority to field commanders during crises would become plausible.[72] The United States and its European allies faced similar dilemmas in dealing with the conventionally superior Soviet Union during the Cold War. The United States also invested in all these technologies, including banking on its nuclear deployment in Europe to signal the virtual inevitability of escalation to a nuclear conflict,[73] much like Pakistan plans to with its tactical nuclear capability. The efficacy of these U.S. strategies was always suspect. The fact that they left too much to chance is widely recognized today.

Unsurprisingly then, the current trajectory of the South Asian nuclear rivalry continues to worry Western capitals. A crisis featuring these technologies and capabilities can reasonably be expected to heighten third-party concerns and further lower their preferred crisis intervention threshold. U.S. crisis managers tend to recognize this. Even as they back active efforts to promote bilateral crisis management mechanisms and feel uncomfortable at the thought of their crisis management becoming a permanent fixture in South Asia, they also see no wisdom in leaving India and Pakistan to manage their own crises in the depicted context.[74] For India and Pakistan, the urge to employ these new technologies in a crisis could conceivably incentivize autonomous behavior. Yet, all the compulsions that forced them to engage the third party in previous South Asian crises would remain as potent.

Second, deployed arsenals will make the third party's conflict management task far more challenging: the time available to external actors to intervene before nuclear weapons are readied for use will shrink drastically, even possibly nearing zero if both sides choose to adopt a launch-on-warning posture. This will be a radical departure from the current situation where the escalation ladder is elongated courtesy of recessed nuclear postures. The multiple-audience problem will be accentuated; the potential costs of misperceiving or miscalculating the third party's or the antagonist's intentions and signals could be astronomically higher. Incidentally, these higher risks may make the antagonists even more interested in banking on third-party mediation rather than testing the consequences of direct conflict. If anything then, brokered bargaining ought to be further cemented at the core of South Asian nuclear crisis management going forward, but with far greater risks of untoward escalation.

7 Beyond South Asia

Generalizing the Application of Brokered Bargaining

THE ANALYSIS THUS FAR HAS TESTED BROKERED BAR-
gaining in the South Asian context. What cases other than India
and Pakistan can be expected to display crisis behavior that fits the contours
of the trilateral framework? The perpetual concerns and realistic possibility of
further nuclear proliferation make this a highly relevant policy question. In
terms of specific proliferation trends, a potential domino effect in the Middle
East has long been of great concern. It is feared a chain reaction may flow
from Iran to its Arab neighbors, principally Saudi Arabia and Egypt, as well
as to Turkey. This could potentially prompt Israel to declare its hitherto covert
nuclear status.[1] An Eastern chain including North Korea (already nuclear) and
U.S. allies Japan and South Korea has also been touted as a real possibility.[2]

The discussion in this chapter explores the general applicability of brokered bargaining beyond South Asia, focusing on various prototypes of
regional rivalries within these chains. In addition, it analyzes the Sino-Indian
equation, the only existing nuclear pair other than India and Pakistan that
resembles a regional rivalry. The spread signifies varying power differentials,
regional contexts, and security arrangements. It includes states stronger and
weaker than the South Asian rivals; regions with and without the presence of
non-state actors or concern about terrorism-related crisis triggers; regional
rivals that are friends as well as foes of the United States; and contexts featuring U.S. extended deterrence guarantees. Specifically, this chapter analyzes

four prototypes of rivalries, each differentiated from the other by the nature of the antagonists' relations with the unipole.

The Middle East

A domino nuclear proliferation effect in the Middle East could end up producing two types of nuclear rivalries: between countries that are considered friends of the unipole; and between a friend and foe of the United States. Each prototype is examined below.

Prototype 1: Crisis Between Two Friends of the U. S.
The brokered bargaining framework ought to apply wholly to nuclear rivals that, like India and Pakistan, enjoy relatively friendly relations with the United States. While no such rivalries are on the horizon yet, one can envision contexts in which Saudi Arabia and Israel, Turkey and Israel, and Egypt and Israel are pitted against one another as nuclear rivals.[3] Admittedly, these are low probability scenarios; the foremost impetus for a Saudi Arabian, Egyptian, or Turkish pursuit of nuclear weapons is likely to be their competition with Iran. Yet, it is not impossible to imagine these countries being ruled by emboldened forces willing to use their nuclear status to compete with Iran and Israel simultaneously. Recognizing this concern, Israel has already repeatedly warned that the presence of any other nuclear power in its neighborhood "would pose an intolerable threat to Israel's survival as a state and society."[4]

Were a crisis to occur between any pair among these countries in the envisioned nuclearized environment, the conflicting parties and the United States will likely face crisis management opportunities and constraints similar to the ones identified in the South Asian case studies. Like South Asia, there is plenty about a Middle Eastern crisis that would deeply worry the United States. The region has a weak security culture, secretive defense establishments, all the above-mentioned potential nuclear states are dictatorships or illiberal democracies, some of these countries are geographically contiguous, politics in the Middle East has strong ideological and religious undertones, and the region is infested with militant outfits that are opposed to Israel's existence and stand to gain from any major regional crises.

Washington's deep ties to and interest in the Middle East should further reinforce its perceived need to intervene to de-escalate a nuclear crisis.[5] Israel, Saudi Arabia, Turkey, and Egypt have all been crucial to America's regional interests for decades. Moreover, the United States maintains military bases in and around the region which, as long as they remain, will keep its forces directly in harm's way of any nuclear incident in the vicinity.[6] The region has also served as the world's energy hub for decades and is likely to remain critical for transshipment of global energy and trade. Combined with the unacceptability of the obvious humanitarian catastrophe that would result from any nuclear exchange, these factors ought to force the United States to intervene to defuse a crisis situation immediately.

U.S. efforts to broker peace can be expected to take a course similar to that observed in the South Asian cases. Washington would rely on its reward-punishment leverage to incentivize de-escalation, with the specific context of the crisis dictating the balance between use of inducements and efforts to raise the adversaries' costs of defiance. Equally, the antagonists' reliance on a strong military and economic relationship with the United States ought to impose limits on their autonomous behavior and heighten their sensitivity to its crisis preferences. In fact, their compulsion not to leave the field open to their opponent should be reinforced by the fact that both sides would be familiar with working Washington's channels and thus equally well positioned to extract concessions from the United States.

The risks entailed in these crises should also be generally comparable to those in South Asia. Given their close relations with America, any of these countries could feel emboldened to create a demonstration crisis to attract its support. Moreover, even though Israel will be operating from a position of conventional military superiority against its adversaries, like India did in South Asia, it may be less keen on adopting a no-first-use (NFU) policy given that its small size and lack of geographical depth makes it exceptionally vulnerable to a decapitating first strike.[7] An aversion to NFU may have implications for force postures (of Israel and its adversaries) during crises. Misinterpretation of signals from an adversary in such a context could lead to desperate or unintended actions from one or both sides, in turn unleashing an escalatory dynamic.

The third party's role as an information conduit, especially its calibrated use of private intelligence information, would be crucial to preventing or removing any misunderstandings between the adversaries and nudging the crisis dynamic toward de-escalation. Washington's familiarity with the regional countries in question ought to make this process somewhat easier, although the South Asian crisis experiences provide sufficient reason to guard against complacency in this regard. Moreover, the assumption of relatively balanced U.S. equities and warm relations with the conflicting parties lowers the risks of these rivals imagining gang up scenarios or perceiving outright U.S. support to use force against the opponent. An antagonist may consider unilateral action if it feels that the United States has sufficient leverage over their opponent to prevent it from retaliating, but the costs of losing third-party support after such a move would not be lost on it. U.S. signaling to ensure that the regional rivals recognize its opposition to any such action would be important to deter them from contemplating this.

Prototype 2: Crisis between a Friend and Foe of the U.S.
The more likely Middle Eastern nuclear rivalry between Israel and Iran offers the most obvious example of this prototype.[8] Israel is already believed to have approximately 80 nuclear warheads and a relatively sophisticated delivery capability.[9] It is also developing a highly advanced, multilayered missile defense system.[10] The prospect of a nuclear-armed Iran is not imminent. A troubled but still operative deal between Tehran and the permanent members of the UN Security Council and Germany (P5+1) in 2015 put a limit on Iran's nuclear activities.[11] Yet, critics believe that the deal opens greater pathways for Iran to revive its quest for nuclear weapons down the road.[12] The depicted scenario assumes a declared Iranian nuclear capability up against Israel's more sophisticated arsenal.

The United States ought to have an immediate interest in managing an Israel-Iran crisis. Its stakes in the Middle East and the risk of major global economic disruptions due to a nuclear crisis will be further accentuated by factors specific to this case. A crucial U.S. partner will be up against a foe whose relations with the United States would have taken another serious hit given its acquisition of nuclear weapons in defiance of international pressure.[13] While the United States does not offer Israel a formal security guarantee, the long-standing "special relationship" between them implies that U.S. alliance credibility will be on the line.[14] Moreover, the threat to U.S. military presence from any nuclear incident will be further heightened given that U.S. bases and personnel in the region could become direct targets of any Iranian nuclear use in an all-out war.

A low U.S. intervention threshold also ought to be dictated by the Western depiction of Iran as a theocracy capable of irrational decision making. The most alarmist views project Iran as an undeterrable, fanatical state holding

apocalyptic beliefs about Israel's total disappearance, and potentially willing
to use its nuclear capability to achieve this goal even at the risk of its own
destruction.[15] Iran has also been an active supporter of powerful non-state
actors against Israel and many fear that it may use its nuclear shield to exploit
the sub-conventional space with greater vigor.[16] While a number of counter-
vailing pressures on Iran suggest that these concerns are exaggerated,[17] one
can reasonably assume Western powers will expect the worst.

U.S. concerns would be further heightened by a number of geographical
and technical imperatives that may threaten crisis stability. Israel's earlier-
mentioned vulnerability to an adversary's first strike will have implications
for its force posture in this case as well. At the same time, Israel's massive
nuclear superiority in the early years of Iran's nuclearization could worry the
Iranian leadership about an Israeli preemptive strike, perhaps even forcing it
to consider dispersal of its arsenal and pre-delegation of launch authority.[18]
Lacking any formal diplomatic relations or direct lines of communication and
entangled in a deeply emotive rivalry marked by cognitive dissonance, these
antagonists would be susceptible to overcooking provocativeness and causing
serious escalation.

The envisioned crisis scenario will present an acute dilemma for the
United States. Israel will expect full U.S. support. However, Washington's
natural and obvious inclination to back its ally outright would be complicated
by the nuclear context. A U.S.-Israel gang up against Iran may force Iran to
buckle, but equally a no-win situation may thrust it into a belligerent mode
and force greater reliance on its nuclear deterrent. Worse yet, an actual act
of military aggression by the U.S.-Israel combine could end up flirting with
Iran's nuclear red lines and bring deliberate nuclear use into play. Even Israel
ought to be wary of such an outcome that could force Iran into a use 'em or
lose 'em mindset.

These dynamics would seriously constrain the United States' ability to
embolden Israel. Instead, its position as the third party interested in ensuring de-escalation above all else ought to lead it to balance between its need
to demonstrate commitment to its ally and ensure the absence of a nuclear
catastrophe by favoring crisis termination. This dual U.S. role would require
careful calibration. On the one hand, the United States would have to signal its opposition to any Israeli display of resolve that may escalate the crisis.
This task would be complicated by Israel's strategic culture that prizes offensive action, specifically preventive and preemptive strikes.[19] Israel's inevitable

nuclear superiority over Iran as well as Iran's track record of blinking in the face of risk in conflict situations may further embolden Israeli leaders.[20] The U.S. toolkit may include persuasion and inducements to incentivize Israel's deference to its preferences but a less flexible Israeli response may also require hints at potential costs of defiance. In contexts where Iran's militant proxies may have had a role in triggering the crisis, the United States could also take a leaf from its South Asian playbook by accepting Iran's plausible deniability to make it harder for Israel to contemplate direct action without it coming across as the aggressor.

Yet, in parallel to efforts aimed at restraining its ally, the United States would have to avoid any impression that these signals are a sign of a waning of the U.S. commitment to Israel in the crisis, lest Israeli leaders feel forced to chart an autonomous crisis strategy. One obvious reassurance from the United States—this would also satisfy alliance credibility considerations—may come in the form of an outward diplomatic and military posture that signals its intent to back Israel fully in case of a confrontation. The United States could also promise to redress any Israeli dissatisfaction through post-crisis actions. America's broken relationship with Iran would offer it far greater post-crisis options to punish it diplomatically, economically, or through other nonmilitary means (military action will remain unlikely given Iran's nuclear capability) than America could afford against Pakistan in South Asia. Even here though, the United States would need to ensure that it distinguishes these post-crisis efforts from its positioning in any future crisis and manages Israel's expectations accordingly. A failure to do so may be misread by Israeli leaders as a promise of fuller U.S. support in future crisis iterations and this may embolden them to provoke and escalate a fresh crisis down the line.

The U.S. role as third-party mediator would also be compromised in this case by its antagonism toward Iran. This may be a context in which the unipole must rely heavily on other third parties with leverage over Tehran to influence its crisis behavior. These actors would have to assume the lead role in employing the reward-punishment leverage vis-à-vis Iran to complement U.S. efforts to convince Israel to bank on U.S. crisis management. As the situation stands today, the P5+1 may be the best third-party grouping to act as lead intermediaries with Iran.

The antagonists can be expected to display the use of both prongs of the resolve-prudence trade-off. It is reasonable to expect both sides to signal their resolve to each other. Their mutual concern about preemption may even lead them to undertake risky force demonstrations and posturing that signals pre-paredness to employ nuclear weapons at short notice. Israel may also seek to exhibit autonomous behavior in the face of U.S. efforts to restrain it, both to express its displeasure to Washington and to force it to reveal its inten-tions more fully. At the same time, it would gain little by testing Washington's patience beyond a point for this would risk denting the inevitable Western diplomatic support for Israel against Iran, and could even force the United States to bring its punishment leverage into play. Equally though, one ought not to rule out the possibility of Israel recognizing the futility of defying the United States and of it voluntarily banking on prudence to extract concessions from Washington.[21]

Iran, on its part, would not be able to ignore the fact that outright defiance of third-party interlocutors could eventually force them to present a united global front against it during the crisis. The most obvious node of third-party leverage over Iran would flow from Tehran's diplomatic and economic isolation, which would likely already have increased because of its weapons program. Iran's leaders would be sensitive to these costs, but equally, induce-ments to the contrary could be attractive as face savers in a crisis context. Iran's almost guaranteed destruction in case of an all-out war would also not be lost on its leadership.

Even if Israel and Iran are deterred from deliberate nuclear use, their nuclear rivalry will carry significant risks of inadvertence during crises. The context will remain crisis prone, both because of the perceived mutual vulner-ability to preemption and because of the complicating presence of non-state actors that could trigger crises. Iran's non-state proxies such as Hezbollah, which operates against Israel from Lebanon and Syria, are far stronger than any of the non-state actors operating in South Asia.[22] There are fears that these groups may feel emboldened by an Iranian nuclear capability, or worse, that Iran could include them under its nuclear security umbrella.[23] Much as in South Asia, these groups could create frequent crises, even without Iran's approval, and still bring Tel Aviv and Tehran to the brink of major war.

The multiple-audience problem will also pose greater challenges than experienced by India and Pakistan in their crises. The collective actor media-tion effort puts a high premium on efficient coordination between the vari-ous third parties. At a minimum, the effort requires a strong enough working relationship and requisite trust between the United States and the other lead intermediaries to convince each other of their sincerity in pursuing de-escalation, and building on this, to allow coordination and messaging discipline during the crisis.

Even if they overcome this significant challenge, the regional rivals may discount their leverage over their adversary and any commitments the mediators may make on its behalf. Iran may feel that the P5+1 group is under Washington's sway and thus it may remain suspicious of its crisis agenda. Or, while trusting its intentions, Iranian leaders may believe that Washington is deliberately misinforming the other P5+1 members of Israel's real designs to use force against Iran. Similarly, Israel could perceive Tehran's willingness to engage the third party as a mere tactic to divert attention from its offensive intent. The result could be provocative posturing by both sides that may cause one of them to panic and act precipitously in desperation.

The same outcome could flow from misinterpreted third-party actions. The envisioned U.S. crisis role entails necessarily contradictory public versus private postures. These mixed signals would be aimed at furthering the de-escalation agenda but they would also be susceptible to misinterpretation. Distrustful of American intentions and expecting an outright partisan U.S. approach against it, Iran may construe any U.S. force demonstrations in Israel's favor as signs of an imminent joint Israel-U.S. action against it. This may push Iranian leaders or local military commanders with pre-delegated launch authority into a use 'em or lose 'em mindset. Even short of that, an Iranian response merely aimed at signaling its preparedness to escalate may still end up provoking Israel's worst fears and force it to act prematurely. In the absence of clearly defined nuclear thresholds—highly likely during the initial phase of their nuclear competition—and any a priori understanding on how to keep a conflict limited, the situation could easily lead to swift and potentially uncontrollable escalation.

The Korean Peninsula

The Korean peninsula represents a prototype where a U.S. foe and formal U.S. allies with extended deterrence guarantees are pitted against each other. A nuclear North Korea threatens South Korea and Japan, both nonnuclear states under the U.S. nuclear umbrella.[24] The U.S. has made itself a direct party to the conflict; it maintains an active troop presence in South Korea and Japan and is committed to using all military means to defend these allies against Pyongyang.[25]

The Korean peninsula has gone through multiple bouts of high tensions over the years. Since 2013, North Korea has provoked the world through repeated missile and four nuclear tests.[26] Its nuclear program has led to multiple UN resolutions and economic and diplomatic sanctions that continue to be championed by the United States as a means of forcing Pyongyang to denuclearize.[27] The country's increasing isolation has left it almost entirely dependent on its neighbor and only significant ally, China, for survival. China accounts for over 90 percent of the country's trade volume and is its only significant diplomatic outlet.[28] North Korean nuclearization and its continued belligerence have tested China's patience, seriously frayed China-North Korea relations, and brought China under increasing global pressure to adopt a harsher approach toward its ally. Yet, China has opposed U.S. calls for North Korea's total isolation, instead seeking patient diplomacy and a policy of inducement to alter the Kim regime's behavior.[29] China's approach toward the hermit kingdom is dictated by its need to prevent Pyongyang's collapse since it offers a useful buffer between China and U.S. allies South Korea and Japan and the U.S. troop presence there.[30] A North Korean collapse or even a major conventional war on the peninsula would also create a massive refugee crisis for China to deal with.[31]

The crisis context on the Korean peninsula does not naturally lend itself to brokered bargaining. The situation is more reminiscent of the Cold War: the United States and China are pitted against one another and committed to defending their allies.[32] Indeed, most observers warn that a conflict on the peninsula could suck the United States and China into a direct confrontation.[33] Yet, the risk of nuclear war ought to force the crisis actors to entertain a number of crisis opportunities and constraints associated with the brokered bargaining framework.

That the United States has troops in and joint defense plans with its East Asian allies implies that it must behave as a "defender" backing its protégés in a crisis. However, it is faced with a nuclear challenger that epitomizes virtually all Western concerns about regional nuclear powers: notably, it is a totalitarian, revisionist state with unsettled borders and an unfinished war agenda; it is ruled by a rogue regime known for its extreme belligerence; this regime is now in charge of a small nuclear arsenal with unknown safety and security redundancies but nonetheless capable of hitting South Korea and Japan; and it is actively pursuing a capability to target the United States directly.[34] Conflict scenarios on the peninsula all confirm that a major war will ultimately lead to the North's total destruction at the hands of the United States and its allies but it will not be before a North Korean conventional military assault has caused a "human catastrophe," including hundreds of thousands of casualties in South Korea.[35] Escalation of the conflict to the nuclear level would take the casualty count into the millions.[36] Not only would the United States be unable to ignore the obviously devastating humanitarian consequences of such a development, but U.S. troops in the region may be a key North Korean target.[37] As in the Israel-Iran dyad posited earlier, these realities would likely bring the tension between the U.S. role as a committed ally versus a third-party broker of peace to the fore. A compulsion to seek de-escalation may therefore override alliance considerations even though the United States will, in parallel, have to be ready to defend its allies, and indeed its own troops, in an eventuality.

Here too, the outright antagonistic relationship between North Korea and the United States implies that Washington must rely on others to mediate with Pyongyang while it works to prevent its protégés from escalating tensions. China's unique leverage over North Korea makes it the obvious, in fact only, realistic mediator vis-à-vis Pyongyang. Despite the Sino-U.S. strategic competition on the peninsula, the dire consequences of a major conflict and China's interest in preventing North Korea's collapse ought to incentivize it to work with Washington to manage tensions.

Washington's task of restraining its allies ought to be relatively easier in this context given Japan and South Korea's formal and heavy reliance on the United States for their protection against North Korea. The recklessness associated with the North Korean leadership and the massive harm its military aggression can inflict on these countries should encourage further caution on their part. In fact, they may also find reason to urge the United States to exercise caution to avoid forcing a desperate North Korea into military action.

The North Korean nuclear capability ought to limit the Sino-U.S. third party's crisis management toolkit in ways similar to those witnessed in the examined South Asian crises. Even though North Korea's excessive dependence on China and the absence of any alternative alignment options for North Korea suggest significant maneuvering room for Beijing to coerce the North Korean leadership, the Kim regime's Hobbesian conception of its surrounding environment and its obsession with emphasizing its strategic independence suggests a need for more careful signaling on China's part. For instance, Beijing must remain wary of signals or actions that may be interpreted by the North Korean leadership as a Chinese decision to gang up with the United States to forcibly disarm it. This would risk undermining all Chinese leverage and forcing an already paranoid North Korean regime into total self-help mode, with potentially disastrous consequences. That said, this Chinese constraint and the North Korean propensity for excessive autonomy ought not to overshadow the Kim regime's need to avoid a major conflict that risks its annihilation. Chinese mediation remains critical as a potential face-saving option for North Korea; forcing China to oppose it outright, especially in an escalated crisis scenario, would be suicidal.

Glimpses of these behavior patterns can be gleaned from recent periods of high tension on the Korean peninsula. In spring 2013, tensions spiked in the wake of a North Korean rocket test in December 2012 followed by a nuclear test in February 2013.[38] The situation was a classic display of North Korean brinkmanship, extending far enough to include a threat of nuclear war and movement of its missiles to its eastern borders to signal its intent to target the United States directly.[39] The United States entered into a tit-for-tat brinkmanship exercise that entailed resolve signals and provocative joint military exercises with South Korea.[40] Throughout, however, its behavior reflected its recognition of the necessity to play the dual role of ally and third party. The United States reached out to China with private and public calls to help restrain North Korea.[41] A number of Western capitals complemented U.S. efforts to persuade China to press the North Korean leadership.[42]

Even as China continued to urge restraint on all sides, it obliged the international community by pressuring Pyongyang to stop its provocations. It also employed its punishment leverage, imposing financial sanctions on North Korea by asking its four largest banks to halt all transactions with the country.[43] Tensions lingered as North Korea undertook provocative military moves and even detained Chinese sailors in an obvious show of defiance.[44] Yet, Chinese diplomacy played an important role in forcing Pyongyang to ultimately back down. North Korea then proposed talks with South Korea and also joined China in calling for a resumption of the stalled six-party talks, the primary diplomatic forum of engagement between North Korea and South Korea, Japan, and the United States.[45]

Another bout of prolonged major tensions began early in 2017. The state of global politics at the time was exceptionally ill-suited for successful international diplomacy on the Korean peninsula. Newly elected U.S. president Donald Trump had created a major upheaval in Sino-U.S. relations, including promising a clean break from China's preferred patient diplomacy with Pyongyang if China did not rein in the North Korean leadership.[46] The United States and China got into a war of words over the crisis. President Trump blamed China for doing "little to help" and threatened, and subsequently imposed, sanctions and blacklisted Chinese companies, banks, and traders engaging with North Korea.[47] North Korea remained defiant and continued to test the Trump administration's resolve by conducting multiple missile tests for months and openly threatening a direct attack against the U.S. homeland.[48] Washington reacted aggressively throughout 2017, signaling its readiness to undertake military action to disarm North Korea and force a regime change.[49] Simultaneously, China's relations with North Korea deteriorated as Pyongyang blamed China for "dancing to the tune of the U.S." and embarrassed Beijing by openly and persistently defying its calls for restraint.[50]

Lost in all this noise, however, was the parallel reality that the fundamentals of crisis management on the Korean peninsula had not changed.[51] Despite extremely harsh rhetoric that stressed that their patience had run out,[52] American officials also continued to stress their preference for diplomacy and constantly banked on the all-too-familiar approach of relying on China to force a change in Pyongyang's behavior.[53] To President Trump's insinuations that the United States may go after North Korea alone, even South Korea raised serious concerns and international partners like the UK and others cautioned against such an approach, arguing instead in favor of cooperating with China to ensure de-escalation of tensions.[54]

Tensions with the United States did not prevent China from responding positively to the world's complaints that it was not doing enough to rein in North Korea. China continued to insist on a diplomatic solution and resisted U.S. pressure to cripple North Korea's economy completely,[55] but it also went further than it had before by imposing major sanctions on Pyongyang.[56] Throughout, China also joined the U.S. in backing the peninsula's denuclearization and calling on the North Korean regime to suspend its nuclear and missile testing to defuse tensions.[57] North Korea complicated China's position by arguing that Chinese behavior had crossed a "red line."[58] It even took the unprecedented step of directly threatening China with "grave consequences."[59] However, even as the North Korean leadership continued to take advantage of China's averseness to a total rupture of ties with North Korea, its dependence on China in active conflict scenarios was too great for it to go beyond such grandstanding. Unsurprisingly then, Pyongyang never dared to consider imposing any of the "grave consequences" it had threatened and there were early signs of a desire to mend relations in late 2017.[60] North Korea also reached out to South Korea with an offer for talks in the beginning of 2018.

The Korean peninsula has escaped a major conflict thus far. Yet, the context remains fraught with extreme risk. The moral hazard problem continues to drive North Korea's attention-seeking provocations that keep the region on the verge of war. The multiple-audience problem is also far more accentuated in this environment than experienced in the South Asian crises. The virtually nonexistent U.S.–North Korea relationship and the unreliability of direct communication channels between North and South Korea implies a critical Chinese role as the information conduit in conjunction with the United States. But as direct strategic competitors on the Korean peninsula, the United States and China are not naturally suited to actively coordinating a crisis management strategy as this requires trust and messaging discipline in the presence of multiple antagonists. Confused signaling or misunderstandings could easily lead to misinterpretations of the situation followed by destabilizing actions by any of the involved actors. On the other hand, the North Korean regime's Hobbesian mindset may prompt it to view close Sino-U.S. coordination suspiciously. Since such an effort will inevitably involve Chinese pressure on North Korea to back down, Pyongyang may misinterpret the situation as a U.S.-China gang up against it. Its hypersensitivity to an American preemptive strike and the fact that the United States will be posturing publicly as a defender of its allies prepared for any eventuality increase the likelihood of North Korea finding itself in a use 'em or lose 'em mindset. A parallel Chinese effort to act as the guarantor of any U.S. private promises and assurances to North Korea may not be sufficient to assuage its concerns given that the North Korean leadership would likely discount China's power to hold the U.S. and its allies to their commitments.

On their part, the United States and its allies remain wary of a surprise attack by North Korea. Given that the opacity of the North Korean state makes it nearly impossible to obtain accurate intelligence, there is a fair possibility of the United States assuming the worst at the first inkling of North Korean plans to aggress. It may therefore choose to attempt preemption. This could happen even if North Korea's characteristic belligerence in such a situation is only intended to force China to reveal its intentions fully or extract greater concessions from the United States and its allies, or perhaps is driven merely by sheer habit.

The risk of a major conflict on the Korean peninsula will remain high. The United States is desperate to prevent further North Korean nuclear modernization. One can therefore expect increased and persistent U.S. pressure on the North Korean regime. This will keep alive the regime's fears of U.S. preemption, and its increased sensitivity to such a possibility during periods of high tensions will continue to threaten crisis stability. Moreover, short of North Korea overplaying its hand in a way that forces China to punish it directly, or more likely, to seek forcible regime change, China's likely continued opposition to any actions that could completely undermine its leverage over its ally or lead to the state's collapse also lends itself to greater Sino-U.S. tensions over North Korea going forward. This would affect their ability to coordinate strategies in subsequent crises, making these episodes even harder to defuse.

The Sino-Indian Dyad

The brokered bargaining framework also holds relevance for a current nuclear rivalry: China and India. In this case, a friend of the unipole is challenged by the unipole's presumptive great power rival. These two giants remain locked in a strategically competitive relationship and have multiple disputes over the demarcation of their 2,175 mile-long border.[61] Spats over troop movements and infrastructure projects along disputed border zones have flared up in the past, including a significant one in 2017, and conflict triggered by sustained border tensions or over broader territorial disagreements like Tibet remains possible.[62]

It goes without saying that a crisis between two countries with huge economies and a huge population (well over two billion people) will force the world to take notice. The global economic losses associated with even a purely conventional conflict between them would be significant. The U.S. interest in this context will be immediate but it may initially be driven more by concerns about the shock of any prolonged Sino-Indian crisis to the global economy and to other U.S. regional interests than by the nuclear dimension. Unlike India and Pakistan, China and India are not on a war footing and their robust conventional capabilities and largely retaliatory nuclear force postures vis-à-vis each other also militate against a sudden escalation of a crisis to the nuclear level.[63] However, U.S. involvement can be expected to transform into the mediatory role expected of third parties in brokered bargaining contexts at the first signs of serious escalatory potential. Realistically, this would require a conventional war beyond a minor crisis.

In a scenario with heightened risk of untoward escalation, the truly global consequences of any nuclear exchange between these two rivals should prompt the United States to call for immediate crisis de-escalation. However, given China's strength and stature, which are more akin to a global rather than regional power, the third party's leverage over China ought to be somewhat blunted. A more typical U.S.-led crisis management effort complemented by other third-party actors could still be effective vis-à-vis India.

Given the limitations on the United States' ability to pressure China directly, U.S. crisis mediation may be focused more on persuasion and inducements to encourage China to de-escalate. The United States could also usefully facilitate communication between the adversaries, including perhaps acting as a guarantor of India's promises and commitments to China, and use its intelligence capabilities to prevent any misunderstanding during a crisis. U.S. punishment leverage such as signaling willingness to inflict trade and business losses on China or even military moves, say naval maneuvering in the South China sea, would remain available. However, China's ability to stand firm in the face of these signals makes them relatively unattractive. They could compromise the already limited U.S. leverage without delivering much in terms of Chinese concessions. Collective pressure from multilateral forums such as the UN may be more effective in raising China's diplomatic costs of defiance than bilateral U.S. efforts.

America's regional policy interests lend themselves to a partisan crisis posture that seeks to embolden India against China. Indeed, the United States can reasonably be expected to try to protect the equities in its relationship with India by attempting to fashion a favorable crisis outcome for New Delhi.[64] Yet, the de-escalation agenda ought to reign supreme. It should force a more balanced use of the reward-punishment leverage on the part of U.S. decision makers. In tandem with offering rewards for prudence, they would have to remain open to raising India's costs if its autonomous actions risk escalation. The United States may have to redress any Indian dissatisfaction through post-crisis support.

Intuitively, one could expect China to resist any U.S. attempts at mediation. China is not enthused by the prospect of U.S. ingress in its affairs. The strong India-U.S. partnership and Washington's interest in using India to check China's rise ought to make Beijing even more reluctant and suspicious of U.S involvement. Indeed, China's initial instinct in a crisis may be to keep the United States at bay and to signal its resolve to achieve its ideal crisis objectives. However, its interest in engaging the third party ought to grow in a crisis scenario that carries real potential of uncontrolled escalation. Faced with such a prospect, Chinese decision makers would not be able to escape the innate factors that tend to force conflicting parties to act within the trilateral framework in nuclear crises.

China's advantage over India would not be absolute; the nuclear overhang will still make all-out conflict irrational. Therefore, even if China were able to hold its own, defying Washington and completely ignoring international concerns about a heightened crisis would serve little purpose as it would leave the field open for India to curry favor with the third party. On the other hand, engaging a third party that is seeking an end to the crisis but largely unable to threaten consequential punishment would offer Beijing an excellent opportunity to extract greater concessions from India as a quid pro quo for de-escalation. As for India, it would likely be keener to elicit U.S. support to offset China's advantage. Since it would gain little by defying the United States in the face of a serious threat, it may prize prudence over resolve to maximize U.S. support.

A Sino-Indian crisis presents a lower-risk scenario than the other three prototypes examined here. Neither side has any incentive to provoke a major conflict to attract third-party attention. China risks compromising its strategic autonomy and stature as a U.S. competitor by creating a demonstration crisis. India would gain little by provoking China given that the third party would be unable to extract major concessions from Beijing on India's behalf. As countries whose global rise is predicated on their economic growth, China and India must also factor in the significant economic disruptions that would inevitably flow from a crisis between them. India's sensitivity to crisis-related economic losses has already been highlighted in the discussion of the 2001–2002 military standoff and the 2008 Mumbai crisis between India and Pakistan.

In terms of possibilities of inadvertence, neither side's arsenal is vulnerable to preemption and neither is likely to see an interest in using nuclear weapons first in a crisis between them. Even as they continue to upgrade their nuclear capabilities to build redundancies into their assured retaliation postures, their current arsenals can, without a doubt, cause unacceptable damage to the other. The crisis dynamics also make it unlikely for India to feel overly emboldened by the prospect of U.S. support or for China to realistically imagine a gang up scenario against it. The one potentially destabilizing factor could be China's and India's misperception about Washington's leverage over their adversary. China could conceivably perceive the United States as having sufficient leverage over India and as willing to use it to prevent it from retaliating against Chinese escalation. This could simply be untrue or China could end up overcooking provocativeness and forcing India's hand to react in defiance of U.S. pressure. India, on its part, is liable to discount U.S. leverage over China to convince it to shelve any plans to escalate or it may construe Washington's inability as a deliberate decision to look the other way as China lets off steam. India could panic and its reaction could unleash a tit-for-tat escalatory dynamic.

China and India experienced a period of prolonged border tensions in 2017. This was never threatening enough to offer a real peek into how China, India, and the United States would react to a major crisis scenario, but hints of expected crisis behavior were still discernable. Even as the standoff lasted months and was accompanied by bellicose rhetoric and military threats, the Chinese and Indian propensity to avoid major escalation was conspicuous throughout. The nuclear angle was nonexistent. The United States expressed a clear preference for de-escalation and continued to push for direct Sino-India talks.[65] Washington's sensitivity to a possible Chinese reaction to any indication of its tilt toward India was also all but apparent. The United States backed India's preference for the territorial status quo ante but it limited its interactions with Indian leaders to private channels and avoided any forceful signals of opposition to China during the crisis.[66] Tellingly, the antagonists negotiated a rather abrupt and unexpected end to their standoff ahead of a major economic summit in China that involved the world's leading emerging economies, including India.[67]

The foregoing analysis establishes the relevance of brokered bargaining in explaining crisis behavior beyond South Asia. The four prototypes examined here represent significantly different contexts. Even as each presents a distinct set of challenges for the third-party actors, the fundamental crisis dynamic whereby the third party works to secure de-escalation without seeking to alienate either conflicting party completely and the antagonists feel compelled not to defy it outright remains valid in each case. Risks of misperceptions and inadvertence emanating from the trilateral framework exist across the cases but crisis management challenges tend to be especially acute in prototypes that involve U.S. allies and foes as the principal antagonists. The analysis ought to provide valuable lessons for policy makers in the United States as well as in the regions covered by these prototypes.

8 Brokered Bargaining

Implications for Theory and Practice

O UR EMPIRICAL ANALYSIS OF THE SOUTH ASIAN CASE studies has provided evidence of patterns of behavior in line with brokered bargaining. The preceding two chapters have further established the applicability of the framework to South Asia's evolving context and generalized its validity beyond the region. This chapter reflects upon the theoretical and practical implications of this work.

Theoretical Implications

As a theory of process centered on the third party, brokered bargaining breaks new ground. It departs from the prevailing tendency to examine third-party involvement through two-actor bargaining models. It is premised on a trilateral framework underpinned by a *process* that entails the recursive interplay of the perceptions, expectations, incentives, strategies, and choices among the three parties involved, but the process cannot be parsed to resemble the more familiar two-actor or two-against-one-actor models. This puts brokered bargaining squarely in the extremely thinly populated category of three-actor bargaining frameworks.[1]

Traditional explanations of nuclear crisis behavior overlook the dual attributes of the resolve-prudence trade-off inherent to brokered bargaining. In this three-cornered framework, theories of classic brinkmanship and behavioral characteristics encompassed by them remain relevant, but actors make crisis choices with very different audiences and motives in mind. The posited framework demands a much deeper understanding of the antagonists' behavior, directed simultaneously at the adversary and the third party and constrained by their desire to attain positive evaluation, and the interplay between this dynamic and the third party's use of its reward-punishment leverage. Traditional explanations rooted in bilateral deterrence models (or for that matter even nonnuclear explanatory factors like conventional deterrence) may seem to provide plausible answers for the absence of major wars and uncontrolled escalation in South Asia but they are unable to accurately explain the processes and mechanisms that shape behavior and ultimately affect these outcomes.

The South Asian case studies reveal aspects of Indian and Pakistani behavior that explanations grounded in traditional models find puzzling. India's and Pakistan's obvious eagerness to use the third party's presence to their advantage; India's propensity to hold back from crossing the Line of Control (LoC) at Kargil despite absorbing additional casualties; the absence of any effort on its part to establish the credibility of its newly declared deterrent more forcefully through resolute signaling during the crisis; its seeming contentment with restraint during the Mumbai crisis despite the huge reputational losses its stance entailed; Pakistan's decision to abandon its troops and its loss of face caused by backing down in the face of the Indian response in the Kargil crisis; its propensity to persist with its cover story of a mujahedeen intrusion during the crisis; and its denial of Ajmal Kasab's nationality despite clear evidence to the contrary at Mumbai, among other seemingly perplexing actions and signals, have all been discussed. Bilateral models discount the antagonists' concern for positive evaluation that helps rationalize these crisis decisions.

The analysis in this book builds on the deductive logic of propositions in literature specific to South Asia that recognize the third-party dynamic.[2] It has for the first time explained the trigger of the three-actor interaction as a function of the mutually reinforcing dynamic involving the third party's concerns about dangers of uncontrolled escalation and either the antagonists' desire to proactively lure the third party or their compulsion not to ignore it as it enters unsolicited. Since the argument suggests a virtual inevitability of third-party involvement independent—but not mutually exclusive—of the desire of the conflicting parties, it ends up ascribing agency to the third-party actors. This is contrary to the inside-out orientation of much of the specialist literature on South Asia that focuses disproportionately on Indian and Pakistani strategies.[3] The posited third-party outlook also makes specific nuclear postures of the regional rivals less relevant than formulations like Narang's posture optimization theory would suggest.[4] Nuclear postures may influence the third party's specific crisis choices and affect the risks involved in a given context but even the most relaxed postures would be unlikely to alter the urge of the external actors to intervene per se. America's keen interventions in the South Asian crises despite recessed postures of the rivals are obvious cases in point.

The relative predictability of third-party engagement also implies that the antagonists need not necessarily outcompete each other in provocativeness to attract its attention. In each of the three studied South Asian cases, both antagonists contested for third-party support. In the Kargil crisis and the 2001–2002 standoff, this entailed brinkmanship, but during the Mumbai crisis, they seemed to compete in outdoing each other in exhibiting restraint as a means of attaining third-party sympathy (India) or of preventing its outright opposition (Pakistan). This emphasis on prudence as attention-seeking behavior is counterintuitive. Not only scholarship on nuclear crisis behavior, but also disciplines like sociology that study the evaluation potential of audiences tend to portray an actor's positive evaluation as being tied to its ability to exhibit resolve.[5]

Moreover, the antagonists' relative eagerness to attract third parties is not necessarily correlated with the type of state in question. This finding differs from formulations like Paul Kapur's "instability-instability paradox," which considers the desire for third-party intervention as necessarily associated with the weaker, revisionist (in terms of territorial preferences) state.[6] The literature on South Asia reaches this conclusion based on the rather prevalent but still unsubstantiated assumption that the Pakistani state was directly involved in the terrorist attacks that triggered the twin peaks and Mumbai crises. Indeed, had the perpetrators of the December 2001 parliament and the November 2008 Mumbai attacks acted on the Pakistani state's orders as Indian alleged, the weaker, revisionist state would be responsible for creating these crises. However, if these non-state actors were operating autonomously, Pakistan would still stand out as the antagonist keener to attract the third party in the Kargil crisis, but India, the state with the status quo territorial preference and stronger military capabilities, would come across as more eager to solicit U.S. attention at the front-end of the twin peaks crisis.

The contention that the antagonists and the third party will tend to engage in brokered bargaining each time a regional nuclear crisis occurs also downplays the importance of specific crisis triggers for the trilateral interaction to be initiated. The framework's validity is not limited to contexts that feature clandestine encroachments on territory or acts by non-state actors as triggers, although these were the only ones operative in the South Asian context. The nature of the triggering event will naturally have implications for the maneuvering space and leverage available to the involved actors, their specific crisis choices, and the risks of escalation, but the trilateral bargaining exercise should take place regardless—as long as the regional rivals have plausible use of force options and there is even the slightest possibility of their employment. Nonetheless, since brokered bargaining is situated within the rationalist framework, it assumes the state to be a unitary actor. While Pakistan was challenged on this count, there was never any question of non-state actors being able to run an independent crisis policy beyond initiating the episode, or of them engaging India as an autonomous crisis interlocutor in parallel with the Pakistani state.[7] Contexts where states lack control over non-state actors operating from their territory to the point that they can be modeled as totally independent players are incomparable to those experienced in South Asia in terms of the crisis dynamics they may unleash. These fall outside the scope of this analysis.

A key contribution of this work is to highlight the risks of escalation emanating from the interaction between the third parties and regional rivals. The discussion has hinted at how the third party could mismanage its role or misperceive the intentions or behavior of the antagonists and end up unleashing an unwanted escalatory dynamic; how regional rivals could misperceive third-party behavior and hence consider actions that can lead to major war; and how the antagonists could be thrown off due to each other's moves intended for the third party. These and the many other new implications for crisis stability pointed out in the case studies demand much deeper exploration. Deterrence optimists and pessimists need to broaden the scope of their inquiries to incorporate three-cornered bargaining exercises much more centrally. Pessimists could continue holding on to their traditional concerns about inadvertence but their focus should expand to examining how brokered bargaining introduces additional risks into the equation, and how these may affect the more recognized risks. Optimists must comprehend the characteristics of the trilateral framework that highlight the drivers of de-escalation and potential for escalation quite apart from the urge for nuclear states to avoid conflict solely because of the presence of nuclear weapons. Indeed, there is room for a new strand of literature focused on the impact of the three-cornered framework on the traditional optimism-pessimism debate to emerge from this book's core arguments.

This book has also engaged aspects of the literature beyond the nuclear realm. The third party's role as "power mediator" has provided an opportunity to test the efficacy of mediation in a context typically consumed by coercive bargaining. In the posited framework, the presence of nuclear weapons constrains the unipole's ability to take an acutely coercive or an outright partisan approach toward the antagonists despite its preponderant position. This absence of extreme coercion as an option of choice for the third party is key to successful crisis management in brokered bargaining. It makes the framework distinct from theories like pivotal deterrence. While Crawford's *uncertainty* and *isolation avoidance* effects are at play in brokered bargaining as well, he explicitly distinguishes pivotal deterrence from mediation and discards the latter for its inability to capture the centrality of coercion to his framework.[8]

Although the analysis here provides no definitive answers for the debate on the characteristics of an effective mediator, it does underscore the partial effectiveness of power mediation as a technique in environments typically believed to be ripe for purely coercive interventions. In evaluating third-party management techniques in international conflicts, William Dixon presents two criteria to determine the effectiveness of the third parties: assessing whether the presence of particular crisis management efforts prevented further escalation of a conflict; and whether those efforts tended to promote peaceful settlements.[9] The U.S.-led third party proved to be effective in South Asia inasmuch as it prevented escalation and achieved crisis termination, but it consistently failed to address larger disputes underpinning these crises.

In terms of Washington's ability to achieve crisis de-escalation, manipulative leverage seems to trump the need for third-party impartiality and trust of the conflicting parties in the mediator.[10] Both India and Pakistan remained suspicious of American intentions and designs throughout the decade spanning the three examined South Asian crises but they still engaged with U.S. crisis management efforts. This confirms the argument in a strand of mediation literature that a lack of better alternatives is a more important consideration than impartiality and trustworthiness for conflicting parties to accept a mediator.[11] Overall though, South Asia's experience seems to conform more closely to Kyle Beardsley's view that by forcing an agreement or consent to end immediate tensions, mediation makes it more likely that the unsatisfied party will later renege on its commitments.[12] Pakistan has failed to follow through on its crisis-time promises to ensure a permanent end to anti-India terrorism as deeper India-Pakistan disputes have lingered on.

The analysis also extends application of the still nascent unipolarity theory to regional nuclear crises and argues that nuclear proliferation adds to the demands on the unipole. It accounts for the unipole's near-compulsion to engage, but also illustrates the limitations of its role in this context, irrespective of the broader global strategy it may be pursuing to maintain its preeminence in the world.[13] Evidence from the South Asian case studies also confirms the unipole's interest in seeking out, and where possible coordinating with, other strong powers that, in turn, tend to rally behind the unipole's de-escalation agenda ahead of any incentives to undermine its influence. The examination of non–South Asian prototypes has further highlighted the importance of these other third-party actors in situations where one of the antagonists is estranged from the unipole. Overall, as Yusuf and Kirk note, "a less-appreciated feature of the nuclear revolution could be that it significantly attenuates incentives for greater power rivals to compete through regional proxies when the latter possess nuclear weapons, and instead creates a basic common interest in preventing potentially catastrophic escalation."[14] Crucially, this feature also takes away the regional rivals' alternative alignment options they could otherwise use to offset the unipole's leverage.

The emphasis on the role of multiple third parties in affecting de-escalation highlights the relevance of Morgan's "collective actor" framework in post–Cold War nuclear contexts.[15] The analysis here substantiates the utility of the "international-hegemony model," one of Morgan's organizational options for collective-actor security management that sees a hegemon allowing a collective actor to play a consequential role in crises. Incidentally, Morgan, arguing that the hegemon would not be willing to share its role with other actors in this manner, has dismissed this option as largely theoretical.[16]

Finally, brokered bargaining casts a shadow on the credibility of U.S. security guarantees to regional allies in nuclearized environments. These contexts will tend to pit the United States' role of defender of its allies against its role as third-party mediator. U.S. signals to manage the expectations of allies under its security umbrella prior to crises would be important to prevent these states from feeling emboldened and increasing the risk of escalation by acting provocatively in anticipation of U.S. support. This may dampen concerns about ambitious allies aggressing against U.S. wishes in a crisis. But the allies may feel the need to resort to self-help during crises or their adversaries may seek to take advantage of the U.S. predicament by exhibiting belligerence to force it to fully reveal its intentions.

The literature already points to credibility problems for U.S. extended deterrence in the post–Cold War era. However, these concerns flow from the United States' presumed lack of strategic interest to intervene on behalf of its protégés in the absence of competing superpower intervention.[17] The analysis here suggests instead that the stakes involved in any nuclear crisis will force the United States to intervene, but that its credibility to fully back the protégé will be suspect due to its compulsion to play defender and third party simultaneously. This dynamic may leave U.S. allies nervous about their patron's ability to defend them. The recourse of nonnuclear allies such as Japan and South Korea could have implications for nuclear proliferation down the road.

Policy Implications

In highlighting the importance of third-party mediation for regional nuclear crisis management, this book argues that practitioners working to reduce the risks of escalation in nuclear crises must not ignore the utility of third-party actors in reducing tensions. The argument is not intended to question the desirability or efficacy of bilateral escalation control per se. Nor does it necessarily present the trilateral crisis management framework as optimal. But the findings of this work do caution against efforts to artificially force bilateral crisis management roles upon the regional antagonists, for instance, by explicitly challenging India's and Pakistan's implied belief that the United States will save them every time as a means of getting them to invest in stronger bilateral protocols.[18] While doing so could help address the earlier-identified moral hazard problem to some extent, it is a highly risky proposition.[19] Instead of prompting the antagonists to focus on strengthening bilateral mechanisms, the expected absence of third parties could prompt them to try even harder to attract external actors by exhibiting excessive provocativeness, or force them into self-help mode. Both would end up adding to the risks of escalation.

To the contrary, crisis management would benefit greatly if the virtual inevitability of U.S. and other third-party involvement were accepted and if regional nuclear rivals also moved beyond any psychological or rhetorical hang-ups about acknowledging their propensity to utilize third-party presence to their advantage. U.S. policy makers must accept that they would have to continue drawing on their policy machinery's bureaucratic impulses to engage in nuclear crisis environments abroad irrespective of their geostrategic interests and alliance considerations. Other strong powers should also internalize their likely roles in promoting de-escalation. The Indian strategic elite must also move beyond its apathy toward third-party mediation in India-Pakistan affairs, at least during crisis moments. Many of them detest the proposition that India keenly used third-party channels in the post-1998 crises with Pakistan, or that it made concessions in return for third-party support.[20] Such a stance unnecessarily adds to the signaling confusion during crises by forcing Indian leaders to posture differently to external actors versus their domestic audience.

There is need for a holistic third-party policy approach to crises between regional nuclear powers. This must focus on three tasks: crisis prevention; efforts to ensure that the conflicting parties prefer using third-party crisis mediation ahead of employing force unilaterally; and efforts to minimize the potency of instability-inducing factors that make escalation likelier in any given crisis situation.

Crisis Prevention
The most assured way to prevent a crisis is through dispute resolution. Since the third party is likely to be hamstrung during a crisis given its compulsion to pursue the tactical objective of de-escalation above all else, it must prioritize deeper strategic engagement to incentivize and assist dispute resolution efforts of the antagonists during peacetime. In the South Asian context, outstanding India-Pakistan territorial disputes—Kashmir being the most crucial—underlie tensions, including motivations for anti-India terrorism from Pakistani soil.[21] Their resolution must therefore be prioritized. As a first step, the United States should consider a more active role in encouraging an uninterrupted India-Pakistan dialogue on Kashmir.

In parallel, the United States should work to eliminate incentives for any actor to provoke crises. Both crisis-time choices and post-crisis diplomacy can help achieve this. Every time the de-escalation agenda in a crisis coincides with the third party's opposition to the provoker's stance, the right message is conveyed. The Kargil crisis, for instance, involved an obvious rejection of an effort by a nuclear state to revise territorial boundaries through crisis-creation. Pakistani military officers realize this and privately acknowledge that the world will be even less sympathetic if Pakistan attempts such direct interventions again. The Kargil and twin peaks experiences also lend themselves to a broader observation: not only is the state actor responsible for initiating the brinkmanship exercise likely to fail in achieving its crisis objectives, but it will also incur reputational costs in the process. In addition, the Mumbai crisis points to restrained and prudent behavior as a viable alternative to risk manipulation to attract third-party support.

The third party also ought to consider post-crisis actions to raise the costs for provokers while providing rewards to the victims. The provoker should be left feeling that, in the end, it lost out even if it managed to escape the crisis with a face saver; the victim must believe that its engagement with the third party paid off even though it may have exited the crisis with its objectives only partially fulfilled. The precise balance between the third party's post-crisis rewards and punishments would depend on the regional rivals in question, the broader regional interests of the third party, and its reputational considerations. Its task would be easiest when the provoker is clearly identifiable and is a foe situated in a region where the third party is not hamstrung in meting out punishment due to any other immediate interests. A plausible scenario would be the United States imposing post-crisis costs on a nuclear Iran for provoking a crisis with Israel. The third party's role becomes far more challenging in situations where the provoker happens to be its ally or friend or where it must rely on this actor to achieve other pressing national objectives. U.S. efforts in South Asia were complicated by the presence of an amorphous non-state provoker in the 2001–2002 and Mumbai crises. Pakistan's importance in Afghanistan added to the complexity. Washington was unable to get Pakistan to successfully achieve permanent elimination of anti-India terrorist outfits from its soil in the post-crisis periods.

Regardless of the U.S. position, Pakistan must make utmost efforts to defeat all forms of terrorism emanating from its territory. Pakistan has scored remarkable successes against domestic terrorism since the Mumbai crisis. Yet, the visible presence of Pakistan-based anti-India militant organizations and their leaders and a seeming lack of urgency and inability on the part of the Pakistani state to prosecute them has led to the world's continued suspicion regarding Pakistan's sincerity about eliminating these outfits.[22] Meanwhile, not only has the danger of fresh crises remained clear and present, but Pakistan's global reputation also continues to be greatly harmed, in turn affecting its ability to garner third-party diplomatic support for deeper dispute resolute.

Equally important, India and Pakistan must work together in defeating the terrorist menace. Absent a synergetic, or in fact a joint approach, non-state actors are likely to continue finding terrorism an attractive proposition. For terrorists, be they India-specific outfits like the Lashkar-e-Taiba) or transnational groups like the Islamic State or Al Qaeda, the dream scenario would be to land a "Muslim Pakistan" in war with a "Hindu India" to galvanize global Muslim sentiment against "infidels" while creating enough instability within Pakistan to engineer an Islamist takeover of the country. This would be catastrophic, not only for Pakistan but also for India and the rest of the world. One can also no longer rule out escalation of bilateral tensions over anti-Pakistan subversive actions by India's Hindu extremist elements who seem increasingly empowered and emboldened under Prime Minister Narendra Modi.[23] Pakistan already regularly alleges active Indian support of terrorist and secessionist outfits in Pakistan.[24] Pakistani citizens have also been targeted in terrorist attacks in India in the past by Hindu extremist outfits to derail India-Pakistan relations.[25] While these have thus far never created crisis situations, Pakistan has lately been more aggressive in raising its concerns about India.

In addition to unilateral domestic counterterrorism efforts aimed at preventing cross-border terrorist attacks in the first place, arguably, the most potent way to undermine terrorist agendas is for India and Pakistan to resurrect their bilateral commitment to insulate their broader relationship from terrorism.[26] If they avoid upping the ante in the face of terrorist strikes, crises will be prevented and non-state actors will sooner or later be forced to question the very rationale for such attacks. To a large extent, the two sides had managed this between the 2001–2002 and Mumbai crises. Had circumstances remained conducive for this to continue, an uninterrupted dialogue between the two sides might eventually have led them to a breakthrough. As it is, they were reportedly extremely close to resolving the Kashmir dispute just months before the Mumbai attacks occurred.[27]

A way forward could be to revitalize the existing joint India-Pakistan antiterrorism mechanism, set up in 2006 to provide a recognized institution for cooperation on investigations and prosecutions of cross-border terrorist incidents.[28] The scope of the collaboration could even be broadened to preventive intelligence that could help thwart terrorist designs.[29] Such information sharing has taken place through informal arrangements in the past. Most recently, the two sides set up a discreet information exchange channel between their national security advisors. In March 2016, Pakistan used this to tip India off about a possible attack at a festival in the Indian state of Gujarat.[30] The same year, it shared specific intelligence on infiltration of LeT-linked militants from Pakistan in time for India to act upon it.[31] However, these efforts have been ad hoc and are exceptions rather than the norm. Another aspect of cooperation could be to create a process to share evidence in real time in the wake of a terrorist attack to help fix attribution for the incident. External actors like the U.S. can also play a helpful role by offering real-time information to ascertain facts surrounding the incident. This is crucial given that past experiences have tended to lead India to reflexively blame the Pakistani state for significant terrorist incidents, especially in Kashmir. Pakistan does much the same by alleging Indian support for the perpetrators of major terrorist acts on its territory. This tendency increases the likelihood of escalation of tensions after serious terrorist episodes and creates a perverse incentive for militant outfits that stand to gain from instigating an India-Pakistan conflict to keep conducting attacks. More broadly, the United States and other third parties ought to help increase India's and Pakistan's capacity to prevent terrorism by further enhancing counterterrorism cooperation with them.

Possible crisis triggers other than terrorism must also be mitigated. For instance, India and Pakistan have engaged in constant, low-level tit-for-tat military activity on the LoC in Kashmir since 2013, in violation of a ceasefire they agreed to in 2003. These actions are usually authorized by local commanders and driven by tactical military considerations peculiar to the LoC but they still carry the potential for triggering a bilateral crisis or escalating an ongoing one. Both sides need to be encouraged to work toward formalizing a permanent ceasefire on the LoC and to develop robust protocols to prevent violations that could heighten tensions.[32]

Incentivizing Diplomacy over Resort to Military Force
The U.S. ability to create incentives for regional nuclear actors to bank on its mediation ahead of adopting autonomous crisis postures in its defiance is relatively greater when dealing with internationally mainstream states like India and Pakistan that have working relationships with the unipole and are not opposed to interacting with it. As discussed in the preceding chapter, globally isolated and recalcitrant states with no ties with the United States and other strong powers present a far greater crisis management challenge. The policy implication is a significant one: once a state has crossed the nuclear Rubicon, the only sensible policy for the international community is to keep it engaged rather than completely shunning it.[33] Forcing such a nuclear capable state into global isolation will only make it more difficult for third parties to influence its crisis (and peacetime) decisions. This suggests the need for a rethink of the

global push to isolate North Korea completely, in favor of continued reliance on diplomacy to find a solution to Pyongyang's belligerence and to prevent it from perfecting a capability that could directly target the U.S. mainland. A fully cornered North Korea may further anchor itself in a self-help mindset, making it even harder to mold its behavior in crises and in peacetime.

This observation leads to a fairly loaded proposition: if total isolation of states that manage to acquire nuclear weapons is counterproductive, it follows that the world's powers will be unable to punish such states as harshly as required to send a strong signal, and thereby deter, other aspirants from pursuing a nuclear capability. The conundrum ends up placing a high premium on prevention. Global powers need to pay far greater attention to raising the costs of aspiring states before they acquire operational nuclear weapons capabilities. The 2015 U.S.-Iran nuclear deal is an example of stringent diplomatic and economic pressure forcing a suspected nuclear aspirant to give up efforts it may have been making to acquire a weapons capability. But these actions—or indeed, even more punitive measures such as preventive use of force—would have to be taken not only against states estranged from the United States, but also against allies that may be dissatisfied with their patron's support and may therefore choose to pursue an independent nuclear capability. Moreover, in no event should third-party actors take steps that may increase the global demand for nuclear weapons. The U.S. military intervention in Iraq under the pretext of a presence of weapons of mass destruction, and more recently, the violent overthrow of Libyan dictator Muammar Gaddafi, who had abandoned his country's nuclear program, and the United States' inability to defend Ukraine, another state that voluntarily gave up its nuclear weapons after the Cold War in return for security guarantees against Russian aggression,[34] were unfortunate in this regard. The North Korean leadership regularly points to the examples of Iraq and Libya as justification for believing a nuclear capability is necessary for the survival of its regime.[35] Perhaps even more disconcerting were the Trump administration's early signals that it may prefer allies like Japan to acquire their own nuclear arsenal.[36] The United States must realize the negative consequences of such a development. Far from absolving America of the need to play sheriff in the region, Washington would still have to engage as a third party seeking de-escalation, albeit in a context marked by an emboldened ally less susceptible to its leverage than before. This would greatly complicate crisis management on the Korean peninsula; it would add to the mix the presently discountable possibility of Japan (or South Korea) acting as an ambitious protégé and triggering a conflict with North Korea. China's experience with North Korea is instructive in this regard. Having tolerated, and even indirectly enabled, North Korea's nuclear program for years,[37] Beijing now finds itself in an extremely awkward position, having to deal with a belligerent North Korean regime, and yet unable to isolate it completely to satisfy the world for fear that doing so would increase the risk of a nuclear catastrophe on its border.

Reducing the Risks of Escalation

Finally, in terms of reducing the potential risks of escalation associated with crisis situations, the third parties must avoid policies that incentivize either antagonist to adopt force structures, postures, or doctrines that weaken crisis stability. U.S. defense and civilian nuclear cooperation with India over the past decade, while serving broader U.S. geostrategic interests, has not only left Pakistan more paranoid about U.S. intentions, but it has prompted Pakistan to upgrade its own military capability at an accelerated pace. As Pakistan's conventional deterrent erodes in the years to come, its tendency to fall back on its nuclear capability will increase. While this may be inevitable, the United States should reconsider support (to both sides) for technologies whose value added is debatable but whose acquisition may still have obvious negative implications for South Asian strategic stability. U.S. interest in backing India's BMD shield would be one avenue worth reexamining in this regard.[38] The third party equally needs to oppose post-crisis measures by the regional rivals that make crisis stability tenuous, and consequently increase its crisis management challenges, in future iterations. India's and Pakistan's ability to develop Cold Start and Nasr, respectively, largely unopposed, speaks to the third party's inability to do so in South Asia.

Furthermore, virtually all ingredients of the traditionally recommended toolkit for bilateral risk reduction and strategic stability measures would also help increase the likelihood of successful escalation control in contexts marked by brokered bargaining. Efforts aimed at injecting some level of transparency in India's and Pakistan's nuclear policies and postures, strengthening of their command and control and safety and security protocols, continuing bilateral discussions on nuclear doctrines and on measures to prevent unauthorized and unintended launches, steps to reduce accidental crisis triggers, measures to limit dual-use missiles, strengthening of pre-notification protocols, and development of common understanding of notions of limited war while working to eliminate limited war options and deliberate exploitation of the sub-conventional space along the conflict spectrum, would all be useful.[39] Perhaps the most worrying reality in this realm is that the current trajectory of nuclear modernization in South Asia promises to eliminate the region's recessed force postures. Any move toward active deployment in peacetime will remove the crucial lag between a decision to mobilize nuclear forces and their actual employment. The situation begs for a non-deployment agreement between India and Pakistan, at least in peacetime, which would force them to undergo mobilization and deployment of nuclear forces during the crisis. This would reduce the dangers of haste, central to virtually all drivers of unintended escalation,[40] associated with ready-to-launch postures at the outset of the crisis. It would also provide the third party time and space to influence the deployment decision of the antagonists.

In addition, the South Asian crisis experience and the theoretical literature in the pessimist vein ought to be used to identify specific behavior patterns that increase the chances of inadvertent escalation within the trilateral framework. The case studies have pointed to a number of critical junctures where the risks were heightened considerably and could easily have led the antagonists to major war. These and other potential scenarios need to be better understood and behavior that tends to create them avoided by the antagonists and the third party when they engage in brokered bargaining.

There is also a need to ensure robust three-way communication channels during crises. It is important for India and Pakistan to develop a shared lexicon of terms and generate a common understanding of signaling, and for the third party to be equally involved, not only in absorbing this understanding but also making the antagonists comfortable with its own signaling language and style. Moreover, relevant officials representing the regional rivals must maintain open and direct communication channels with important third-party capitals during peacetime. These preexisting mechanisms and rapport should allow for relatively easier transition to crisis communication if and when the need arises.

On their part, third-party interlocutors must not underestimate the challenges involved in performing their role as go-betweens. The bureaucratic impulse within the U.S. system that quickly pushed decision making in the South Asian nuclear crises to the very top of the chain of command was important in ensuring coordinated messaging among U.S. crisis managers and between the United States and other third parties. Other third-party capitals ought to emulate this U.S. approach. There is also high premium on the ability of third parties to gather information from both antagonists, obtain timely private information from their own sources, and collate, sanitize, and utilize it with extreme discretion to further the crisis de-escalation agenda. This implies a need for the United States and other third parties to invest in maintaining robust intelligence gathering capabilities in geographical zones home to current or potential nuclear rivals. They also need to maintain deep regional expertise that allows their crisis managers to communicate in a manner that is sensitive to the norms, requirements, and limitations of the operative environments.

Third-party expertise in regions of interest is also needed to be able to predict potential crisis triggers, anticipate crises, and prepare the most suitable, context specific, crisis engagement strategies. Third parties can benefit in this regard by continuing to invest in simulations to study potential crisis trajectories and plan contingencies for various plausible scenarios.[41] Moreover, they need to establish mechanisms to retain institutional memory from their past crisis management experiences. The current U.S. system is ad hoc and often leaves crisis managers learning on the job amid crises.[42] One possible fix could be to convert the notional U.S. playbook on India-Pakistan crises U.S. principals drew upon during the Mumbai crisis into an actual, live document. This will be even more important going forward given that future South Asian crises promise to leave the third party with far more challenging crisis management tasks than in the past. In addition, the United States must invest in creating mechanisms that allow it to coordinate crisis strategies with other third parties in peacetime. This is especially needed for cases where the United States must lean on others to lead crisis management efforts with one of the antagonists. The United States should consider constituting third-party contact groups consisting of countries with leverage over the nuclear rivals in question.[43] These groups ought to plan for contingencies and be prepared to spring into collective action as soon as a crisis situation is believed to be brewing.

Brokered bargaining is inherently fraught with risk. Without a clear understanding of the drivers of crisis behavior and the options and tools available to ensure peaceful outcomes, regional rivals and third-party actors risk creating greater confusion and instability during crisis moments. These policy prescriptions can help alter the incentives, and in turn, behavior of regional nuclear rivals and the United States and other strong powers in ways that make crises less likely, and crisis management less challenging.

Avenues for Future Research

The analysis in this book is limited to a single dyad and the three cases that form the universe of crises between regional nuclear states. A diversity of dyads with a larger set of cases (thankfully absent) would have allowed for the posited theory to be tested in more varied contexts. That said, the use of the structured focus comparison method to investigate the case studies will allow additional comparisons to be drawn with ease, should fresh crises occur in South Asia or elsewhere.

This study has said little about two important policy questions. First, it does not systematically explore the intersection of nuclear weapons and terrorism. While the assumption of states being unitary actors applied to the South Asian context given that Pakistan had control over its crisis actions despite the complicating presence of non-state actors, this condition may not always hold in the future. The presence of a terrorist group with a high degree of operational independence and one that does not conform to a classic rational calculus will alter crisis dynamics fundamentally. A logical next step in terms of scholarship would be to examine the relevance of brokered bargaining in a context where a terrorist outfit interested in triggering a war is modeled as an independent fourth player.

Second, the analysis has limited the application of the brokered bargaining framework to dyads whose nuclear capabilities are *employable and known*. The crisis demeanor of the actors involved is dependent on their shared recognition of the realistic possibility of escalation to the nuclear level. Removing this condition would amount to a qualitatively different crisis environment, at least for the crisis player(s) that is oblivious to the presence of nuclear weapons. The model would now encompass opaque deterrence contexts. Since future nuclear powers may choose to maintain opacity to avoid international sanction unless forced otherwise, examining precisely how behavior patterns may be affected by less-than-full confidence in the presence of a nuclear dynamic for any or all of the involved actors holds significant policy relevance. There would be value in examining the various degrees of opacity and the likely behavior patterns and implications for crisis stability at each level.

Finally, even though America's global preponderance is unquestionable at present, the growing debate about the longevity of unipolarity points to the need for a study examining the impact on regional nuclear crisis management in a more multipolar global setting. What if China and Russia solidify their hegemonic reach in their extended neighborhoods in ways that begin to eclipse U.S. power in multiple regions? Would these countries still forego positional interests and line up behind the United States to manage a regional nuclear crisis in their backyards in this context? Or would they expect the United States to play second fiddle to them? Would the United States accept this? Would these strong powers end up creating real alternative alignment options for the rivals; how might this alter the crisis dynamic? The emphasis in this book on the special nature of a nuclear crisis moment would suggest that management of nuclearized crises may be one of the last things the world's strongest powers cease to converge on, even in a post-unipolar world. Yet, third-party configurations and specific approaches may become different in this transformed global context. This prediction needs more rigorous analysis.

This book has sought to enhance understanding of nuclear crisis behavior among regional powers nested in a unipolar global order. It has introduced brokered bargaining to explain crisis dynamics in such contexts and has argued that three-way bargaining may be the norm in regional nuclear crisis settings. It is crucial that policy makers internalize this lesson and pursue options to minimize the risks associated with the trilateral framework. Their ability to prevent nuclear war in future crises may depend on it.

Appendix

List of Interviews

Richard Armitage, U.S. Deputy Secretary of State, 2001–2005. November 14, 2014; Washington, DC.

Rana Banerji, former Special Secretary, Cabinet Secretariat, India. March 21, 2013; New Delhi.

Salman Bashir, Foreign Secretary of Pakistan, 2008–2012, and Pakistan's High Commissioner to India, 2012–2014. October 26, 2016; Washington, DC.

Donald Camp, U.S. Deputy Assistant Secretary of State for South Asia, 2001–2004. June 14, 2013; Washington, DC.

Wendy Chamberlain, U.S. Ambassador to Pakistan, 2001–2002. June 12, 2013; Washington, DC.

Satish Chandra, India's High Commissioner to Pakistan, 1995–1998, and Deputy National Security Adviser, 2002–2005. March 25, 2013; New Delhi (group interview with Sushant Sareen and Prabath Shukla).

Shamila Chaudhary, Director for Afghanistan and Pakistan, U.S. National Security Council, 2010–2011. June 12, 2013; Washington, DC.

Shahzad Chaudhry, Director General Air Force Strategic Command, Pakistan, 2001–2005. June 17, 2013; Copenhagen.

Paolo Cotta-Ramusino, Secretary General, Pugwash Conferences on Science and World Affairs, 2002–present. March 8, 2014; interview by Skype.

Amarjit S. Dulat, Secretary, Research and Analysis Wing, India, 1999–2000. March 22, 2013; New Delhi.

Mahmud Durrani, Pakistan's Ambassador to the United States, 2006–2008, and National Security Adviser, 2008–2009. May 14, 2013 and August 18, 2016; Lahore (2013) and Rawalpindi (2016).

Tariq Fatemi, Special Assistant to the Pakistani Prime Minister on Foreign Affairs, 2013–2017, and Additional Secretary in the office of the Prime Minister, 1998–1999. February 25, 2014; Islamabad.

Sajit Gandhi, Foreign Affairs Officer, U.S. Department of State, 2004–2010. June 13, 2013; Washington, DC.

Tariq Waseem Ghazi, Commander V Corps, Pakistan Army, 2001–2004. June 18, 2013; Copenhagen.

Anish Goel, Director for South Asia, U.S. National Security Council, 2008–2011. November 3, 2017; Washington, DC.

Stephen J. Hadley, U.S. National Security Advisor, 2005–2009. June 6, 2013; Washington, DC.

Ejaz Haider, senior Pakistani journalist and security expert. August 15, 2016; interview by phone.

Husain Haqqani, Pakistan's Ambassador to the United States, 2008–2011. June 27, 2016; Washington, DC.

Michael Hayden, Director, U.S. Central Intelligence Agency, 2006–2009. December 10, 2015; Washington, DC.

Karl F. Inderfurth, U.S. Assistant Secretary of State for South Asian Affairs, 1997–2001. June 13, 2013; Washington, DC.

Jalil Abbas Jilani, Foreign Secretary of Pakistan, 2012–2013, and Pakistan's Ambassador to the United States, 2013–2017. December 11, 2017; interview by phone.

Manoj Joshi, senior Indian journalist. March 23, 2013; New Delhi (group interview with C. Raja Mohan, Pranab D. Samanta, and Praveen Swami).

Vivek Katju, Joint Secretary, Ministry of External Affairs, India, 1999, and former Indian Ambassador. March 23, 2013; New Delhi.

Dhruv C. Katoch, former Director, Center for Land Warfare Studies, and former Indian army officer. March 25, 2013; New Delhi (roundtable organized at the Delhi Policy Group for discussion of this research).

Ashfaq Parvez Kayani, Chief of Army Staff, Pakistan Army, 2007–2013. August 18, 2016; Rawalpindi.

Aziz Ahmed Khan, Pakistan's High Commissioner to India, 2003–2006. February 6, 2014; interview by phone.

Feroz H. Khan, Director, Arms Control and Disarmament Affairs, Strategic Plans Division, Pakistan, 1999–2001. June 16, 2013 and March 9, 2014; Copenhagen (2013) and by phone (2014).

Riaz Muhammad Khan, Foreign Secretary of Pakistan, 2005–2008. June 18, 2013; Copenhagen.

Shamshad Ahmad Khan, Foreign Secretary of Pakistan, 1997–2000. April 23, 2013; Lahore.

Riaz Khokhar, Pakistan's Ambassador to the United States, 1997–1999, and Foreign Secretary of Pakistan, 2002–2005. May 9, 2013; Islamabad.

Khalid Kidwai, Director General, Strategic Plans Division, Pakistan, 2000–2014. July 10, 2013; Rawalpindi.

Michael Krepon, American nonproliferation expert. June 5, 2013; Washington, DC.

Radha Kumar, Indian security expert. March 25, 2013; New Delhi (roundtable organized at the Delhi Policy Group for discussion of this research).

A. S. Lamba, Vice Chief of Army Staff, Indian Army, 2010–2011. July 18, 2013; Bangkok.

Peter R. Lavoy, Special Assistant to the President and Senior Director for South Asia, U.S. National Security Council, 2015–2017. November 10, 2014 and June 1, 2017; Washington, DC.

Maleeha Lodhi, Pakistan's Ambassador to the United States, 1999–2002. August 7, 2013; Islamabad.

Thomas F. Lynch III, Special Assistant to U.S. Chairman Joint Chiefs of Staff, Michael Mullen, 2008–2010. June 14, 2013; Washington, DC.

Tariq Majid, Chairman, Joint Chiefs of Staff Committee, Pakistan Army, 2007–2010. May 13, 2013; Lahore.

Fali Homi Major, Chief of Air Staff, Indian Air Force, 2007–2009. August 10, 2014; interview by phone and e-mail.

Achal Malhotra, former Indian Ambassador. March 25, 2013: New Delhi (roundtable organized at the Delhi Policy Group for discussion of this research).

Shahid Malik, Pakistan's High Commissioner to India, 2006–2012. May 21, 2013, August 8, 2013, and August 31, 2016; Lahore.

V. P. Malik, Chief of Army Staff, Indian Army, 1997–2000. January 6, 2017; interview by e-mail.

Lalit Mansingh, Foreign Secretary of India, 1999–2001, and India's Ambassador to the United States, 2001–2004. June 18, 2013; Copenhagen.

Raja Menon, former Indian navy officer and strategic expert. June 17, 2013; Copenhagen.

Shiv Shankar Menon, Foreign Secretary of India, 2006–2009, and India's National Security Adviser, 2011–2014. September 6, 2016; interview by Skype.

William B. Milam, U.S. Ambassador to Pakistan, 1998–2001. June 7, 2013; Washington, DC.

C. Raja Mohan, senior Indian journalist. March 23, 2013; New Delhi (group interview with Manoj Joshi, Pranab D. Samanta, and Praveen Swami).

Cameron Munter, U.S. Ambassador to Pakistan, 2010–2012. May 26, 2013; interview by Skype.

Milan Naidu, Vice Chief of Army Staff, Indian Army, 2007–2009. November 21, 2014; interview by Skype.

Polly Nayak, American strategic expert. June 15, 2013; interview by phone.

John Negroponte, U.S. Deputy Secretary of State, 2007–2009. December 4, 2014; Washington, DC.

Satyabrata Pal, India's High Commissioner to Pakistan, 2006–2009. August 7, 2014; Noida, India.

G. Parthasarthy, India's High Commissioner to Pakistan, 1998–2000. July 18, 2013; Bangkok.

Anne W. Patterson, U.S. Ambassador to Pakistan, 2007–2010. June 14, 2013; interview by phone.

Balli S. Pawar, former Indian army officer. March 25, 2013; New Delhi (roundtable organized at the Delhi Policy Group for discussion of this research).

George Perkovich, American nonproliferation expert. April 15, 2015; Washington, DC.

Leena Ponnappa, India's Deputy National Security Adviser, 2007–2009. March 25, 2013; New Delhi (roundtable organized at the Delhi Policy Group for discussion of this research).

Ashraf Jehangir Qazi, Pakistan's High Commissioner to India, 1997–2002. December 16, 2015; Islamabad.

Shah Mahmood Qureshi, Foreign Minister of Pakistan, 2008–2011. July 22, 2010; Islamabad.

Nirupama Rao, Foreign Secretary of India, 2009–2011, and India's Ambassador to the United States, 2011–2013. December 20, 2017; interview by e-mail.

Sherry Rehman, Federal Minister for Information and Broadcasting, Pakistan, 2008–2009. February 9, 2014; interview by phone.

Condoleezza Rice, U.S. National Security Advisor, 2001–2005, and Secretary of State, 2005–2009. March 4, 2016; interview by phone.

Bruce Riedel, former CIA official and Special Assistant to the President and Senior Director for Near East and South Asian Affairs, U.S. National Security Council, 2001–2002. April 30, 2015; Washington, DC.

Arun Sahgal, former Indian army officer. March 25, 2013; New Delhi (roundtable organized at the Delhi Policy Group for discussion of this research).

Naeem Salik, Director, Arms Control and Disarmament Affairs, Strategic Plans Division, Pakistan, 2001–2005. March 9, 2014; interview by Skype.

Tamanna Salikuddin, Political Officer, U.S. Embassy, Islamabad, 2008–2009, and Director of Afghanistan and Pakistan, U.S. National Security Council, 2011–2013. June 14, 2013; Washington, DC.

Pranab D. Samanta, senior Indian journalist. March 23, 2013; New Delhi (group interview with Manoj Joshi, C. Raja Mohan, and Praveen Swami).

Shyam Saran, Foreign Secretary of India, 2004–2006. August 8, 2014; New Delhi.

Sushant Sareen, Indian strategic expert. March 25, 2013; New Delhi (group interview with Satish Chandra and Prabath Shukla).

Prabath Shukla, former Indian Ambassador. March 25, 2013; New Delhi (group interview with Satish Chandra and Sushant Sareen).

Kanwal Simbal, Foreign Secretary of India, 2002–2003. March 25, 2013; New Delhi (roundtable organized at the Delhi Policy Group for discussion of this research).

Aditya Singh, former Indian army officer and member of the National Security

Advisory Board, 2008–2010. March 25, 2013; New Delhi (roundtable organized at the Delhi Policy Group for discussion of this research).

Arun K. Singh, India's Ambassador to the United States, 2015 2016. November 22, 2017; interview by Skype.

K. C. Singh, former Indian Ambassador. March 25, 2013; New Delhi (roundtable organized at the Delhi Policy Group for discussion of this research).

David Smith, U.S. defense attaché, Islamabad, 1994–1997 and 2000–2003. November 6, 2014; Istanbul.

Vishnu Som, senior Indian journalist. June 24, 2017; interview by phone.

Vikram Sood, Secretary, Research and Analysis Wing, India, 2001–2003. January 12, 2017; interview by phone.

Praveen Swami, senior Indian journalist. March 23, 2013; New Delhi (group interview with Manoj Joshi, C. Raja Mohan, and Pranab D. Samanta).

Strobe Talbott, U.S. Deputy Secretary of State, 1994–2001. November 19, 2014; Washington, DC.

B. G. Verghese, senior Indian journalist and member of the Kargil Review Committee. March 25, 2013; New Delhi (roundtable organized at the Delhi Policy Group for discussion of this research).

Mark Webber, Special Assistant to the President and Senior Director for South and Central Asian Affairs, U.S. National Security Council, 2007–2009. June 14, 2013; Washington, DC.

Thomas West, Special Assistant to the Under Secretary for Political Affairs, U.S. Department of State, 2008–2010, and Director of Afghanistan and Pakistan, U.S. National Security Council, 2012–2014. June 14, 2013; Washington, DC.

Joshua T. White, Senior Advisor and Director for South Asian Affairs, U.S. National Security Council, 2015–2017. June 5, 2017; Washington, DC.

Edward Wittenstein, Special Assistant to U.S. Deputy Secretary of State John Negroponte, 2006–2009. October 31, 2014; interview by Skype.

Asif Ali Zardari, President of Pakistan, 2008–2013. February 10, 2016; Washington, DC.

Notes

Introduction

1 Jonathan Marcus, "Analysis: The World's Most Dangerous Place," BBC News, March 23, 2000.

2. Kenneth N. Waltz, "The Stability of a Bipolar World," *Daedalus* 93, 3 (1964): 888.

3. Stephen G. Brooks and William Wohlforth, *World Out of Balance: International Relations and the Challenge of American Primacy* (Princeton, NJ: Princeton University Press, 2008), 27–28.

4. Nuno P. Monteiro, *Theory of Unipolar Politics* (New York: Cambridge University Press, 2014), 123–26.

5. Individually, China is the only country with the economic resources to develop power projection capabilities approximating those of a superpower, but it has little interest in subverting the international political and economic order that it greatly depends on and benefits from. It has therefore deliberately avoided such investments at an accelerated pace, instead signaling its willingness to compete with the United States under the unipolar umbrella. Ho-fung Hung, *The China Boom: Why China Will Not Rule the World* (New York: Columbia University Press, 2016); Monteiro, *Theory of Unipolar Politics*, 126–43. Also see Stephen G. Brooks and William C. Wohlforth, "The Once and Future Superpower: Why China Won't Overtake the United States," *Foreign Affairs* 95, 3 (May–June 2016): 91–104.

6. India controls 45 percent of the erstwhile Jammu and Kashmir state's territory, Pakistan holds 35 percent, and China is in control of the remaining 20 percent. "Kashmir Fast Facts," CNN, March 31, 2016. Part of the territory

under China's control was ceded to it by Pakistan in 1963 under a bilateral agreement.

7. See Victoria Schofield, *Kashmir in Conflict: India, Pakistan and the Unending War* (London: I. B. Tauris, 2003); Sumit Ganguly, *Conflict Unending: India-Pakistan Tensions Since 1947* (New York: Columbia University Press, 2002).

8. On the 1971 war and the events surrounding it, see Richard Sisson and Leo E. Rose, *War and Secession: Pakistan, India, and the Creation of Bangladesh* (Berkeley: University of California Press, 1990).

9. On the Pakistani security establishment's (principally its army's) fixation on India, see Shuja Nawaz, *Pakistan, Its Army, and the Wars Within* (Karachi: Oxford University Press, 2008); T. V. Paul, *The Warrior State: Pakistan in the Contemporary World* (New York: Oxford University Press, 2014); C. Christine Fair, *Fighting to the End: The Pakistan Army's Way of War* (New York: Oxford University Press, 2014).

10. Feroz H. Khan, *Eating Grass: The Making of the Pakistani Bomb* (Stanford, CA: Stanford University Press, 2012), 75–92.

11. These included skirmishes on the Siachen glacier in the north of Kashmir in 1984, which has been occupied by India since; a mini-crisis sparked by fears of an Indian preventive strike on Pakistan's nuclear facilities later in the year; the Brasstacks crisis of 1987, which was triggered by a threatening Indian military exercise near the international border; and the "compound crisis" of 1990, which was fueled by Indian accusations of Pakistani support of an armed insurgency in Indian Kashmir. On the background of the Siachen dispute, see Raspal S. Khosa, "The Siachen Glacier Dispute: Imbroglio on the Roof of the World," *Contemporary South Asia* 8, 2 (July 1999): 187–209. Also see Robert G. Wirsing, *Pakistan's Security under Zia, 1977–1988: The Policy Imperatives of a Peripheral Asian State* (New York: St. Martin's Press, 1991), 143–94. On the "preventive strikes" episode, see Sumit Ganguly and Devin T. Hagerty, *Fearful Symmetry: India-Pakistan Crisis in the Shadow of Nuclear Weapons* (Seattle: University of Washington Press, 2005), 44–67. On Brasstacks, see Kanti P. Bajpai et al., *Brasstacks and Beyond: Perception and Management of Crisis in South Asia* (New Delhi: Manohar, 1995). On the compound crisis, see P. R. Chari, Pervaiz I. Cheema, and Stephen P. Cohen, *Perception, Politics and Security in South Asia: The Compound Crisis of 1990* (London: Routledge, 2003); P. R. Chari, Pervaiz I. Cheema, and Stephen P. Cohen, *Four Crises and a Peace Process: American Engagement in South Asia* (Washington, DC: Brookings Institution Press, 2007), 80–117.

12. On the Indo-Soviet relationship during the Cold War, see Robert C. Horn, *Soviet-Indian Relations: Issues and Influence* (New York: Praeger, 1982); Peter J. S. Duncan, *The Soviet Union and India* (London: Routledge, 1989).

13. Chari, Cheema, and Cohen, *Four Crises and a Peace Process*, 218.

14. See Teresita C. Schaffer, *India and the United States in the 21st Century: Reinventing Partnership* (Washington, DC: CSIS Press, 2010).

15. On the U.S.-Pakistan relationship until the turn of the century, see Dennis Kux, *The United States and Pakistan, 1947–2000: Disenchanted Allies* (Washington, DC: Woodrow Wilson Center Press, 2001).

16. Elisabeth Bumiller and Jane Perlez, "Pakistan's Spy Agency Is Tied to Attack on U.S. Embassy," *New York Times*, September 22, 2011. More generally, on the U.S.-Pakistan relationship since 9/11, see Daniel S. Markey, *No Exit from Pakistan: America's Tortured Relationship with Islamabad* (New York: Cambridge University Press, 2013).

17. Pervez Musharraf, *In the Line of Fire: A Memoir* (New York: Free Press, 2006), 202.

18. For some of these concerns, as the West sees them, see Bruno Tertrais, *Pakistan's Nuclear Programme: A Net Assessment*, Recherches and Documents no. 04/2012 (Paris: Fondation pour la Recherche Strategique, June 13, 2012); Christopher Clary, *Thinking about Pakistan's Nuclear Security in Peacetime, Crisis and War*, Occasional Paper no. 12 (New Delhi: Institute for Defence Studies and Analyses, September 2010). Also see Henry D. Sokolski, ed., *Pakistan's Nuclear Future: Worries Beyond War* (Carlisle, PA: U.S. Army War College, 2008).

19. China and India have remained strategic rivals throughout and continue to have active border disputes. Most notably, they fought a major war in 1962. For a comprehensive recounting of the war, see Steven Hoffmann, *India and the China Crisis* (Berkeley: University of California Press, 1990).

20. Howard B. Schaffer and Teresita C. Schaffer, *How Pakistan Negotiates with the United States: Riding the Roller Coaster* (Washington, DC: United States Institute of Peace Press, 2011), 23–24. For a typical, positive Pakistani statist view of Sino-Pakistan relations, see Ahmed H. Shah and Ishtiaq A. Choudhry, "Pak-China Diplomatic and Military Relations: An Analysis," *Berkeley Journal of Social Science* 3 (Spring 2013). For a more objective view of the contours of the relationship, see Andrew Small, *The Pakistan-China Axis: Asia's New Geopolitics* (New York: Oxford University Press, 2015).

21. Small, *The China-Pakistan Axis*, 27–46. Also see Khan, *Eating Grass*.

22. Ashley J. Tellis, "The Merits of Dehyphenation: Explaining U.S. Success in Engaging India and Pakistan," *Washington Quarterly* 31, 4 (Autumn 2008): 21–42.

23. For the role of moral hazard in third-party interventions, see Alan J. Kuperman, "The Moral Hazard of Humanitarian Intervention: Lessons from the Balkans," *International Studies Quarterly* 52, 1 (March 2008): 49–80; Timothy W. Crawford and Alan J. Kuperman, eds., *Gambling on Humanitarian Intervention: Moral Hazard, Rebellion and Civil War* (Abingdon: Routledge, 2006).

24. Scott Sagan points to the "vulnerability/invulnerability paradox" to argue that moves like mating and dispersal of nuclear assets that may make an arsenal more likely to survive a decapitating first strike in a crisis situation increase the vulnerability of the arsenal to terrorist breaches. Scott D. Sagan, "Introduction: Inside Nuclear South Asia," in *Inside Nuclear South Asia*, ed. Scott D. Sagan (Stanford, CA: Stanford University Press, 2009), 16.

Chapter 1

1. Vipin Narang, *Nuclear Strategy in the Modern Era: Regional Powers and International Conflict* (Princeton, NJ: Princeton University Press, 2014), 2–3, 5–6.

2. Arvind Kumar, "Theories of Deterrence and Nuclear Deterrence in the Subcontinent," in *The India-Pakistan Nuclear Relationship: Theories of Deterrence and International Relations*, ed. E. Sridharan (New Delhi: Routledge, 2007), 254.

3. For a discussion of definitional issues regarding crises, see P. R. Chari, Pervaiz I. Cheema, and Stephen P. Cohen, *Four Crises and a Peace Process: American Engagement in South Asia* (Washington, DC: Brookings Institution Press, 2007), 4–8; Charles F. Hermann, "International Crisis as a Situational Variable," in *International Politics and Foreign Policy: A Reader in Research and Theory*, ed. James N. Rosenau (New York: Free Press, 1969), 411–16; Oran R. Young, *The Politics of Force: Bargaining during International Crises* (Princeton, NJ: Princeton University Press, 1968), 6–15. For other important works on international crises, see Michael Brecher and Jonathan Wilkenfeld, *A Study of Crisis* (Ann Arbor: University of Michigan Press, 1997); Michael Brecher, *Crises in World Politics: Theory and Reality* (New York: Pergamon, 1993); Glenn H. Snyder and Paul Diesing, *Conflict Among Nations: Bargaining, Decision Making, and System Structure in International Crises* (Princeton, NJ: Princeton University Press, 1977).

4. Dan Snodderly, ed., *Peace Terms: Glossary of Terms for Conflict Management and Peacebuilding* (Washington, DC: United States Institute of Peace Press, 2011), 17.

5. For seminal works on how the advent of nuclear weapons revolutionized thinking about crises and war, see Bernard Brodie, "War in the Atomic Age," in *The Absolute Weapon: Atomic Power and World Order*, ed. Bernard Brodie (New York: Harcourt, Brace, 1946), 21–69; Bernard Brodie, "Implications for Military Policy," in *The Absolute Weapon: Atomic Power and World Order*, ed. Bernard Brodie (New York: Harcourt, Brace, 1946), 70–107; Robert Jervis, *The Meaning of Nuclear Revolution: Statecraft and the Prospect of Armageddon* (Ithaca, NY: Cornell University Press, 1989).

6. For classic writings on nuclear deterrence, see Bernard Brodie, *Strategy in the Missile Age* (Princeton, NJ: Princeton University Press, 1959); Glenn

H. Snyder, *Deterrence and Defense: Toward a Theory of National Security* (Princeton, NJ: Princeton University Press, 1961); William W. Kaufmann, "The Requirements of Deterrence," in *Military Policy and National Security*, ed. William W. Kaufmann (Princeton, NJ: Princeton University Press, 1956), 12–38; Herman Kahn, *On Thermonuclear War* (Princeton, NJ: Princeton University Press, 1960); Thomas C. Schelling, *The Strategy of Conflict* (Cambridge, MA: Harvard University Press, 1960); Thomas C. Schelling, *Arms and Influence* (New Haven, CT: Yale University Press, 1966). For more recent perspectives, see T. V. Paul, Patrick M. Morgan, and James J. Wirtz, eds., *Complex Deterrence: Strategy in the Global Age* (Chicago: University of Chicago Press, 2009); Keith B. Payne, *Deterrence in the Second Nuclear Age* (Lexington: University Press of Kentucky, 1996); Patrick M. Morgan, *Deterrence Now* (Cambridge: Cambridge University Press, 2003).

7. Kenneth N. Waltz, *The Spread of Nuclear Weapons: More May Be Better*, Adelphi Paper 171 (London: International Institute for Strategic Studies, 1981). Also see Waltz's writings in Scott D. Sagan and Kenneth N. Waltz, *The Spread of Nuclear Weapons: A Debate Renewed* (New York: W.W. Norton, 2003), 3–45, 125–55.

8. Snyder, *Deterrence and Defense*, 239–40.

9. Ibid., 239; Schelling, *Arms and Influence*, 33 (and more generally, 18–34).

10. Robert J. Art, "To What Ends Military Power?" *International Security* 4, 4 (Spring 1980): 7–8. For the origins of the term "compellence," its comparison with deterrence, and its application in the Cold War context, see Schelling, *Arms and Influence*, 69–91.

11. For seminal works on the credibility-of-commitment issue, see Robert Jervis, *The Logic of Images in International Relations* (Princeton, NJ: Princeton University Press, 1970); Schelling, *Arms and Influence*, 35–91. Also see Frank C. Zagare and D. Marc Kilgour, *Perfect Deterrence* (Cambridge: Cambridge University Press, 2000), 65–81, 296–301.

12. See Snyder, *Deterrence and Defense*, 239–58.

13. Ibid., 246–49.

14. John J. Mearsheimer, *Conventional Deterrence* (Ithaca, NY: Cornell University Press, 1983), 18.

15. On the origins of MAD and its use in practice during the Cold War, see Henry D. Sokolski, ed., *Getting MAD: Nuclear Mutual Assured Destruction, Its Origins and Practice* (Carlisle, PA: U.S. Army War College, 2004).

16. Another solution to the credibility problem that informed nuclear strategizing during the Cold War was "limited war." Limited war theory envisioned a "war of endurance" where less than total destruction was to be inflicted on the opponent to raise its costs—enough to force it to back down but not so high that it would deem an all-out nuclear retaliation necessary. For a brief discussion of limited war and its theorists, see Arpit Rajain,

Nuclear Deterrence in Southern Asia: China, India and Pakistan (New Delhi: Sage Publications, 2005), 82–93. Also see Robert E. Osgood, *Limited War: The Challenge to American Strategy* (Chicago: University of Chicago Press, 1957); Robert E. Osgood, *Limited War Revisited* (Boulder, CO: Westview Press, 1979); Robert Powell, "Nuclear Deterrence and the Strategy of Limited Retaliation," *American Political Science Review* 83, 2 (June 1989): 503–19.

17. Young, *The Politics of Force*, 96–97; Snyder and Diesing, *Conflict Among Nations*, 27.

18. Schelling, *The Strategy of Conflict*, 187–203. Also see T. C. Schelling, "Nuclear Strategy in Europe," *World Politics* 14, 3 (April 1962): 421–25. On feigning irrationality, see Richard N. Lebow, *The Art of Bargaining* (Baltimore: Johns Hopkins University Press, 1996), 96.

19. On brinkmanship, see Schelling, *Arms and Influence*, 91, 99–105. Also see Schelling, *The Strategy of Conflict*, 199–201; Robert Jervis, "Why Nuclear Superiority Doesn't Matter," *Political Science Quarterly* 94, 4 (Winter 1979–1980): 617–33; Robert Powell, "The Theoretical Foundation of Strategic Nuclear Deterrence," *Political Science Quarterly* 100, 1 (1985): 75–96; Robert Powell, "Nuclear Brinkmanship with Two-Sided Incomplete Information," *American Political Science Review* 82, 1 (March 1988): 155–78; Robert Powell, "Nuclear Deterrence Theory, Nuclear Proliferation, and National Missile Defense," *International Security* 27, 4 (Spring 2003): 91–97.

20. Much of the crisis modeling aimed at understanding escalation and crisis stability dynamics has been premised on playing chicken. See, for example, Steven J. Brams and D. Mark Kilgour, "Threat Escalation and Crisis Stability: A Game-Theoretic Analysis," *American Political Science Review* 81, 3 (1987): 833–50.

21. Daniel S. Geller, "Nuclear Weapons, Deterrence, and Crisis Escalation," *Journal of Conflict Resolution* 34, 2 (1990): 293–95. For a discussion of the effectiveness of nuclear coercion, see Matthew Kroenig, "Nuclear Superiority and the Balance of Resolve: Explaining Nuclear Crisis Outcomes," *International Organization* 67, 1 (2013): 141–71. For the opposite view, see Todd S. Sechser and Matthew Fuhrmann, *Nuclear Weapons and Coercive Diplomacy* (Cambridge: Cambridge University Press, 2017).

22. Robert Jervis, *The Illogic of American Nuclear Strategy* (Ithaca, NY: Cornell University Press, 1984), 11.

23. There is vast and diverse literature on the U.S. nuclear buildup and the evolution of U.S. nuclear strategy during the Cold War, the dilemmas facing American thinkers, strategists, and decision makers that shaped U.S. thinking, and critiques of the strategy. See Lawrence Freedman, *The Evolution of Nuclear Strategy* (London: Macmillan and the International Institute for Strategic Studies, 1989); James E. Goodby, *At the Borderline of Armageddon: How American Presidents Managed the Atom Bomb* (Lanham, MD: Rowman

& Littlefield, 2006); McGeorge Bundy, *Danger and Survival: Choices about the Bomb in the First Fifty Years* (New York: Random House, 1988); John Lewis Gaddis, *The Long Peace: Inquiries into the History of the Cold War* (New York: Oxford University Press, 1987); David Schwartzman, *Games of Chicken: Four Decades of U.S. Nuclear Policy* (New York: Praeger, 1988); David Alan Rosenberg, "The Origins of Overkill: Nuclear Weapons and American Strategy, 1945–1960," *International Security* 7, 4 (Spring 1983): 3–71; John Lewis Gaddis, *The Cold War: A New History* (New York: Penguin Books, 2005); Alexander L. George and Richard Smoke, *Deterrence in American Foreign Policy: Theory and Practice* (New York: Columbia University Press, 1974); Fred Desmond Ball and Jeffrey Richelson, eds., *Strategic Nuclear Targeting* (Ithaca, NY: Cornell University Press, 1986); Jervis, *The Illogic of American Nuclear Strategy*; Jervis, *The Meaning of Nuclear Revolution*.

24. Christoph Bluth, "Reconciling the Irreconcilable: Alliance Politics and the Paradox of Extended Deterrence in the 1960s," *Cold War History* 1, 2 (January 2001): 73–102; Stephen J. Cimbala, *Extended Deterrence: The United States and NATO Europe* (Lexington, MA: Lexington Books, 1987). Also see the suggested readings in note 23, above.

25. David O. Smith, "The US Experience with Tactical Nuclear Weapons: Lessons for South Asia," in *Deterrence Stability and Escalation Control in South Asia*, eds. Michael Krepon and Julia Thompson (Washington, DC: Henry L. Stimson Center, 2013), 73–74. Also see John J. Mearsheimer, "Nuclear Weapons and Deterrence in Europe," *International Security* 9, 3 (Winter 1984–1985): 19–46; David Holloway, "Nuclear Weapons and the Cold War in Europe," in *Imposing, Maintaining, and Tearing Open the Iron Curtain: The Cold War and East-Central Europe, 1945–1989*, eds. Mark Kramer and Vit Smetana (Lanham, MD: Lexington Books, 2013), 437–55.

26. For a discussion of the most significant Cold War nuclear crises, see Richard K. Betts, *Nuclear Blackmail and Nuclear Balance* (Washington, DC: Brookings Institution Press, 1987); Kurt Gottfried and Bruce G. Blair, *Crisis Stability and Nuclear War* (New York: Oxford University Press, 1988), 161–225.

27. For an authoritative firsthand account of the Cuban missile crisis, see Robert F. Kennedy, *Thirteen Days: A Memoir of the Cuban Missile Crisis* (New York: W.W. Norton, 1969). For a summary of the key developments and elements of behavior, see Betts, *Nuclear Blackmail and Nuclear Balance*, 109–23; Honoré M. Catudal, *Nuclear Deterrence: Does It Deter?* (Berlin: Berlin Verlag, 1985), 462–84. For a discussion of the risks that were not recognized at the time, see Len Scott and R. Gerald Hughes, eds., *The Cuban Missile Crisis: A Critical Appraisal* (New York: Routledge, 2015); Sheldon M. Stern, *The Week the World Stood Still: Inside the Secret Cuban Missiles Crisis* (Stanford, CA: Stanford University Press, 2005); Scott. D. Sagan, *The Limits of Safety:*

Organizations, Accidents, and Nuclear Weapons (Princeton, NJ: Princeton University Press, 1993), 53–155.

28. Betts, *Nuclear Blackmail and Nuclear Balance*, 83–109.

29. For a discussion of the conflict, see Thomas W. Robinson, "The Sino-Soviet Border Conflict," in *Diplomacy of Power: Soviet Armed Forces as a Political Instrument*, ed. Stephen S. Kaplan (with Michel Tatu et al.) (Washington, DC: Brookings Institution Press, 1981), 265–313; Thomas W. Robinson, "The Sino-Soviet Border Dispute: Background, Development, and the March 1969 Border Clashes," *American Political Science Review* 66, 4 (December 1972): 1175–1202.

30. Brodie, *Strategy in the Missile Age*, 397.

31. Robert Jervis, *Perception and Misperception in International Politics* (Princeton, NJ: Princeton University Press, 1976); Robert Jervis, Richard N. Lebow, and Janice G. Stein, *Psychology and Deterrence* (Baltimore: Johns Hopkins University Press, 1985); Scott D. Sagan, "The Perils of Proliferation: Organization Theory, Deterrence Theory and the Spread of Nuclear Weapons," *International Security* 18, 4 (Spring 1994): 66–107; Sagan and Waltz, *The Spread of Nuclear Weapons*, 46–87, 156–84; Barry R. Posen, *Inadvertent Escalation: Conventional War and Nuclear Risks* (Ithaca, NY: Cornell University Press, 1991), 1–27; Daniel Frei, *Risks of Unintentional Nuclear War* (Totawa, NJ: Allanheld, Osmun, 1983). For a definition of crisis stability, see James J. Wirtz, "Beyond Bipolarity: Prospects for Nuclear Stability after the Cold War," in *The Absolute Weapon Revisited: Nuclear Arms and the Emerging International Order*, eds. T. V. Paul, Richard J. Harknett, and James J. Wirtz (Ann Arbor: University of Michigan Press, 1998), 143. Also see Robert Powell, "Crisis Stability in the Nuclear Age," *American Political Science Review* 83, 1 (March 1989): 61–76.

32. On the role of reputation in deterrence contexts, see Jonathan Mercer, *Reputation and International Politics* (Ithaca, NY: Cornell University Press, 1996), 14–43. For a more general discussion of reputation in bargaining, see Fred C. Iklé, *How Nations Negotiate* (New York: Frederick A. Praeger, 1968), 76–86.

33. Snyder and Diesing, *Conflict Among Nations*, 188. On reputation for resolve, see Alex Weisiger and Keren Yarhi-Milo, "Revisiting Reputation: How Past Actions Matter in International Politics," *International Organization* 69 (Spring 2015): 473–95; Joshua D. Kertzer, *Resolve in International Politics* (Princeton, NJ: Princeton University Press, 2016).

34. Herman Kahn, *On Escalation: Metaphors and Scenarios* (Baltimore: Penguin Books, 1968). For examples of prominent Cold War literature on escalation, see Bernard Brodie, *Escalation and the Nuclear Option* (Princeton, NJ: Princeton University Press, 1966); Schelling, *The Strategy of Conflict*; Schelling, *Arms and Influence*; Richard Smoke, *War: Controlling Escalation*

(Cambridge, MA: Harvard University Press, 1977). Also see the suggested readings in note 23, above.

35. Michael Krepon, "Is Cold War Experience Applicable to South Asia?" in *Nuclear Risk Reduction in South Asia*, ed. Michael Krepon (New York: Palgrave Macmillan, 2004), 7–14. Also see Victor A. Kremenyuk, "The Cold War as Cooperation," in *From Rivalry to Cooperation: Russian and American Perspectives on the Post–Cold War Era*, eds. Manus I. Midlarsky, John A. Vasquez, and Peter V. Gladkov (New York: HarperCollins, 1994), 3–25; Allan S. Krass, *The United States and Arms Control: The Challenge of Leadership* (Westport, CT: Praeger, 1997), 9–27.

36. David Holloway, "Nuclear Weapons and the Escalation of the Cold War, 1945–1962," in *The Cambridge History of the Cold War*, eds. Melvyn P. Leffler and Odd Arne Westad (Cambridge: Cambridge University Press, 2010), 384.

37. Patrick M. Morgan and T. V. Paul, "Deterrence among Great Powers in an Era of Globalization," in *Complex Deterrence: Strategy in the Global Age*, eds. T. V. Paul, Patrick M. Morgan, and James J. Wirtz (Chicago: University of Chicago Press, 2009), 260–61; Lebow, *The Art of Bargaining*, 96.

38. Sagan, *The Limits of Safety*; Bruce G. Blair, *The Logic of Accidental Nuclear War* (Washington: DC: Brookings Institution Press, 1993).

39. Glenn H. Snyder, *Alliance Politics* (Ithaca, NY: Cornell University Press, 1997), 180–92; Glenn H. Snyder, "The Security Dilemma in Alliance Politics," *World Politics* 36, 4 (July 1984), 461–95.

40. Stephen L. Quackenbush, "Not Only Whether But Whom: Three-Party Extended Deterrence," *Journal of Conflict Resolution* 50, 4 (August 2006): 563. Also see Paul K. Huth, *Extended Deterrence and the Prevention of War* (New Haven, CT: Yale University Press, 1988), 28–55.

41. Timothy W. Crawford, "The Endurance of Extended Deterrence: Continuity, Change and Complexity in Theory and Policy," in *Complex Deterrence: Strategy in the Global Age*, eds. T. V. Paul, Patrick M. Morgan, and James J. Wirtz (Chicago: University of Chicago Press, 2009), 292.

42. Morgan and Paul, "Deterrence among Great Powers," 261.

43. Ralph B. Levering, *The Cold War: A Post–Cold War History* (Arlington Heights, IL: Harlan Davidson, 2005), 76–77.

44. Betts, *Nuclear Blackmail and Nuclear Balance*, 123–29; Gottfried and Blair, *Crisis Stability and Nuclear War*, 198–206.

45. Scott D. Sagan and Jeremi Suri, "The Madman Nuclear Alert: Secrecy, Signaling, and Safety in October 1969," *International Security* 27, 4 (Spring 2003): 152–53.

46. The most high-profile instance was the U.S. decision to dispatch an impressive naval taskforce including USS *Enterprise*, the world's largest nuclear aircraft carrier, to the Bay of Bengal as a show of strength to deter

Soviet-backed India in the 1971 India-Pakistan War that ultimately led to Pakistan's dismemberment. Asaf Siniver, *Nixon, Kissinger, and U.S. Foreign Policy Making: The Machinery of Crisis* (Cambridge: Cambridge University Press, 2008), 177–80; Henry A. Kissinger, *White House Years* (Boston: Little, Brown, 1979), 909–10.

47. Sharad Joshi, "The Practice of Coercive Diplomacy in the Post 9/11 Period" (PhD diss., School of Public and International Affairs, University of Pittsburgh, 2006), 26–27. For detailed discussions on the Laotian crisis and Vietnam intervention, see, respectively, David K. Hall, "The Laos Crisis, 1960–61," in *The Limits of Coercive Diplomacy: Laos, Cuba, Vietnam*, eds. Alexander L. George, David K. Hall, and William E. Simons (Boston: Little, Brown, 1971), 36–85; William E. Simons, "The Vietnam Intervention, 1964–65," in *The Limits of Coercive Diplomacy: Laos, Cuba, Vietnam*, eds. Alexander L. George, David K. Hall, and William E. Simons (Boston: Little, Brown, 1971), 144–210.

48. Rajain, *Nuclear Deterrence in Southern Asia*, 46–47; Kissinger, *White House Years*, 172.

49. Glenn H. Snyder, *Alliance Politics* (Ithaca, NY: Cornell University Press, 1997), 332–34.

50. Timothy W. Crawford, *Pivotal Deterrence: Third-Party Statecraft and the Pursuit of Peace* (Ithaca, NY: Cornell University Press, 2003), 18.

51. Ibid., 15–17.

52. Nuno P. Monteiro, *Theory of Unipolar Politics* (New York: Cambridge University Press, 2014).

53. Sumit Ganguly and Devin T. Hagerty, *Fearful Symmetry: India-Pakistan Crises in the Shadow of Nuclear Weapons* (Seattle: University of Washington Press, 2005).

54. Peter R. Lavoy, "Introduction: The Importance of the Kargil Conflict," in *Asymmetric Warfare in South Asia: The Causes and Consequences of the Kargil Conflict*, ed. Peter R. Lavoy (New York: Cambridge University Press, 2009), 29.

55. Robert Jervis, "What Do We Want to Deter and How Do We Deter It?" in *Turning Point: The Gulf War and U.S. Military Strategy*, eds. L. Benjamin Ederington and Michael J. Mazarr (Boulder, CO: Westview Press, 1994), 122–23.

56. Morgan, *Deterrence Now*, 172–202; Patrick M. Morgan, "Collective-Actor Deterrence," in *Complex Deterrence: Strategy in the Global Age*, eds. T. V. Paul, Patrick M. Morgan, and James J. Wirtz (Chicago: University of Chicago Press, 2009), 158–81.

57. Morgan, "Collective-Actor Deterrence," 163–64.

58. Crawford, *Pivotal Deterrence*, 5.

59. Ibid., 20–21.

60. Ibid., 37–40.

61. For this discussion, see ibid., 158–68.

62. Frank C. Zagare and D. Marc Kilgour, "The Deterrence-Versus-Restraint Dilemma in Extended Deterrence: Explaining British Policy in 1914," *International Studies Review* 8 (2006): 623–41.

63. See Devin T. Hagerty, *The Consequences of Nuclear Proliferation: Lessons from South Asia* (Cambridge: The MIT Press, 1998), 133–70.

64. Crawford, *Pivotal Deterrence*, 171–72.

65. Moeed Yusuf and Jason Kirk, "Keeping an Eye on South Asian Skies: America's Pivotal Deterrence in Nuclearized India-Pakistan Crises," *Contemporary Security Policy* 37, 2 (2016): 246–72.

66. Narang, *Nuclear Strategy in the Modern Era*.

67. Ibid., 15–17.

68. Ibid., 17–21.

69. C. Raja Mohan, "Drawing America into Kashmir," *Hindu*, June 6, 2002.

70. For example, S. Paul Kapur, *Dangerous Deterrent: Nuclear Weapons Proliferation and Conflict in South Asia* (Stanford, CA: Stanford University Press, 2007), 215n115; Bhumitra Chakma, "Escalation Control, Deterrence Diplomacy and America's Role in South Asia's Nuclear Crises," *Contemporary Security Policy* 33, 3 (2012): 573; Feroz H. Khan, "The Independence-Dependence Paradox: Stability Dilemmas in South Asia," *Arms Control Today* 33, 8 (October 2003); Andrew C. Winner and Toshi Yoshihara, *Nuclear Stability in South Asia* (n.p.: Institute for Foreign Policy Analysis, January 2002), 76; Robert Jervis, "Kargil, Deterrence, and International Relations Theory," in *Asymmetric Warfare in South Asia: The Causes and Consequences of the Kargil Conflict*, ed. Peter R. Lavoy (New York: Cambridge University Press, 2009), 396; Dinshaw Mistry, "Tempering Optimism about Nuclear Deterrence in South Asia," *Security Studies* 18, 1 (2009): 180–81; Chari, Cheema, and Cohen, *Four Crises and a Peace Process*, 217.

71. Jervis, "Kargil, Deterrence, and International Relations Theory," 396. Jervis makes this point specifically in the India-Pakistan context and predicts that the United States is likely to side with India each time Pakistan, the likely provoker, triggers a crisis.

72. See Chari, Cheema, and Cohen, *Four Crises and a Peace Process*, 99–108; P. R. Chari, *Nuclear Crisis, Escalation Control, and Deterrence in South Asia*, Working Paper 1.0 (Washington, DC: Henry L. Stimson Center, August 2003), 17.

73. Chari, Cheema, and Cohen, *Four Crises and a Peace Process*, 97–98; Hagerty, *The Consequences of Nuclear Proliferation*, 150–52.

74. Chari, Cheema, and Cohen, *Four Crises and a Peace Process*, 98; Hagerty, *The Consequences of Nuclear Proliferation*, 161–63.

75. Bhumitra Chakma, "South Asia's Nuclear Deterrence and the USA," in *The Politics of Nuclear Weapons in South Asia*, ed. Bhumitra Chakma (Burlington, VT: Ashgate, 2011), 134.

76. Yusuf and Kirk, "Keeping an Eye on South Asian Skies."

77. Rabia Akhtar and Debak Das, *Nuclear Learning in South Asia: The Levels of Analysis*, Policy Studies no. 57 (Colombo: Regional Centre for Strategic Studies, 2015), 13.

78. Ganguly and Hagerty, *Fearful Symmetry*.

79. Chakma, "Escalation Control"; Kapur, *Dangerous Deterrent*; Mistry, "Tempering Optimism."

80. Akhtar and Das, *Nuclear Learning in South Asia*, 90.

81. Sumit Ganguly and R. Harrison Wagner, "India and Pakistan: Bargaining in the Shadow of Nuclear War," *Journal of Strategic Studies* 27, 3 (2004): 500.

82. S. Paul Kapur, "India and Pakistan's Unstable Peace: Why Nuclear South Asia Is Not Like Cold War Europe," *International Security* 30, 2 (Fall 2005): 127–52; Kapur, *Dangerous Deterrent*. Kapur uses "revisionist" in the context of Pakistan's dissatisfaction with the territorial status quo in Kashmir and its desire to alter it. Kapur, *Dangerous Deterrent*, 198n54.

83. T. Negeen Pegahi, "Dangerous Deterrent? Assessing the Risk That Nuclear Acquisition Will Embolden Weak States" (PhD diss., Department of Political Science, University of Chicago, June 2013), 151.

84. Chakma, "South Asia's Nuclear Deterrence"; Ganguly and Wagner "Bargaining in the Shadow of Nuclear War."

85. Dinshaw Mistry, "Complexity of Deterrence among New Nuclear States: The India-Pakistan Case," in *Complex Deterrence: Strategy in the Global Age*, eds. T. V. Paul, Patrick M. Morgan, and James J. Wirtz (Chicago: University of Chicago Press, 2009), 190.

86. Khan, "The Independence-Dependence Paradox."

87. Crawford, *Pivotal Deterrence*, 161–62.

88. Abdul Sattar, *Pakistan's Foreign Policy, 1947–2005: A Concise History* (Karachi: Oxford University Press, 2007), 96–98. On the Chinese role in the war, see Paul M. McGarr, *The Cold War in South Asia: Britain, the United States and the Indian Subcontinent, 1945–1965* (New York: Cambridge University Press, 2013), 326–33.

89. McGarr, *The Cold War in South Asia*, 159. Also see Steven Hoffmann, *India and the China Crisis* (Berkeley: University of California Press, 1990), 196–200, 206–10.

90. Kapur, *Dangerous Deterrent*, 60–61, 215n115.

91. Satu Limaye, "Mediating Kashmir: A Bridge Too Far," *Washington Quarterly* 26, 1 (Winter 2002–2003): 159.

92. Yusuf and Kirk, "Keeping an Eye on South Asian Skies."

Chapter 2

1. Michael Mastanduno, "Preserving the Unipolar Moment: Realist Theories and U.S. Grand Strategy after the Cold War," in *Unipolar Politics: Realism and State Strategies after the Cold War*, eds. Ethan B. Kapstein and Michael Mastanduno (New York: Columbia University Press, 1999), 144; I. William Zartman and Saadia Touval, "International Mediation in the Post–Cold War Era," in *Managing Global Chaos: Sources of and Responses to International Conflict*, eds. Chester A. Crocker, Fen O. Hampson, and Pamela Aall (Washington, DC: United States Institute of Peace Press, 1996), 448.

2. Nuno P. Monteiro, *Theory of Unipolar Politics* (New York: Cambridge University Press, 2014).

3. For example, Neil Joeck, "The Kargil War and Nuclear Deterrence," in *Nuclear Proliferation in South Asia: Crisis Behaviour and the Bomb*, eds. Sumit Ganguly and S. Paul Kapur (New York: Routledge, 2009), 138–39; Polly Nayak and Michael Krepon, *The Unfinished Crisis: US Crisis Management after the 2008 Mumbai Attacks* (Washington, DC: Henry L. Stimson Center, 2012), 64.

4. Author's interview of Joshua T. White, senior advisor and director for South Asian Affairs, U.S. National Security Council (2015–2017), Washington, DC, June 5, 2017.

5. Author's interview of Strobe Talbott, U.S. deputy secretary of state during the Kargil crisis, Washington, DC, November 19, 2014.

6. "Economic Impacts of a Nuclear Weapon," *Article 36*, Briefing paper, March 2015; Ira Helfand, *An Assessment of the Extent of Projected Global Famine Resulting from Limited, Regional Nuclear War* (London: Physicians for Social Responsibility, 2007).

7. Alan Robock, Luke Oman, and Georgiy L. Stenchikov, "Nuclear Winter Revisited with a Modern Climate Model and Current Nuclear Arsenals: Still Catastrophic Consequences," *Journal of Geophysical Research* 112, D13107 (2007); Alan Robock et al., "Climatic Consequences of Regional Nuclear Conflicts," *Atmospheric Chemistry and Physics* 7 (2007): 2003–12; Helfand, "An Assessment of the Extent of Projected Global Famine." Also see Lynn Eden, *Whole World on Fire: Organizations, Knowledge, and Nuclear Weapons Devastation* (Ithaca, NY: Cornell University Press, 2004).

8. James Doyle, "Why Eliminate Nuclear Weapons?" *Survival* 55, 1 (2013): 8.

9. Alan Robock and Owen B. Toon, "Local Nuclear War, Global Suffering," *Scientific American* (January 1, 2010): 74.

10. Some have argued that "altruism—the desire to save the lives of millions of innocent civilians" may be the principal reason for the U.S. concern about ensuring absence of nuclear weapons use in regional crises. Robert Jervis, "Kargil, Deterrence, and International Relations Theory," in *Asymmetric Warfare in South Asia: The Causes and Consequences of the Kargil Conflict*, ed. Peter R. Lavoy (New York: Cambridge University Press, 2009), 391.

11. Nina Tannenwald, *The Nuclear Taboo: The United States and the Non-Use of Nuclear Weapons since 1945* (Cambridge: Cambridge University Press, 2007), 16; T. V. Paul, "Taboo or Tradition? The Non-Use of Nuclear Weapons in World Politics," *Review of International Studies* 36, 4 (2010): 855–56.

12. Gregory D. Koblentz, *Strategic Stability in the Second Nuclear Age*, Special Report no. 71 (New York: Council on Foreign Relations, November 2014), 5.

13. Michael Krepon, "Is Cold War Experience Applicable to South Asia?" in *Nuclear Risk Reduction in South Asia*, ed. Michael Krepon (New York: Palgrave Macmillan, 2004), 8–12.

14. Stephen Van Evera, "Primed for Peace: Europe after the Cold War," *International Security* 15, 3 (Winter 1990–1991): 45.

15. Steven Pifer, "A Realist's Rationale for a World Without Nuclear Weapons," in *The War That Must Never Be Fought: Dilemmas of Nuclear Deterrence*, eds. George P. Shultz and James E. Goodby (Stanford, CA: Hoover Institution Press, 2015), 86–93; Krepon, "Is Cold War Experience Applicable to South Asia?" 12.

16. For a summary of the concerns raised by proliferation pessimists in terms of new nuclear weapon states as well as a rebuttal of these arguments, see Devin T. Hagerty, *The Consequences of Nuclear Proliferation: Lessons from South Asia* (Cambridge, MA: MIT Press, 1998), 16–37. For a longer, seminal optimism-pessimism debate, see Scott D. Sagan and Kenneth N. Waltz, *The Spread of Nuclear Weapons: A Debate Renewed* (New York: W.W. Norton, 2003). For examples of more detailed discussions of various aspects of the pessimist contentions, see Scott D. Sagan, "The Perils of Proliferation: Organization Theory, Deterrence Theory and the Spread of Nuclear Weapons," *International Security* 18, 4 (Spring 1994): 66–107; David J. Karl, "Proliferation Pessimism and Emerging Nuclear Powers," *International Security* 21, 3 (Winter 1996–1997): 87–98; Lewis A. Dunn, *Controlling the Bomb* (New Haven, CT: Yale University Press, 1982), 69–94; Karl Kaiser, "Non-proliferation and Nuclear Deterrence," *Survival* 31, 2 (March–April 1989): 123–36.

17. Sagan, "The Perils of Proliferation," 66–107; Hagerty, *The Consequences of Nuclear Proliferation*, 28–33.

18. T. V. Paul, "Complex Deterrence: An Introduction," in *Complex Deterrence: Strategy in the Global Age*, eds. T. V. Paul, Patrick M. Morgan, and James J. Wirtz (Chicago: University of Chicago Press, 2009), 9; Luis Dunn, *Containing Nuclear Proliferation*, Adelphi paper 263 (London; International Institute for Strategic Studies, Winter 1991), 4.

19. Jeffrey W. Knopf, "The Importance of International Learning," *Review of International Studies* 29, 2 (April 2003): 185–207; Jack S. Levy, "Learning and Foreign Policy: Sweeping a Conceptual Minefield," *International Organization* 48, 2 (1994): 279–312.

20. Author's interviews of U.S. interlocutors confirmed an unwavering consensus in line with the pessimists' view. Even those who accept that new nuclear powers may behave rationally perceive the risk to be too high for the world not to be alarmed by any nuclear crisis, irrespective of the shape or form it takes.

21. Patrick M. Morgan, *Deterrence Now* (Cambridge: Cambridge University Press, 2003), 172–202; Patrick M. Morgan, "Collective-Actor Deterrence," in *Complex Deterrence: Strategy in the Global Age*, eds. T. V. Paul, Patrick M. Morgan, and James J. Wirtz (Chicago: University of Chicago Press, 2009), 158–81.

22. Timothy W. Crawford, *Pivotal Deterrence: Third-Party Statecraft and the Pursuit of Peace* (Ithaca, NY: Cornell University Press, 2003), 2.

23. Fetter explains this dynamic aptly: if "one side believes that war is inevitable, it may try to preemptively destroy the other side's vulnerable but valuable weapons of mass destruction. Even if both sides prefer not to pre-empt, each may fear that the other side will; consequently, both may decide to launch at the first (perhaps false) indication of an attack." Steve Fetter, "Ballistic Missiles and Weapons of Mass Destruction: What Is the Threat? What Should Be Done?" *International Security* 16, 1 (Summer 1991): 29.

24. Ronald J. Fisher, "Methods of Third-Party Intervention," in *Berghof Handbook for Conflict Transformation*, eds. Norbert Ropers, Martina Fischer, and Eric Manton (Berlin: Berghof Center for Conflict Management, 2001), 165–66; J. G. Stein, "Structures, Strategies, and Tactics of Mediation: Kissinger and Carter in the Middle East," *Negotiation Journal* 1 (1985): 331–47.

25. Zartman and Touval, "International Mediation in the Post–Cold War Era," 445–47. On mediation in international crises, also see Oran R. Young, *The Intermediaries: Third Parties in International Crises* (Princeton, NJ: Princeton University Press, 1967); Jacob Bercovitch, "Mediation in International Conflicts: Theory, Practice, and Developments," in *Peacemaking in International Conflict: Methods and Techniques*, ed. I. William Zartman (Washington, DC: United States Institute of Peace Press, 2007), 163–94; Kyle C. Beardsley et al., "Mediation Style and Crisis Outcomes," *Journal of Conflict Resolution* 50, 1 (February 2006): 58–86; Marieke Kleibor, "Understanding the Success and Failure of International Mediation," *Journal of Conflict Resolution* 40, 2 (1996): 360–89; Jacob Bercovitch and Jeffery Z. Rubin, eds., *Mediation in International Relations: Multiple Approaches to Conflict Management* (New York: St. Martin's Press, 1992).

26. Fisher, "Methods of Third-Party Intervention," 165; Saadia Touval and I. William Zartman, "Introduction: Mediation in Theory," in *International Mediation in Theory and Practice*, eds. Saadia Touval and I. William Zartman (Boulder, CO: Westview Press, 1985), 12–14. On the mediator as a manipulator, see Saadia Touval and I. William Zartman, eds., *International Mediation in Theory*

and Practice (Boulder, CO: Westview Press, 1985). Of the three roles mediators are known to perform—communication, formulation, and manipulation—
manipulation is the most aggressive. Jacob Bercovitch, "The Structure and
Diversity of Mediation in International Relations," in *Mediation in International
Relations: Multiple Approaches to Conflict Management*, eds. Jacob Bercovitch
and Jeffrey S. Rubin (New York: St. Martin's Press, 1992), 14–21.

27. Saadia Touval, "The Superpowers as Mediators," in *Mediation in International Relations: Multiple Approaches to Conflict Management*, eds. Jacob
Bercovitch and Jeffery Z. Rubin (New York: St. Martin's Press, 1992), 232–
48; Zartman and Touval, "International Mediation," 454–58; Beardsley et al.,
"Mediation Style," 64–65; Kleibor, "Understanding the Success," 371.

28. The role of a face saver is also well-established in literature on bargaining games: "mediation provides the negotiator with a face-saving device
whereby he can retreat without feeling that he has capitulated. Presumably,
this face-saving results from throwing the blame for one's own concessions
onto the mediator." Dean G. Pruitt and Douglas F. Johnson, "Mediation as an
Aid to Face Saving in Negotiation," *Journal of Personality and Social Psychology* 14, 3 (1970): 246.

29. Saadia Touval, *The Peace Brokers: Mediators in the Arab-Israeli Conflict, 1948–1979* (Princeton, NJ: Princeton University Press, 1982), 321.

30. Kyle Beardsley, "Agreement Without Peace? International Mediation
and Time Inconsistency Problems," *American Journal of Political Science* 52,
4 (October 2008): 737.

31. There is vast and deeply contested literature on the effectiveness
of mediators and the role of impartiality versus bias in mediation. See, for
example, Young, *The Intermediaries*; Ronald J. Fisher, "Pacific, Impartial
Third-Party Intervention in International Conflict: A Review and Analysis,"
in *Beyond Confrontation: Learning Conflict Resolution in the Post–Cold War
Era*, eds. John A. Vasquez et al. (Ann Arbor: University of Michigan Press,
1995), 39–59; Peter J. Carnevale and Sharon Arad, "Bias and Impartiality in
International Mediation," in *Resolving International Conflicts: The Theory and
Practice of Mediation*, ed. Jacob Bercovitch (London: Lynne Rienner, 1996),
39–53; Robert W. Rauchhaus, "Asymmetric Information, Mediation, and
Conflict Management," *World Politics* 58, 2 (January 2006): 207–41; Saadia
Touval and I. William Zartman, "Mediation in International Conflicts," in
Mediation Research: The Process and Effectiveness of Third-Party Intervention,
eds. Kenneth Kressel, Dean Pruitt, and associates (San Francisco: Jossey-Bass,
1989), 115–37; Touval, *The Peace Brokers*, 10–16; Andrew Kydd, "Which Side
Are You On? Bias, Credibility, and Mediation," *American Journal of Political
Science* 47, 4 (October 2003): 597–611.

32. Touval, *The Peace Brokers*, 10–16; Zartman and Touval, "International
Mediation," 453.

33. Muthiah Alagappa, "Exploring Roles, Strategies, and Implications: Historical and Conceptual Perspectives," in *The Long Shadow: Nuclear Weapons and Security in 21st Century Asia*, ed. Muthiah Alagappa (Stanford, CA: Stanford University Press, 2008), 85; Michael Handel, *Weak States in the International System* (London: Frank Cass, 1990), 204.

34. Handel, *Weak States*, 12. Also see Robert L. Rothstein, *Alliances and Small Powers* (New York: Columbia University Press, 1968), 265–323.

35. Glenn H. Snyder and Paul Diesing, *Conflict Among Nations: Bargaining, Decision Making, and System Structure in International Crises* (Princeton, NJ: Princeton University Press, 1977), 204.

36. Richard K. Ashley, *The Political Economy of War and Peace: The Sino-Soviet-American Triangle and the Modern Security Problematique* (London: Francis Pinter, 1980), 41–43; Crawford, *Pivotal Deterrence*, 20.

37. Robert Gilpin, *Global Political Economy: Understanding the International Economic Order* (Princeton, NJ: Princeton University Press, 2001), 7.

38. Sameer Lalwani, "Danger Zone: Posturing against Pakistan Can Be Costly for India," *Hindustan Times*, September 23, 2015.

39. See S. Paul Kapur, "India and Pakistan's Unstable Peace: Why Nuclear South Asia Is Not Like Cold War Europe," *International Security* 30, 2 (Fall 2005): 127–52; S. Paul Kapur, *Dangerous Deterrent: Nuclear Weapons Proliferation and Conflict in South Asia* (Stanford, CA: Stanford University Press, 2007); Bhumitra Chakma, "South Asia's Nuclear Deterrence and the USA," in *The Politics of Nuclear Weapons in South Asia*, ed. Bhumitra Chakma (Burlington, VT: Ashgate, 2011); Sumit Ganguly and R. Harrison Wagner, "India and Pakistan: Bargaining in the Shadow of Nuclear War," *Journal of Strategic Studies* 27, 3 (2004); Dinshaw Mistry, "Complexity of Deterrence among New Nuclear States: The India-Pakistan Case," in *Complex Deterrence: Strategy in the Global Age*, eds. T. V. Paul, Patrick M. Morgan, and James J. Wirtz (Chicago: University of Chicago Press, 2009); Feroz H. Khan, "The Independence-Dependence Paradox: Stability Dilemmas in South Asia," *Arms Control Today* 33, 8 (October 2003).

40. Mediation literature notes that a decision by a party to a conflict to accept a mediator is a function of the evaluation of available alternatives. Ignoring or denying a stronger third party that has expressed interest in mediating would risk forcing it to move closer to the opponent. Touval, *The Peace Brokers*, 14; Touval, "The Superpowers as Mediators," 239–40.

41. For an analysis of the multiple-audience problem from the strategic communication perspective, see John. H. Fleming and John. M. Darley, "Mixed Messages: The Multiple Audience Problem and Strategic Communication," *Social Cognition* 9, 1 (1991): 25–46.

42. See James Fearon, "Rationalist Explanations of War," *International Organization* 49, 3 (Summer 1995): 379–414; Burcu Savun, "Mediator Types

and the Effectiveness of Information-Provision Strategies in the Resolution of International Conflict," in *International Conflict Mediation: New Approaches and Findings*, eds. Jacob Bercovitch and Scott Sigmund Gartner (London: Routledge, 2009), 96–112.

43. Limited war theory envisions an a priori understanding between the rivals in terms of the concept of war limitation. Henry A. Kissinger, *The Necessity of Choice: Prospects of American Foreign Policy* (New York: Harper & Row, 1960), 60.

44. Jeffrey Z. Rubin and Bert R. Brown, *The Social Psychology of Bargaining and Negotiating* (New York: Academic Press, 1975), 44–48.

45. Ibid., 44.

46. Ibid.

47. Ibid.

48. Ibid., 46.

49. Ibid., 48–50.

50. Ibid., 48.

51. See, for example, Dinshaw Mistry, "Tempering Optimism about Nuclear Deterrence in South Asia," *Security Studies* 18, 1 (2009): 148–82; Bhumitra Chakma, "Escalation Control, Deterrence Diplomacy and America's Role in South Asia's Nuclear Crises," *Contemporary Security Policy* 33, 3 (2012): 554–76; Kapur, *Dangerous Deterrent*. On nuclear weapons being *the* principal factor determining behavior, see Karl, "Proliferation Pessimism," 91.

52. Endogeneity refers to a situation whereby the values an explanatory variable takes on are a consequence, rather than a cause, of the dependent variable. Such situations are common when observing political processes but they create misleading conclusions about the direction of causality. Garry King, Robert O. Keohane, and Sidney Verba, *Designing Social Inquiry: Scientific Inference in Qualitative Research* (Princeton, NJ: Princeton University Press, 1994), 185 (and 185–96 for a more in-depth discussion of the endogeneity problem).

53. For a timeline of related developments and tensions on the Korean peninsula dating back to 2002, see "Timeline: North Korea Nuclear Standoff," BBC News, April 2, 2013; "Chronology of U.S.-North Korean Nuclear and Missile Diplomacy," Arms Control Association, Fact Sheets and Briefs, January 2018. For references on the 1987 and 1990 India-Pakistan crises, see note 11 in the Introduction. On the concept of opaque deterrence, see Hagerty, *The Consequences of Nuclear Proliferation*, 39–62; Avner Cohen and Benjamin Frankel, "Opaque Nuclear Proliferation," *Journal of Strategic Studies* 133, 3 (September 1990): 14–44.

54. King, Keohane, and Verba, *Designing Social Inquiry*, 209.

55. Alexander L. George, "Case Studies and Theory Development: The Method of Structured, Focused Comparison," in *Diplomacy: New Approaches*

in History, Theory, and Policy, ed. Paul G. Lauren (New York: Free Press, 1979), 43–68; Alexander L. George and Andrew Bennett, *Case Studies and Theory Development in the Social Sciences* (Cambridge, MA: MIT Press, 2005), 67–72.

56. For a basic introduction to the method of process tracing, see Stephen V. Evera, *Guide to Methods for Students of Political Science* (Ithaca, NY: Cornell University Press, 1997), 64–67; John Gerring, *Case Study Research: Principles and Practices* (Cambridge: Cambridge University Press, 2007), 172–85.

57. "Soaking and poking" is a methodological term brought to prominence by Richard Fenno's work on members of the U.S. Congress. It describes a technique that relies on "thick" and detailed description of any mechanisms or occurrences relevant to the research question. For Fenno's seminal work, see Richard F. Fenno, *Home Style: House Members in Their Districts* (Boston: Little, Brown, 1978).

58. Two English language daily newspapers each were selected from India and Pakistan as the primary press sources: the *Hindu* and *Indian Express* in India; and *Dawn* and *News* in Pakistan. The Associated Press was selected as the international outlet. Multiple sources permitted triangulation of the information. Relevant material from the following periods was included in the database: Kargil crisis: April 1–August 15, 1999; 2001–2002 standoff: December 13, 2001–April 13, 2003; and Mumbai crisis: November 26, 2008–March 15, 2009.

59. For an introduction to the various methods of content analysis in qualitative research, see Hsiu-Fang Hsieh and Sarah E. Shannon, "Three Approaches to Qualitative Content Analysis," *Qualitative Health Research* 15, 9 (November 2005): 1277–88. Also see B. Devi Prasad, "Content Analysis: A Method in Social Science Research," in *Research Methods for Social Work*, eds. D. K. Lal Das and V. Bhaskaran (New Delhi: Rawat, 2008), 173–93.

Chapter 3

1. Robert G. Wirsing, *Kashmir in the Shadow of War: Regional Rivalries in a Nuclear Age* (Armonk, NY: M. E. Sharpe, 2003), 36–37; Samuel Black, "The Structure of South Asian Crises from Brasstacks to Mumbai," Appendix I, in *Crises in South Asia: Trends and Potential Consequences*, eds. Michael Krepon and Nate Cohn (Washington, DC: Henry L. Stimson Center, 2011), 41.

2. Feroz H. Khan, *Eating Grass: The Making of the Pakistani Bomb* (Stanford, CA: Stanford University Press, 2012), 310.

3. Wirsing, *Kashmir in the Shadow of War,* 42–43.

4. D. Suba Chandran, *Limited War: Revisiting Kargil in the Indo-Pak Conflict* (New Delhi: India Research Press, 2005), 61.

5. Waheguru Pal Singh Sidhu, "Operation Vijay and Operation Parakram: The Victory of Theory?" in *The India-Pakistan Nuclear Relationship: Theories of Deterrence and International Relations*, ed. E. Sridharan (New Delhi:

Routledge, 2007), 220. Estimates of the number of Indian soldiers killed vary from 449 to 1,717. Pakistani casualty figures range from 97 to 772. For various estimates, see John H. Gill, "Military Operations in the Kargil Conflict," in *Asymmetric Warfare in South Asia: The Causes and Consequences of the Kargil Conflict*, ed. Peter R. Lavoy (New York: Cambridge University Press, 2009), 122; Chandran, *Limited War*, 61; Sumit Ganguly and Devin T. Hagerty, *Fearful Symmetry: India-Pakistan Crises in the Shadow of Nuclear Weapons* (Seattle: University of Washington Press, 2005), 143.

6. The United States initiated separate nonproliferation dialogues with India and Pakistan. Between June 1998 and January 2000, twelve rounds of talks were conducted with India and ten rounds with Pakistan. Wirsing, *Kashmir in the Shadow of War*, 94–95.

7. For analyses of the insurgency, India's counterinsurgency campaign and Pakistan's role, see Rekha Chowdhary, "India's Response to the Kashmir Insurgency: A Holistic Perspective," in *Insurgency and Counterinsurgency in South Asia: Through a Peacebuilding Lens*, ed. Moeed Yusuf (Washington, DC: United States Institute of Peace Press, 2014), 45–76; Happymon Jacob, "Conflict in Kashmir: An Insurgency with Long Roots," in *Insurgency and Counterinsurgency in South Asia: Through a Peacebuilding Lens*, ed. Moeed Yusuf (Washington, DC: United States Institute of Peace Press, 2014), 23–44.

8. Chowdhary, "India's Response to the Kashmir Insurgency," 54.

9. The full text of the Lahore Declaration is available at http://peacemaker.un.org/sites/peacemaker.un.org/files/IN%20PK_990221_The%20Lahore%20Declaration.pdf.

10. Hassan Abbas, *Pakistan's Drift into Extremism: Allah, the Army, and America's War on Terror* (Armonk: NY: M. E. Sharpe, 2005), 168–69. For a more detailed account of the backchannel, see Wirsing, *Kashmir in the Shadow of War*, 25–33.

11. Devin T. Hagerty, "The Kargil War: An Optimistic Assessment," in *Nuclear Proliferation in South Asia: Crisis Behaviour and the Bomb*, eds. Sumit Ganguly and S. Paul Kapur (New York: Routledge, 2009), 103.

12. Timothy D. Hoyt, "Kargil: The Nuclear Dimension," in *Asymmetric Warfare in South Asia: The Causes and Consequences of the Kargil Conflict*, ed. Peter R. Lavoy (New York: Cambridge University Press, 2009), 150, 154.

13. Kaiser Tufail, "Kargil Conflict and Pakistan Air Force," *Aeronaut*, blogspot, January 28, 2009. There is still a great deal of controversy about the extent to which the Pakistani prime minister and his team were aware of the Kargil operation. The prime minister was reportedly briefed only once by the army top brass and the true scope of the intrusion was not shared with him. Sartaj Aziz, *Between Dreams and Realities: Some Milestones in Pakistan's History* (Karachi: Oxford University Press, 2009), 253.

14. Feroz H. Khan, Peter R. Lavoy, and Christopher Clary, "Pakistan's Motivations and Calculations for the Kargil Conflict," in *The Causes and Consequences of the Kargil Conflict*, ed. Peter R. Lavoy (New York: Cambridge University Press, 2009), 90. Aside from Musharraf, those in the know about the Kargil plan were limited to his chief of general staff, General Aziz Khan; the director general of military operations, General Tauqir Zia; and the force commanders of the two geographically relevant deployments, General Mahmud Ahmed of X Corps, and General Javed Hasan, force commander Northern Areas, which included the Northern Light Infantry unit that actually intruded into Kargil. Sanjay Dutt, *War and Peace in Kargil Sector* (New Delhi: A.P.H., 2000), 415.

15. Information about Pakistan's nuclear program was restricted to the very top civilian and military leaders until the May 1998 tests. The army took charge of nuclear oversight in the 1990s but nuclear matters were still managed by a tightly controlled and opaque Combat Development Directorate. It was only after the Kargil crisis that Pakistan's nuclear decision making and command and control were truly formalized and the nuclear program was socialized within the military. Khan, *Eating Grass*, 323–37.

16. Khan, Lavoy, and Clary, "Pakistan's Motivations," 76–78.

17. Pervez Musharraf, *In the Line of Fire: A Memoir* (New York: Free Press, 2006), 88–90.

18. Ibid., 87.

19. Hagerty, "The Kargil War," 103.

20. Statement of the U.S. State Department's senior advisor, Mathew Daley, during the Kargil conflict. Quoted in Tara Kartha, "Chronology," in *Kargil 1999: Pakistan's Fourth War for Kashmir*, ed. Jasjit Singh (New Delhi: Knowledge World, 1999), 282–83.

21. S. Paul Kapur, *Dangerous Deterrent: Nuclear Weapons Proliferation and Conflict in South Asia* (Stanford, CA: Stanford University Press, 2007), 130.

22. Government of India, *From Surprise to Reckoning: The Kargil Review Committee Report* (New Delhi: Sage Publications, 2000), 242.

23. J. N. Dixit, "A Defining Moment," in *Guns and Yellow Roses: Essays on the Kargil War* (New Delhi: HarperCollins, 1999), 193.

24. Khan, *Eating Grass*, 311.

25. Peter R. Lavoy, "Introduction: The Importance of the Kargil Conflict," in *Asymmetric Warfare in South Asia: The Causes and Consequences of the Kargil Conflict*, ed. Peter R. Lavoy (New York: Cambridge University Press, 2009), 6–8.

26. Dutt, *War and Peace in Kargil Sector*, 415.

27. Kartha, "Chronology," 271.

28. Lavoy, "Introduction," 21. Also see Gill, "Military Operations," 114–15.

29. Jasjit Singh, "The Fourth War," in *Kargil 1999: Pakistan's Fourth War for Kashmir*, ed. Jasjit Singh (New Delhi: Knowledge World, 1999), 141.

30. John Lancaster, "Kashmir Crisis Was Defused on Brink of War," *Washington Post*, July 26, 1999; Kartha, "Chronology," 267.

31. Only a brigade's worth of troops was moved into the northern command area of operations to recreate reserves. Fresh forces were transferred to this area again in mid-June but these only began to arrive toward the end of the month and therefore had little impact on the conflict. Musharraf, *In the Line of Fire*, 93.

32. Shakil Shaikh, "PM, COAS Discuss Indian Build-up at LoC," *News*, May 23, 1999, quoted in Chandran, *Limited War*, 44–45.

33. Bhumitra Chakma, "Escalation Control, Deterrence Diplomacy and America's Role in South Asia's Nuclear Crises," *Contemporary Security Policy* 33, 3 (2012): 563.

34. Amit Baruah, "Any Weapon Will Be Used, Threatens Pakistan," *Hindu*, June 1, 1999.

35. Sidhu, "Operation Vijay and Operation Parakram," 222.

36. "U.S. Involvement Essential: PM," *Dawn*, July 10, 1999.

37. During these conversations that took place while Musharraf was on a trip to China, the two talked about Musharraf's war objectives quite explicitly. General Aziz even assured Musharraf that he had told the foreign minister not to make any commitments on the situation on the ground in Kargil during his interactions in New Delhi. Jaswant Singh, *A Call to Honour: In Service of Emergent India* (New Delhi: Rupa, 2006), 213–19.

38. Ibid., 220.

39. Aziz, *Between Dreams and Realities*, 274. Pakistan's foreign secretary, Shamshad Ahmad Khan, had convinced Prime Minister Sharif to activate the backchannel to seek a way out of the crisis. Author's interview of Shamshad Ahmad Khan, Lahore, April 23, 2013.

40. Wirsing, *Kashmir in the Shadow of War*, 30–31.

41. Ibid., 32–33.

42. The July 16 date was ultimately extended by a day. Lavoy, "Introduction," 22.

43. Ashley J. Tellis, *India's Emerging Nuclear Posture: Between Recessed Deterrent and Ready Arsenal* (Santa Monica, CA: RAND, 2001), 131.

44. Bruce Riedel, *American Diplomacy and the 1999 Kargil Summit at Blair House* (Philadelphia: Center for the Advanced Study of India, University of Pennsylvania, 2002), 3.

45. William Milam, "Kargil Revisited," *Friday Times* 25, 3, March 1–7, 2013.

46. Anwar Iqbal, "Pakistan Reserves Right to Retaliate: Foreign Office," *News*, May 27, 1999, quoted in D. Suba Chandran, "Why Kargil? Pakistan's

Objectives and Motivations," in *Kargil: The Tables Turned*, eds. Ashok Krishna and P. R. Chari (New Delhi: Institute of Peace & Conflict Studies, 2001), 32.

47. "Pakistan Forces Not Operating in Valley," *Dawn*, June 16, 1999; "Pakistan Deflects Clinton's Call on Militants," Reuters, June 17, 1999.

48. Author's interview of Shamshad Ahmad Khan, April 23, 2013.

49. "Kargil Conflict Timeline," BBC News, July 13, 1999; Chandran, *Limited War*, 63.

50. Chandran, "Why Kargil?" 32.

51. Aziz, *Between Dreams and Realities*, 274.

52. The military had failed to inform Sharif about this and some other key losses and Sharif had begun to receive this information from American and even Indian diplomats. Peter R. Lavoy, "Why Kargil Did Not Produce General War: The Crisis-Management Strategies of Pakistan, India, and the United States," in *Asymmetric Warfare in South Asia: The Causes and Consequences of the Kargil Conflict*, ed. Peter R. Lavoy (New York: Cambridge University Press, 2009), 186.

53. Singh, *A Call to Honour*, 224.

54. M. K. Akbar, *Kargil: Cross Border Terrorism* (New Delhi: Mittal, 1999), 386.

55. Tom Clancy, Tony Zinni, and Tony Koltz, *Battle Ready* (New York: Penguin, 2004), 347.

56. M. Siddique-ul-Farooque, *Kargil: Adventure or Trap! White Paper* (Lahore, Sagar Publishers, 2006), 47. In response to a question on the possibility of a Pakistani pullout from Kargil, Musharraf stated on June 26: "It is too early to say [but] it's a government decision. It is the Prime Minister's decision. We will not withdraw unilaterally." "No Unilateral Withdrawal from Kargil: Pak," *Rediff*, June 26, 1999.

57. Author's interview of Shamshad Ahmad Khan, April 23, 2013. For a detailed list of interactions between Pakistan and China during the crisis, see William Shimer, "Chinese Involvement in South Asian Crises," Appendix V, in *Crises in South Asia: Trends and Potential Consequences*, eds. Michael Krepon and Nate Cohn (Washington, DC: Henry L. Stimson Center, 2011), 94–95.

58. Hagerty, "The Kargil War," 105.

59. Ibid.

60. Siddique-ul-Farooque, *Kargil*, 47.

61. Strobe Talbott, *Engaging India: Diplomacy, Democracy, and the Bomb* (Washington, DC: Brookings Institution Press, 2004), 164.

62. Ibid., 168.

63. Akbar, *Kargil*, 277; "Nawaz Sharif's Visit to Washington," *Frontier Post*, July 6, 1999.

64. Owen Bennett-Jones, *Pakistan: Eye of the Storm* (New Haven, CT: Yale University Press, 2002), 100.

65. Dinshaw Mistry, "Tempering Optimism about Nuclear Deterrence in South Asia," *Security Studies* 18, 1 (2009): 159–60; D. Suba Chandran, "Role of the United States: Mediator or Mere Facilitator?" in *Kargil: The Tables Turned*, eds. Ashok Krishna and P. R. Chari (New Delhi: Institute of Peace & Conflict Studies, 2001), 219.

66. Talbott, *Engaging India*, 159.

67. Mariana Baabar, "Pakistan's Dilemma," *Outlook India*, July 12, 1999.

68. This phase entailed a number of Indian patrols, artillery exchanges, and some troop deployment but the mood was marked by complacency about the severity of the challenge. Based on military briefings, the Indian defense minister was promised on May 16 that the "intruders will be evicted in 48 hours." The estimate went up to another two days a day later and to 2–3 weeks when the prime minister received his first full briefing on the intrusions two days hence. Dutt, *War and Peace in Kargil Sector*, 414; Singh, *A Call to Honour*, 203.

69. "Blasting Peace," *India Today*, June 7, 1999; L. K. Advani, *My Country, My Life* (New Delhi: Rupa, 2008), 564.

70. Tufail, "Kargil Conflict." Pakistani and Indian leaders have traditionally viewed air warfare as escalatory. George Perkovich and Toby Dalton, "Modi's Strategic Choice: How to Respond to Terrorism from Pakistan," *Washington Quarterly* 38, 1 (Spring 2015): 24; R. Sukumaran, "The 1962 India-China War and Kargil 1999: Restrictions on the Use of Air Power," *Strategic Analysis* 27, 3 (July–September 2003): 354.

71. Dutt, *War and Peace in Kargil Sector*, 423; "1999 Kargil Conflict," *Global Security.org*, undated, http://www.globalsecurity.org/military/world/war/kargil-99.htm. For a detailed analysis of Indian use of air power during the Kargil crisis, see Benjamin S. Lambeth, *Airpower at 18,000: The Indian Air Force in the Kargil War* (Washington, DC: Carnegie Endowment for International Peace, 2012).

72. Quoted in Hagerty, "The Kargil War," 104.

73. Quoted in ibid.

74. Raj Chengappa with Rohit Saran and Harinder Baweja, "Will the War Spread?" *India Today International*, July 5, 1999.

75. "1999 Kargil Conflict"; Dutt, *War and Peace in Kargil Sector*, 423–24.

76. Vishnu Som, "In Kargil War, India Was Minutes Away from Bombing Pak Bases," NDTV, July 19, 2016. NDTV broke this story based on the narration of events in the original "squadron diary" of the Srinagar-based 17th squadron of the IAF, which was assigned targets in Pakistani Kashmir and in Rawalpindi, where the Pakistan army is headquartered. Author's interview

(by phone) of Vishnu Som, the NDTV journalist who acquired the squadron diary and revealed the facts, June 24, 2017.

77. Author's interview of Vishnu Som, June 24, 2017.

78. V. P. Malik, *Kargil: From Surprise to Victory* (New Delhi: HarperCollins, 2006), 147.

79. Other important heights reclaimed included Point 5140 in Dras on June 20; Point 5203 in Batalik on June 22; strategic peaks Three Pimples and Point 4700 in Dras on June 28; and Khalubar on July 6. Lavoy, "Introduction," 12–13; Mistry, "Tempering Optimism," 155; "1999 Kargil Conflict."

80. While the Indian military managed to break the Pakistani resistance on Tiger Hill by July 4, the hilltop was not completely secured till four days later. Gill, "Military Operations," 115.

81. Ashley J. Tellis, C. Christine Fair, and Jamison J. Medby, *Limited Conflicts under the Nuclear Umbrella: Indian and Pakistani Lessons from the Kargil Crisis* (Santa Monica, CA: RAND, 2001), 56.

82. Dutt, *War and Peace in Kargil Sector*, 414.

83. D. Azhagarasu, Deepa Rajkumar, and Anju S. Alex, "Chronology of Events during the Kargil Crisis," in *Kargil: The Tables Turned*, eds. Ashok Krishna and P. R. Chari (New Delhi: Institute of Peace & Conflict Studies, 2001), 266.

84. Malik, *From Surprise to Victory*, 146.

85. Advani, *My Country*, 565.

86. Singh, *A Call to Honour*, 226.

87. Wirsing, *Kashmir in the Shadow of War*, 30.

88. Ibid., 30–31.

89. Indo-U.S. relations were not completely out of the Cold War hangover even though the Clinton administration and multinational corporations were attracted by India's potential. The nonproliferation lobby remained a major obstacle in Washington. Wirsing, *Kashmir in the Shadow of War*, 107–8. With China, India's relations reached their nadir after India surprisingly blamed China, not Pakistan, to justify its May 1998 nuclear tests. "Nuclear Anxiety; Indian's Letter to Clinton on Nuclear Testing," *New York Times*, May 13, 1998.

90. Wirsing, *Kashmir in the Shadow of War*, 82.

91. Suzzane Goldenberg, "India's Balancing Act on Kashmir," *Guardian*, June 1, 1999.

92. Lavoy, "Why Kargil Did Not Produce General War," 194; Sumit Ganguly and R. Harrison Wagner, "India and Pakistan: Bargaining in the Shadow of Nuclear War," *Journal of Strategic Studies* 27, 3 (2004): 492; Advani, *My Country*, 569.

93. Singh, *A Call to Honour*, 212.

94. Tellis, Fair, and Medby, *Limited Conflicts under the Nuclear Umbrella*, 25.

95. Andrew C. Winner and Toshi Yoshihara, *Nuclear Stability in South Asia* (n.p.: Institute for Foreign Policy Analysis, January 2002), 71.

96. Arpit Rajain, "India's Political and Diplomatic Responses to the Kargil Crisis," in *Kargil: The Tables Turned*, eds. Ashok Krishna and P. R. Chari (New Delhi: Institute of Peace & Conflict Studies, 2001), 188.

97. Singh, *A Call to Honour*, 222.

98. Author's interview of Riaz Khokhar, Pakistan's ambassador to the United States during the Kargil crisis, Islamabad, May 9, 2013.

99. Wirsing, *Kashmir in the Shadow of War*, 94–95. For details of negotiations and diplomacy between Strobe Talbott and Jaswant Singh, see Talbott, *Engaging India*.

100. Hagerty, "The Kargil War," 105.

101. Sidhu, "Operation Vijay and Operation Parakram," 222.

102. Malik, *From Surprise to Victory*, 147.

103. Wirsing, *Kashmir in the Shadow of War*, 82. Part of the quote is from Thomas W. Lippman, "India Hints at Attack in Pakistan; U.S. Acts to Ease Tension on Kashmir," *Washington Post*, June 27, 1999.

104. A.G. Noorani, "Kargil Diplomacy," *Frontline* 16, 16 (July 31–August 31, 1999). Mishra's trip was deliberately timed to coincide with the G-8 meeting. Aziz, *Between Dreams and Realities*, 260.

105. Chandran, *Limited War*, 64–65; Singh, *A Call to Honour*, 227.

106. Key Indian officials involved in managing the Kargil crisis have since argued along these lines. For examples, see Paul Kapur's recounting of Prime Minister Vajpayee and Army Chief V. P. Malik's remarks echoing this sentiment. Kapur, *Dangerous Deterrent*, 130, 128.

107. Chandran, *Limited War*, 65; "Vajpayee Loses Confidence Vote by 1 Vote," *Rediff*, April 17, 1999.

108. Chakma, "Escalation Control," 563; Malik, *From Surprise to Victory*, 147.

109. S. Paul Kapur, "Ten Years of Instability in a Nuclear South Asia," *International Security* 33, 2 (Fall 2008): 78.

110. Kapur, *Dangerous Deterrent*, 128.

111. Ibid., 127–28.

112. Ibid., 128.

113. Singh, *A Call to Honour*, 227; Sumit Ganguly, *Deadly Impasse: Indo-Pak Relations at the Dawn of a New Century* (Cambridge: Cambridge University Press, 2016), 39n25.

114. Singh, *A Call to Honour*, 227.

115. Malik, *From Surprise to Victory*, 259–60.

116. Ibid., 260.

117. Quoted in Noorani, "Kargil Diplomacy."

118. Author's interview of Strobe Talbott, U.S. deputy secretary of state during the Kargil crisis, Washington, DC, November 19, 2014.

119. Riedel, *American Diplomacy and the 1999 Kargil Summit at Blair House*, 3–4.

120. Author's interview of Karl F. Inderfurth, U.S. assistant secretary of state for South Asian affairs during the Kargil crisis, Washington, DC, June 13, 2013.

121. Talbott, *Engaging India*, 157.

122. Bill Clinton, *My Life* (New York: Vintage Books, 2005), 865.

123. P. R. Chari, Pervaiz I. Cheema, and Stephen P. Cohen, *Four Crises and a Peace Process: American Engagement in South Asia* (Washington, DC: Brookings Institution Press, 2007), 131.

124. Author's interview of Karl F. Inderfurth, June 13, 2013.

125. Howard B. Schaffer and Teresita C. Schaffer, *How Pakistan Negotiates with the United States: Riding the Roller Coaster* (Washington, DC: United States Institute of Peace Press, 2011), 155–56; author's interview of Riaz Khokhar, May 9, 2013; author's interview of Karl F. Inderfurth, June 13, 2013.

126. N. C. Menon, "Ultras Will Have to Go: Inderfurth," *Hindustan Times*, May 31, 1999, quoted in Chandran, "Role of the United States," 205–6.

127. Azhagarasu, Rajkumar, and Alex, "Chronology of Events during the Kargil Crisis," 268.

128. Talbott, *Engaging India*, 158.

129. Kartha, "Chronology," 270.

130. "France, Annan Say LoC Must be Respected," *Statesman* (India), June 2, 1999, quoted in Lavoy, "Why Kargil Did Not Produce General War," 198.

131. Author's interview of Strobe Talbott, November 19, 2014.

132. Azhagarasu, Rajkumar, and Alex, "Chronology of Events during the Kargil Crisis," 269.

133. Akbar, *Kargil*, 391.

134. Singh, *A Call to Honour*, 206–7.

135. Author's interview of William Milam, U.S. ambassador to Pakistan during the Kargil crisis, Washington, DC, June 7, 2013.

136. Lavoy, "Why Kargil Did Not Produce General War," 200.

137. Ganguly, *Deadly Impasse*, 41.

138. Singh, *A Call to Honour*, 208.

139. Ibid.

140. Malik, *From Surprise to Victory*, 147.

141. Akbar, *Kargil*, 281.

142. Wirsing, *Kashmir in the Shadow of War*, 82.

143. "G-8 Appeals for Talks to End Kargil Crisis," *Rediff*, June 20, 1999.

144. Aziz, *Between Dreams and Realities*, 275.

145. Noorani, "Kargil Diplomacy."

146. Clancy, Zinni and Koltz, *Battle Ready*, 347.

147. William B. Milam, *Bangladesh and Pakistan: Flirting with Failure in South Asia* (London: Hurst, 2009), 157.

148. Talbott, *Engaging India*, 159.

149. Kapil Kak, "International Responses," in *Kargil 1999: Pakistan's Fourth War for Kashmir*, ed. Jasjit Singh (New Delhi: Knowledge World, 1999), 197–98.

150. Singh, *A Call to Honour*, 224.

151. Bhumitra Chakma, "South Asia's Nuclear Deterrence and the USA," in *The Politics of Nuclear Weapons in South Asia*, ed. Bhumitra Chakma (Burlington, VT: Ashgate, 2011), 122.

152. Ibid.

153. Rodney W. Jones and Joseph McMillan, "The Kargil Crisis: Lessons Learned by the US," in *Asymmetric Warfare in South Asia: The Causes and Consequences of the Kargil Conflict*, ed. Peter R. Lavoy (New York: Cambridge University Press, 2009), 367.

154. A senior Pakistani diplomat posted to the prime minister's office had informed U.S. ambassador Milam of the presence of the backchannel early on and Milam had reported this back to Washington. Author's interview of William Milam, June 7, 2013.

155. Ibid.

156. "Sharif, Clinton Discuss Kargil," *Dawn*, July 5, 1999.

157. Riedel, *American Diplomacy and the 1999 Kargil Summit at Blair House*, 8.

158. Ibid.

159. Talbott, *Engaging India*, 165.

160. Riedel, *American Diplomacy and the 1999 Kargil Summit at Blair House*, 7, 12.

161. Clinton, *My Life*, 865.

162. Riedel, *American Diplomacy and the 1999 Kargil Summit at Blair House*, 8.

163. Talbott, *Engaging India*, 162.

164. Riedel, *American Diplomacy and the 1999 Kargil Summit at Blair House*, 11.

165. Author's interview of Bruce Riedel, former CIA official and special assistant to the U.S. president and senior director for Near East and South Asian Affairs at the National Security Council during the Kargil crisis, Washington, DC, April 30, 2015.

166. Feroz H. Khan, "Nuclear Signaling, Missiles, and Escalation Control in South Asia," in *Escalation Control and the Nuclear Option in South Asia*, eds. Michael Krepon, Rodney W. Jones, and Ziad Haider (Washington, DC:

Henry L. Stimson Center, 2004), 86–87. Indian army chief V. P. Malik argues that "the coverage of the nuclear danger factor was speculative and exaggerated. The 'doomsday forecasting' suited the non-proliferation policy of the West, and, after 4 July 1999, helped in claiming much greater success for President Clinton's personal intervention in the crisis than it deserved." Malik, *From Surprise to Victory*, 276.

167. For the full text of the Clinton-Sharif statement, see "The Kashmir Crisis," Acronym Institute, *Disarmament Diplomacy* 38 (June 1999).

168. Wirsing, *Kashmir in the Shadow of War*, 83; Talbott, *Engaging India*, 169.

169. Talbott, *Engaging India*, 168–69; Riedel, *American Diplomacy and the 1999 Kargil Summit at Blair House*, 12.

170. Author's interview of Riaz Khokhar, May 9, 2013. U.S. sources deny this and claim that the Indian prime minister was only in listening mode and was never asked to provide or volunteered any input. Author's interview of Karl F. Inderfurth, June 13, 2013.

171. Author's interview of Bruce Riedel, April 30, 2015.

172. Singh, *A Call to Honour*, 223.

173. Ibid.

174. Hasan Akhtar, "Delhi Has Suffered Diplomatic Setback: India Asked to Heed G8 Call, End Hostilities," *Dawn*, June 22, 1999; "Islamabad's Stand Vindicated, Says FO," *Dawn*, June 21, 1999.

175. Akhtar, "Delhi Has Suffered Diplomatic Setback."

176. Kak, "International Responses," 198.

177. A. Mallika Joseph, "The Kargil Crisis and the G-8," in *Kargil: The Tables Turned*, eds. Ashok Krishna and P. R. Chari (New Delhi: Institute of Peace & Conflict Studies, 2001), 235–36.

178. Talbott, *Engaging India*, 162.

179. Ibid., 168.

180. "US Opposes Pre-conditions for Talks," *Dawn*, July 27, 1999.

181. U.S. Department of State, "Daily Press Briefing," DPB no. 101, August 10, 1999.

182. Riedel, *American Diplomacy and the 1999 Kargil Summit at Blair House*, 3–4.

183. The Indian strategic elite tends to see Pakistan as a Chinese proxy propped up to keep India in check. There is also a lingering belief that China could intervene militarily on Pakistan's side in a conflict despite the presence of nuclear weapons. Author's interview of Rana Banerji, former Indian civil servant specializing in intelligence and security issues, New Delhi, March 21, 2013; author's interview of Shyam Saran, India's foreign secretary (2004–2006), New Delhi, August 8, 2014. Also see Sidhu, "Operation Vijay and Operation Parakram," 231.

184. Swaran Singh, "The Kargil Conflict: Why and How of China's Neutrality," *Strategic Analysis* 23, 7 (October 1999): 1090–91.

185. Milam, "Kargil Revisited."

186. Jones and McMillan, "The Kargil Crisis," 359. The United States was at the forefront of mobilizing and leading a coalition into war in the Balkans against Serbian leader Slobodan Milosevic, who had ruthlessly targeted his ethnic Albanian Muslim majority population in Kosovo. Talbott, *Engaging India*, 154.

187. Chari, Cheema, and Cohen, *Four Crises and a Peace Process*, 132.

188. Noorani, "Kargil Diplomacy."

189. Author's interview of Karl Inderfurth, June 13, 2013.

190. A prototypical limited war is marked by limited objectives and geographical scope, use of military force that is restricted in quantum and type, selective choice of targets, commitment of only a fraction of the resources available to the belligerents, and a conscious decision to ensure that the fundamental patterns of existence of the antagonists are not under serious threat. Robert E. Osgood, *Limited War: The Challenge to American Strategy* (Chicago: University of Chicago Press, 1957), 1–2.

191. Tellis, Fair, and Medby, *Limited Conflicts under the Nuclear Umbrella*, 6. The authors use these attributes to define India's perception of Pakistan but it is equally true for how the world saw it during the crisis.

192. Lavoy, "Introduction," 12–13.

193. On Pakistan's worry about India threatening its territorial integrity, see C. Christine Fair, *Fighting to the End: The Pakistan Army's Way of War* (New York: Oxford University Press, 2014), 154–59; Anatol Lieven, *Pakistan: A Hard Country* (New York: PublicAffairs, 2011), 186–88.

194. Singh, *A Call to Honour*, 224–25.

195. Author's interview of Riaz Khokhar, May 9, 2013.

Chapter 4

1. Celia W. Dugger, "Suicide Raid in New Delhi; Attackers among 12 Dead," *New York Times*, December 13, 2001.

2. Sharad Joshi, "The Practice of Coercive Diplomacy in the Post 9/11 Period" (PhD diss., School of Public and International Affairs, University of Pittsburgh, 2006), 53.

3. Sumit Ganguly and Devin T. Hagerty, *Fearful Symmetry: India-Pakistan Crisis in the Shadow of Nuclear Weapons* (Seattle: University of Washington Press, 2005), 168; Joshi, "Practice of Coercive Diplomacy," 53.

4. For basic information on these groups, see their profiles in Stanford University's Mapping Militant Organizations database, available at http://web.stanford.edu/group/mappingmilitants/cgi-bin/groups/view/79; and

http://web.stanford.edu/group/mappingmilitants/cgi-bin/groups/view/95. For a comprehensive analysis of the history of LeT and the threat posed by the group, see Stephen Tankel, *Storming the World Stage: The Story of Lashkar-e-Taiba* (New York: Columbia University Press, 2011).

5. "Lashkar Was 'Involved' in Kaluchak Attack," *Tribune*, May 18, 2002.

6. Polly Nayak and Michael Krepon, *US Crisis Management in South Asia's Twin Peaks Crisis*, Report 57 (Washington DC: Henry L. Stimson Center, September 2006).

7. "Lashkar Was 'Involved' in Kaluchak Attack."

8. V. K. Sood and Pravin Sawhney, *Operation Parakram: The War Unfinished* (New Delhi: Sage Publications, 2003), 85.

9. Shujaat Bukhari, "PM Extends 'Hand of Friendship' to Pakistan," *Hindu*, April 19, 2003.

10. Rajesh M. Basrur, "Coercive Diplomacy in a Nuclear Environment: The December 13 Crisis," in *Prospects for Peace in South Asia*, eds. Rafiq Dossani and Henry S. Rowen (Stanford, CA: Stanford University Press, 2005), 303.

11. C. Raja Mohan, "Fernandes Unveils 'Limited War' Doctrine," *Hindu*, January 25, 2002.

12. S. Paul Kapur, *Dangerous Deterrent: Nuclear Weapons Proliferation and Conflict in South Asia* (Stanford, CA: Stanford University Press, 2007), 132–33.

13. As many as five thousand people were killed in insurgency-related violence in 1999–2000 in Indian Kashmir. Amit Gupta and Kaia Leather, *Kashmir: Recent Developments and U.S. Concerns* (Washington, DC: Congressional Research Service, June 21, 2002), 6. The years 1999–2001 saw some of the highest fatalities of Indian security forces and the number of foreign (non-Kashmiri) terrorists operating in Kashmir saw a commensurate increase. Praveen Swami, "The Roots of Crisis—Post-Kargil Conflict in Kashmir and the 2001–2002 Near-War," in *The India-Pakistan Military Standoff: Crisis and Escalation in South Asia*, ed. Zachary S. Davis (New York: Palgrave Macmillan, 2011), 31–33. The latter was seen as an indication of Pakistan's support of the infiltration of foreign militants across the Line of Control.

14. Swami, "The Roots of Crisis," 30; "India Court Confirms Death Penalty for Red Fort Attack," BBC News, August 10, 2011.

15. Nayak and Krepon, *US Crisis Management in South Asia's Twin Peaks Crisis*, 14. For Indian and Pakistani views on the Agra summit, see, respectively, Jaswant Singh, *A Call to Honour: In Service of Emergent India* (New Delhi: Rupa, 2006), 248–60; Khurshid Mahmud Kasuri, *Neither a Hawk nor a Dove: An Insider's Account of Pakistan's Foreign Relations Including Details of the Kashmir Framework* (Karachi: Oxford University Press, 2015), 157–60.

16. Sood and Sawhney, *Operation Parakram*, 89.

17. Rajesh Kumar, "Revisiting the Kashmir Insurgency, Kargil, and the Twin Peak Crisis: Was the Stability/Instability Paradox at Play?" *New England Journal of Political Science* 3, 1 (Fall 2008): 79.

18. S. Kalyanaraman, "Operation Parakram: An Indian Exercise in Coercive Diplomacy," *Strategic Analysis* 26, 4 (2002): 483; Zafar N. Jaspal, "Understanding the Political-Military Context of the 2002 Military Standoff—A Pakistani Perspective," in *The India-Pakistan Military Standoff: Crisis and Escalation in South Asia*, ed. Zachary S. Davis (New York: Palgrave Macmillan, 2011), 60.

19. Feroz H. Khan, "Pakistan's Nuclear Force Posture and the 2001–2002 Military Standoff," in *The India-Pakistan Military Standoff: Crisis and Escalation in South Asia*, ed. Zachary S. Davis (New York: Palgrave Macmillan, 2011), 137.

20. For a detailed account of A. Q. Khan's "nuclear black market," see *Nuclear Black Markets: Pakistan, A.Q. Khan and the Rise of Proliferation Networks—A Net Assessment* (London: International Institute of Strategic Studies, 2007).

21. David Albright and Holly Higgins, *Pakistani Nuclear Scientists: How Much Nuclear Assistance to Al Qaeda* (Washington, DC: Institute for Science and International Security, August 30, 2002).

22. Joshi, "Practice of Coercive Diplomacy," 97.

23. For examples of Pakistani official statements rebuking the world's concerns in the weeks following 9/11, see "No Danger to Nuclear Assets: FO," *News*, October 30, 2001; "Pakistan's Nuclear Assets in Safe Hands, Says Sattar," *News*, November 2, 2001; "No Country Can Find Location of Pak N-assets," *News*, November 8, 2001.

24. Zahid Hussain, *Frontline Pakistan: The Struggle with Militant Islam* (New York: Columbia University Press, 2007), 37.

25. David Smith, "The 2001–2002 Standoff: A Real Time View from Islamabad," in *The India-Pakistan Military Standoff: Crisis and Escalation in South Asia*, ed. Zachary S. Davis (New York: Palgrave Macmillan, 2011), 191.

26. Joshi, "The Practice of Coercive Diplomacy," 71; Khalid Hasan, "US Forces at Jacobabad Airbase: Pakistan Agreed to Long Term Use," *Daily Times*, October 29, 2002.

27. Pervez Musharraf, *In the Line of Fire: A Memoir* (New York: Free Press, 2006), 202.

28. Ibid., 201.

29. Joshi, "Practice of Coercive Diplomacy," 66–67.

30. The Bush administration's preemption doctrine was codified in the *National Security Strategy of the United States of America*, a document released in September 2002. National Security Council, *The National Security*

Strategy of the United States of America (Washington DC: National Security Council, September 20, 2002).

31. Steve Coll, "The Standoff: How Jihadi Groups Helped Provoke the Twenty-First Century's First Nuclear Crisis," *New Yorker*, February 13, 2006. For the text of CIA director George J. Tenet's testimony before the U.S. Senate Select Committee on Intelligence in which this assessment was presented, see George Tenet, "Worldwide Threat—Converging Dangers in a Post 9/11 World," testimony before the Senate Select Committee on Intelligence, 107th Cong., 2nd sess., February 6, 2002.

32. Patrick Bratton, "Signals and Orchestration: India's Use of Compellence in the 2001–2002 Crisis," *Strategic Analysis* 34, 4 (2010): 596.

33. Sood and Sawhney, *Operation Parakram*, 95.

34. Feroz H. Khan, *Eating Grass: The Making of the Pakistani Bomb* (Stanford, CA: Stanford University Press, 2012), 347.

35. Bratton, "Signals and Orchestration," 600.

36. Sood and Sawhney, *Operation Parakram*, 73, 77.

37. When asked what the goal of the order was, the prime minister reportedly responded by saying *"Wo baad mein batayein gey"* (That we'll tell you later). Ibid., 62.

38. Khan, *Eating Grass*, 347; Wallace J. Thies and Dorle Hellmuth, "Critical Risk and the 2002 Kashmir Crisis," *Nonproliferation Review* 11, 3 (Fall–Winter 2004): 7; Vishal Thapar, "Prithvi Missiles Moved Near Border in Punjab," *Hindustan Times*, December 25, 2001; Sujit Chatterjee and V. S. Chandrasekar, "India's Missile System in Position: Fernandes," *Rediff*, December 26, 2001; Basrur, "Coercive Diplomacy," 307.

39. Smith, "The 2001–2002 Standoff," 194–95.

40. Bratton, "Signals and Orchestration," 601; Alex Stolar, *To the Brink: Indian Decision-Making and the 2001–2002 Standoff*, Report no. 68 (Washington, DC: Henry L. Stimson Center, February 2008), 14.

41. P. R. Chari, *Nuclear Crisis, Escalation Control, and Deterrence in South Asia*, Working Paper 1.0 (Washington, DC: Henry L. Stimson Center, August 2003), 21.

42. Sood and Sawhney, *Operation Parakram*, 80.

43. Ibid.

44. Feroz H. Khan, "Nuclear Signaling, Missiles, and Escalation Control in South Asia," in *Escalation Control and the Nuclear Option in South Asia*, eds. Michael Krepon, Rodney W. Jones, and Ziad Haider (Washington, DC: Henry L. Stimson Center, 2004), 88.

45. Celia W. Dugger, "Terrorists Attack Parliament in India, Killing Seven People," *New York Times*, December 13, 2001.

46. "All Options Are Open: PM," *Hindu*, December 20, 2001.

47. "India Recalls High Commissioner to Pakistan: Samjhauta Express, Lahore Bus Service to be Terminated," *Tribune*, December 21, 2001; "India Cuts Strengths of Missions by Half: Bans Overflights by Pakistani Planes," *Tribune*, December 28, 2001.

48. Author's interview of Mahmud Durrani, May 14, 2013, Lahore.

49. For the salient features of India's nuclear doctrine, see "Cabinet Committee on Security Reviews Progress in Operationalizing India's Nuclear Doctrine," press release, Government of India, January 4, 2003.

50. "Pak Designs Will Be Foiled: Omar," *Hindu*, December 19, 2001.

51. J. P. Shukla, "No Weapon Will Be Spared for Self-Defence: PM," *Hindu*, January 3, 2002.

52. "No War, But Troops to Stay Where They Are: George," *Indian Express*, January 7, 2002.

53. Sridhar Krishnaswami, "Bush Expects Musharraf to Take All Steps against Terrorism," *Hindu*, January 11, 2002.

54. "We Are Prepared: Army Chief," *Hindu*, January 12, 2002; Celia W. Dugger, "A Blunt-Speaking General Says India Is Ready for War," *New York Times*, January 11, 2002; P. R. Chari, Pervaiz I. Cheema, and Stephen P. Cohen, *Four Crises and a Peace Process: American Engagement in South Asia* (Washington, DC: Brookings Institution Press, 2007), 177.

55. "Uncalled for Concerns: Fernandes," *Hindu*, January 12, 2002.

56. Srinath Raghavan, "A Coercive Triangle: India, Pakistan, the United States, and the Crisis of 2001–2002," *Journal of Defence Studies* 9, 2 (June 2009): 247.

57. "All Options Are Open."

58. Chari, Cheema, and Cohen, *Four Crises and a Peace Process*, 167.

59. Stolar, *To the Brink*, 12–13. The quote is from Lalit Mansingh, India's ambassador to the United States during the crisis.

60. Ashok K. Mehta, "More Bark Than Bite," *Rediff*, December 31, 2001.

61. K. Subrahmanyam, "Indo-Pak Nuclear Conflict Unlikely," *Times of India*, January 2, 2002.

62. Sood and Sawhney, *Operation Parakram*, 77.

63. Basrur, "Coercive Diplomacy," 313.

64. Stolar, for instance, reports that India's National Security Advisory Board had a consensus that India should adopt a restrained approach to maintain favorable international opinion. Stolar, *To the Brink*, 13. External Affairs Minister Jaswant Singh, who remained a voice of restraint throughout the crisis, recalled later that his greatest challenge was to get Indian military chiefs to see "'restraint' . . . as a strategic asset, for avoiding conflict." Singh, *A Call to Honour*, 268.

65. Sood and Sawhney, *Operation Parakram*, 80.

66. Bratton, "Signals and Orchestration," 601.

67. Stolar, *To the Brink*, 18.

68. Ibid.

69. Ibid.

70. Dinshaw Mistry, "Tempering Optimism about Nuclear Deterrence in South Asia," *Security Studies* 18, 1 (2009): 165–66.

71. David E. Sanger and Judith Miller, "Bush Meets India's Envoy; Fears of Pakistan War Deepen," *New York Times*, January 11, 2002.

72. On Padmanabhan's statement having this dual audience, see Sumit Ganguly and Michael R. Kraig, "The 2001–2002 Indo-Pakistani Crisis: Exposing the Limits of Coercive Diplomacy," *Security Studies* 14, 2 (April–June, 2005): 301.

73. Stolar, *To the Brink*, 19.

74. Author's interview of Lalit Mansingh, India's ambassador to the United States during the 2001–2002 standoff, Copenhagen, June 18, 2013.

75. Smith, "The 2001–2002 Standoff," 195.

76. Peter Lavoy, "Pakistan's Nuclear Posture: Security and Survivability," Nonproliferation Education Center, 2007, 2.

77. Nayak and Krepon, *US Crisis Management in South Asia's Twin Peaks Crisis*, 16.

78. "Pak. Rules Out Nuclear War," *Hindu*, December 28, 2001.

79. Thies and Hellmuth, "Critical Risk," 7.

80. Bill Gertz, "Pakistan Builds Missile Sites Near Border with India; Bush Asks Nations to Ease Tensions," *Washington Times*, January 14, 2002.

81. Author's interview (by Skype) of Naeem Salik, director, Arms Control and Disarmament Affairs, Strategic Plans Division, the secretariat of Pakistan's National Command Authority, during the 2001–2002 standoff, March 9, 2014; author's interview (by phone) of Feroz Hassan Khan, former director, Arms Control and Disarmament Affairs, Strategic Plans Division, March 9, 2014.

82. "President Rules Out Falling of N-assets into Wrong Hands," *Dawn*, December 22, 2001.

83. "Nuclear Pakistan Is Alert : Musharraf," *News*, December 27, 2001.

84. "Islamabad Adheres to Norms of Coexistence: Freedom to Struggle Confused with Terrorism: Sattar," *Dawn*, December 30, 2001.

85. "No Action to Be Taken in Haste, Says Sattar," *Dawn*, December 31, 2001.

86. Paolo Cotta-Ramusino and Maurizio Martellini, "Nuclear Safety, Nuclear Stability, and Nuclear Strategy in Pakistan, A Concise Report of a Visit by Landau Network—Centro Volta," Landau Network-Centro Volta, Italy, January 14, 2002. Although Kidwai's interview was given in a private, ostensibly off-the-record setting, the Italian scientists had informed Pakistani officials that they wanted to publish it. They shared the to-be-published

version of their recounting with the Pakistani Foreign Ministry, which raised no objections to its publication. Author's interview (by Skype) of Paolo Cotta-Ramusino, one of the participants of the meeting with Kidwai, March 8, 2014.

87. While Kidwai maintains that the interview was never meant to be made public, he agrees that the statement conveyed both resolve and prudence and therefore may have worked to Pakistan's advantage once it was out in the public domain. Author's interview of Khalid Kidwai, director general, Strategic Plans Division, during the 2001–2002 standoff, Rawalpindi, July 10, 2013.

88. Basrur, "Coercive Diplomacy," 307.

89. The full text of Musharraf's speech is available at "President General Pervez Musharraf's Address to the Nation, January 12, 2002," South Asia Terrorism Portal, http://www.satp.org/satporgtp/countries/pakistan/document/papers/2002Jan12.htm.

90. Mistry, "Tempering Optimism," 169.

91. Author's interview of Tariq Waseem Ghazi, commander of Pakistan army's V Corps during the 2001–2002 standoff, Copenhagen, June 18, 2013.

92. Smith, "The 2001–2002 Standoff," 194.

93. Ibid., 194–95.

94. Ibid., 195.

95. Ibid., 195–96.

96. Ibid., 196.

97. Nayak and Krepon, *US Crisis Management in South Asia's Twin Peaks Crisis*, 31.

98. Author's interview of Tariq Waseem Ghazi, June 18, 2013.

99. Author's interview of Khalid Kidwai, July 10, 2013.

100. Nayak and Krepon, *US Crisis Management in South Asia's Twin Peaks Crisis*, 25; Bratton, "Signals and Orchestration," 604.

101. Nayak and Krepon, *US Crisis Management in South Asia's Twin Peaks Crisis*, 22–23.

102. C. Raja Mohan, "Diplomacy Precedes Military Response," *Hindu*, December 15, 2001.

103. Author's interview (by phone) of Condoleezza Rice, U.S. national security advisor during the 2001–2002 standoff, March 4, 2016; author's interview of Richard Armitage, U.S. deputy secretary of state during the 2001–2002 standoff, Washington, DC, November 14, 2014.

104. Author's interview of Richard Armitage, November 14, 2014.

105. Ibid.

106. For instance, the U.S. defense attaché in Islamabad, David Smith, reports that their focus remained on ensuring that the military campaign in Afghanistan did not get impacted by the India-Pakistan crisis. Author's interview of David Smith, Istanbul, November 6, 2014.

107. Author's interview of Condoleezza Rice, March 4, 2016.

108. Author's interview of former senior Indian official who wishes to remain anonymous.

109. David E. Sanger, *The Inheritance: The World Obama Confronts and the Challenges to American Power* (New York: Harmony Books, 2009), 221.

110. Author's interview of Condoleezza Rice, March 4, 2016.

111. Author's interview of Richard Armitage, November 14, 2014.

112. Nayak and Krepon, *US Crisis Management in South Asia's Twin Peaks Crisis*, 27–28.

113. Michael Krepon, "Crises in South Asia: Trends and Potential Consequences," in *Crises in South Asia: Trends and Potential Consequences*, eds. Michael Krepon and Nate Cohn (Washington, DC: Henry L. Stimson Center, 2011), 21. For a brief chronology of interaction between Pakistani and Chinese officials during the crisis, see William Shimer, "Chinese Involvement in South Asian Crises," Appendix V, in *Crises in South Asia: Trends and Potential Consequences*, eds. Michael Krepon and Nate Cohn (Washington, DC: Henry L. Stimson Center, 2011), 95–97.

114. Nayak and Krepon, *US Crisis Management in South Asia's Twin Peaks Crisis*, 24; Zachary S. Davis, "Introduction," in *The India-Pakistan Military Standoff: Crisis and Escalation In South Asia*, ed. Zachary S. Davis (New York: Palgrave Macmillan, 2011), 11.

115. Condoleezza Rice, *No Higher Honour: A Memoir of My Years in Washington* (London: Simon and Schuster, 2011), 124.

116. Davis, "Introduction," 11–12.

117. Chari, Cheema, and Cohen, *Four Crises and a Peace Process*, 167.

118. "India Must Exercise Restraint: Powell," *Hindu*, December 17, 2001.

119. U.S. Department of State, "Daily Press Briefing for December 18," December 18, 2001, quoted in Chari, Cheema, and Cohen, *Four Crises and a Peace Process*, 168.

120. Rajiv Chandrasekaran, "Pakistan, India Mass Troops: Tensions Escalate as New Delhi Considers Strike," *Washington Post*, December 24, 2001.

121. "Delhi Attack Was to Harm Pakistan: US," *News*, December 21, 2001.

122. "Bush Hails Action against Extremists," *Dawn*, January 1, 2002.

123. "Powell Hails Musharraf's Move against Militants," *Dawn*, January 5, 2002.

124. Chari, Cheema, and Cohen, *Four Crises and a Peace Process*, 168; "War Not to End Crisis in S. Asia: Powell Banks on Diplomacy," *Dawn*, January 11, 2002.

125. "Stop Aiding Terrorism, U.K. Tells Pak.," *Hindu*, December 17, 2001.

126. Hassan Suroor, "Straw Wants Pak. to Take 'More Effective' Steps," *Hindu*, December 29, 2001.

127. Chari, Cheema, and Cohen, *Four Crises and a Peace Process*, 166–67.

128. Coll, "The Standoff."

129. "Bush Blocks Lashkar Finances," *Hindu*, December 22, 2001.

130. Sridhar Krishnaswami, "U.S. Brands Lashkar, Jaish Terrorist Outfits," *Hindu*, December 27, 2001.

131. Author's interview of Condoleezza Rice, March 4, 2016.

132. Nayak and Krepon, *US Crisis Management in South Asia's Twin Peaks Crisis*, 25.

133. Author's interview of Wendy Chamberlain, U.S. ambassador to Pakistan during phase I of the 2001–2002 standoff, Washington, DC, June 12, 2013.

134. Erik Eckholm, "The India-Pakistan Tension: Islamabad; Pakistan Pledges to Bar any Groups Linked to Terror," *New York Times*, January 13, 2002.

135. "US Wants Peace Efforts to Go On: Bush Rings Musharraf, Vajpayee," *Dawn*, January 14, 2002; Rice, *No Higher Honour*, 126.

136. Todd S. Purdum, "The India-Pakistan Tension: The Diplomacy; Bush Speaks to Leaders and Urges Negotiation," *New York Times*, January 14, 2002.

137. S. Paul Kapur, "Ten Years of Instability in a Nuclear South Asia," *International Security* 33, 2 (Fall 2008): 81.

138. Bhumitra Chakma, "South Asia's Nuclear Deterrence and the USA," in *The Politics of Nuclear Weapons in South Asia*, ed. Bhumitra Chakma (Burlington, VT: Ashgate, 2011), 130.

139. Kanti Bajpai, "To War or Not to War: The India-Pakistan Crisis of 2001–02," in *Nuclear Proliferation in South Asia: Crisis Behaviour and the Bomb*, eds. Sumit Ganguly and S. Paul Kapur (New York: Routledge, 2009), 175.

140. Jawed Naqvi, "India Softens Tone after Powell's Visit: Jaswant Wants Action on Terrorists' List," *Dawn*, January 19, 2002.

141. See, for example, "Musharraf Calls for Third-Party Mediation on Kashmir," *Hindu*, February 14, 2002; "Musharraf Seeks US Mediation on Kashmir," *Dawn*, February 14, 2002.

142. "India Iterates Opposition to Third-Party Mediation," *Hindu*, February 15, 2002.

143. "Indo-US Wargames," *Dawn*, May 5, 2002; "Joint Indo-US Naval Exercise," BBC News, May 5, 2002.

144. Even when in prison, the militant with the highest profile, LeT's leader Hafiz Saeed, was reportedly given access to international phone facilities and was allowed to remain connected with his sympathizers abroad. Hassan Abbas, *Pakistan's Drift into Extremism: Allah, the Army, and America's War on Terror* (Armonk, NY: M. E. Sharpe, 2005), 225. JeM chief Maulana Masood Azhar was also released by the Pakistani courts. Coll, "The Standoff."

145. Mistry, "Tempering Optimism," 166.

146. Nayak and Krepon, *US Crisis Management in South Asia's Twin Peaks Crisis*, 17.

147. Waheguru Pal Singh Sidhu, "Operation Vijay and Operation Parakram: The Victory of Theory?" in *The India-Pakistan Nuclear Relationship: Theories of Deterrence and International Relations*, ed. E. Sridharan (New Delhi: Routledge, 2007), 227.

148. Ganguly and Kraig, "The 2001–2002 Indo-Pakistan Crisis," 305.

149. Mistry, "Tempering Optimism," 166–67.

150. Author's interview (by phone) of Vikram Sood, India's Research and Analysis Wing (RAW) chief during the 2001–2002 standoff, January 12, 2017.

151. Nayak and Krepon, *US Crisis Management in South Asia's Twin Peaks Crisis*, 18.

152. Luv Puri, "Be Ready for Decisive Battle, PM Tells Jawans," *Hindu*, May 23, 2002.

153. Nayak and Krepon, *US Crisis Management in South Asia's Twin Peaks Crisis*, 18.

154. Chari, Cheema, and Cohen, *Four Crises and a Peace Process*, 169.

155. The bulk of this aspect of Indian signaling was pointed at the United States. For examples and a sense of the themes covered in this messaging effort, see quotes from Indian officials in Rahul Bedi, "A Strike Staunched," *Frontline* 19, 12 (June 8–21, 2002); "Vajpayee Rejects Talks Offer," *Dawn*, June 5, 2002; "India Not to Be Impulsive, George Tells Security Conference," *Tribune*, June 3, 2002; "Delhi Reacts to Musharraf's Remark," *Dawn*, June 19, 2002; Sridhar Krishnaswami, "Every Country Has the Right to Pre-emption: Jaswant," *Hindu*, October 1, 2002; "Address by Shri Atal Bihari Vajpayee, Prime Minister of India," 57th session of the U.N. General Assembly, September 13, 2002; P. S. Suryanarayana, "Sinha Rules Out Talks with Pak.," *Hindu*, September 26, 2002.

156. Jawed Naqvi, "Delhi Sees No Chance of N-weapons Use," *Dawn*, June 3, 2002.

157. "Indian Official Says Attack Plan Ready: Defense Ministry Plays Down Report," *Dawn*, June 4, 2002.

158. "India Rules Out Use of Nuclear Weapons," *Times of India*, June 3, 2002.

159. Polly Nayak, *Reducing Collateral Damage to Indo-Pakistani Relations from the War on Terrorism*, Policy Brief 107 (Washington, DC: Brookings Institution, September 2002), 2.

160. "BJP Won't Rule Out War If Terrorist Acts Continue," *Hindu*, May 16, 2002.

161. Jim Hoagland, "Misreading Musharraf," *Washington Post*, May 23, 2002.

162. Ashok Mehta, "Operation Parakram: The Real Winner Was the US," *Tribune*, August 13, 2005.

163. Mistry, "Tempering Optimism," 167.

164. Celia W. Dugger, "India Tones Down War Talks as U.S. Presses Pakistanis," *New York Times*, June 4, 2002.

165. Stolar, *To the Brink*, 21.

166. Stolar reports that while Mishra was convinced that the worst of the crisis was over, Jaswant Singh was not. He thus continued to churn out hawkish rhetoric, including publicly disparaging Musharraf's speech. Ibid., 21–22.

167. Chari, Cheema, and Cohen, *Four Crises and a Peace Process*, 170.

168. Sameer Lalwani, "Danger Zone: Posturing against Pakistan Can Be Costly for India," *Hindustan Times*, September 23, 2015.

169. Coll, "The Standoff."

170. "Infiltration Has Not Declined: Fernandes," *Hindu*, June 6, 2002.

171. Bajpai, "To War or Not to War," 176.

172. Nayak and Krepon, *US Crisis Management in South Asia's Twin Peaks Crisis*, 36.

173. Howard B. Schaffer and Teresita C. Schaffer, *How Pakistan Negotiates with the United States: Riding the Roller Coaster* (Washington, DC: United States Institute of Peace, 2011), 153.

174. Nayak and Krepon, *US Crisis Management in South Asia's Twin Peaks Crisis*, 36–37.

175. Coll, "The Standoff."

176. Mistry, "Tempering Optimism," 170.

177. Ibid., 171.

178. Joshi, "Practice of Coercive Diplomacy," 107–8.

179. Ibid., 100–101.

180. Kapur, *Dangerous Deterrent*, 136.

181. Singh, *Call to Honour*, 269.

182. Chari, Cheema, and Cohen, *Four Crises and a Peace Process*, 179.

183. Joshi, "Practice of Coercive Diplomacy," 92–94.

184. Author's interview of Tariq Waseem Ghazi, June 18, 2013.

185. Basrur, "Coercive Diplomacy," 320.

186. "Pakistan Will Be Stupid to Consider Nukes: Omar," *Times of India*, May 17, 2002.

187. Khan, "Nuclear Signaling, Missiles, and Escalation Control," 88–89; "Pak. Test-Fires Another Missile," *Hindu*, May 27, 2002; "Series of Missile Tests Completed," *Dawn*, May 28, 2002.

188. Author's interview of Khalid Kidwai, July 10, 2013.

189. Smith, "The 2001–2002 Standoff," 203; Feroz H. Khan and Peter R. Lavoy, "Pakistan: The Dilemma of Nuclear Deterrence," in *The Long Shadow: Nuclear Weapons and Security in 21st Century Asia*, ed. Muthiah Alagappa (Stanford, CA: Stanford University Press, 2008), 228.

190. Khan, *Eating Grass*, 350–51.

191. "India Threatens to Scrap Indus Water Treaty," *Dawn*, May 24, 2002.

192. Khan, *Eating Grass*, 350.

193. "Pakistan's Ghauri Missile Is Deterrent for India's Prithvi Missile," *Daily Jang*, May 26, 2002, quoted in Thies and Hellmuth, "Critical Risk," 13.

194. "Press Conference by New Permanent Representative of Pakistan," United Nations, news briefing, May 29, 2002.

195. The text of Musharraf's speech is available at, "Pakistan President General Pervez Musharraf's Address to the Nation," May 27, 2002, http://www.satp.org/satporgtp/countries/pakistan/document/papers/Pervez_May272002.htm.

196. "New Delhi Reaction to Speech Regretted," *Dawn*, May 29, 2002; Ganguly and Kraig, "The 2001–2002 Indo-Pakistani Crisis," 305.

197. Sridhar Krishnaswami, "We Can Take Offensive into Indian Territory: Musharraf," *Hindu*, May 27, 2002.

198. "Musharraf Rules Out Possibility of Nuclear War," *Hindu*, June 2, 2002.

199. "Pakistan Move to Rein in India: World Community Asked to Intervene," *Dawn*, May 19, 2002.

200. Khan, *Eating Grass*, 350; "Pakistan Asks UN to Intervene: War-like Situation," *Dawn*, May 24, 2002.

201. Khan, *Eating Grass*, 350.

202. Smith, "The 2001–2002 Standoff," 200.

203. "We Should Avoid War: Musharraf," *Hindu*, May 31, 2002.

204. Smith, "The 2001–2002 Standoff," 201.

205. Chakma, "South Asia's Nuclear Deterrence," 131.

206. Ibid.

207. Ibid.

208. Mistry, "Tempering Optimism," 169. Mistry's observation was made for Pakistan's concessions in both phases of the crisis but it encapsulates these concessions.

209. Nayak and Krepon, *US Crisis Management in South Asia's Twin Peaks Crisis*, 32.

210. Sanger, *The Inheritance*, 221.

211. Ibid.

212. Nayak and Krepon, *US Crisis Management in South Asia's Twin Peaks Crisis*, 36–37; Schaffer and Schaffer, *How Pakistan Negotiates*, 153.

213. Author's interview of Richard Armitage, November 14, 2014. U.S. ambassador to Pakistan Wendy Chamberlain reported to her staff at the embassy in Islamabad that the consensus in Washington was that India would be justified in acting militarily under the circumstances. Smith, "The 2001–2002 Standoff," 199.

214. Nayak and Krepon, *US Crisis Management in South Asia's Twin Peaks Crisis*, 31.

215. Ibid., 32. Deputy Secretary Armitage also agreed with Powell but these two were in the minority among Washington's crisis managers.

216. Praveen Swami, "A War to End a War: The Causes and Outcomes of the 2001–2 India-Pakistan Crisis," in *Nuclear Proliferation in South Asia: Crisis Behaviour and the Bomb*, eds. Sumit Ganguly and S. Paul Kapur (New York: Routledge, 2009), 152; Chakma, "South Asia's Nuclear Deterrence," 131.

217. Author's interview of David Smith, November 6, 2014.

218. Smith, "The 2001–2002 Standoff," 202.

219. David E. Sanger and Celia W. Dugger, "Bush Intervenes in Effort to Stop a Kashmir War," *New York Times*, June 6, 2002.

220. Elisabeth Bumiller and Thom Shanker, "Bush Presses Pakistan on Kashmir and Orders Rumsfeld to Region," *New York Times*, May 31, 2002.

221. Jim Lehrer's interview of Colin Powell, May 30, 2002, quoted in Raghavan, "A Coercive Triangle," 253.

222. Smith, "The 2001–2002 Standoff," 202.

223. Author's interview of Bruce Riedel, special assistant to the president and senior director for Near East and North African Affairs, National Security Council (2001–2002), Washington. DC, April 30, 2015.

224. Chari, Cheema, and Cohen, *Four Crises and a Peace Process*, 170.

225. Deputy Secretary Armitage deliberately used the advisories as a crisis management tool once they had been issued. Author's interview of Richard Armitage, November 14, 2014.

226. Author's interview of Maleeha Lodhi, Islamabad, August 7, 2013.

227. Author's interview of Richard Armitage, November 14, 2014.

228. Smith, "The 2001–2002 Standoff," 203.

229. Chari, Cheema, and Cohen, *Four Crises and a Peace Process*, 160–61, 170–71; Thomas L. Friedman, "India, Pakistan, and GE," *New York Times*, August 11, 2002; author's interview (by phone) of Jalil Abbas Jilani, Pakistan's head of mission in New Delhi during part of the 2001–2002 standoff, December 11, 2017. Jilani met a senior repesentative of the Federation of Indian Chambers of Commerce and Industry at the time who informed him of the chambers' petition.

230. Nayak and Krepon, *US Crisis Management in South Asia's Twin Peaks Crisis*, 34.

231. John Daniszewski, "Putin Fails in India-Pakistan Peace Bid," *Los Angeles Times*, June 5, 2002.

232. "Bush Makes Personal Appeal for Peace," *Dawn*, June 6, 2002.

233. Chari, Cheema, and Cohen, *Four Crises and a Peace Process*, 169.

234. Ibid.

235. Author's interview of Richard Armitage, November 14, 2014.

236. Nayak and Krepon, *US Crisis Management in South Asia's Twin Peaks Crisis*, 36.

237. Ibid.; Schaffer and Schaffer, *How Pakistan Negotiates*, 153.

238. Nayak and Krepon, *US Crisis Management in South Asia's Twin Peaks Crisis*, 36.

239. Schaffer and Schaffer, *How Pakistan Negotiates*, 153.

240. Ibid.

241. Bhavna Vij and Jyoti Malhotra, "US Puts Money to Musharraf's Mouth," *Indian Express*, June 8, 2002.

242. Seth Mydans, "U.S. Envoy Spells Out to Pakistan Steps to Lower Tension," *New York Times*, June 7, 2002.

243. Mehta, "Operation Parakram." Schaffer and Schaffer analyze the disconnect between U.S. and Pakistani perceptions of what each promised the other during Armitage's visit. For Armitage, the key was to take an attractive message to New Delhi. What Pakistan saw as an American assurance to get India to negotiate on Kashmir was, for Armitage, no more than an agreement to suggest to India that it should resume a dialogue with Pakistan. Musharraf's priority was exactly the opposite—getting Armitage to help force India back to the Kashmir question. Schaffer and Schaffer, *How Pakistan Negotiates*, 153.

244. Coll, "The Standoff."

245. Nayak and Krepon, *US Crisis Management in South Asia's Twin Peaks Crisis*, 37.

246. Ibid.; author's interview of Richard Armitage, November 14, 2014.

247. Author's interview of Richard Armitage, November 14, 2014.

248. Bajpai, "To War or Not to War," 169.

249. Chari, Cheema, and Cohen, *Four Crises and a Peace Process*, 169.

250. Author's interview of Lalit Mansingh, June 18, 2013.

251. Chari, Cheema, and Cohen, *Four Crises and a Peace Process*, 171.

252. Celia W. Dugger, "The Kashmir Brink," *New York Times*, June 20, 2002.

253. Author's interview of Vikram Sood, January 12, 2017.

254. Joshi, "Practice of Coercive Diplomacy," 103.

255. Zhang Guihong argues, more generally, that Chinese policy on South Asian nuclear deterrence at this time was driven by the sole consideration of preventing escalation of an India-Pakistan conflict. Zhang Guihong, "US Security Policy towards South Asia after September 11 and Its Implications for China: A Chinese Perspective," *Strategic Analysis* 27, 2 (2003): 145–71.

256. Mark Fitzpatrick, *Overcoming Pakistan's Nuclear Dangers* (London: Routledge, 2014), 63.

257. Author's interview of Lalit Mansingh, June 18, 2013.

258. Mistry, "Tempering Optimism," 171.

259. See Scott D. Sagan, "The Perils of Proliferation: Organization Theory, Deterrence Theory and the Spread of Nuclear Weapons," *International Security* 18, 4 (Spring 1994): 66–107.

260. Sood and Sawhney, *Operation Parakram*, 80.
261. Nayak, *Reducing Collateral Damage to Indo-Pakistani Relations from the War on Terrorism*, 2.
262. Thies and Hellmuth, "Critical Risk," 7.
263. Sidhu, "Operation Vijay and Operation Parakram," 227; author's interview of Tariq Waseem Ghazi, June 18, 2013.
264. Joshi, "Practice of Coercive Diplomacy," 72.
265. Author's interview of Richard Armitage, November 14, 2014.
266. Ibid.

Chapter 5

1. Arabinda Acharya, Sujoyini Mandal, and Akanksha Mehta, *Terrorist Attacks in Mumbai: Picking Up the Pieces* (Singapore: International Centre for Political Violence and Terrorism Research, S. Rajaratnam School for International Studies, Nanyang Technological University, 2009), 6. For a complete chronology of the Mumbai attacks, see John Wilson et al., *Mumbai Attacks: Response and Lessons* (New Delhi: Observer Research Foundation, n.d.), 11–15.
2. Acharya, Mandal, and Mehta, *Terrorist Attacks in Mumbai*, 21–22.
3. Tushar Srivastava, "I Was Being Trained in Pak, Reveals Kasab," *Hindustan Times*, December 4, 2008.
4. Jayadeva Uyangoda, "After the Mumbai Tragedy," *Economic and Political Weekly* 43, 51 (December 20–26, 2008): 8. Also see Sukumar Muralidharan, "Mumbai, Militarism and the Media," *Economic and Political Weekly* 43, 49 (December 6–12, 2008): 15–18.
5. Amit Baruah and Sandeep Dikshit, "India, Pak. Ceasefire Comes into Being," *Hindu*, November 26, 2003.
6. The 2003–2005 period saw an absence of any major terrorist incidents on mainland India that were attributable to Pakistan. Cross-LoC infiltration also decreased. B. Raman, *Mumbai 26/11: A Day of Infamy* (New Delhi: Lancer Publishers, 2009), 62; Anit Mukherjee, "A Brand New Day or Back to the Future? The Dynamics of India-Pakistan Relations," *India Review* 8, 4 (October–December 2009): 422–23.
7. See Moeed Yusuf (with contributions from Megan Neville, Ayesha Chugh, and Stephanie Flamenbaum), "Pakistan's Militancy Challenge: From Where, to What," in *Pakistan's Counterterrorism Challenge*, ed. Moeed Yusuf (Washington, DC: Georgetown University Press, 2014), 15–33.
8. For a summary of the "capacity" versus "will" debate in terms of Pakistan's approach to counterterrorism, see ibid., 33–41.
9. Pakistan had formally banned LeT after the 2001–2002 standoff but most of its cadres who were rounded up during the crisis and the several

crackdowns thereafter were let go. Tony Karon, "After Mumbai, Can the US Cool India-Pakistan Tension?" *Time*, December 4, 2008. Organizationally too, LeT escaped the crackdowns as it got enough time to move and conceal its funds and immediately began operating under its alias, Jama'at-ud-Dawa, which had existed as a registered charity organization since the 1980s. See Stephen Tankel, *Lashkar-e-Taiba: From 9/11 to Mumbai* (London: International Centre for the Study of Radicalisation and Political Violence, April–May 2009).

10. U.S. intelligence sources later claimed to have unearthed evidence that pointed to involvement of ISI personnel in planning the Kabul attack. Bill Roggio, "41 Killed in Kabul Suicide Strike at Indian Embassy," *Long War Journal*, July 7, 2008; "Report: U.S. Officials Say Pakistan Helped Plan Indian Embassy Blast," Fox News, August 1, 2008. LeT was suspected of having a role in terrorist attacks in New Delhi in October 2005, in Bangalore in December 2005, in Varanasi in March 2006, in Nagpur in June 2006, and in Mumbai in July 2007. Ashley J. Tellis, "Lessons from Mumbai—Part II," Testimony before the Senate Homeland Security and Governmental Affair Committees, January 28, 2009, in *Mumbai, India and Terrorism*, ed. Elena N. Popov (New York: Nova Science, 2010), 78.

11. Neil Joeck, "The Indo-Pakistani Nuclear Confrontation: Lessons from the Past, Contingencies for the Future," in *Pakistan's Nuclear Future: Reining in the Risk*, ed. Henry Sokolski (Carlisle, PA: Strategic Studies Institute, 2009), 40.

12. For details of Cold Start and the thinking behind the doctrine, see Walter C. Ladwig III, "A Cold Start for Hot Wars? The Indian Army's New Limited War Doctrine," *International Security* 32, 3 (Winter 2007–2008): 163–67; Subhash Kapila, *India's New "Cold Start" War Doctrine Strategically Reviewed*, Paper no. 991 (n.p.: South Asia Analysis Group, May 4, 2004).

13. Polly Nayak and Michael Krepon, *The Unfinished Crisis: US Crisis Management after the 2008 Mumbai Attacks* (Washington, DC: Henry L. Stimson Center, 2012), 27.

14. The nuclear deal required a change in U.S. law and in the regulations of the Nuclear Suppliers Group, which controls the global export of nuclear material, equipment, and technology and prohibits supply to countries like India that are non-signatories to the Nuclear Nonproliferation Treaty. For background and analysis of various technical and political facets of the nuclear deal, see Carl Paddock, *India-US Nuclear Deal: Prospects and Implications* (New Delhi: Epitome Books, 2009). Also see Dinshaw Mistry, *The US-India Nuclear Agreement: Diplomacy and Domestic Politics* (Cambridge: Cambridge University Press, 2014).

15. Raman, *Mumbai 26/11*, 107.

16. Daniel S. Markey, *No Exit from Pakistan: America's Tortured Relationship with Islamabad* (New York: Cambridge University Press, 2013), 105–68.

17. For a representation of the official Pakistani view, see Adil Sultan Muhammad, *Indo-US Civilian Nuclear Cooperation Agreement: Implications on South Asian Security Environment* (Washington, DC: Henry L. Stimson Center, July 2006). Pakistan officially conveyed its concerns to the International Atomic Energy Commission through a formal letter written by its permanent representative to the commission on July 18, 2008. The text of the letter is available at http://carnegieendowment.org/files/pakistanletter_iaea_20080718.pdf.

18. For an insight into the line of thinking in the United States that fuels Pakistani concerns about nefarious U.S. designs on Pakistan's program, see Frederick W. Kagan and Michael O'Hanlon, "Pakistan's Collapse, Our Problem," *New York Times*, November 18, 2007.

19. Michael V. Hayden, *Playing to the Edge: American Intelligence in the Age of Terror* (New York: Penguin Press, 2016), 345–51.

20. Uyangoda, "After the Mumbai Tragedy," 8. For a typical representation of this sentiment at the time, see the *Hindustan Times* editorial "Dealing with the Neighbor," December 2, 2008.

21. Emily Wax and Rama Lakshmi, "Indian Official Says Pakistan's ISI Trained, Supported Mumbai Attackers," *Washington Post*, December 6, 2008.

22. George Friedman, "Strategic Motivations for the Mumbai Attack," *Geopolitical Weekly* 12, 18 (December 1, 2008).

23. Ibid.

24. Shivshankar Menon, *Choices: Inside the Making of India's Foreign Policy* (Washington, DC: Brookings Institution Press, 2016), 62.

25. Author's interview (by Skype) of Milan Naidu, India's officiating army chief during the initial days of the Mumbai crisis, November 21, 2014.

26. Pranab Dhal Samanta, "26/11: How India Debated a War with Pakistan That November," *Indian Express*, November 26, 2010.

27. Ibid.; author's interview of Milan Naidu, November 21, 2014.

28. Barbara Starr, "U.S.: India's Air Force 'On Alert' after Mumbai Attacks," CNN, December 15, 2008; Samanta, "26/11."

29. Samanta, "26/11."

30. Nandini R. Iyer, "PM: Our Neighbours Will Have to Pay If . . . ," *Hindustan Times*, November 27, 2008.

31. "India Serves Demarche on Pakistan," *Hindu*, December 2, 2008.

32. Rajesh Basrur et al., *The 2008 Mumbai Terrorist Attacks: Strategic Fallout*, Monograph no. 17 (Singapore: S. Rajaratnam School of International Studies, Nanyang Technological University, 2009), 18.

33. "No Military Action against Pakistan: Mukherjee," *Dawn*, December 2, 2008.

34. "War with Pakistan Not a Solution: India," *Dawn*, December 11, 2008.

35. "Indian Envoy Summoned Over Airspace Violation," *Dawn*, December 18, 2008.

36. Jawed Naqvi, "War Not an Option, says India," *Dawn*, December 17, 2008.

37. "Disinformation Campaign, Says India," *Hindu*, December 19, 2008; "India Will Be Obliged to Consider All Options," *Indian Express*, December 19, 2008.

38. Jawed Naqvi, "India Threatens to Act If World Doesn't," *Dawn*, December 23, 2008.

39. "India, Pakistan: Signs of a Coming War," Stratfor, December 24, 2008; "Geopolitical Diary: Countdown to a Crisis on the Subcontinent," Stratfor, December 22, 2008; "India May Still Strike at Pakistan: US Report," *Times of India*, December 19, 2008.

40. Jawed Naqvi, "India Denies Issuing Ultimatum; DGMOs Hold Talks," *Dawn*, December 29, 2008; "India, Pakistan: Signs"; Ramesh Vinayak, "India Amassing Troops on Rajasthan Border, Claims Pak Portal," *India Today*, December 22, 2008; Sachin Parashar, "Not Safe to Be in Pakistan, India Tells Its Citizens," *Times of India*, December 27, 2008.

41. "Singh Calls Military Meet as Tensions Escalate," *Dawn*, December 26, 2008; Iftikhar Gilani, "Indian NCA Discusses All Available Options," *Daily Times*, December 26, 2008.

42. Naqvi, "India Denies Issuing Ultimatum."

43. "India's Gift to Pakistan on New Year," *Hindu*, December 31, 2008.

44. Nayak and Krepon, *The Unfinished Crisis*, 49.

45. Raman, *Mumbai 26/11*, 115.

46. Basrur et al., *The 2008 Mumbai Terrorist Attacks*, 17.

47. V. Krishna and Amit Baruah, "Tensions Mount as Zardari Rules Out Handing over Fugitives to India," *Hindustan Times*, December 4, 2008.

48. "Pakistan's Lashkar Arrests, An Eyewash: India," IBN Live, December 10, 2008.

49. Jawed Naqvi, "India Hands Over Mumbai 'Evidence' to Pakistan," *Dawn*, January 6, 2009.

50. "PM Singh: Attacks Supported by 'Official Agencies,'" *Dawn*, January 6, 2009; "We Want Actual Action," *Outlook India*, January 5, 2009.

51. "A 'Friendly' Handshake to Defuse Tension," *Dawn*, January 20, 2009.

52. Vinay Kumar, "Diplomacy Has Prevailed, Asserts Pranab," *Hindu*, February 19, 2009.

53. Menon, *Choices*, 60–61.

54. Nayak and Krepon, *The Unfinished Crisis*, 46.

55. Ejaz Haider, "Indo-U.S. Ties and Washington's Crisis Brokering," *Newsweek Pakistan*, September 16, 2016.

56. Author's interview of a senior crisis manager during the Mumbai crisis who wishes to remain anonymous.

57. Roundtable interaction at the Delhi Policy Group organized for the author to discuss this research, New Delhi, March 25, 2013.

58. Menon, *Choices*, 62–63.

59. Sumit Ganguly, *Deadly Impasse: Indo-Pak Relations at the Dawn of a New Century* (Cambridge: Cambridge University Press, 2016), 100.

60. Nayak and Krepon, *The Unfinished Crisis*, 35.

61. Anita Joshua, "Manmohan Apologizes for 'Failing' to Prevent Attacks," *Hindu*, December 12, 2008.

62. Naqvi, "India Threatens."

63. "India Asks UN to Ban Jamaatud Dawa," *Dawn*, December 10, 2008.

64. Pakistan had immediately responded to one demarche by merely reiterating its proposal to set up a joint investigation under the NSAs of the two countries. It responded to the second one a week later by presenting a counter-demarche in which it simply refused to extradite individuals India had demanded. Baqir Sajjad Syed, "Pakistan's Response to India's Demand Likely in a Couple of Days," *Dawn*, December 8, 2008; Baqir Sajjad Syed, "Extradition Demand Rejected in Response to Demarche," *Dawn*, December 9, 2008.

65. K. Alan Kronstadt, "Terrorist Attacks in Mumbai, India, and Implications for U.S. Interests," in *Mumbai, India and Terrorism*, ed. Elena N. Popov (New York: Nova Science, 2010), 5. For the text of the U.S. House of Representatives Resolution 1532, see "US Congress Passes Resolution Condemning Mumbai Attacks," December 12, 2008, http://www.thefreelibrary.com/US+C ongress+passes+resolution+condemning+Mumbai+attacks.-a0199282375.

66. "Outlawed Jamaat Gets New Avatar," *Hindustan Times*, January 2, 2008.

67. Author's interview (by Skype) of Shiv Shankar Menon, India's foreign secretary during the Mumbai crisis, September 6, 2016; Basrur et al., *The 2008 Mumbai Terrorist Attacks*, 21.

68. Author's interview of Shiv Shankar Menon, September 6, 2016.

69. Jawed Naqvi, "Singh Hopes Pakistan Will Hand Over Mumbai Masterminds," *Dawn*, January 4, 2009.

70. Nayan Chanda, "On Top of Their Game," *Times of India*, December 25, 2010.

71. Haider, "Indo-U.S. Ties."

72. Ibid.

73. For an official version of the FBI's role in the Mumbai investigations, see the testimony of FBI's chief intelligence officer, Donald Van Duyn, before the U.S. Senate Committee on Homeland Security and Governmental Affairs, January 8, 2009.

74. Haider, "Indo-U.S. Ties."

75. Siddarth Varadarajan, "India Does U-turn on Extradition of Mumbai Suspects," blogpost on *Reality, One Bite at a Time,* January 16, 2009, http://svaradarajan.blogspot.com/2009/01/india-does-u-turn-on-extradition-of.html; Kamal Siddiqi and Amit Baruah, "Pakistan Says It's Cooperating," *Hindustan Times,* January 16, 2009.

76. Ganguly, *Deadly Impasse,* 103.

77. Raza Khan, "Pakistan-India: U.S. Pressure to Thaw Relations," *World Politics Review,* June 23, 2009; Saeed Shah, "Pakistan, India Resume Dialogue, But Not Peace Talks," McClatchy DC Bureau, July 16, 2009; "U.S. Careful on India-Pakistan," United Press International, July 21, 2009.

78. Author's interview of Mahmud Durrani, Pakistan's NSA during the Mumbai crisis, Lahore, May 14, 2013.

79. "We Feared Indian Strike: ISI Chief," *Hindu,* January 8, 2009.

80. Zaffar Abbas, "A Hoax Call That Could Have Triggered War," *Dawn,* December 6, 2008.

81. Author's interview of Asif Ali Zardari, Pakistan's president during the Mumbai crisis, Washington, DC, February 10, 2016; author's interview of Ashfaq Parvez Kayani, Pakistan's army chief during the Mumbai crisis, Rawalpindi, August 18, 2016; Saeed Shah, "Mysterious Phone Call Brought Nuclear Rivals to the Brink after Mumbai," *Guardian,* December 8, 2008.

82. Author's interview of Shahid Malik, Pakistan's high commissioner to India during the Mumbai crisis, Lahore, August 31, 2016.

83. Abbas, "Hoax Call"; author's interview of Ashfaq Parvez Kayani, August 18, 2016.

84. Syed I. Raza, "No Alarming Indian Military Buildup: ISPR," *Dawn,* December 1, 2008.

85. Syed I. Raza, "Govt Convenes All Party Conference," *Dawn,* December 1, 2008.

86. "IAF Denies Pak Claims of Airspace Violation," *Times of India,* December 15, 2008; "Govt. Downplays Indian Jets' Airspace Breach," *Dawn,* December 14, 2008.

87. Iftikhar A. Khan, "Indian Planes Intrude into Pakistan's Airspace," *Dawn,* December 14, 2008.

88. Khalid Tanveer, "Pakistan Warns India It Will Respond to Any Attack," Associated Press, December 25, 2008.

89. "Will Retaliate 'Within Minutes' If India Strikes: Kayani," *Indian Express,* December 24, 2008.

90. Iftikhar A. Khan, "'Surgical Strike' Speculation Quashed," *Dawn,* December 25, 2008.

91. "Pakistan Military on 'High Alert,'" *Al Jazeera,* December 23, 2008.

92. Ibid.; Zein Basravi, "Pakistan Moves Troops to India Border," CNN, December 26, 2008; "Pakistan Deploying More Troops along Border: BSF," *Times of India,* December 25, 2008.

93. Naqvi, "India Denies Issuing Ultimatum"; Basravi, "Pakistan Moves Troops."

94. Author's interview of Mahmud Durrani, May 14, 2013.

95. Salman Masood, "Pakistan's Spy Chief to Visit India," *New York Times*, November 28, 2008.

96. Nirupama Subramanian, "Our Hands Are Clean: Pakistan," *Hindu*, November 30, 2009.

97. Pakistani president Zardari expounded on Pakistan's stance two days after receiving the demarches: "At the moment these are just names of individuals. No proof, no investigation, nothing has been brought forward." "We have not been given any tangible proof to say that he is definitely a Pakistani. I very much doubt . . . that he's [Ajmal Kasab] a Pakistani." Krishna and Baruah, "Tensions Mount." For an example of the denial of Kasab's identity much later in December, see Syed I. Raza, "No Counsellor Access for Kasab: Malik," *Dawn*, December 24, 2008.

98. For instance, Pakistan's leading news channel, Geo TV, revealed on December 12 that its team had visited Kasab's village and confirmed his identity. Nirupama Subramanian, "Ajmal Is a Pakistani: Geo TV," *Hindu*, December 13, 2008.

99. Nirupama Subramanian, "Furnish Evidence, Says Pakistan," *Hindu*, December 13, 2008.

100. Angel Rabasa et al., *The Lessons of Mumbai* (Santa Monica, CA: RAND, 2009), 17.

101. Syed I. Raza, "JuD Leaders Arrested, Camps Shut Down: Rehman Malik," *Dawn*, January 9, 2016; Siddiqi and Baruah, "Pakistan Says It's Cooperating."

102. "Pakistan Backtracks on Link to Mumbai Attacks: NY," *Nation*, February 13, 2009.

103. Within a week of announcing the investigation's findings, Pakistan set up special proceedings of the Anti-Terrorism Court in the central jail where the Mumbai accused were being detained. "Lakhvi, Two Others Remanded to FIA," *Nation*, February 20, 2009.

104. "India Urged to Respond Quickly to Pakistan's Queries," *Dawn*, February 25, 2016; "India Delayed 26/11 Probe: Pakistan," *Times of India*, July 11, 2009.

105. Nayak and Krepon, *The Unfinished Crisis*, 51; Raman, *Mumbai 26/11*, 122.

106. Author's interview of Husain Haqqani, Pakistan's ambassador to the United States during the Mumbai crisis, Washington, DC, June 27, 2016.

107. List of countries collated from author's interviews of Pakistani and U.S. officials involved in the Mumbai crisis.

108. Author's interview of Mahmud Durrani, Rawalpindi, August 18, 2016. Durrani had conveyed these points to acting U.S. ambassador in Islamabad, Gerald Feierstein.

109. Acting U.S. ambassador Gerald Feierstein and U.S. officials in Washington were the first ports of call. Author's interview (by phone) of Anne W. Patterson, U.S. ambassador to Pakistan during the Mumbai crisis, June 14, 2013; author's interview of Asif Ali Zardari, February 10, 2016.

110. Author's interview of Shahid Malik, August 31, 2016.

111. Author's interview of Anne W. Patterson, June 14, 2013.

112. Author's interview of Condoleezza Rice (by phone), U.S. secretary of state during the Mumbai crisis, March 4, 2016; Bob Woodward, *Obama's Wars* (New York: Simon and Schuster, 2010), 46.

113. Author's interview of Husain Haqqani, June 27, 2016.

114. Siobhan Gorman and Matthew Rosenberg, "Terror in Mumbai: Attacks Linked to Pakistan Group," *Wall Street Journal*, December 1, 2008; Eric Schmitt, Somini Sengupta, and Jane Perlez, "U.S. and India See Link to Militants in Pakistan," *New York Times*, December 2, 2008; Wax and Lakshmi, "Indian Official Says Pakistan's ISI Trained, Supported Mumbai Attacker."

115. White House spokesperson Dana Perino affirmed during a press conference: "We have no reason not to trust Pakistan right now. I've heard nothing that says the Pakistani government was involved." Anwar Iqbal, "US Trusts Pakistan, Says White House," *Dawn*, December 1, 2008.

116. The transcript of the interview, aired on December 2, 2008, is available as "Interview with President Asif Ali Zardari/Eyewitness to Terror," CNN, http://transcripts.cnn.com/TRANSCRIPTS/0812/02/lkl.01.html.

117. Hayden, *Playing to the Edge*, 352.

118. Author's interview of Michael V. Hayden, CIA director during the Mumbai crisis, Washington, DC, December 10, 2015.

119. "Pak May Relocate 100,000 Army Personnel to Border," *Rediff India Abroad*, November 29, 2008.

120. Syed I. Raza, "Pakistan Delivers Clear Message to Mullen," *Dawn*, December 4, 2008.

121. Nayak and Krepon, *The Unfinished Crisis*, 45.

122. Ibid.

123. Author's interview of Mahmud Durrani, May 14, 2013.

124. Ibid.

125. Nayak and Krepon, *The Unfinished Crisis*, 45.

126. Khan, "'Surgical Strike' Speculation Quashed."

127. Khurshid Mahmud Kasuri, *Neither a Hawk nor a Dove: An Insider's Account of Pakistan's Foreign Relations Including Details of the Kashmir Framework* (Karachi: Oxford University Press, 2015), 429–30; Imtiaz Gul, "Surgical Strikes Post-Uri?" *Express Tribune*, September 30, 2016.

128. Author's interview of Ashfaq Parvez Kayani, August 18, 2016.

129. Author's discourse with Ahmed Shuja Pasha, ISI chief during the Mumbai crisis, August 19, 2016; author's interview of Ashfaq Parvez Kayani, August 18, 2016.

130. Khan, "'Surgical Strike' Speculation Quashed."

131. Author's interview of Asif Ali Zardari, February 10, 2016.

132. Haider, "Indo-U.S. Ties."

133. "India Failed to Provide Information for Listing Militants as Terrorists," *Dawn*, June 6, 2011.

134. Amit Baruah, "Pakistan 'Shared Mumbai Attacks Research with India,'" BBC News, December 4, 2010.

135. President Zardari authorized the ISI to share the information after ISI chief General Pasha briefed him on his recent meeting with CIA director Michael Hayden. Baruah, "Pakistan 'Shared Mumbai Attacks Research with India.'" Zardari acknowledged to the U.S. ambassador in Pakistan that he did so to signal his commitment. "Pak Agreed to Share Information on Mumbai Attacks with India: WikiLeaks," *Thaindian News*, December 5, 2010.

136. Haider, "Indo-U.S. Ties."

137. Ibid.

138. Author's interview of Asif Ali Zardari, February 10, 2016.

139. Haider, "Indo-U.S. Ties."

140. U.S. officials conveyed this to visiting Pakistani NSA Mahmud Durrani in a meeting at the State Department in mid-December. Author's interview of a senior interlocutor during the Mumbai crisis who wishes to remain anonymous.

141. "India Delayed 26/11 Probe."

142. Author's interview of Condoleezza Rice, March 4, 2016; Samanta, "26/11."

143. Rice, *No Higher Honour*, 719.

144. Author's interview of Anne W. Patterson, June 14, 2013.

145. Nayak and Krepon, *The Unfinished Crisis*, 27.

146. Ibid., 58.

147. For a detailed account of the initial frenzy and the difficulties in coordinating a response due to the vacation, see ibid., 5–10.

148. Hayden, *Playing to the Edge*, 352.

149. Author's interview of a senior U.S. interlocutor during the Mumbai crisis who wishes to remain anonymous.

150. Woodward, *Obama's Wars*, 45.

151. Author's interview of a senior U.S. interlocutor during the Mumbai crisis who wishes to remain anonymous.

152. Author's interview of Michael V. Hayden, December 10, 2015.

153. Author's interview of Anne W. Patterson, June 14, 2013.

154. Author's interview of Anish Goel, director for South Asia, U.S. National Security Council (2008–2011), Washington, DC, November 3, 2017.

155. Author's interview of a senior U.S. interlocutor during the Mumbai crisis who wishes to remain anonymous.

156. Author's interview of a senior U.S. interlocutor during the Mumbai crisis who wishes to remain anonymous.

157. Nayak and Krepon, *The Unfinished Crisis*, 57.

158. Author's interview of Condoleezza Rice, March 4, 2016; author's interview of Michael V. Hayden, December 10, 2015.

159. Author's interview of Condoleezza Rice, March 4, 2016.

160. Rice, *No Higher Honour*, 719.

161. Haider, "Indo-U.S. Ties."

162. Kavitha Rao, "Travel Update: Some Advice for Visitors to Mumbai," *New York Times*, November 29, 2008.

163. Raman, *Mumbai 26/11*, 213–14.

164. Nayak and Krepon, *The Unfinished Crisis*, 20.

165. Woodward, *Obama's Wars*, 46.

166. Author's e-mail correspondence (in the follow up to an interview) with Bruce Riedel, May 8, 2015.

167. Author's interview of Michael V. Hayden, December 10, 2015.

168. Author's e-mail correspondence with Bruce Riedel, May 8, 2015.

169. "'Pak State Not Behind Mumbai Attacks,'" *Hindustan Times*, January 14, 2008.

170. Nayak and Krepon, *The Unfinished Crisis*, 13.

171. Rice, *No Higher Honour*, 720.

172. Ibid.

173. Ibid.

174. "Need for Direct and Tough Action by Pak: Rice," *India Today*, December 3, 2008.

175. Rice, *No Higher Honour*, xviii.

176. "Rice Warns India against Unintended Consequences," Reuters, December 3, 2008.

177. Haider, "Indo-U.S. Ties."

178. Author's interview of Anish Goel, November 7, 2017.

179. Haider, "Indo-U.S. Ties."

180. Sandeep Dikshit, "Pranab Rules Out Military Action," *Hindu*, December 3, 2008.

181. Nayak and Krepon, *The Unfinished Crisis*, 38; author's interview (by phone) of Polly Nayak, co-author of Nayak and Krepon, *The Unfinished Crisis*, June 15, 2013.

182. Quoted in Basrur et al., *The 2008 Mumbai Terrorist Attacks*, 22; "Pakistan Will Act If Evidence Is Credible: Gilani," *Dawn*, January 5, 2009.

183. Raman, *Mumbai 26/11*, 125.

184. The list has been collated and triangulated based on interviews of U.S. officials involved in managing the Mumbai crisis.

185. Author's interview of Mahmud Durrani, May 14, 2013.

186. Nayak and Krepon, *The Unfinished Crisis*, 26.

187. "Rice Call Prompted Hasty Decision to Send DG ISI," *News*, November 30, 2008.

188. Author's interview of Ashfaq Parvez Kayani, August 18, 2016; "ISI Representative to Visit India Instead of Pasha," *Dawn*, November 29, 2008.

189. "U.S. Pushed for Pasha's India Visit," *Hindu*, May 21, 2011.

190. Author's interview of a senior interlocutor directly involved in this conversation who wishes to remain anonymous.

191. Author's interview of Michael V. Hayden, December 10, 2015.

192. Ambassador Haqqani had communicated this assessment formally to Islamabad. Author's interview of Husain Haqqani, June 27, 2016.

193. Author's interview of Thomas F. Lynch III, special assistant to the chairman of the U.S. Joint Chiefs of Staff, Admiral Michael Mullen, Washington, DC, June 14, 2013.

194. Rice's meeting with the Pakistani prime minister got especially heated. Upon Prime Minister Gilani's denial of any Pakistani links, she told him "Mr. Prime Minister, either you're lying to me or your people are lying to you." She also let it be known that the United States was not blaming the Pakistani government but that rogue elements from within could have been involved. Rice, *No Higher Honour*, 721.

195. Author's interview of Husain Haqqani, June 27, 2016.

196. Basrur et al., *The 2008 Mumbai Terrorist Attacks*, 20.

197. Author's interview of Anne W. Patterson, June 14, 2013.

198. Author's interview (by phone) of Ejaz Haider, one of the attendees of the meeting in which McCain made these remarks, August 15, 2016; Nirupama Subramaniam, "McCain Warns Pakistan of Indian Air Strikes," *Hindu*, December 7, 2008.

199. Author's interview of Ejaz Haider, August 15, 2016.

200. Nayak and Krepon, *The Unfinished Crisis*, 42.

201. Kasuri, *Neither a Hawk nor a Dove*, 428–30.

202. Wilson et al., "Mumbai Attacks," 37.

203. Nayak and Krepon, *The Unfinished Crisis*, 43; author's interview of a senior Pakistani interlocutor during the Mumbai crisis who wishes to remain anonymous.

204. Saibal Dasgupta, "China Quizzes Pakistan Over Mumbai Attack," *Times of India*, December 2, 2008.

205. "Pakistan Has Taken Positive Steps: US," *Dawn*, December 9, 2008.

206. On the European Union's reaction, see Shada Islam, "EU Welcomes Crackdown," *Dawn*, December 9, 2008.

207. Nayak and Krepon, *The Unfinished Crisis*, 45.

208. Author's interview of Mahmud Durrani, May 14, 2013; author's interview of Stephen J. Hadley, U.S. NSA during the Mumbai crisis, Washington, DC, June 6, 2013.

209. Anwar Iqbal, "US Urges Pakistan to Understand 'Gravity' of Situation," *Dawn*, December 21, 2008.

210. Anwar Iqbal, "Rice Urges Restraint as Relocation of Troops Alarms US," *Dawn*, December 29, 2008.

211. Anwar Iqbal, "Zardari and Singh Ease Bush Worries: US Phone Diplomacy," *Dawn*, January 1, 2009.

212. "Pak Army 'Paid Wages' to Lashkar," *Tribune*, December 19, 2010.

213. Author's interview of a senior Pakistani interlocutor during the Mumbai crisis who wishes to remain anonymous.

214. "General Kayani Calls for Calm with India," *Dawn*, December 29, 2008; Nirupama Subramanian, "Zardari Calls for De-escalation of Tensions," *Hindu*, December 30, 2008.

215. Nayak and Krepon, *The Unfinished Crisis* 46; Basrur et al., *The 2008 Mumbai Terrorist Attacks*, 22.

216. Author's interview of Asif Ali Zardari, February 10, 2016.

217. "India Warned of Response to Pakistan Attack: Wikileaks," *Dawn*, May 20, 2011.

218. Author's interview of Stephen J. Hadley, June 6, 2013.

219. The war approach lay at the heart of the Bush administration's doctrine of preemption that informed U.S. strategy in the war in Afghanistan (and Iraq). See National Security Council, *The National Security Strategy of the United States of America* (Washington DC: National Security Council, September 20, 2002).

220. See, for example, Carlos Lozada, "A Conversation with David Kilcullen," *Washington Post*, March 22, 2009; David E. Sanger, "Pakistan Overshadows Afghanistan on US Agenda," *New York Times*, May 6, 2009.

221. Brian M. Jenkins, "Terrorists Can Think Strategically: Lessons Learned from the Mumbai Attacks," Testimony before the U.S. Senate Homeland Security and Governmental Affairs Committee, January 28, 2009, 3.

222. Nayak and Krepon, *The Unfinished Crisis*, 56.

223. Hayden, *Playing to the Edge*, 345–51.

224. Raman, *Mumbai 26/11*, 213–14.

225. David Carter, "The Compellence Dilemma: International Disputes with Violent Groups," *International Studies Quarterly* 59, 3 (2015): 472–74.

226. Rice, *No Higher Honour*, 720.

227. Author's interview of Shahid Malik, August 31, 2016.

228. Author's interview of a senior Pakistani interlocutor during the Mumbai crisis who wishes to remain anonymous.

229. Rice, *No Higher Honour*, 720.

230. Author's interview of Shah Mahmood Qureshi, Islamabad, July 22, 2010. Mukherjee and Qureshi had only one conversation on November 28 but no such threat had been communicated according to Qureshi. See "Statement by External Affairs Minister Mr. Pranab Mukherjee on the Hoax Telephone Call to President Zardari of Pakistan," Embassy of India, Washington, DC, Embassy Archives, December 7, 2008.

231. Author's interview of Condoleezza Rice, March 4, 2016.

232. "Jailed Militant's Hoax Calls Drove India, Pakistan to Brink of War," *Dawn*, November 26, 2009.

233. Hayden, *Playing to the Edge*, 352.

Chapter 6

1. Author's interviews of former U.S. interlocutors revealed a firm and deeply held consensus on this point. There was not a single dissenting view.

2. Author's interview (by phone) of Condoleezza Rice, U.S. national security advisor during the 2001–2002 standoff and U.S. secretary of state during the Mumbai crisis, March 4, 2016; author's interview of Stephen J. Hadley, U.S. national security advisor during the Mumbai crisis, Washington, DC, June 6, 2013.

3. Author's interview of Peter R. Lavoy, special assistant to the U.S. president and senior director for South Asia, National Security Council (2015–2017), Washington, DC, June 1, 2017.

4. Nayak and Krepon use the term "issue competition" to warn of the possible distraction competing priorities may cause for U.S. policy makers when a crisis erupts in South Asia. Polly Nayak and Michael Krepon, *The Unfinished Crisis: US Crisis Management after the 2008 Mumbai Attacks* (Washington, DC: Henry L. Stimson Center, 2012), 64.

5. On Washington's de-hyphenation policy, see Ashley J. Tellis, "The Merits of Dehyphenation: Explaining U.S. Success in Engaging India and Pakistan," *Washington Quarterly* 31, 4 (Autumn 2008): 21–42.

6. Bruce Riedel, *American Diplomacy and the 1999 Kargil Summit at Blair House* (Philadelphia: Center for the Advanced Study of India, University of Pennsylvania, 2002), 3–4.

7. Michael Krepon, "Crises in South Asia: Trends and Potential Consequences" in *Crises in South Asia: Trends and Potential Consequences*, eds. Michael Krepon and Nate Cohn (Washington, DC: Henry L. Stimson Center, 2011), 21.

8. Andrew Small, "As Indo-Pak Tensions Simmer, China Adopts Diplomatic Balancing Act," *Wire*, September 30, 2016.

9. Timothy W. Crawford, *Pivotal Deterrence: Third-Party Statecraft and the Pursuit of Peace* (Ithaca, NY: Cornell University Press, 2003), 1–2.

10. The term "contract out" comes from Moeed Yusuf, "Banking on an Outsider: Implications for Escalation Control in South Asia," *Arms Control Today* 41, 5 (June 2011): 21–27.

11. P. R. Chari, Pervaiz I. Cheema, and Stephen P. Cohen, *Four Crises and a Peace Process: American Engagement in South Asia* (Washington, DC: Brookings Institution Press, 2007), 218.

12. Prime Minister Vajpayee's government had lost a vote of confidence in the parliament shortly before the Kargil crisis and was thus bound to hold elections in the coming months. "Vajpayee Loses Confidence Vote by 1 Vote," *Rediff*, April 17, 1999.

13. James D. Fearon, "Domestic Political Audiences and the Escalation of International Disputes," *American Political Science Review* 88, 3 (September 1994): 577–92. Also see Kenneth Schultz, "Domestic Opposition and Signaling in International Crises," *American Political Science Review* 92, 4 (December 1998): 829–44.

14. Nayak and Krepon, *The Unfinished Crisis*, 66. Author's interviews of several former Indian officials and experts also confirmed the prevalence of this view.

15. On the importance of individual leaders in international politics, see Daniel Byman and Kenneth Pollack, "Let Us Now Praise Great Men: Bringing the Statesman Back In," *International Security* 25, 4 (Spring 2001): 107–46. For a contrary view, see Robert Jervis, "Do Leaders Matter and How Would We Know?" *Security Studies* 22, 2 (2013): 153–79.

16. For a comprehensive analysis of India's economic performance during this period and its future potential, see Tushar Poddar and Evi Yi, "India's Rising Growth Potential," in *BRICs and Beyond* (n.p.: Goldman Sachs, 2007), 9–25.

17. David Carter, "The Compellence Dilemma: International Disputes with Violent Groups," *International Studies Quarterly* 59, 3 (2015); Shivshankar Menon, *Choices: Inside the Making of India's Foreign Policy* (Washington, DC: Brookings Institution Press, 2016), 72.

18. George Perkovich and Toby Dalton, *Not War, Not Peace: Motivating Pakistan to Prevent Cross-Border Terrorism* (New Delhi: Oxford University Press, 2016).

19. This line of reasoning was the single most frequently cited counter-argument to brokered bargaining in the author's conversations with Indian interlocutors. The author finds this view to be pervasive among India's strategic elite more generally as well.

20. Dinshaw Mistry, "Tempering Optimism about Nuclear Deterrence in South Asia," *Security Studies* 18, 1 (2009): 180.

21. V. K. Sood and Pravin Sawhney, *Operation Parakram: The War Unfinished* (New Delhi: Sage Publications, 2003), 22, 25–26; Rajesh Kumar, "Revisiting the Kashmir Insurgency, Kargil, and the Twin Peak Crisis: Was the Stability/Instability Paradox at Play?" *New England Journal of Political Science* 3, 1 (Fall 2008): 79.

22. Author's interviews of former Indian and Pakistani crisis managers confirmed their normative preference for direct communication but also revealed their strong conviction that indirect communication through the third party will remain necessary in light of the mistrust between the two rivals.

23. This particular task of acting as the information conduit is also known as "informational mediation" and is well recognized as an effective tool for the most part. Kyle Beardsley, "Agreement without Peace? International Mediation and Time Inconsistency Problems," *American Journal of Political Science* 52, 4 (October 2008): 726–27.

24. For a brief discussion of the Indo-U.S. nuclear and security cooperation during this period, see K. Alan Kronstadt, *India-U.S. Relations* (Washington, DC: Congressional Research Service, August 12, 2008), 36–51.

25. Feroz H. Khan, "Pakistan's Nuclear Force Posture and the 2001–2002 Military Standoff," in *The India-Pakistan Military Standoff: Crisis and Escalation in South Asia*, ed. Zachary S. Davis (New York: Palgrave Macmillan, 2011), 133.

26. Ellen Barry and Salman Masood, "India Claims 'Surgical Strikes' across Line of Control in Kashmir," *New York Times*, September 29, 2016; "18 Jawans Killed at Pre-Dawn Strike at Uri," *Hindu*, September 18, 2016.

27. George Perkovich and Toby Dalton, "Modi's Strategic Choice: How to Respond to Terrorism from Pakistan," *Washington Quarterly* 38, 1 (Spring 2015), 23; Menon, *Choices*, 66.

28. Author's interview/correspondence with Fali Homi Major (by phone and e-mail), India's air force chief during the Mumbai crisis, August 10, 2014.

29. Siddharth Varadarajan, "Indian Surgical Strikes against Terrorists in Pakistan: What We Know, What We Don't Know," *Wire*, September 29, 2016.

30. M. Ilyas Khan, "India's 'Surgical Strikes' in Kashmir: Truth or Illusion?" BBC News, October 23, 2016; Shashank Joshi, "Kashmir: Why Is India's Modi Going on the Offensive?" CNN, September 29, 2016; Samrudhi Ghosh, "BJP, Opposition Debate Over Evidence of Indian Army's Surgical Strikes," *India Today*, October 5, 2016.

31. Sushant Singh, "Surgical Strikes: Significant Casualties among Terrorists and Their Backers, Says Indian Army," *Indian Express*, September 30, 2016; Siddharth Varadarajan, "Surgical Strikes: The Questions That Still Remain," *Wire*, October 3, 2016.

32. Suhasini Haidar and Kallol Bhattacherjee, "India Carries Out Surgical Strikes against Terror 'Launch Pads' Across LoC," *Hindu*, September 29, 2016; Khan, "India's 'Surgical Strikes' in Kashmir."

33. Varadarajan, "Indian Surgical Strikes"; Haidar and Bhattacherjee, "India Carries Out Surgical Strikes."

34. Author's interview of Peter R. Lavoy, June 1, 2017.

35. Ibid.

36. Saikat Datta, "Behind the Scenes: How India Went About Planning 'Surgical Strikes' after the Uri Attack," *Scroll.in*, September 29, 2016, https://scroll.in/article/817807/behind-the-scenes-how-india-went-about-planning-surgical-strikes-after-the-uri-attack; Sushil Aaron, "What Are India, BJP Trying to Achieve with the Surgical Strikes across the LoC?" *Hindustan Times*, September 30, 2016.

37. White House, "Statement by NSC Spokesperson Ned Price on National Security Advisor Susan E. Rice's Call with National Security Advisor Ajit Doval of India," September 28, 2016.

38. Jayanth Jacob, "Russia Backs India's Surgical Strikes, Says Uri 'Terrorists' from Pakistan," *Hindustan Times*, October 3, 2016.

39. Author's interview of Peter R. Lavoy, June 1, 2017.

40. Author's interview of Joshua T. White, senior advisor and director for South Asian Affairs, U.S. National Security Council during the Uri episode, Washington, DC, June 5, 2017.

41. "'Surgical' Farce Blows Up in India's Face," *Express Tribune*, September 30, 2016.

42. Author's interview of Joshua T. White, June 5, 2017.

43. Yashwant Raj, "Uri Attack an Act of Cross-Border Terror, India Has Right to Defend Itself: US," *Hindustan Times*, October 13, 2016.

44. "United States Urges India, Pakistan to Avoid Steps That Escalate Tensions," *Dawn*, September 30, 2016; "Uri Attack: Avoiding Direct Reference to Pak, China Voices Concern over Rising Tensions in Kashmir," *Indian Express*, September 19, 2016.

45. Author's interview of Joshua T. White, June 5, 2017.

46. Sadanand Dhume, "A More Assertive India Is Good for the West," *Wall Street Journal*, October 6, 2016.

47. Varadarajan, "Indian Surgical Strikes."

48. Vikram Sood, "Perpetual Restraint against Unending Provocation?" *Book Review Journal* 41, 3 (March 2017): 37.

49. Toby Dalton and George Perkovich, "Is a Pakistan-India War Just One Attack Away?" *Herald*, January 23, 2017.

50. See, for example, Feroz H. Khan and Ryan W. French, *South Asian Stability Workshop: A Crisis Simulation Exercise*, Report no. 2013–008 (Monterey, CA: Project on Advanced Systems and Concepts for Countering WMD,

October 2013); Feroz Hassan Khan, *South Asian Stability Workshop 2.0: A Crisis Simulation Report*, Report no. 2016–001 (Monterey, CA: Project on Advanced Systems and Concepts for Countering WMD, February 2016); Feroz H. Khan and Diana Wueger, *Escalation Management and Crisis De-Escalation in South Asia*, workshop report (National Nuclear Safety Administration, December 2015); Gurmeet Kanwal, "Worst-Case Scenarios: What Would Happen If Indo-Pak War Breaks Out?" *Hindustan Times*, October 8, 2015.

51. Khan and French, *South Asian Stability Workshop*; Khan, *South Asian Stability Workshop 2.0.*

52. Author's interview (by phone) of Vikram Sood, India's Research and Analysis Wing (RAW) chief during the 2001–2002 standoff, January 12, 2017.

53. Yusuf, "Banking on an Outsider."

54. Khan and Wueger, *Escalation Management and Crisis De-Escalation*; Khan, *South Asian Stability Workshop 2.0.*

55. On learning in international relations, see Jeffrey W. Knopf, "The Importance of International Learning," *Review of International Studies* 29, 2 (April 2003): 185–207. For a brief discussion of nuclear learning, see Rabia Akhtar and Debak Das, *Nuclear Learning in South Asia: The Levels of Analysis*, Policy Studies no. 57 (Colombo: Regional Centre for Strategic Studies, 2015), 9–16. Specifically on learning by the superpowers during the Cold War, see Vladislav Zubok, "Soviet Nuclear Learning: Peculiar Patterns," in *From Rivalry to Cooperation: Russian and American Perspectives on the Post–Cold War Era*, eds. Manus I. Midlarsky, John A. Vasquez, and Peter V. Gladkov (New York: HarperCollins, 1994), 40–55; Jack S. Levy, "Learning from Experience in U.S. and Soviet Foreign Policy," in *From Rivalry to Cooperation: Russian and American Perspectives on the Post–Cold War Era*, eds. Manus I. Midlarsky, John A. Vasquez, and Peter V. Gladkov (New York: HarperCollins, 1994), 56–86.

56. Rajesh M. Basrur, *South Asia's Cold War: Nuclear Weapons and Conflict in Contemporary Perspective* (London: Routledge, 2008), 7.

57. Victor Asal and Kyle Bearsley, "Proliferation and International Crisis Behaviour," *Journal of Peace Research* 44, 2 (March 2007): 142.

58. On constructivism, see Alexander Wendt, *Social Theory of International Politics* (Cambridge: Cambridge University Press, 1999).

59. Knopf, "The Importance of International Learning"; Jack S. Levy, "Learning and Foreign Policy: Sweeping a Conceptual Minefield," *International Organization* 48, 2 (1994): 279–312.

60. See Akhtar and Das, *Nuclear Learning in South Asia*, 40–48.

61. Rabia Akhtar, "Outsourcing Escalation Control," *South Asian Voices*, blogpost, September 23, 2013, http://southasianvoices.org/outsourcing-escalation-control/. For an analysis of nuclear learning in South Asia, including some of the positive lessons, see Feroz Hassan Khan, Ryan Jacobs, and

Emily Burke, eds., *Nuclear Learning in South Asia: The Next Decade* (Monterey, CA: Naval Postgraduate School, 2014).

62. Christopher Clary, "Deterrence Stability and the Conventional Balance of Forces in South Asia," in *Deterrence Stability and Escalation Control in South Asia*, eds. Michael Krepon and Julia Thompson (Washington, DC: Henry L. Stimson Center, 2013), 136. On inefficiencies in India's defense sector and the dysfunctional politico-military equation that contributes to it, see Stephen P. Cohen and Sunil Dasgupta, *Arming Without Aiming: India's Military Modernization* (Washington DC: Brookings Institution Press, 2010); Perkovich and Dalton, *Not War, Not Peace*.

63. Chari, Cheema, and Cohen, *Four Crises and a Peace Process*, 198; Vipin Narang, "Posturing for Peace? Pakistan's Nuclear Postures and South Asian Stability," *International Security* 34, 3 (Winter 2009–2010): 73–76.

64. Baqir Sajjad Syed, "NCA Stresses Full-Spectrum Deterrence," *Dawn*, September 6, 2013.

65. For a discussion of Nasr and its likely impact on India-Pakistan deterrence and crisis stability, see Rajaram Nagappa, Arun Vishwanathan, and Adit Malhotra, *Hatf-IX/Nasr- Pakistan's Tactical Nuclear Weapon: Implications for Indo-Pak Deterrence* (Bangalore: International Strategic and Security Studies Programme, National Institute of Advanced Studies, July 2013). For a scorching critique of Pakistan's decision to develop and test Nasr, see Ejaz Haider, "Stupidity Gone Nuclear-I," *Express Tribune*, April 25, 2011; Ejaz Haider, "Stupidity Gone Nuclear-II," *Express Tribune*, April 26, 2011. For the opposing view, see Mansoor Ahmed, "Why Pakistan Needs Tactical Nuclear Weapons," *Weekly Pulse*, May 6, 2011.

66. Naeem Salik, *Learning to Live with the Bomb—Pakistan: 1998–2016* (Karachi: Oxford University Press, 2017), 16.

67. Moeed Yusuf and Khalid Banuri, "India's Quest for Ballistic Missile Defense: A Slippery Slope," in *South Asia at a Crossroads: Conflict or Cooperation in the Age of Nuclear Weapons, Missile Defense, and Space Rivalries*, eds. Subrata Ghoshroy and Gotz Neuneck (Hamburg: Nomos, 2010), 103–10.

68. On instability arising from counterforce targeting, see Sumit Ganguly and S. Paul Kapur, *India, Pakistan, and the Bomb: Debating Nuclear Stability in South Asia* (New York: Columbia University Press, 2012), 88. More generally on this subject, see Keir A. Lieber and Daryl G. Press, "The New Era of Counterforce: Technological Change and the Future of Nuclear Deterrence," *International Security* 41, 4 (Spring 2017): 9–49. For a brief discussion of the destabilizing aspects of cruise missiles in South Asia, see Basrur, *South Asia's Cold War*, 73.

69. See Rajesh Basrur and Jaganath Sankaran, "India's Slow and Unstoppable Move to MIRV," in *The Lure and Pitfalls of MIRVs: From the First to the Second Nuclear Age*, eds. Michael Krepon, Travis Wheeler, and Shane Mason (Washington, DC: Henry L. Stimson Center, 2016), 119–47; Feroz H. Khan and Mansoor Ahmed, "Pakistan MIRVs and Counterforce Targeting," in

The Lure and Pitfalls of MIRVs: From the First to the Second Nuclear Age, eds. Michael Krepon, Travis Wheeler, and Shane Mason (Washington, DC: Henry L. Stimson Center, 2016), 149–75.

70. Perkovich and Toby Dalton, *Not War, Not Peace*, 199.

71. "Why Bind Ourselves to 'No First Use Policy', Says Parrikar on India's Nuke Doctrine," *Hindu*, November 10, 2016; "India May Abandon Its 'No First Use' Nuclear Policy: Expert," *Indian Express*, March 21, 2017; Sameer Lalwani and Hannah Haegeland, "The Debate Over Indian Nuclear Strategy Is Heating Up," *War on the Rocks*, April 15, 2017.

72. Narang, "Posturing for Peace?" 75; Feroz H. Khan and Peter R. Lavoy, "Pakistan: The Dilemma of Nuclear Deterrence," in *The Long Shadow: Nuclear Weapons and Security in 21st Century Asia*, ed. Muthiah Alagappa (Stanford, CA: Stanford University Press, 2008), 228.

73. David O. Smith, "The US Experience with Tactical Nuclear Weapons: Lessons for South Asia," in *Deterrence Stability and Escalation Control in South Asia*, eds. Michael Krepon and Julia Thompson (Washington, DC: Henry L. Stimson Center, 2013), 73–74.

74. Author's interviews of U.S. interlocutors confirmed a normative belief that these crises would be best managed bilaterally but also a virtual consensus that the United States cannot ignore the risks in the South Asian equation and must therefore continue to intervene to ameliorate them unless the situation stabilizes drastically.

Chapter 7

1. Erid S. Edelman, Andrew F. Krepinvich, and Evan Braden Montgomery, "The Dangers of a Nuclear Iran: The Limits of Containment," *Foreign Affairs* 90, 1 (January–February 2011): 69.

2. For a comprehensive analysis of the projections about horizontal proliferation since the beginning of the atomic age, see Moeed Yusuf, *Predicting Proliferation: The History of the Future of Nuclear Weapons*, Policy Paper 9 (Washington, DC: Brookings Institution, January 2009). Specifically on these "chains," see ibid., 39–40.

3. For background on Arab-Israeli relations, including their conflicts, see Avi Shalom, *The Iron Wall: Israel and the Arab World* (New York: W. W. Norton, 2014); *A Survey of Arab-Israeli Relations*, 2nd ed. (London: Europa Publications, 2004). Specifically on Israel-Turkey relations, which have followed a very different trajectory than Israel's relations with the Arab countries in the neighborhood, see Hasan Kosebalaban, "The Crisis in Turkish-Israeli Relations: What Is Its Strategic Significance?" *Middle East Policy* 17, 3 (Fall 2010): 36–50; Ilker Ayturk, "The Coming of an Ice Age? Turkish–Israeli Relations since 2002," *Turkish Studies* 12, 4 (2011): 675–87.

4. Steven Simon, *An Israeli Strike on Iran*, Contingency Planning Memorandum no. 5 (New York: Council on Foreign Relations, November 2009), 1.

5. On U.S. foreign policy and ties with Middle Eastern countries over the decades, see David W. Lesch and Mark L. Haas, eds., *The Middle East and the United States: History, Politics, and Ideologies* (Boulder, CO: Westview, 2012).

6. For a map of U.S. military bases in and around the Middle East, see https://www.google.com/maps/d/viewer?mid=1XmUD73hHQVBbdm8UcIrR tAcCgTg&hl=en_US.

7. As early as 1966, Israel's undeclared nuclear red lines included nuclear weapon use against massive conventional attacks. Avner Cohen, *Israel and the Bomb* (New York: Columbia University Press, 1998), 237. Israel is also believed to have considered a demonstration nuclear blast in the 1967 Arab-Israeli Six-Day War. William J. Broad and David E. Sanger, "'Last Secret' of 1967 War: Israel's Doomsday Plan for Nuclear Display," *New York Times*, June 3, 2017.

8. For background on Israel-Iran relations, including their intensifying rivalry since the turn of the century, see Dalia Dassa Kaye, Alireza Nader, and Parisa Roshan, *Israel and Iran: A Dangerous Rivalry*, (Santa Monica, CA: RAND, 2011). For more detailed analyses of the Iran-Israel-U.S. triangle, see Jalil Roshandel with Nathan Chapman Lean, *Iran, Israel, and the United States: Regime Security vs. Political Legitimacy* (Santa Barbara, CA: Praeger, 2011).

9. "Nuclear Weapons: Who Has What at a Glance," Arms Control Association, July 2017; "Israel," Nuclear Threat Initiative, Country Profile. For an authoritative account of Israel's nuclear weapons program, see Cohen, *Israel and the Bomb*.

10. Ruth Eglash and William Booth, "Israel to Launch One of the Most Advanced Missile Defense Systems in the World, With U.S. Help," *Washington Post*, March 3, 2016.

11. The text of the deal is available at https://www.state.gov/e/eb/tfs/spi/iran/jcpoa/. For a detailed account of the deal and the diplomatic negotiations to achieve it, see Trita Parsi, *Losing an Enemy: Obama, Iran, and the Triumph of Diplomacy* (New Haven, CT: Yale University Press, 2017). For a timeline of international diplomacy with Iran that culminated in this deal, see "Timeline of Nuclear Diplomacy with Iran," Arms Control Association, Fact Sheets and Briefs, January 2018. The deal has been heavily criticized by U.S. president Donald Trump. He officially decertified the deal in 2017 but allowed it to remain in effect. Mark Landler and David E. Sanger, "Trump Disavows Nuclear Deal, But Doesn't Scrap It," *New York Times*, October 13, 2017.

12. Carol Morello and Karen DeYoung, "Nuclear Deal with Iran Scrutinized by Experts," *Washington Post*, July 17, 2015; David Albright, "Iran on

Notice," testimony at the U.S. House Foreign Affairs Committee hearing, "Iran on Notice," February 16, 2017.

13. For an account of the U.S.-Iran relationship, see Seyed Hossein Mousavian with Shahir Shahidsaless, *Iran and the United States: An Insider's View of the Failed Past and Road to Peace* (New York: Bloomsbury, 2014).

14. On the U.S.-Israel relationship, see Dennis Ross, *Doomed to Succeed: The U.S.-Israel Relationship from Truman to Obama* (New York: Farrar, Straus and Giroux, 2015). Also see Robert O. Freedman, ed., *Israel and the United States: Six Decades of U.S.-Israeli Relations* (Boulder, CO: Westview, 2012).

15. Suzanne Maloney, *Thinking the Unthinkable: The Gulf States and the Prospect of a Nuclear Iran*, Middle East Memo 27 (Washington, DC: Brookings Institution, January 2013): 10–13; Jahangir Amuzegar, "Nuclear Iran: Perils and Prospects," *Middle East Policy* 13, 2 (Summer 2006): 97–98.

16. Jeffrey Goldberg, "The Iranian Regime on Israel's Right to Exist," *Atlantic*, March 9, 2015.

17. Colin H. Kahl, Melissa G. Dalton, and Matthew Irvine, *Risk and Rivalry: Iran, Israel and the Bomb* (Washington, DC: Center for a New American Security, June 2012), 13–18; Paul Pillar, "We Can Live With a Nuclear Iran," *Washington Monthly* (March–April 2012); Fareed Zakaria, "Is Iran Rational?" *Washington Post*, April 9, 2015.

18. Edelman, Krepinvich, and Montgomery, "The Dangers of a Nuclear Iran," 68; Kahl, Dalton, and Irvine, *Risk and Rivalry*, 24.

19. Edelman, Krepinvich, and Montgomery, "The Dangers of a Nuclear Iran," 68.

20. Kahl, Dalton, and Irvine, *Risk and Rivalry*, 25–26.

21. Israel has exhibited a recognition of the benefits of this approach in the past. For instance, despite being under direct attack from Iraqi Scud missiles during the first Gulf War, it deferred to firm U.S. demands for restraint. In return, the United States agreed to work on alternative ways to target Iraq's missiles. Ross, *Doomed to Succeed*, 238–42.

22. On Iran's support to militant proxies, see Marius Deeb, *Syria, Iran, and Hezbollah: The Unholy Alliance and Its War on Lebanon* (Stanford, CA: Hoover Institution Press, 2013), 54–81; Keith A. Petty, "Veiled Impunity: Iran's Use of Non-State Armed Groups," *Denver Journal of International Law and Policy* 36, 2 (2008): 191–219. Specifically on Hezbollah, see James Worrall, Simon Mabon, and Gordon Clubb, *Hezbollah: From Islamic Resistance to Government* (Santa Barbara, CA: Praeger, 2010); Matthew Levitt, *Hezbollah: The Global Footprint of Lebanon's Party of God* (Washington, DC: Georgetown University Press, 2013).

23. Massimiliano Fiore, *Israel and Iran's Nuclear Programme: Roll Back or Containment*, Istituto Affari Internazionali, IAI Working Papers 11, 18 (July 2011), 4; Gili Cohen, "IDF Official: Nuclear Iran Will Limit Israel's Ability to

Protect Its Border," *Haaretz*, January 17, 2012; Ronen Bergman, "Will Israel Attack Iran?" *New York Times*, January 25, 2012.

24. On North Korea, see Victor D. Cha and David C. Kang, *Nuclear North Korea: A Debate on Engagement Strategies* (New York: Columbia University Press, 2003); Victor Cha, *The Impossible State: North Korea, Past and Future* (New York: Ecco, 2013); Sung Chull Kim and Michael D. Cohen, eds., *Nuclear Korea and Nuclear Weapons: Entering the New Era of Deterrence* (Washington, DC: Georgetown University Press, 2017). On the state of the U.S. alliance with South Korea and Japan, see Gilbert Rozman, *Asia's Alliance Triangle: US-Japan-South Korea Relations at a Tumultuous Time* (New York: Palgrave Macmillan, 2015).

25. Richard C. Bush, *The U.S. Policy of Extended Deterrence in East Asia: History, Current Views, and Implications*, Arms Control Series Paper 5 (Washington, DC: Brookings Institution, February 2011).

26. For a comprehensive list of North Korean missile and nuclear tests and diplomacy around its nuclear program dating back to 1985, see "Chronology of U.S.-North Korean Nuclear and Missile Diplomacy," Arms Control Association, Fact Sheets and Briefs, January 2018.

27. For a list of U.N. Security Council sanctions against North Korea since its first nuclear test in 2006, see "UN Security Council Resolutions on North Korea," Arms Control Association, Fact Sheets and Briefs, January 2018.

28. Eleanor Albert, "The China-North Korea Relationship," Backgrounder, Council on Foreign Relations, September 27, 2017.

29. Carla Freeman, "Assessing China's Leadership in the North Korean Crisis," *38 North*, May 12, 2017.

30. Cha and Kang, *Nuclear North Korea*, 157.

31. Albert, "The China-North Korea Relationship."

32. China is also committed to defending North Korea under a 1961 treaty, but its willingness to do so remains unclear, especially after Pyongyang's nuclearization. Albert, "The China-North Korea Relationship"; Carrie Gracie, "Why Beijing Should Lead on the North Korean Crisis," BBC News, April 21, 2017.

33. Paul B. Stares, *Military Escalation in Korea*, Contingency Planning Memorandum no. 10 (New York: Council on Foreign Relations, November 2010), 4.

34. North Korea has been explicit in revealing its intent to develop a nuclear capability to strike the U.S. homeland. In 2017, it tested intercontinental ballistic missiles capable of reaching the U.S. mainland. Ankit Panda and Vipin Narang, "North Korea's ICBM: A New Missile and a New Era," *War on the Rocks*, July 6, 2017; Christine Kim and Phil Stewart, "North Korea Says 'Breakthrough' puts U.S. Mainland Within Range of Nuclear Weapons," Reuters, November 28, 2017.

35. Cha, *The Impossible State*, 212–13; Bill Powell, "Madman Across the Water: Taking Out North Korea's Nuclear Weapons Won't Be Quick, And It Won't Be Easy," *Newsweek*, May 5, 2017, 36–39; Uri Friedman, "North Korea: The Military Options. What Would a Strike Actually Entail?" *Atlantic*, May 17, 2017.

36. Kathleen J. McInnis et al., *The North Korean Nuclear Challenge: Military Options and Issues for Congress* (Washington, DC: Congressional Research Service, October 27, 2017).

37. Friedman, "North Korea."

38. "US Vows to Defend Itself, Allies amid North Korea Threats," ABC News, April 3, 2013.

39. Matt Smith, "North Korea Warns 'Moment of Explosion' Nears," CNN, April 4, 2013; Malcolm Moore, "North Korea Moves Missiles to East Coast amid Threats of Attack on US Bases," *Telegraph*, April 4, 2013.

40. Thom Shanker, "U.S. Runs Practice Sortie in South Korea," *New York Times*, March 28, 2013; "S. Korea Hails New Military Pact with U.S.," *Japan Times*, March 26, 2013; Foster Klug, "U.S., South Korean Military Drills Inspire North Korea's Anger," *World Post*, November 4, 2013; Arshad Mohammad and Jack Jim, "U.S. Tells North Korea New Missile Launch Would Be 'Huge Mistake,'" Reuters, April 12, 2013.

41. Jill Dougherty, Jethro Mullen, and Laura Smith, "China, United States to Work Together to Calm Down North Korea," CNN, April 14, 2013.

42. Tania Branigan and Peter Beaumont, "North Korea's Aggressive Stance Condemned by G8 in 'Strongest Terms,'" *Guardian*, April 11, 2013.

43. Keith Bradsher and Nick Cumming-Bruce, "China Cuts Ties with Key North Korean Bank," *New York Times*, May 7, 2013; Simon Rabinovitch, "China Banks Rein in Support for North Korea," *Financial Times*, May 13, 2013.

44. "Detained Chinese Fishermen, Boat Released by North Korea," VOA News, May 21, 2013.

45. Jethro Mullen and K. J. Kwon, "North and South Korea Tentatively Agree to Talks on Shuttered Industrial Zone," CNN, June 7, 2013; "North Korea, China Want to Resume Nuclear Talks," CNN, June 19, 2013.

46. Tom Phillips, "China 'Seriously Concerned' after Trump Questions Taiwan Policy," *Guardian*, December 12, 2016; Dominic Rushe and Benjamin Haas, "Could Trump's Chest Thumping over China Trigger a Trade War?" *Guardian*, December 10, 2016; Eli Watkins, "Trump: US Will Act Unilaterally on North Korea If Necessary," CNN, April 3, 2017.

47. "Trump Says North Korea 'Behaving Very Badly,' China Has Done Little to Help," Reuters, March 17, 2017; Nicole Gaouette and Elise Labott, "Tillerson to Warn China of Sanctions over North Korea," CNN, March 16, 2017; "Turning the Screws on North Korea; New Sanctions and a Turn by China may Finally Isolate

the Kim Regime," *Wall Street Journal*, September 22, 2017; "China Slams 'Wrong' US Sanctions on North Korea-Tied Traders," *Guardian*, November 22, 2017.

48. Joshua Berlinger, "North Korea's Missile Tests: What You Need to Know," CNN, December 3, 2017; Zachary Cohen and Euan McKirdy, "North Korea Threatens Strike on Guam," CNN, August 9, 2017; Carol Morello, "North Korea's Top Diplomat Says Strike against U.S. Mainland Is 'Inevitable,'" *Washington Post*, September 23, 2017.

49. Kim Hjelmgaard, "Tillerson: Military Action against North Korea 'Option Is on the Table,'" *USA Today*, March 17, 2017; Nic Robertson, "Trump and Kim's War of Words Is Rattling South Koreans," CNN, September 30, 2017.

50. "North Korea Says China 'Dancing to the Tune of the US,'" BBC News, February 23, 2017; James Griffiths, "North Korea Blights China's One Belt, One Road Party with Missile Launch," CNN, May 14, 2017.

51. Jeffrey Lewis, "Rex Tillerson's 'New Approach' to North Korea Sounds a Lot Like the Old Approach," *Washington Post*, March 24, 2017.

52. Peter Baker and Choe Sang-Hun, "Trump Threatens 'Fire and Fury' against North Korea If It Endangers U.S.," *New York Times*, August 8, 2017.

53. "Jim Mattis: US Wants Diplomatic End to North Korea Crisis," *Times of India*, September 26, 2017; "Trump Urges China's Xi to Work 'Hard' and Fast on North Korea," *Guardian*, November 9, 2017; Ambassador Nikki Haley, "Remarks at an Emergency UN Security Council Meeting on North Korea," United States Mission to the United Nations, November 29, 2017.

54. Choe Sang-Hun, "Allies for 67 Years, U.S. and South Korea Split Over North Korea," *New York Times*, September 4, 2017; F. Brinley Bruton, "War with Kim Jong Un 'Must Not Happen,' South Korea Says," NBC News, November 7, 2017; Matthew Weaver et al., "Trump Says US Will Act Alone on North Korea If China Fails to Help," *Guardian*, April 3, 2017.

55. Somini Sengupta, "After U.S. Compromise, Security Council Strengthens North Korea Sanctions," *New York Times*, September 11, 2017.

56. China banned North Korea's crucial mineral and other exports, suspended vital oil sales to North Korea, citing worries about nonpayment, curtailed financial activities with the country, and went along with the "toughest-ever" UN sanctions against North Korea imposed in the wake of Pyongyang's sixth nuclear test in September 2017 and after another test launch of its intercontinental ballistic missile in December 2017. Albert, "The China-North Korea Relationship"; Simon Denyer, "China Bans North Korean Iron, Lead, Coal, Imports as Part of U.N. Sanctions," *Washington Post*, August 14, 2017; Carol Morello, Michelle Ye Hee Lee, and Emily Rauhala, "U.N. Agrees to Toughest-Ever Sanctions against North Korea," *Washington Post*, September 11, 2017. Rick Gladstone and David E. Sanger, "Security Council Tightens Economic Vise on North Korea, Blocking Fuel, Ships and Workers," *New York Times*, December 22, 2017.

57. "China Calls on N Korea to Suspend Missile and Nuclear Tests," BBC, March 8, 2017; Anna Fifield, "In Latest Test, North Korea Detonates Its Most Powerful Nuclear Device Yet," *Washington Post*, September 3, 2017.

58. Brad Lendon, Chieu Luu, and Sol Han, "North Korea: China Stomping on 'Red Line' in Relations," CNN, May 4, 2017.

59. Neil Connor, "North Korea Warns China of 'Grave Consequences' in First Direct Rebuke to Beijing over Criticism," *Telegraph*, May 4, 2017.

60. "Xi Jinping Sends Rare Message to Kim Jong-Un in Sign Relations Could Be Improving," *Telegraph*, November 2, 2017; Simon Denyer, "China to Send Envoy to North Korea, Reopening Dialogue with the Isolated Regime," *Washington Post*, November 15, 2017.

61. Waheguru Pal Singh Sidhu and Jing-Dong Yuan, *China and India: Cooperation or Conflict?* (Boulder, CO: Lynne Rienner, 2003). Also see M. Taylor Fravel, *Strong Borders, Secure Nation: Cooperation and Conflict in China's Territorial Disputes* (Princeton, NJ: Princeton University Press, 2008).

62. Julie McCarthy, "In a Remote Himalayan Corner, Tensions Rise between India and China," NPR, July 10, 2017; Loulla-Mae Eleftheriou-Smith, "India and China 'Preparing for Armed Conflict' If Bhutan Solution Not Found," *Independent*, August 15, 2017. On possible conflict scenarios between China and India, see Daniel S. Markey, *Armed Confrontation between China and India*, Contingency Planning Memorandum no. 27 (New York: Council on Foreign Relations, November 2015).

63. For basic information on China's and India's nuclear capabilities, see the Nuclear Threat Initiative's country profiles, available, respectively, at http://www.nti.org/learn/countries/china/ and http://www.nti.org/learn/countries/india/. On their nuclear force postures, see Vipin Narang, *Nuclear Strategy in the Modern Era: Regional Powers and International Conflict* (Princeton, NJ: Princeton University Press, 2014), 94–152.

64. Markey, *Armed Confrontation between China and India*.

65. Tanvi Madan, "The US and Doklam: Look Beyond Rhetoric," Brookings Institution, September 26, 2017.

66. Ibid.

67. Ankit Panda, "Disengagement at Doklam: Why and How Did the India-China Standoff End?" *Diplomat*, August 29, 2017.

Chapter 8

1. For a discussion of the bias toward analyzing trilateral relationships through two-actor or two-against-one-actor models, see Timothy W. Crawford, *Pivotal Deterrence: Third-Party Statecraft and the Pursuit of Peace* (Ithaca, NY: Cornell University Press, 2003), 15–19.

2. For example, Feroz H. Khan, "The Independence-Dependence Paradox: Stability Dilemmas in South Asia," *Arms Control Today* 33, 8 (October 2003); Peter R. Lavoy, "Introduction: The Importance of the Kargil Conflict," in *Asymmetric Warfare in South Asia: The Causes and Consequences of the Kargil Conflict*, ed. Peter R. Lavoy (New York: Cambridge University Press, 2009), 29; Bhumitra Chakma, "South Asia's Nuclear Deterrence and the USA," in *The Politics of Nuclear Weapons in South Asia*, ed. Bhumitra Chakma (Burlington, VT: Ashgate, 2011), 134–35.

3. For example, Khan, "The Independence-Dependence Paradox."

4. Vipin Narang, *Nuclear Strategy in the Modern Era: Regional Powers and International Conflict* (Princeton, NJ: Princeton University Press, 2014).

5. This bias is partly a result of the fact that literature on "evaluation" tends to focus disproportionately on domestic audiences whereby actors often have to exhibit resolve to obtain positive evaluation. See Dean G. Pruitt and Douglas F. Johnson, "Mediation as an Aid to Face Saving in Negotiation," *Journal of Personality and Social Psychology* 14, 3 (1970): 239–46; Jeffery Z. Rubin and Bert R. Brown, *The Social Psychology of Bargaining and Negotiating* (New York: Academic Press, 1975), 48–54.

6. S. Paul Kapur, *Dangerous Deterrent: Nuclear Weapons Proliferation and Conflict in South Asia* (Stanford, CA: Stanford University Press, 2007).

7. For an original analysis of the complexity of Pakistan's unitary actor problem, see George Perkovich, "The Non-Unitary Model and Deterrence Stability in South Asia," in *Deterrence Stability and Escalation Control in South Asia*, eds. Michael Krepon and Julia Thompson (Washington, DC: Henry L. Stimson Center, 2013), 21–40.

8. Crawford, *Pivotal Deterrence*, 2.

9. William J. Dixon, "Third-Party Techniques for Preventing Conflict Escalation and Promoting Peaceful Settlement," *International Organization* 50, 4 (Autumn 1996): 653–81.

10. Saadia Touval, *The Peace Brokers: Mediators in the Arab-Israeli Conflict, 1948–1979* (Princeton, NJ: Princeton University Press, 1982).

11. Ibid., 14.

12. Kyle Beardsley, "Agreement without Peace? International Mediation and Time Inconsistency Problems," *American Journal of Political Science* 52, 4 (October 2008): 723–40.

13. On broader unipolar strategies and their implications for U.S. involvement around the world, see Nuno P. Monteiro, *Theory of Unipolar Politics* (New York: Cambridge University Press, 2014).

14. Moeed Yusuf and Jason Kirk, "Keeping an Eye on South Asian Skies: America's Pivotal Deterrence in Nuclearized India-Pakistan Crises," *Contemporary Security Policy* 37, 2 (2016): 263.

15. Patrick M. Morgan, *Deterrence Now* (Cambridge: Cambridge University Press, 2003), 172–202; Patrick M. Morgan, "Collective-Actor Deterrence," in *Complex Deterrence: Strategy in the Global Age*, eds. T. V. Paul, Patrick M. Morgan, and James J. Wirtz (Chicago: University of Chicago Press, 2009), 158–81.

16. Morgan, "Collective-Actor Deterrence," 163–64.

17. Timothy W. Crawford, "The Endurance of Extended Deterrence: Continuity, Change, and Complexity in Theory and Policy," in *Complex Deterrence: Strategy in the Global Age*, eds. T. V. Paul, Patrick M. Morgan, and James J. Wirtz (Chicago: University of Chicago Press, 2009), 286–88.

18. P. R. Chari, *Nuclear Crisis, Escalation Control, and Deterrence in South Asia*, Working Paper 1.0 (Washington, DC: Henry L. Stimson Center, August 2003), 25.

19. Dinshaw Mistry, "Tempering Optimism about Nuclear Deterrence in South Asia," *Security Studies* 18, 1 (2009): 181.

20. This was a recurring theme in the author's interviews of Indian interlocutors. Specifically, at the roundtable interaction at the Delhi Policy Group, New Delhi, March 25, 2013; author's interview of Indian experts and journalists, Raja Mohan, Manoj Joshi, Praveen Swami, and Pranab Samanta, New Delhi, March 23, 2013; and author's interview of Shyam Saran, India's foreign secretary (2004–2006), New Delhi, August 8, 2014.

21. Toby Dalton and George Perkovich, "Is a Pakistan-India War Just One Attack Away?" *Herald*, January 23, 2017.

22. Yatish Yadav, "Pakistan Stalls 26/11 Attacks Trial to Buy Lakhvi Time, Seeks 'More Evidence,'" *Indian Express*, July 1, 2016; "India Protests after Pak's Hafiz Saeed Warns of Pathankot-Style Attacks," *Hindustan Times*, February 4, 2016; Mehreen Zahra-Malik, "Militant Leader Hafiz Saeed Is Released by Pakistani Court," *New York Times*, November 23, 2017.

23. Michael Safi, "Rise of Hindu 'Extremist' Spooks Muslim Minority in India's Heartland," *Guardian*, March 25, 2017; "India's Hindu Fundamentalists," *Al Jazeera*, October 8, 2015.

24. "Pakistan Submits Proofs of India's Involvement in Cross Border Terrorism to UN Chief," *Dawn*, January 6, 2017.

25. The most high profile of these attacks in recent times was the bombing of the Samjhauta Express train in 2007, which killed 68 people, mostly Pakistanis. The perpetrators, including a serving Indian army colonel, were members of Hindu extremist outfits. "Bring Perpetrators of Samjhauta Blasts to Justice: Pakistan to India," *Indian Express*, March 9, 2017.

26. Minu Jain, "India, Pakistan Delink Terrorism from Dialogue," *Indian Express*, July 16, 2009.

27. Steve Coll, "The Back Channel," *New Yorker*, March 2, 2009. Also see Khurshid Mahmud Kasuri, *Neither a Hawk nor a Dove: An Insider's Account*

of Pakistan's Foreign Relations Including Details of the Kashmir Framework (Karachi: Oxford University Press, 2015).

28. N. Ravi, "India, Pakistan to Set Up Anti-Terrorism Mechanism," *Hindu*, September 17, 2006.

29. On the desirability of such collaboration, see Anand Arni and Shaukat Javed, "India-Pakistan Intelligence Cooperation to Counter Terrorism," paper prepared for the Ottawa Dialogue, intelligence dialogue meeting, October 2014.

30. Praveen Swami, "Pakistan NSA Warned Ajit Doval of 26/11-Type Hit on Maha Shivratri," *Indian Express*, March 7, 2016.

31. Author's interview (by phone) of Jalil Abbas Jilani, Pakistan's ambassador to the United States (2013–2017), December 11, 2017.

32. See Happymon Jacob, *Ceasefire Violations in Jammu Kashmir: A Line on Fire* (Washington, DC: United States Institute of Peace, 2017).

33. Paul Bracken, *Fire in the East: The Rise of Asian Military Power and the Second Nuclear Age* (New York: HarperCollins, 1999), xiii; Muthiah Alagappa, "Reinforcing National Security and Regional Stability: The Implications of Nuclear Weapons and Strategies," in *The Long Shadow: Nuclear Weapons and Security in 21st Century Asia*, ed. Muthiah Alagappa (Stanford, CA: Stanford University Press, 2008), 536–37.

34. "Putin Reveals Secrets of Russia's Crimea Takeover Plot," BBC News, March 9, 2015. These guarantees that extended to protection against threats to territorial integrity or political independence were provided in the Budapest Memorandum on Security Assurances concluded in 1994 under which Ukraine (and Belarus and Kazakhstan) agreed to give up the nuclear weapons they had inherited from the erstwhile Soviet Union.

35. Bruce Klingner and Sue Mi Terry, "We Participated in Talks with North Korean Representatives. This is What We Learned," *Washington Post*, June 22, 2017.

36. Gene Gerzhoy and Nick Miller, "Donald Trump Thinks More Countries Should Have Nuclear Weapons. Here's What the Research Says," *Washington Post*, April 6, 2016.

37. Charles Lee, "North Korean and Chinese Nuclear Development: Two Peas in a Pod," *Diplomat*, November 10, 2016.

38. Samir Nair and Guru Amrit Khalsa, "Towards U.S.-India Missile Defense Cooperation," *CogitAsia*, Center for Strategic and International Studies, June 6, 2013. Also see Sumit Ganguly, *Deadly Impasse: Indo-Pak Relations at the Dawn of a New Century* (Cambridge: Cambridge University Press, 2016), 124–26.

39. See Michael Krepon, Rodney W. Jones, and Ziad Haider, eds., *Escalation Control and the Nuclear Option in South Asia* (Washington, DC: Henry L. Stimson Center, 2004); Michael Krepon and Julia Thompson, eds., *Deterrence*

Stability and Escalation Control in South Asia (Washington, DC: Henry L. Stimson Center, 2013); Shaun Gregory and Maria Sultan, "Towards Strategic Stability in South Asia," *Contemporary South Asia* 14, 2 (June 2005): 135–40, and the collection of articles in *Contemporary South Asia* 14, 2 (June 2005); "Confidence-building and Nuclear Arms Control" (Part IV), in *The Politics of Nuclear Weapons in South Asia*, ed. Bhumitra Chakma (Burlington, VT: Ashgate, 2011), Part IV, 155–229; Zachary S. Davis, "A Decade of Nuclear Learning: Ten Years after the South Asian Nuclear Test," Conference Report, Center on Contemporary Conflict, Naval Postgraduate School, February 12–13, 2009; Mario E. Carranza, *South Asian Security and International Nuclear Order: Creating a Robust Indo-Pakistani Nuclear Arms Control Regime* (Farnham, Surrey: Ashgate, 2009), 177–230; Moeed Yusuf, "Persevering towards Nuclear Stability," in *Security and Nuclear Stabilization in South Asia*, ed. Imtiaz Alam (Lahore: Free Media Foundation, 2006), 16–42; Chari, "Nuclear Crisis, Escalation Control, and Deterrence in South Asia"; Moeed Yusuf, "Banking on an Outsider: Implications for Escalation Control in South Asia," *Arms Control Today* 41, 5 (June 2011); Neil Joeck, *Maintaining Nuclear Stability in South Asia*, Adelphi Paper 312 (London: International Institute for Strategic Studies, September 1997); Feroz H. Khan, "Reducing the Risk of Nuclear War in South Asia," in *Pakistan's Nuclear Future: Reining in the Risk*, ed. Henry Sokolski (Carlisle, PA: Strategic Studies Institute, 2009), 63–101.

40. Thomas C. Schelling, "Nuclear Strategy in Europe," *World Politics* 14, 3 (April 1962): 428.

41. Polly Nayak and Michael Krepon, *The Unfinished Crisis: US Crisis Management after the 2008 Mumbai Attacks* (Washington, DC: Henry L. Stimson Center, 2012), 62.

42. Polly Nayak and Michael Krepon, *US Crisis Management in South Asia's Twin Peaks Crisis*, Report 57 (Washington DC: Henry L. Stimson Center, September 2006). A number of the author's interviews of former U.S. officials confirmed this as well.

43. The concept of informal partnerships created by the global sheriff to perform specific international tasks in today's unipolar world is most elaborately discussed by Richard N. Haass, *The Reluctant Sheriff: The United States after the Cold War* (New York: Council on Foreign Relations, 1997), 93–100.

Index

ladders, 17, 180; manipulation of
risk of war, 6, 15, 35–37, 40, 43, 45,
59, 65, 66, 79, 84, 94–95, 102, 105,
117, 128–29, 135–36, 158, 159, 162,
163; by preemptive strikes, 15, 17, 30,
33, 40, 74, 139, 187, 193, 194, 235n23;
reduction in, 17, 30, 205, 210–13;
relationship to U.S. intervention,
29–32, 113–14, 211–12; risk
reduction protocols, 17, 30
Robock, Alan: on regional nuclear war,
29
Rubin, Jeffrey: on evaluation in
bargaining frameworks, 41–42
Russia: during India-Pakistan military
standoff of 2001–2002, 109, 110;
relations with India, 75, 174;
relations with United States, 2, 214

Saeed, Hafiz, 84, 133, 143, 258n144
Sagan, Scott: on vulnerability/
invulnerability paradox, 224n24
Salik, Naeem, 179
Samjhauta Express train bombing,
290n25
Sattar, Abdul, 93
Saudi Arabia, 181, 182; relations with
Pakistan, 73, 140, 146
Sawhney, Pravin, 88, 90, 118
Schaffer, Howard B., 263n243
Schaffer, Teresita C., 263n243
Schelling, Thomas: on threats and
chance, 15
Shaheen missiles, 105
Sharif, Nawaz: during Kargil conflict,
57–58, 59–60, 61–62, 64, 71, 72–74,
75, 77, 78, 81–82, 240n13, 242n39,
243n52; and Lahore Declaration, 54,
57–58
Sheikh, Omar Saeed, 154
Sidhu, Waheguru, 66
Singh, Jaswant: during India-Pakistan
military standoff of 2001–2002, 90,

100, 104, 254n64, 260n166; during
Kargil crisis, 65, 66, 68, 70, 71, 82
Singh, Manmohan: during Mumbai
crisis, 121, 124–25, 126, 130, 141, 147,
151, 165, 173
Singh, Swaran, 75
Sino-Indian relations: brokered
bargaining in, 181, 194–97
Sino-Indian War of 1962, 25, 223n19
Sino-Soviet Ussuri River conflict, 16–17,
19–20, 46, 53
Smith, David, 256n106
Snyder, Glenn: on straddle strategy, 20
soaking and poking, 48, 239n57
Sood, V. K., 88, 90, 92, 118
South Korea, 210; relations with United
States, 181, 188–94, 204
Soviet Union: relations with India, 4,
22, 25, 229n46; Ussuri River conflict
with China, 16–17, 19–20, 46, 53
Stolar, Alex, 103, 254n64, 260n166
Stratfor, 125–26
Straw, Jack, 98, 102, 109
structured focus comparison method,
48, 212
Subrahmanyam, K., 90
Suez crisis, 19

tactical nuclear weapons, 16, 179, 180
Talbott, Strobe, 66, 70
Tellis, Ashley J., 63
third parties: as balancers, 161–62,
168; crisis prevention by, 205–6,
208; face savers provided by, 34,
58, 61, 62, 72, 74, 75, 78, 110, 114,
161, 162, 187, 206, 236n28; during
future crises, 176–77; impact of
regional nuclearization on, 33–34;
as information conduit, 7–8, 34, 38,
70, 114, 119, 137, 142, 148, 153–54,
171–72, 183–84, 278n23; pivotal
deterrence by, 21–22, 24, 32, 202;
positive evaluation by, 41–42, 47, 82,